CompTIA A+ Certification: 220-603

Instructor's Edition

THOMSON ™

COURSE TECHNOLOGY

Australia • Canada • Mexico • Singapore
Spain • United Kingdom • United States

CompTIA A+ Certification: 220-603

VP and GM, Training Group:	Michael Springer
Series Product Managers:	Charles G. Blum and Adam A. Wilcox
Developmental Editor:	Andy LaPage
Copyeditor:	Robert Tillett and Ken Maher
Keytester:	Gail Sandler
Series Designer:	Adam A. Wilcox
Cover Designer:	Abby Scholz

For more information contact:

Course Technology
25 Thomson Place
Boston, MA 02210

Or find us on the Web at: www.course.com

For permission to use material from this text or product, submit a request online at: www.thomsonrights.com

Any additional questions about permissions can be submitted by e-mail to: thomsonrights@thomson.com

Trademarks

Course ILT is a trademark of Course Technology.

Some of the product names and company names used in this book have been used for identification purposes only and may be trademarks or registered trademarks of their respective manufacturers and sellers.

Disclaimers

Course Technology reserves the right to revise this publication and make changes from time to time in its content without notice.

he logo of the CompTIA Authorized Quality Curriculum (CAQC) program and the status of this or other training material as "Authorized" under the CompTIA Authorized Quality Curriculum program signifies that, in CompTIA's opinion, such training material covers the content of CompTIA's related certification exam.

The contents of this training material were created for the CompTIA A+ 220-603 exam covering CompTIA certification objectives that were current as of October 2006.

CompTIA has not reviewed or approved the accuracy of the contents of this training material and specifically disclaims any warranties of merchantability or fitness for a particular purpose. CompTIA makes no guarantee concerning the success of persons using any such "Authorized" or other training material in order to prepare for any CompTIA certification exam.

ISBN 10: 1-4239-5444-0
ISBN 13: 978-1-4239-5444-6

Printed in the United States of America

1 2 3 4 5 6 7 8 9 PM 08 07 06

Contents

Introduction

After reading this introduction, you will know how to:

A Use Course Technology ILT manuals in general.

B Use prerequisites, a target student description, course objectives, and a skills inventory to properly set students' expectations for the course.

C Set up a classroom to teach this course.

D Get support for setting up and teaching this course.

Topic A: About the manual

Course Technology ILT philosophy

Our goal at Course Technology is to make you, the instructor, as successful as possible. To that end, our manuals facilitate students' learning by providing structured interaction with the software itself. While we provide text to help you explain difficult concepts, the hands-on activities are the focus of our courses. Leading the students through these activities will teach the skills and concepts effectively.

We believe strongly in the instructor-led class. For many students, having a thinking, feeling instructor in front of them will always be the most comfortable way to learn. Because the students' focus should be on you, our manuals are designed and written to facilitate your interaction with the students, and not to call attention to manuals themselves.

We believe in the basic approach of setting expectations, then teaching, and providing summary and review afterwards. For this reason, lessons begin with objectives and end with summaries. We also provide overall course objectives and a course summary to provide both an introduction to and closure on the entire course.

Our goal is your success. We encourage your feedback in helping us to continually improve our manuals to meet your needs.

Manual components

The manuals contain these major components:

- Table of contents
- Introduction
- Units
- Appendices
- Course summary
- Glossary
- Index

Each element is described below.

Table of contents

The table of contents acts as a learning roadmap for you and the students.

Introduction

The introduction contains information about our training philosophy and our manual components, features, and conventions. It contains target student, prerequisite, objective, and setup information for the specific course. Finally, the introduction contains support information.

Units

Units are the largest structural component of the actual course content. A unit begins with a title page that lists objectives for each major subdivision, or topic, within the unit. Within each topic, conceptual and explanatory information alternates with hands-on activities. Units conclude with a summary comprising one paragraph for each topic, and an independent practice activity that gives students an opportunity to practice the skills they've learned.

The conceptual information takes the form of text paragraphs, exhibits, lists, and tables. The activities are structured in two columns, one telling students what to do, the other providing explanations, descriptions, and graphics. Throughout a unit, instructor notes are found in the left margin.

Appendices

This course has two appendices. Appendix A lists all CompTIA A+ 220-603 exam objectives along with references to corresponding coverage in this manual. Appendix B provides list of acronyms that appear on all four CompTIA A+ exams covering 2006 objectives—Essentials, 220-602, 220-603, and 220-604.

Course summary

This section provides a text summary of the entire course. It is useful for providing closure at the end of the course. The course summary also indicates the next course in this series, if there is one, and lists additional resources students might find useful as they continue to learn about the software.

Glossary

The glossary provides definitions for all of the key terms used in this course.

Index

The index at the end of this manual makes it easy for you and your students to find information about a particular software component, feature, or concept.

Manual conventions

We've tried to keep the number of elements and the types of formatting to a minimum in the manuals. We think this aids in clarity and makes the manuals more classically elegant looking. But there are some conventions and icons you should know about.

Instructor note/icon

Item	Description
Italic text	In conceptual text, indicates a new term or feature.
Bold text	In unit summaries, indicates a key term or concept. In an independent practice activity, indicates an explicit item that you select, choose, or type.
`Code font`	Indicates code or syntax.
`Longer strings of ▶` `code will look ▶` `like this.`	In the hands-on activities, any code that's too long to fit on a single line is divided into segments by one or more continuation characters (▶). This code should be entered as a continuous string of text.
Instructor notes.	In the left margin, provide tips, hints, and warnings for the instructor.
Select **bold item**	In the left column of hands-on activities, bold sans-serif text indicates an explicit item that you select, choose, or type.
Keycaps like (↵ ENTER)	Indicate a key on the keyboard you must press.
⚠ *Warning icon.*	Warnings prepare instructors for potential classroom management problems.
✔ *Tip icon.*	Tips give extra information the instructor can share with students.
Setup icon.	Setup notes provide a realistic business context for instructors to share with students, or indicate additional setup steps required for the current activity.
Projector icon.	Projector notes indicate that there is a PowerPoint slide for the adjacent content.

Hands-on activities

The hands-on activities are the most important parts of our manuals. They are divided into two primary columns. The "Here's how" column gives short directions to the students. The "Here's why" column provides explanations, graphics, and clarifications. To the left, instructor notes provide tips, warnings, setups, and other information for the instructor only. Here's a sample:

Do it!

A-1: Creating a commission formula

Here's how	Here's why
1 Open Sales	This is an oversimplified sales compensation worksheet. It shows sales totals, commissions, and incentives for five sales reps.
2 Observe the contents of cell F4	F4 ▼ = =E4*C_Rate
	The commission rate formulas use the name "C_Rate" instead of a value for the commission rate.

Take the time to make sure your students understand this worksheet. We'll be here a while.

For these activities, we have provided a collection of data files designed to help students learn each skill in a real-world business context. As students work through the activities, they will modify and update these files. Of course, students might make a mistake and therefore want to re-key the activity starting from scratch. To make it easy to start over, students will rename each data file at the end of the first activity in which the file is modified. Our convention for renaming files is to add the word "My" to the beginning of the file name. In the above activity, for example, students are using a file called "Sales" for the first time. At the end of this activity, they would save the file as "My sales," thus leaving the "Sales" file unchanged. If students make mistakes, they can start over using the original "Sales" file.

In some activities, however, it might not be practical to rename the data file. Such exceptions are indicated with an instructor note. If students want to retry one of these activities, you will need to provide a fresh copy of the original data file.

PowerPoint presentations

Each unit in this course has an accompanying PowerPoint presentation. These slide shows are designed to support your classroom instruction while providing students with a visual focus. Each presentation begins with a list of unit objectives and ends with a unit summary slide. We strongly recommend that you run these presentations from the instructor's station as you teach this course. A copy of PowerPoint Viewer is included, so it is not necessary to have PowerPoint installed on your computer.

The Course ILT PowerPoint add-in

The CD also contains a PowerPoint add-in that enables you to do two things:

- Create slide notes for the class
- Display a control panel for the Flash movies embedded in the presentations

To load the PowerPoint add-in:

1   Copy the Course_ILT.ppa file to a convenient location on your hard drive.
2   Start PowerPoint.
3   Choose Tools, Macro, Security to open the Security dialog box. On the Security Level tab, select Medium (if necessary), and then click OK.
4   Choose Tools, Add-Ins to open the Add-Ins dialog box. Then, click Add New.
5   Browse to and double-click the Course_ILT.ppa file, and then click OK. A message box will appear, warning you that macros can contain viruses.
6   Click Enable Macros. The Course_ILT add-in should now appear in the Available Add-Ins list (in the Add-Ins dialog box). The "x" in front of Course_ILT indicates that the add-in is loaded.
7   Click Close to close the Add-Ins dialog box.

After you complete this procedure, a new toolbar will be available at the top of the PowerPoint window. This toolbar contains a single button labeled "Create SlideNotes." Click this button to generate slide-notes files in both text (.txt) and Excel (.xls) format. By default, these files will be saved to the folder that contains the presentation. If the PowerPoint file is on a CD-ROM or in some other location to which the slide-notes files cannot be saved, you will be prompted to save the presentation to your hard drive and try again.

When you run a presentation and come to a slide that contains a Flash movie, you will see a small control panel in the lower-left corner of the screen. You can use this panel to start, stop, and rewind the movie, or to play it again.

Topic B: Setting student expectations

Properly setting students' expectations is essential to your success. This topic will help you do that by providing:

- Prerequisites for this course
- A description of the target student
- Guidelines for CompTIA certification
- A list of the objectives for the course
- A skills assessment for the course

Course prerequisites

Students taking this course should be familiar with personal computers and the use of a keyboard and a mouse. Furthermore, this course assumes that students have completed the *CompTIA A+ Certification: Essentials* course or have equivalent experience.

Target student

This course will prepare students for the CompTIA A+ 220-603 certification exam (2006 objectives). It is designed to prepare students to assist users remotely as a help desk or call center support technician.

How to become CompTIA certified

In order to achieve CompTIA A+ certification, a student must register for and pass the CompTIA A+ Essentials exam and any one of the following certification exams:

- CompTIA A+ 220-602
- CompTIA A+ 220-603
- CompTIA A+ 220-604

In order to become CompTIA certified, students must:

1   Select a certification exam provider. For more information, students should visit http://certification.comptia.org/resources/registration.aspx.
2   Register for and schedule a time to take the CompTIA certification exam(s) at a convenient location.
3   Read and sign the Candidate Agreement, which will be presented at the time of the exam. The complete text of the Candidate Agreement can be found at http://certification.comptia.org/resources/canidate_agreement.aspx.
4   Take and pass the CompTIA certification exam(s).

For more information about CompTIA's certifications, such as its industry acceptance, benefits or program news, students should visit http://certification.comptia.org.

CompTIA is a not-for-profit information technology (IT) trade association. CompTIA's certifications are designed by subject matter experts from across the IT industry. Each CompTIA certification is vendor-neutral, covers multiple technologies and requires demonstration of skills and knowledge widely sought after by the IT industry.

To contact CompTIA with any questions or comments, please call (630) 678-8300 or e-mail questions@comptia.org.

Course objectives

You should share these overall course objectives with your students at the beginning of the day. This will give the students an idea about what to expect, and it will help you identify students who might be misplaced. Students are considered misplaced when they lack the prerequisite knowledge or when they already know most of the subject matter to be covered.

Note: In addition to the general objectives listed below, specific CompTIA A+ 220-603 exam objectives are listed at the beginning of each topic. For a complete mapping of exam objectives to course content, see Appendix A.

After completing this course, students will know how to:

- Install expansion cards.
- Install, maintain, and troubleshoot hard drives and data storage devices.
- Install and troubleshoot printers and scanners.
- Manage and monitor files, operating system settings, and the Registry.
- Maintain and troubleshoot a Windows operating system.
- Configure and troubleshoot networking.
- Secure the computing environment.
- Maintain a level of professionalism and ensure customer satisfaction.

Skills inventory

Use the following form to gauge students' skill levels entering the class (students have copies in the introductions of their student manuals). For each skill listed, have students rate their familiarity from 1 to 5, with five being the most familiar. Emphasize that this is not a test. Rather, it is intended to provide students with an idea of where they're starting from at the beginning of class. If a student is wholly unfamiliar with all the skills, he or she might not be ready for the class. A student who seems to understand all of the skills, on the other hand, might need to move on to the next course in the series.

Skill	1	2	3	4	5
Installing a video card					
Installing a sound card					
Installing an internal modem					
Installing a PC Card					
Installing a mini PCI card					
Installing a non-PnP device					
Overriding PnP settings					
Troubleshooting expansion card problems					
Searching for and installing updated drivers					
Choosing a file system					
Physically installing a hard drive					
Partitioning and formatting a hard drive					
Changing the file system type					
Converting to a dynamic disk					
Maintaining your hard drive					
Troubleshooting data storage devices					
Examining the dot-matrix printing process					
Examining how inkjet printers work					
Examining how laser printers work					
Identifying other printer technologies					
Examining the Windows printing process					

Skill	1	2	3	4	5
Installing a printer					
Installing printer add-ons and upgrades					
Performing printer maintenance					
Optimizing printing					
Troubleshooting printer problems					
Connecting a scanner					
Troubleshooting scanner problems					
Optimizing scanners					
Using the command prompt					
Navigating a directory tree					
Creating directories					
Copying a directory and its contents					
Removing directories					
Creating a text file					
Modifying file attributes					
Editing a text file					
Managing temporary files					
Running Windows diagnostics					
Running msinfo32 from a command line					
Managing applications					
Ending a process					
Monitoring performance					
Monitoring network utilization					
Managing users					
Configuring Windows XP services					
Managing the Startup program group					
Disabling error reporting					

Skill	1	2	3	4	5
Enabling error reporting for specific programs					
Viewing the event logs					
Viewing the event logs of a remote computer					
Controlling the display of an event log					
Clearing an event log					
Changing event log properties					
Viewing Registry information					
Searching the Registry					
Backing up Registry files					
Backing up files using Wizard mode					
Restoring information from a backup					
Backing up System State data					
Creating a System Restore point					
Booting to System Restore					
Installing a Windows XP service pack					
Using Windows Update to install hotfixes					
Configuring Automatic Updates					
Troubleshooting operating system startup					
Booting the computer in different startup modes					
Using the System Configuration Utility					
Creating an MS-DOS startup disk					
Running the Recovery Console					
Creating an ASR recovery set					
Using System File Checker					
Enabling Remote Desktop					
Making a Remote Desktop Connection					
Using Remote Assistance					

Skill	1	2	3	4	5
Discussing network models					
Installing a NIC					
Viewing installed network protocols					
Configuring an IP address and subnet mask					
Configuring additional TCP/IP properties					
Joining a Windows domain					
Viewing network resources					
Installing and configuring NWLink					
Sharing a folder					
Setting access permissions					
Connecting to a shared folder					
Sharing a printer					
Connecting to a shared printer					
Installing the NetWare client					
Selecting a connection technology					
Discussing WAN bandwidth technologies					
Configuring a browser to use a proxy server					
Configuring Windows Firewall					
Identifying the technology used to implement WLANs					
Configuring a wireless access point					
Configuring a wireless client					
Verifying the NIC device in Device Manager					
Identifying the TCP/IP utilities used for troubleshooting					
Using Ipconfig to display TCP/IP settings					
Testing TCP/IP connectivity					
Using Nslookup and Tracert to verify settings					
Determining effective NTFS permissions					

Skill	1	2	3	4	5
Joining a workgroup					
Securing access to the operating system					
Choosing the correct file system for security					
Configuring file access restrictions					
Encrypting files					
Understanding authentication technologies					
Using local security policies to set password restrictions					
Enabling an audit policy					
Auditing an event					
Installing a fingerprint reader					
Installing a card reader					
Installing the IdentiPHI Basic software					
Configuring IdentiPHI Basic to accept smart cards					
Enrolling a smart card with IdentiPHI Basic					
Using a smart card					
Uninstalling the smart card reader and software					
Implementing physical access restrictions					
Managing social engineering attacks					
Examining network security					
Maintaining professionalism					
Ensuring customer satisfaction					
Tracking problems and resolutions					

Topic C: Classroom setup

All our courses assume that each student has a personal computer to use during the class. Our hands-on approach to learning requires they do. This topic gives information on how to set up the classroom to teach this course. It includes minimum requirements for the students' personal computers, setup information for the first time you teach the class, and setup information for each time that you teach after the first time you set up the classroom.

Classroom configuration

This course is hardware intensive. It contains activities that require the students to install and remove hardware, and configure an operating system. Due to the amount of hardware required for this course, we recommend that you create the following classroom configuration:

1   Assign a personal computer (designated as a **Student PC**) to each student for Internet access as well as the hardware installation and operating system configuration activities.

2   Designate an **Instructor PC** to be used as a file and print server and for demonstration purposes.

3   If you don't have enough hardware for each student to work independently for every hardware activity, assign an additional PC (designated as a **Group PC**) to each group of two to four students for the hardware installation and configuration activities.

4   Connect all PCs to a **single classroom hub**, which, in turn, is connected to the institution's backbone to allow for Internet connectivity and dynamic IP address assignment.

Instructor PC hardware requirements

Initial configuration

The hardware requirements for the instructor PC are as follows:

- Intel Pentium II or Intel-compatible processor, running at 400 MHz or higher (Pentium III or better strongly recommended)
- At least 256 MB RAM
- SVGA display adapter, supporting at least 256 colors and 800×600 resolution
- Keyboard and mouse
- 10/100 Mb network card (NIC), plus associated cabling to attach to a network (RJ-45 connectors)
- 20 GB hard drive
- 1.44 MB 3.5" floppy disk drive
- CD-ROM drive supported by Windows XP (or 2000) — check the Hardware Compatibility List (HCL)

Additional equipment for classroom

General

- Overhead projector connected to the Instructor PC
- Whiteboard or blackboard
- Printer paper
- Floppy disks for each student and the instructor
- Computer toolkit (including non-magnetic Phillips-head screwdriver)
- Assorted screwdrivers
- Grounding straps
- Grounding mats
- Multimeters
- A copy of Windows XP Professional installation CD for each student

Hardware (for activities on the instructor, student, or group computers)

- Variety of video cards (ISA, PCI, AGP)
- Variety of sound cards
- Variety of modems (internal and external)
- Notebook computer(s) with Windows XP Professional or Windows 2000 Professional installed (you might choose to complete the notebook activities as a group)
- Notebook documentation
- Type I and/or III PC Cards
- Mini-PCI cards
- A variety of legacy (non-PnP) devices
- Combination of drives (hard drives, CD-ROM drive, floppy drive, ZIP drive, DVD drive), controller cards, related media, and cables
- Inkjet or laser printer(s) (you might choose to complete the printer activities as a group)
- Scanner(s) (you might choose to complete the scanner activities as a group)
- NIC cards for each student
- Wireless network card for the instructor computer
- Wireless access router or hub
- Wireless network card
- USB fingerprint scanner, such as the APC Biopod or Microsoft Fingerprint Reader
- SCR331 card reader, from SCM Microsystems and available from www.securityworkplace.com/p-35-scr331-usb-smart-card-reader.aspx
- IdentiPHI Pilot software, available from www.securityworkplace.com/pc-14-2-identiphi-pilot.aspx
- One smart card that is compatible with IdentiPHI Pilot. Contact www.securityworkplace.com for more information or to purchase such a card.

- Appropriate cables for connecting devices (including serial, parallel, USB, FireWire, SCSI)
- Non-working versions of any of the equipment that can be used for troubleshooting labs

Optional hardware

- Phone lines
- Phone cord with RJ-11 connectors on both ends that are long enough to reach the wall outlet
- Dot-matrix printer
- Ink-jet printer
- Laser printer
- Dye-sublimation printer and ink
- Thermal printer and paper
- Solid ink printer and ink
- NICs other than those used in the classroom network (i.e. Token Ring, FDDI)
- Samples of twisted pair, coaxial, fiber cables
- Network card for laser printer
- SCSI cables
- SCSI terminators
- Wireless hub and wireless adapters

Instructor PC software requirements

You will need to install one of the following operating systems on the Instructor's PC. Installation instructions are provided in the section titled "Initial setup instructions." Keep in mind that this course was developed using Windows XP Professional, so the graphics might look different if you use Windows 2000 Professional.

- Windows XP Professional or Windows 2000 Professional

In addition, you will need to install the following software:

- Latest Service Packs
- Latest version of Internet Explorer (www.microsoft.com/windows/ie)
- Device drivers for all installed hardware
- Class presentation files (included on the accompanying CD)
- Microsoft PowerPoint Viewer (included on the accompanying CD)

Student PC hardware requirements

Initial configuration

The hardware requirement for the student PC is as follows:

- Intel Pentium II or Intel-compatible processor, running at 400 MHz or higher (Pentium III or better strongly recommended)
- At least 256 MB RAM
- SVGA display adapter, supporting at least 256 colors and 800×600 resolution
- Keyboard and mouse
- 10/100 Mb Network card (NIC), plus associated cabling to attach to a network (RJ-45 connectors)
- 10 GB hard-disk space
- 1.44 MB 3.5" floppy disk drive
- CD-ROM drive supported by Windows XP or Windows 2000—check the Hardware Compatibility List (HCL)

Student PC software requirements

You will need to install one of the following operating systems on each Student PC. Installation instructions are provided in the section titled "Initial setup instructions." Keep in mind that this course was developed using Windows XP Professional, so the graphics might look different if you use Windows 2000 Professional.

- Windows XP Professional or Windows 2000 Professional

Note: You will need to have the installation files on CD or in a network share for each of these operating systems handy during class.

In addition, you will need the following software:

- Latest Service Packs
- Latest version of Internet Explorer (www.microsoft.com/windows/ie)
- Drivers for all hardware

Group PC hardware requirements

Initial configuration

The hardware requirements for the group PC is as follows:

- Intel Pentium II or Intel-compatible processor, running at 400 MHz or higher (Pentium III or better strongly recommended)
- At least 256 MB RAM
- SVGA display adapter, supporting at least 256 colors and 800×600 resolution
- Keyboard and mouse
- 10/100 Mb Network card (NIC), plus associated cabling to attach to a network (RJ-45 connectors)
- 10 GB hard-disk space
- 1.44 MB 3.5" floppy disk drive
- CD-ROM drive supported by Windows XP (or 2000)—check the Hardware Compatibility List (HCL)

Group PC software requirements

In addition, you will need to install the following software:

- Windows 2000 Professional or Windows XP Professional and the latest service packs
- Latest version of Internet Explorer (www.microsoft.com/windows/ie)
- Drivers for all hardware

Network requirements

The following network components and connectivity are also required for this course:

- Internet access, for the following purposes:
  - Downloading the latest critical updates and service packs from www.windowsupdate.com
  - Completing activities where students download drivers from the Internet (in the case of not having them on disk in the classroom)
  - Downloading the Student Data files from www.courseilt.com (if necessary)
- Analog phone line for testing modem

First-time setup instructions

Classroom server setup

If you have already taught this course and are preparing to teach it again, you can use the abbreviated setup instructions provided in the following section. See "Guidelines for setting up subsequent classes."

The first time you teach this course, you will need to perform the following steps to set up the classroom's Active Directory domain controller.

1 Install Windows Server 2003 or Windows 2000 Server, with the latest Service Pack for your chosen NOS, according to the software manufacturer's instructions. Use the following variables during installation:
   - Format the installation partition to NTFS.
   - Use **Per server** licensing, allowing sufficient connections for your class.
   - Enter **RSTSRV** as the computer name.
   - Enter **Pa$$321** as the Administrator password.
   - Accept the default Windows components, if prompted.
   - Set the Date, Time, and Time Zones for your area.
   - Use Custom settings to enter **192.168.100.254** as the IP Address for the computer. If your network requires you to use another IP address, substitute that address.
   - Enter the default gateway address appropriate to your company.
   - Enter **192.168.100.254** in the Preferred DNS server box to point the computer to itself as its DNS server. If your network requires you to enter a different IP address for this server, substitute that address.
   - Put the server in the default workgroup.
   - Log on as Administrator with a password of Pa$$321.
   - In the Windows Server Post-Setup Security Updates dialog box, click Finish and click Yes.
2 If your copy of Windows Server 2003 or Windows 2000 Server did not include the latest Service Pack, install the appropriate Service Pack.

3 After the installation process is complete, use Device Manager to ensure that all devices are functioning correctly. You might have to download and install drivers for devices listed with a yellow question-mark icon.

4 Promote the computer to an Active Directory domain controller for the RSTDomain.class domain. Here's how (if you're using Windows 2000 Server the steps might be slightly different):

   a In the Manage Your Server Wizard, click "Add or remove a role."

   b On the Preliminary Steps page, click Next. If necessary, on the Configuration Options page, select Custom configuration and click Next.

   c From the Server Role list, select "Domain Controller (Active Directory)" and click Next.

   d Click Next to run the Active Directory Installation Wizard. Then, click Next.

   e On the Operating System Compatibility page, click Next.

   f On the Domain Controller Type page, verify that "Domain controller for a new domain" is selected and click Next. If prompted, created a new domain tree.

   g On the New Domain page, verify that "Domain in a new forest" is selected and click Next.

   h On the New Domain Name page, in the "Full DNS name for new domain" box, type **RSTDomain.class**. Then, click Next.

   i On the NetBIOS Domain Name page, accept the default domain NetBIOS name by clicking Next.

   j On the Database and Log Folders page, accept the default locations by clicking Next.

   k On the Shared System Volume page, accept the default folder location by clicking Next.

   l On the DNS Registration Diagnostics page, select "Install and configure DNS server on this computer, and set this computer to use this DNS server as its preferred DNS server." Click Next.

   m On the Permissions page, accept the default permissions by clicking Next.

   n On the Directory Services Restore Mode Administrator Password page, enter **Pa$$321** in both the Restore mode password and Confirm password text boxes. Click Next.

   o On the Summary page, click Next.

   p Click Finish, and then click Restart Now.

   q After the computer reboots and you log back in as Administrator with a password of **Pa$$321**, click Finish.

5 If necessary, install DHCP to lease IP address information to the instructor and student client computers. To do so:

   a In the Manage Your Server Wizard, click "Add or remove a role."

   b On the Preliminary Steps page, click Next.

   c From the Server Role list, select DHCP server, and then click Next.

   d On the Summary of Selections page, click Next.

   e In the New Scope Wizard, click Next.

   f On the Scope Name page, in the Name box, type **APlusRST**. In the Description box, type **Scope for APlusRST class**.

   g Click Next.

h   In the Start IP address box, enter **192.168.100.200**.
In the End IP address box, enter **192.168.100.240**.
These addresses should be on the same subnet as your classroom server. If your network requires you to enter a different IP address for the classroom server, substitute addresses on that subnet.

i   Click Next. Click Next again to skip the Add Exclusions page.

j   If your class will continue past 8 days, then on the Lease Duration page, under "Limited to," increase the number of days as needed. Then, click Next.

k   On the Configure DHCP Options page, verify that "Yes, I want to configure these options now" is selected and click Next.

l   Enter the default gateway address appropriate to your company, and click Add. Then, click Next.

m   On the Domain Name and DNS Servers page, in the IP address box, enter this computer's IP address (**192.168.100.254**). Click Add and then click Next.
If your network requires you to enter a different IP address for the classroom server, substitute that address.

n   Click Next to skip WINS Servers configuration.

o   On the Activate Scope page, verify that "Yes, I want to activate this scope now" is selected and click Next.

p   Click Finish twice.

6   Authorize the DHCP server in Active Directory. To do so:

a   From Manage Your Server, click Manage this DHCP Server.

b   In the console tree, select and then right-click your RSTSRV.RSTDomain.class server and choose Authorize.

c   Right-click your RSTSRV.RSTDomain.class server and choose Refresh. A green arrow should now be displayed on the server icon. Your scope's status is listed as **Active** in the details pane.

d   Close DHCP.

The first time you teach this course, you will need to perform the following steps to set up each student computer.

1   Use a third-party disk management utility to configure the hard disk as follows:

- A 6 GB partition for the installation of Windows XP Professional, drive letter C:
- A 4 GB partition, drive letter D:
- Leave the remaining as free space.

2   Install Windows XP on an NTFS partition according to the software manufacturer's instructions. If the student machines have Internet access, and they are behind a software or hardware firewall, install the latest critical updates and service packs from www.windowsupdate.com.

- Format the partition to NTFS.
- Set regional settings appropriate for your environment.
- Enter a name and organization appropriate for your environment.
- Name the instructor's computer **RST00**; name each student computer **RST##**, where ## is a unique number assigned to each student starting with 01.
- Use an Administrator password of **Pa$$321**.

- Set the Date, Time, and Time Zones for your area.
- Use Custom network settings to configure the computer to use IP address information appropriate to your environment.
  Note: If Setup does not detect your network card during installation, you will need to manually install the network card and configure networking after setup is complete.
- Make the computer a member of the **TechSupport** workgroup.
- If necessary, turn off Automatic Updates.
- Create a **RSTADMIN##** administrative user on the computer. Use the ## that matches the computer number. Set the password to **Pa$$321**.

Note: You can also use Windows 2000, although the screen shots in this course were taken using Windows XP, so students' screens might look somewhat different.

3 If your copy of Windows XP Professional did not include SP2, install SP2 now.

4 After the installation process is complete, use Device Manager to ensure that all devices are functioning correctly. You might have to download and install drivers for devices listed with a yellow question mark.

5 From the Control Panel, open the Display Properties dialog box and apply the following settings:

- Theme — Windows XP
- Screen resolution — 1024 by 768 pixels
- Color quality — High (24 bit) or higher

6 Format drive D: to NTFS. Students will use this drive for backup activities.

7 Configure Windows Firewall:

   a In Control Panel, click Security Center.

   b Under "Manage security settings for," click Windows Firewall.

   c In the Windows Firewall dialog box, on the Exceptions tab, check File and Printer Sharing.

   d Click OK.

   e Close Windows Security Center and Control Panel.

8 If you don't have the data CD that came with this manual, download the Student Data files for the course. You can download the data directly to student machines or to a central location on your own network.

   a Connect to www.courseilt.com/instructor_tools.html.

   b Click the link for CompTIA to display a page of course listings, and then click the link for CompTIA A+ Certification: 220-603.

   c Click the link for downloading the Student Data files, and follow the instructions that appear on your screen.

9 Create a folder named Student Data at the root of the hard drive. For a standard hard-drive setup, this will be C:\Student Data.

10 Copy the data files to the Student Data folder.

Guidelines for setting up subsequent classes

To set up subsequent classes:

1 Reinstall Windows XP Professional or Windows 2000 Professional on the instructor computer and each student computer and the Group PCs. You do not need to reinstall the domain controller; it can be used from one class to another without re-installation or reconfiguration.

2 Obtain all necessary hardware components and drivers.

Troubleshooting lab setup suggestions

Many of the units in this course include a troubleshooting lab. In each of these labs, students are asked to solve problems related to the material of that unit. Each of the following sections presents ideas for problems that can be implemented.

We suggest two possible means for implementing these problems. In the first, you would send students off to a break while you induce these problems in their computers. In the second scenario, you would divide students into two groups. Each group would implement problems in a set of computers. The groups would switch places and solve the problems that the other group created.

When determining which problems to implement, make sure to take into consideration the technical proficiency of your students.

Unit 1: Expansion cards

For the lab activity entitled "Troubleshooting expansion card problems," you could implement an idea of your own or one of these problems:

- Set the video mode to a mode that the monitor cannot support.
- Set the video refresh rate to a value that the monitor cannot support.
- Install a failing monitor that is blurry or displays an unsteady image.
- Install an out-of-date and buggy version of the video driver.
- Install the wrong video driver for the video adapter.
- Mute the sound.
- Disconnect the speaker power cord.
- Loosen the adapter card in its slot so that its connectors do not make full contact.
- Disconnect the CD-to-sound card audio cable.
- Turn off all Windows sounds in the Control Panel.
- Disconnect the phone cable from the modem.
- Use a bad phone cable to connect the modem to the jack.
- Give students a voice or fax number to dial into instead of another modem line.
- Install damaged or non-functioning adapter cards, such as video cards, modem cards, sound cards, and so forth.
- (Advanced) Put tape over the adapter's edge connector or paint some of the connector's pins with nail polish so that they cannot make contact.

Unit 2: Hard disks

For the activity entitled "Troubleshooting data storage devices," you could implement an idea of your own or one of these problems:

- Disable the floppy drive in the BIOS.
- Disconnect the power cable from the floppy drive.
- Install a damaged, failing, or dead hard drive.
- Install the hard drive cable's connector backward (force the connector backward into the socket).
- Install the hard drive cable backward (connect the motherboard connector to the drive and the master drive connector to the motherboard).
- Install a bad hard drive cable.
- Disconnect the power cable from the hard drive.
- In the BIOS, configure the boot order to not include the primary hard drive.
- Remove the "active" designation from the primary hard drive so that the system won't boot.
- Install a new drive that is partitioned, but not formatted so that the system cannot boot from that drive.
- Install or provide to students an extremely large hard drive (160 GB or larger) in a system that cannot support it.
- With an older, slower drive, configure the BIOS to speed the boot process to the point where the drive cannot spin up and be ready by the time the startup process accesses it.

Unit 3: Printers and scanners

For the activity "Troubleshooting printer problems," you could implement an idea of your own or one of these problems:

- Replace the ink or toner cartridges with empty ones or ones that produce poor quality output.
- Install a printer that prints stray marks on output.
- Disconnect or loosely connect the interface cable.
- Disconnect or loosely connect the power cord.
- Leave the cover or door open, off, or slightly ajar.
- Plug the printer into the power strip, but turn off the strip.
- Create a paper jam.
- Remove the printer driver.
- Install the wrong printer driver.
- Remove the ink cartridge(s).
- Turn the printer off mid-way through a cleaning cycle or while printing.
- Provide the wrong interface cable, power cord, and/or drivers.
- Disable the port in the BIOS to which the printer connects.
- Add paper that is either very static laden or humid (to produce poor images and possibly printer jams).

- If the printer requires setup on the printer, change the settings to use a different interface, or other settings. (For example on a LaserJet printer, use the menu on the printer to specify that it is connected via the serial port while it is actually connected via parallel, or a similar change.)
- Disable the port in the BIOS to which the printer connects.

For the independent practice activity, choose from any of the problems above, or come up with additional ones as appropriate to the level of student understanding of the troubleshooting process and of the equipment.

For the activity "Troubleshooting scanner problems," you could implement an idea of your own or one of these problems:

- Provide the wrong power cord.
- Provide the wrong data cable.
- Remove the drivers.
- Install the wrong driver.
- Remove the software.
- Provide a damaged power or data cable.
- Plug it in using the power cable, but turn off the power strip.

Unit 4: Operating system management

This unit has no troubleshooting lab or requires no setup.

Unit 5: OS Maintenance and troubleshooting

This unit has no troubleshooting lab or requires no setup.

Unit 6: Networking

This unit has no troubleshooting lab or requires no setup.

Unit 7: Security

This unit has no troubleshooting lab or requires no setup.

Unit 8: Professionalism and communication

This unit has no troubleshooting lab or requires no setup.

CertBlaster exam prep software

CertBlaster pre- and post-assessment software is available for this course. To download and install this free software, complete the following steps:

1 Go to www.courseilt.com/certblaster.
2 Click the link for CompTIA A+ 220-603.
3 Save the .EXE file to a folder on your hard drive. (Note: If you skip this step, the CertBlaster software will not install correctly.)
4 Click Start and choose Run.
5 Click Browse and then navigate to the folder that contains the .EXE file.
6 Select the .EXE file and click Open.
7 Click OK and follow the on-screen instructions. When prompted for the password, enter **c_603**.

Topic D: Support

Your success is our primary concern. If you need help setting up this class or teaching a particular unit, topic, or activity, please don't hesitate to get in touch with us. Please have the name of the course available when you call, and be as specific as possible about the kind of help you need.

Phone support

You can call for support 24 hours a day at (888) 672-7500. If you do not connect to a live operator, you can leave a message, and we pledge to return your call within 24 hours (except on Saturday and Sunday).

Web-based support

The Course ILT Web site provides several instructor's tools for each course, including course outlines and answers to frequently asked questions. To download these files, go to www.courseilt.com/instructor_tools.html. For additional Course ILT resources, including our online catalog and contact information, go to http://www.course.com/ilt.

Unit 1

Expansion cards

Unit time: 120 minutes

Complete this unit, and you'll know how to:

A Install a video adapter, sound card, and internal modem, as well as other types of expansion cards.

B Install expansion cards, including PC Card and internal adapters, into laptops.

C Install legacy and non-Plug and Play expansion cards into desktop systems.

D Identify the symptoms, probable causes, and potential solutions to expansion card-related problems.

Topic A: Expansion cards

This topic covers the following CompTIA A+ 220-603 exam objective.

#	Objective
1.1	**1.1 Install, configure, optimize, and upgrade personal computer components** • Add, remove, and configure display devices, input devices and adapter cards including basic input and multimedia devices.

Card installation

Explanation

 This material is covered in CompTIA A+: Essentials.

To install an expansion card, you must consider how to handle the cards safely as well as how to configure the device if Plug-and-Play (PnP) doesn't do it for you.

Safe handling

Expansion cards are sensitive to electrostatic discharge (ESD). You should always follow ESD precautions when working with these cards or any device that must be installed inside your PC's chassis. As usual, follow these guidelines when handling expansion cards:

- Unplug your computer before opening it.
- Ground yourself to the chassis before touching internal components.
- Keep expansion cards inside static-protective bags or packaging until you're ready to install them.
- Handle cards by their edges or slot cover plate. Don't touch board components, traces, or edge-connector pins.

Drivers

Drivers are a form of software that interacts with hardware to enable that device's functionality. It's the responsibility of a driver, for example, to read the data received over the network via a network interface card. Every expansion device or adapter card in your PC requires a driver. (Basically, any device not controlled by the BIOS requires a driver.)

Some drivers are supplied with the operating system. For example, the drivers that are needed to enable onboard serial or parallel ports are supplied with the operating system. Other devices require drivers supplied by the device manufacturer.

In many cases, these vendors will supply their driver to Microsoft, who includes it in the set of files that comprise the operating system or makes it available on the Windows Update Web site. In other cases, you will need to use the drivers supplied with your expansion device, either on a CD that comes with it or on the vendor's Web site.

Card insertion

In general, you will follow these steps to install an expansion card in your PC:

1 If you're not using a PnP-compatible expansion card or operating system, determine the available system resources (IRQs, I/O addresses, and so forth). Configure the DIP switches or jumpers on the card, as necessary, to assign it available system resources.

    If you're using a PnP-compatible card and operating system, the vendor might direct you to run an installation utility before installing their device. This installation program puts the necessary drivers in a location where Windows can find them once you're done installing the device. If appropriate, run that setup program now.

2 Shut down your PC, unplug it, remove peripheral cables, and open the case.

3 Locate an empty and available expansion slot of the correct type.

4 Remove the slot cover for that slot. They are generally either screwed in place or held by spring-clips.

5 If necessary, temporarily move or remove wires or other expansion cards that are in the way so that you can access the slot.

6 If you need to connect wire assemblies to the expansion board—not to its back slot cover plate, but to the board itself—connect that end of the wire assembly before installing the card. In this way, you can easily reach the connector and be sure you're installing the wire assembly in its correct orientation. Connect the other end after you have installed the card.

7 Begin inserting the end of the edge connector furthest from the slot cover. Then, gently push the card into place in the slot. This will help you line up the connector correctly. Inserting the card at an angle like this is usually easier than pushing it straight into the slot.

8 Fix the card in place with screws or clips, as appropriate to your case design.

9 Connect any wiring assemblies, including those you temporarily removed to install this card. Close the case, connect peripherals, and start the system.

10 Depending on your operating system, version, and adapter card technology, configure the card. If you're using PnP-compatible components, PnP will handle this for you.

11 If necessary, install required drivers. If you have to install drivers yourself, you will most likely need to configure them to use the same hardware resources you configured the card to use.

When you're done, some devices and operating system versions will also require you to restart your computer. This fully loads the drivers and configures the operating system to support your new device.

Video adapters

Video adapters convert computer data to the signals required to produce the images that you see on your screen. With the early generations of PCs, video adapters created just text output, and often monochrome output at that. Nowadays, video adapters create the signals necessary to display full color and full motion images and video.

Due to the enormous amount of information that must be manipulated by the adapter to produce these signals, modern video adapters are almost computers in their own right. They often feature a specialized processor chip and lots of onboard memory. Perhaps even more than the CPU type or amount of memory in your system, the video adapter is the component most responsible for the overall performance of your PC.

Creating an image

A traditional TV-style monitor creates an image when a stream of electrons hits a phosphorescent coating on the inside of the front of the screen.

In the earliest monitors, this coating would glow green in the presence of the electron beam and remain black when it wasn't being hit with electrons, hence the green and black of early monitors. Later developments in phosphor coatings permitted the display of red, green, and blue glows that when combined produce a full range of colors.

This electron beam is very narrow, hitting a spot on the screen barely a quarter of a millimeter across at any particular time. To create a full screen image, the beam is moved rapidly back and forth across the screen, from the top to the bottom of the screen many times a second. To create a flicker-free image, the beam must paint out the full screen image at least 60 times every second.

The rate at which the image is painted is called the *refresh rate*. With some early video display standards, the full image could not be refreshed entirely in a single pass. These systems used *interlacing*, in which the odd lines of the image were painted during one pass of the beam and the even lines painted during a second pass. Such interlaced displays often suffered badly from flickering.

Resolution

An image to be displayed on the screen, be it text or a picture, is divided by the display adapter into a series of dots called *pixels* (adapted from "picture element"). Officially, a pixel is the smallest addressable unit of a picture. A monitor's *resolution* is the number of pixels across and down that an adapter can create.

Pixel depth

To create the full range of colors you see, the display adapter must create, and your monitor must be capable of showing, many shades of each color. Such shades are determined by the intensity that each red, green, or blue dot is made to glow. The number of shades that each component can be set to is determined by the *pixel depth*, or bits per pixel devoted to each shade.

Consider a display adapter that devotes 8 bits to each of the red, green, and blue components of an image. Each pixel could be set to one combination of 256 shades of red (8 bits gives 256 possible values), 256 shades of green, plus 256 shades of blue. The total colors displayable equals 256 x 256 x 256, or 16,777,216.

Pixel depth (bits per pixel)	Maximum colors	Bytes of storage per pixel	Descriptive name
1	2	1/8	Monochrome
4	16	1/2	Standard VGA
8	256	1	256-color "Super VGA"
16	65,536	2	High color
24	16,777,216	3	True color

Video display standards

In the earliest years of the PC, IBM was the only significant source of personal computers for business use. Thus, the video adapters and associated standards that they created were adopted as the official standards to be implemented by third-party manufacturers.

The following table lists the popular video standards developed by IBM.

Standard	Text mode resolution	Graphics mode resolution	Text mode matrix (w x h)	Max. colors	Max refresh
Monochrome Display Adapter (MDA)	80 x 25	n/a	9 x 14	2 (black and green/amber/white)	50 Hz
Hercules Graphics Card (HGC)	80 x 25	720 x 348	9 x 14	2 (black and green/amber/white)	50 Hz
Color Graphics Adapter (CGA)	80 x 25	640 x 200 (mono) or 160 x 200 (color)	8 x 8	16 in text or low-res graphics modes, 4 colors in high-res graphics	60 Hz
Enhanced Graphics Adapter (EGA)	80 x 25	640 x 350	8 x 8	16 out of a palette of 64	60 Hz
Video Graphics Adapter (VGA)	Emulation of EGA and other early modes, or via graphics emulation of text mode	640 x 480	Emulation of EGA and other early modes	16 at 640 x 480 or 256 at 320 x 240 resolution out of a 262,144 color palette	60 Hz

SuperVGA

IBM's standards like 8514/a and XGA were never widely implemented.

VGA was the last widely accepted standard created by IBM. Shortly after it was introduced, VGA was superseded by the capabilities of third-party graphics adapters. While the offerings from many of these vendors came to be called "SuperVGA," there was no official standard beyond VGA.

To settle any confusion, the Video Electronics Standards Association created their own video standards. Their standards, officially known as the VESA BIOS Extensions, or VBE, are probably what most people think of when using the term SuperVGA.

The VBE supports various resolutions and color depths. The lowest is 640 x 400 at 8 bits per pixel and the highest is 1600 x 1200 at 16 bits per pixel. Extensions of these specifications could push resolutions and color support even higher.

Connectors

MDA, HGC, CGA, and EGA video adapters produced a digital signal. This signal was sent to the monitor via a 9-pin DIN connector. Beginning with VGA and continuing to modern video displays, video out signals are typically analog signals. The typical VGA or SuperVGA connector is a 15-pin DIN connector, as shown in Exhibit 1-1.

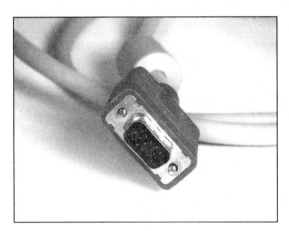

Exhibit 1-1: A 15-pin VGA or SuperVGA connector

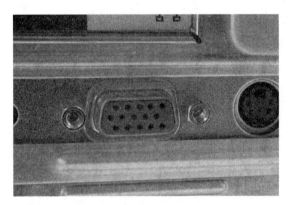

Exhibit 1-2: VGA/SuperVGA socket

Flat panel monitors are connected via either analog or digital lines. Most ship with a 15-pin VGA connection cable even if they are equipped to handle digital video interface (DVI) connections. Some do come with cables for both connection types.

If you want to use this interface, you might need to purchase a video card with a DVI connection. You also need to determine if it uses a DVI-D or DVI-I connection.

DVI-D

DVI-D is a digital only connection. A dual link DVI-D connection contains 24 pins in 3 rows of 8, plus a grounding slot. A single link DVI-D connection contains 18 pins.

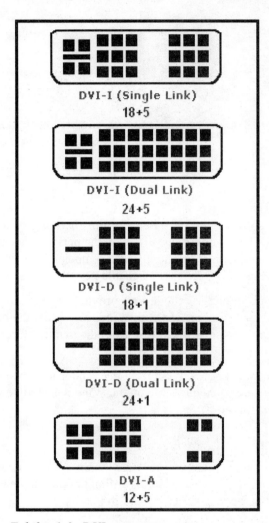

Exhibit 1-3: DVI connector types

DVI-I

DVI-I supports both digital and analog signals. The DVI-I connector contains 4 additional pins over what the DVI-I connector contains. These 4 pins carry analog signals. The analog signal pins are located above and below the grounding slot. Exhibit 1-4 shows an example of a DVI-I connector.

Exhibit 1-4: DVI-I connector

Video drivers

Video drivers are the software interface between the operating system and the video adapter. Such drivers have an enormous effect on the performance and proper operation of your computer. Manufacturers frequently release updated drivers that provide performance improvements, fix errors, and enable new features.

Whenever possible, you should use the drivers provided by the adapter card's manufacturer rather than those bundled with Windows. While the bundled or generic Windows drivers might work just fine, those from the manufacturer frequently offer more features and better operation.

You can typically download new drivers from the vendor's Web site. Drivers for popular video adapters are often available on the Windows Update site (windowsupdate.microsoft.com).

Integrated vs. add-on

Many motherboards include video adapter functionality. Such integrated video cards provide all the regular video adapter features without taking up an expansion slot. Many emulate adapters that you can purchase as add-in boards.

The BIOS often includes functions to disable the on-board video adapter. You might do this if you suspect a problem lies with it or if you want to use a specialized add-in adapter. For example, gamers often use very high performance aftermarket video adapters to speed their games.

Video adapter slot types

Some video adapters are built into the motherboard. This is common on low-end systems in which the manufacturer's main goal is to make the machine as inexpensive to the customer as possible. On other machines, there are three types of slots into which the video adapter might be installed. These include PCI, PCIe, and AGP slots.

PCI slot-based adapters are the slowest of the three types. These have to share the PCI bus with all the other PCI-based devices in the system. However, they work well for implementing a two-monitor system if you are using two separate video cards. If there is not an AGP or PCIe slot on your motherboard, this is your only option for upgrading the video on your system.

AGP is a special slot specifically designed for video adapters. The speed of an 8x AGP slot is 2.1 Gbps. Older systems might use AGP 2x or 4x which run at 533 Mbps and 1.07 Gbps respectively. Some AGP cards are available with two connectors to enable you to connect two monitors to the system. There is only one AGP slot in the system. This can be identified by color as it is a brown slot as compared to the white PCI slots. An example of an AGP video card is shown in Exhibit 1-5.

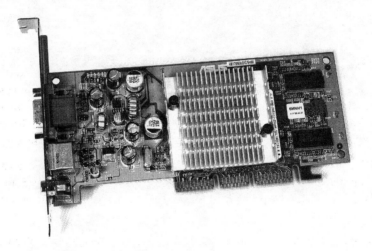

Exhibit 1-5: AGP video card

PCI Express (PCIe) cards are designed to replace AGP video cards in new systems. Motherboards that support PCIe video cards became available in 2004. A 16x PCIe video card has a 4 Gbps bandwidth in each direction. Since this is a dual line technology, you can theoretically achieve 8 Gbps capacity with data moving upstream and downstream at the same time. The high transfer speeds make this an ideal solution for multimedia applications such as gaming and photography/videography. This fits into a 164-pin slot on motherboards equipped with PCIe. An example of a 16x PCIe video card is shown in Exhibit 1-6.

Exhibit 1-6: PCIe video card

Do it!

A-1: Installing a video card

Here's how	Here's why
1 If specified by the adapter's manufacturer, run the adapter's setup utility	To copy the driver installation files to your hard disk where Windows can locate them.
2 If necessary, shut down your PC and open its case	(Make sure to follow electrical and ESD safety precautions.)
3 If necessary, remove the existing video adapter from its expansion slot	
4 Install the video adapter	
5 Close the PC case	
6 If your PC has an integrated video adapter, boot your PC and load the system's BIOS setup program	You will need to disable the onboard video adapter.
Disable the onboard video adapter and save your changes	
7 If your PC doesn't have an integrated video adapter, or after you have disabled the onboard adapter, start your PC	
8 If necessary, configure the driver	You will probably have to choose a resolution and color depth at which you want the driver to operate.
9 Remove the video adapter and reinstall or re-enable the original adapter	Unless your instructor directs you to do otherwise.

Provide students with a variety of video adapters to install.

Be sure students have the correct username and password to log on to their computers. Students should be using the RSTADMIN## user account and password.

Sound and your PC

Explanation

Prior to the introduction of the sound card, PCs were capable of producing simple beeps and clicks through an onboard speaker. Such a speaker is still included in nearly every PC. However, that speaker has never been capable of producing music, computerized voices, and other tunes.

The ProAudio AdLib sound card, and later the Creative Labs SoundBlaster card, revolutionized PC sound. These cards provided the ability to output music in addition to the various beeps and other tones. With such cards, you could also input sound by connecting an audio device, such as a tape player, to the input jack. The card would digitize the sound for use or storage within your computer.

The SoundBlaster Pro is still considered the base standard to which all other sound cards typically comply. Many sound cards provide features beyond what was available in the SoundBlaster Pro, too.

Sound card functions

To produce a signal for your speakers, a sound card must convert digital data into analog sound waves. To enable you to input, or capture, audio, it must convert analog sound signals into digital signals. Many sound cards also enable you to connect a game device, such as a joystick or game paddle, and many also enable you to connect MIDI (Musical Instrument Digital Interface) instruments.

Components

To perform its functions, a typical sound card includes these components:

- Digital signal processor (DSP), sort of like a CPU for sound processing functions.
- Analog to digital converter (ADC), which converts analog signals (like sound waves) to digital signals.
- Digital to analog converter (DAC), which converts digital signals to analog—producing the signals needed by speakers or other analog audio devices.
- Various jacks to connect speakers, microphones, line input or line output devices, game adapters (joysticks), and sometimes MIDI devices.

The sound card you use must be compatible with the expansion bus available in your computer. For example, you'll need a PCI sound card if your computer has only PCI slots available. Many motherboards include integrated sound card functionality.

Exhibit 1-7: A sound card

Sound card connectors

Sound cards typically feature connectors for speakers, microphones, line input or line output devices, and game adapters (joysticks). Some sound cards include connectors for MIDI devices or the game adapter port also supports MIDI device input. The function of each connector is typically labeled with a small icon. Exhibit 1-8 illustrates these connectors and their functions.

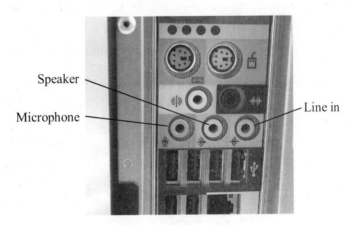

Exhibit 1-8: Standard sound card connectors

Speakers

Sound cards are designed to work with external speakers (or special built-in speakers in a laptop computer). Typically, these speakers require an external source of power. You must connect a cable from the speakers to the speaker out jack on the sound card and plug the speakers' power adapter into an outlet.

Exhibit 1-9: External speakers

CD audio

Internal CD drives include an audio out cable that you can connect to your sound card. When you do so, you can play audio CDs in your drive and have the sound played through your PC's speakers. If you don't connect this cable, you won't be able to play audio CDs (no sound will come from the speakers).

Drivers

As with any add-on hardware, sound cards require device drivers. Typically, you install the drivers to your system before installing the hardware. This puts the driver files where Windows, specifically Plug and Play, can find them after you install the card.

A-2: Installing a sound card

Here's how	Here's why
1 If specified by the adapter's manufacturer, run the adapter's setup utility	To copy the driver installation files to your hard disk where Windows can locate them.
2 If necessary, shut down your PC and open its case	(Make sure to follow electrical and ESD safety precautions.)
3 If necessary, remove the existing sound card from its expansion slot	
4 Install the sound card	
5 Close the PC case	
6 If your PC has an integrated sound card, boot your PC and load the system's BIOS setup program	You will need to disable the onboard sound card.
Disable the onboard sound card and save your changes	
7 If your PC doesn't have an integrated sound card, or after you have disabled the onboard adapter, start your PC	
8 If necessary, configure the driver	
9 Connect the external speakers and plug their power adapter into an outlet	
10 In the System Tray, click the speaker	To display the volume control.
Slide the volume slider up or down and release it	The computer should play a "ding" sound through your speakers.
11 Remove the sound card and reinstall or re-enable the original adapter	Unless your instructor directs you to do otherwise.

Modems

Modems are devices that enable you to connect your computer to another computer through a phone line. The modem in the sending computer must convert the digital signals within the computer to analog signals that are compatible with the phone system. The receiving modem must convert analog signals to digital signals.

Modulation and demodulation

Modems convert a digital signal into an analog one through a process called *modulation*. The digital signal is layered over a standard analog wave to produce a composite analog wave. To convert the composite signal back to digital, the receiving modem demodulates it. *Demodulation* is a process by which the modem electronically subtracts the carrier analog wave revealing the digital signal it carries.

A modem gets its name from this process. It *mod*ulates and *dem*odulates, hence it's called a modem.

Forms

A modem can be an external component that you connect to your PC through a serial port. (In fact, that was the original purpose of serial ports on PCs.) Internal modems are also common. These modems can be built into the motherboard, implemented on an adapter card that you insert into your PC's expansion bus, or implemented on a card that you insert into a riser slot.

Riser cards

The early internal modems were implemented as adapter cards that plugged into a PC/XT or ISA slot. While ISA and PCI-based internal modems are still sold, many modern computers use special expansion buses designed specifically for internal modems. The most popular are:

- The Audio Modem Riser (AMR) slot
- The Communications and Networking Riser (CNR) slot
- The Advanced Communications Riser (ACR) slot

AMR

Intel developed this riser slot standard to support modems and audio cards. This slot moved analog input/output functions off of the motherboard and onto an external card.

An AMR-compatible motherboard includes no other analog I/O functions. Such motherboards don't have to be subjected to time-consuming Federal Communications Commission (FCC) certification tests. Thus, AMR-compatible motherboards are faster and cheaper to produce.

CNR

Intel developed the CNR riser slot standard as an expansion of the AMR slot idea. This expansion slot supports specialized modems, audio cards, and network cards. CNR also provides for extensions that would enable manufacturers to create CNR-based cards that support new technologies, such as cable modems or DSL modems.

ACR

Motherboards from ASUSTeK Computer Inc. (ASUS), sometimes come with a proprietary riser slot called the Advanced Communications Riser slot. This expansion slot supports specialized modems, audio cards, and network cards. This slot type is not nearly as popular as the other, standardized, riser types.

Physical comparisons

Holding an AMR card vertically while looking at the faceplate (slot) cover, you'll see that its components are located on the right side of the circuit board. CNR cards have their components on the left when held the same way.

AMR slots are typically located in the middle of the motherboard. CNR slots are normally near the edge of the motherboard. A motherboard will have either an AMR or CNR slot, not both.

CNR and AMR slots are normally brown. ACR slots are normally white like the PCI slots they mimic.

Benefits of riser cards

Any of these riser slots are designed with the goal of simplifying the expansion card, thus lowering its price. The tradeoff is that the CPU must perform many of the functions that a dedicated controller chip would handle on a "normal" expansion card.

The CPU must handle all the processing for an AMR, CNR, or ACR modem, sound card, or network card. The result is that modems for these slots cost a few dollars while PCI or ISA-based modems typically cost tens of dollars.

Most times, a computer's manufacturer will populate a riser slot with a modem or other add-on card. Riser slot-based aftermarket add-ons are less popular. Unless one fails, you might never need to install a riser slot-based modem or expansion device.

WinModems

Whether they are implemented with a riser slot or PCI slot, modems must perform some basic core functions. These include modulating and demodulating the signal, as well as interfacing with the operating system. This latter function includes things like error correction, compression, command set interpretation, and so forth.

A modem could implement all those functions with hardware, and many do. Another approach is to implement those functions in software. The most popular software-based modem, or softmodem, is the WinModem.

A *WinModem* is Windows-based combination of simple hardware (basically, just physical components to interface with the motherboard and phone lines) and modem function emulation software. The term linmodem (all lowercase) is sometimes used to describe a Linux-based softmodem.

Benefits

Softmodems are inexpensive because less hardware is required. Additionally, you can easily upgrade softmodems by installing new software.

Detractions

Softmodems are tied to their operating systems. You might be able to run a Windows 95-based WinModem under Windows 2000, or you might not. Only with extreme efforts can you run a WinModem under Linux or another non-Windows operating system.

Additionally, software is slower than hardware. Softmodems are slower as a result. To make matters worse, softmodems use CPU power that could be dedicated to other applications running on your computer.

When a modem isn't a modem

The term modem is sometimes used in inappropriate ways. The term is an abbreviation of modulate/demodulate, which is a digital-to-analog (or vice-versa) conversion process. Modems for use over telephone lines do just that. However, the term is sometimes applied to cable and DSL (digital subscriber line) Internet connectivity devices.

Cable and DSL are digital media. There is no need to modulate and demodulate signals sent over those lines. Thus, the connectivity devices you use with those media should not be called modems. Technically, such devices are transceivers. However, most people still call them modems.

Modem installation

As with any add-on hardware, internal modems require device drivers. Softmodems require their software to be installed, for without it, the hardware components are worthless. And in most cases, you can't use the functions of a modem without communications software to provide the dialing and connection management functions you need to actually connect to a remote computer.

Typically, you install the drivers to your system before installing the hardware. This puts the driver files where Windows, specifically Plug and Play, can find them after you install the card.

Resources used by modems

Usually modems use the system resources listed in the following table. You'll quickly notice that COM ports 1 and 3, and COM ports 2 and 4 share the same resources. This means that you cannot have COM ports 1 and 3 (or 2 and 4) enabled at the same time unless you reconfigure one of the ports to use different resources.

Port	IRQ	I/O address
COM1	4	03F8-03FF
COM2	3	02F8-02FF
COM3	4	03F8-03FF
COM4	3	02F8-02FF

Do it!

A-3:   Installing an internal modem

Here's how	Here's why
1 If specified by the adapter's manufacturer, run the modem's setup utility	To copy the driver installation files to your hard disk where Windows can locate them.
2 If necessary, shut down your PC and open its case	(Make sure to follow electrical and ESD safety precautions.)
3 If necessary, remove an existing modem from its riser slot	
4 Install the modem card	
5 Close the PC case	
6 Start your PC	
7 If necessary, configure the driver	

Provide students with a variety of "hard" and softmodems to install.

Topic B: Laptop expansion cards

This topic covers the following CompTIA A+ 220-603 exam objective.

#	Objective
1.1	**1.1 Install, configure, optimize, and upgrade personal computer components**
	• Add, remove, and configure display devices, input devices and adapter cards including basic input and multimedia devices.

PC Cards

Explanation

The expansion cards used in notebook computers are PC Cards. These are roughly the size of a credit card with varying thickness based on the type of card. There are three types of PC Cards. They all have a 68-pin female connector that plugs into a connector in the PC Card slot on the side of the computer. The Personal Computer Memory Card International Association (PCMCIA) developed and maintains the standards for PC Card adapters.

PC Card types

The three types of PC Card adapters are Type I at 3.3 mm thick, Type II at 5 mm thick, and Type III at 10.5 mm thick. Most often, you'll encounter Type II PC Card adapters. These are typically used for network adapters, modems, adding ports such as FireWire and SCSI, and sometimes for memory. Some of the cards use a dongle to attach to a network cable or to other cables. Other cards use a pop-out port for the connector to plug into. An example of a Type II PC Card is shown in Exhibit 1-10.

Exhibit 1-10: A Type II PC Card

Type I cards typically are used for memory, but most computers use SODIMM memory modules instead, so these aren't commonly found. Type III cards are typically used for additional storage, such as a small hard drive. These aren't very common either.

There are three types of bus connections that PC Cards might use. They're described in the following table.

Bus type	Description
CardBus	Provides 32-bit bus mastering, which allows direct communication between the card and other cards without requiring access to the computer CPU. Uses Card and Socket Services automatically to allocate resources required by the add-on.
Zoomed Video (ZV)	Communicates directly between the PC card and the video controller without accessing the system bus.
eXecute In Place (XIP)	Runs commands directly from code stored on the PC Card without using system RAM.

Inserting and removing PC Cards

Insert the card straight into the slot, and it should connect to the pins in the back of the slot. Prior to removing the card, you should stop the services it's using. This is accomplished using the Safely Remove Hardware icon in the System Tray. Press the eject button on the case to pop the card out of the slot.

Card and Socket Services

The PC Card specification includes specifications for software support of the physical cards. This is a three-layer structure that provides plug-and-play functionality. The following table describes the software layers.

Layer	Description
Metaformat, also known as Card Information Structure (CIS)	This is composed of the Basic Compatibility, Data Recording, Data Organization, and System-Specific layers. The purpose of CIS is to provide a method for data organization and data recording format compatibility for a variety of PC Cards.
Card Services	An API that enables sharing of device drivers and other software by PC Cards and sockets. Card Services is designed to provide support for PC Card devices to share device drivers, configuration utilities, and application programs. It's also designed to provide a single resource for functions shared by the software.
Socket Services	Provides a common interface to the hardware that controls the socket into which PC Cards are connected. It provides the upper layers with information about the socket, including the number of sockets, the number of windows and the power needed for the PC Card.

B-1:   Installing a PC Card

Here's how	Here's why
1 Locate the PC Card slot on your notebook	You'll insert and remove a PC Card adapter.
2 How many slots are there? What type(s) of PC Cards can be installed?	*Answers will vary, but there are usually one or two. A single PC Card slot usually enables you to install Type I or Type II. Two slots enable you to install two Type I or Type II cards or one Type III card.*
3 Insert the PC Card in the slot	If you need more precise information on installing the card, refer to the notebook documentation and the PC Card documentation.
Install drivers or software	If prompted to do so.
4 Locate the Safely Remove Hardware icon	It should be located in the System Tray.
5 Double-click the **Safely Remove Hardware** icon	You can also right-click and choose Safely Remove Hardware.
6 Click the device you installed	All of the removable hardware devices are listed.
7 Click **Stop**	To stop the services.
8 Eject the card	By pressing the eject button on the case near the PC Card slot.

Be sure that students have a username and password so they can log on.

Mini PCI cards

Explanation

Another expansion card you might find in notebooks and other portable computer equipment is the mini PCI card. This type of card has the same functionality as a desktop PCI card, just in a smaller format. It's typically used for communications that are integrated into the notebook, including modems and network cards. These cards are installed inside the notebook case rather than being installed externally like the PC Cards. Exhibit 1-11 shows a built-in modem and network adapter provided by a mini PCI card. Further information can be found at pcisig.com/news_room/faqs#mini_pci.

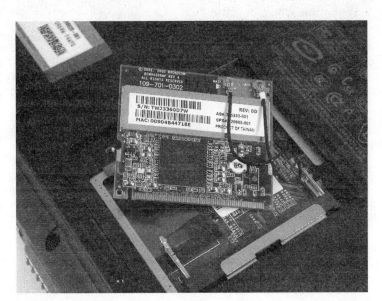

Exhibit 1-11: Built-in modem and network is provided by mini PCI cards

Network adapters and modems

Network adapters are standard equipment on notebook computers now. They used to be PC Cards that you added to a computer. Now they're typically built into the notebook computer. Ethernet 10/100 network cards are the network adapters found in most cases.

Modems are typically built-in adapters as well. If they're PC Cards, then the card usually has a pull-out plug into which the phone cable is connected. If they are on mini PCI cards, then the connector is built into the case.

On some notebooks, the power to a wireless network adapter can be turned off. This helps conserve battery power when you're traveling and don't have access to a network. Be sure to turn it back on when you're ready to connect to a network next time!

Installing mini PCI cards

In most cases, the mini PCI card is accessed through a panel on the underside of the computer case. In other instances, however, you will need to remove the keyboard to access the mini PCI card slot. Refer to the documentation for your laptop computer on where and how to access the mini PCI card slot.

In either case, the mini PCI card is held in place by two arms which are also used to release the card from the slot should you need to remove it. Most mini PCI cards are for network adapters or modems, so there are usually one or more cables that connect to the card as well.

To install the mini PCI card, refer to the instructions that come with the card as well as the instructions for the laptop computer. In most instances, the card is placed at approximately a 45 degree angle to engage with the connectors, and then pressed down until the arms lock it into place.

Do it!

B-2: Installing a mini PCI card

Here's how	Here's why
1 Determine where the mini PCI card access cover is located	This could be on the bottom of the case or under the keyboard.
2 Remove the access cover for the mini PCI slot	If the slot is located under the keyboard, you will likely need to remove a panel before you can remove the keyboard.
3 Turn off the power and unplug the power cord, then remove the battery from the laptop	Removing the battery ensures that the laptop will not accidentally be turned on as you handle it during the procedure.
4 Remove any mini PCI card already installed in the slot	Refer to the laptop computer documentation for the procedure for your system.
Disconnect any wires attached to the mini PCI card	
5 Insert the mini PCI card into the slot	Be sure that any wires that connect to it are not trapped under the card.
6 Press the card into place until the arms lock it in place	
7 Connect any wires to the card as needed	
8 Re-install the battery	

Topic C: Legacy devices

This topic covers the following CompTIA A+ 220-603 exam objective.

#	Objective
1.1	**1.1 Install, configure, optimize, and upgrade personal computer components**
	• Add, remove, and configure display devices, input devices and adapter cards including basic input and multimedia devices.

Legacy devices

Explanation

Legacy devices are older devices that do not support the modern computing standards, such as Plug and Play. An ISA bus adapter card is an example of a legacy device, even though many of them support Plug and Play.

Manual installation

When you can't install a device with Plug and Play, you must install it manually. There are a variety of reasons a device won't install with PnP:

- The device does not support Plug and Play.
- Windows can't recognize the device.
- Windows doesn't have a driver for the device.
- Windows has a driver for the device, but the device still doesn't work because the driver is outdated.

To manually install a non-PnP device:

1 If you're installing an expansion card that will use system resources, you will need to determine the following information:
   - Which resources the card will use—consult the expansion card's owner's manual, vendor's Web site, or other resource to determine this information.
   - Which resource values the card supports—consult the same sources noted previously.
   - Which resources values are available on your PC—use Device Manager to determine this information.

2 If the expansion card you're installing requires physical configuration (through DIP switches or jumpers), configure the card.

3 If you're installing an internal device, such as an expansion card, shut down your PC, physically install the device, and then restart your PC. Otherwise, attach the external device (e.g. printer) to your computer.

4 Open Control Panel, Add Hardware (it's called Add/Remove Hardware or Add New Hardware in some Windows versions). If you're installing a printer, open the Add Printer wizard instead.

5 If Windows can detect the hardware, it will prompt you to install the proper drivers. Follow the wizard's prompts to install the drivers.

6 If Windows cannot detect the hardware, click Have Disk and install the drivers from a floppy, CD-ROM, or hard disk location.

7 Finish the installation by following the remaining prompts from the hardware installation wizard. You might have to restart your PC.

C-1: Installing a non-PnP device

Here's how

1 Obtain a device from your instructor.

2 Determine which resources it requires and what values it supports. Use Device Manager to determine which of those resources are available in your PC. If necessary, configure the device by setting DIP switches or jumpers.

3 If necessary, shut down and unplug your computer. Follow your instructor's directions to discharge static electricity and open your computer case.

4 Attach the new device. If necessary, close the computer case and power up your computer.

5 Log on and open Control Panel. Double-click **Add Hardware**, and use the Add Hardware Wizard to install drivers for the new device. After telling Windows that you've connected the new device, in the Installed hardware list, select **Add a new hardware device**.

6 Choose to install the hardware manually, and then choose to show all devices. Click **Have Disk**, and then enter the path to the drivers. Complete the wizard.

7 Use Device Manager to verify that the hardware has been installed.

Overriding PnP

Sometimes a legacy device is hard-coded to use a specific IRQ or memory address. If that turns out to be the case, you might find that the newly installed legacy device interferes with an existing device. If that happens, you'll have to manually adjust IRQ and memory settings to ensure that all your devices work properly. For the most part, newer devices accept the settings assigned by Windows, so this type of problem isn't as frequent as it once was.

Tell students that not all modern devices support manual resource assignments.

1 Open Device Manager.

2 Expand the necessary category and double-click the device whose settings you need to adjust.

3 Activate the Resources tab.

4 Clear Use automatic settings.

5 From the Setting based on list, choose a configuration other than Current configuration.

6 In the Resource settings list, select the resource type to modify.

7 Click Change Setting.

8 Enter the new configuration data into the Value box.

9 Click OK three times. You might have to restart your PC for the change to take effect.

C-2:   Overriding PnP settings

Here's how	Here's why
1 If necessary, log on to your computer Open Device Manager	
2 Expand **Floppy disk controllers**	
3 Double-click **Standard floppy disk controller**	You cannot adjust resources for many modern devices. The floppy controller is an example of a legacy device that you can adjust.
4 Activate the Resources tab	
5 Clear **Use automatic settings**	
6 From Setting based on, select **Basic configuration 0001**	You might need to select a different configuration option—if so, you will be prompted with a dialog box telling you so.
7 From the Resource settings list, select **IRQ**	You will adjust the interrupt settings for the floppy controller.
8 Click **Change Setting...**	
9 In the Value box, enter **7**	Or, click the up arrow on the spinner control.
10 Click **OK** twice	You are prompted to confirm your intent to assign the resource.
Click **Yes**	To manually assign the resource.
11 Do not restart your PC	(If you're prompted.)
12 Reconfigure the floppy disk controller to use automatic settings If prompted, restart your PC Close Device Manager	You won't leave the device manually configured.

Topic D: Troubleshooting

This topic covers the following CompTIA A+ 220-603 exam objective.

#	Objective
1.2	**Identify tools, diagnostic procedures, and troubleshooting techniques for personal computer components**

- Identify and apply basic diagnostic procedures and troubleshooting techniques, for example:
  - Identify and analyze the problem/potential problem
  - Test related components and evaluate results
  - Identify additional steps to be taken if/when necessary
  - Document activities and outcomes
- Recognize and isolate issues with display, peripheral, multimedia, specialty input device and storage.
- Apply steps in troubleshooting techniques to identify problems (e.g. physical environment, functionality and software/driver settings) with components including display, input devices and adapter cards.

Basic troubleshooting

Explanation

When troubleshooting issues with expansion cards or any computer component, it's best to apply the ASID troubleshooting method.

1 Acquire information about the problem.
 - Ask the user what symptoms she or he is experiencing. This will help you identify and analyze the problem.
 - Verify functionality by testing the component yourself to re-create the problem. Test other components and other expansion cards to see if they're operational. Evaluate the results to determine if the problem is specific to one component.
 - Evaluate the physical environment and software and driver settings.
 - Review Windows 2000 and Windows XP error codes, such as those in Event Viewer.

2 Simplify by removing any non-critical components, shut down unnecessary running programs, disconnect from the Internet or network, and so on. If the problem goes away, its cause lies with one of the components you removed. If not, then you have simplified the system, which will make troubleshooting easier.

3 Implement by identifying probable causes and implementing potential solutions one at a time. Check available reference materials for potential solutions, and check existing service documentation for the component. Available resources might include manuals and product documentation, Web resources such as the Microsoft Knowledge Base and manufacturers' Web sites and users' forums, and training materials. When you define a specific cause, apply the fix. After you have solved the problem, have the user sign off that the problem has been solved to his or her satisfaction.

4 Document the error symptoms, the components you removed from the computer, and the solutions you tried and whether they were successful. At the end of this process, you must fully document the resolution for later reference. It's just as important to record any significant or obvious solutions that turned out not to be the cause of this problem so that you can avoid dead ends in the future.

Troubleshooting expansion cards

As a PC technician, you should be familiar with the most common symptoms, probable causes, and suggested "first try" solutions. You might encounter problems not listed in this table. But, the tables that follow will give you a few scenarios to consider when troubleshooting actual problems.

The following tables list problems, probable causes, and suggested solutions for the following expansion card types:

- Video adapters
- Sound cards
- Internal modems

Video cards

The following table lists video adapter-related problems that you might encounter.

Symptom	Probable cause	Suggested solution
No video at all	Monitor turned off or disconnected, video card failed, cable is bad, wrong video mode.	Make sure the monitor is connected and turned on. Attach a different monitor that is capable of very high resolution modes. If video is displayed, configure a lower resolution mode and then reattach the original monitor. Check for bent or broken pins in the video connector. Replace the video card.
Video scrolls, flips, wavers, is too large, lines doubled up, and so forth	Video card set to a refresh rate or resolution mode that the monitor can't support.	Either replace the monitor with a better one or reconfigure the driver to use a lower resolution mode or lower refresh rate.
Video flickers	Refresh rate too low.	Configure driver to use higher refresh rate.
Video is blurry	Monitor is failing.	Replace the monitor.
Image artifacts are displayed across the screen	Software is at fault, either driver software or your application software.	Update the video card drivers. Check for application updates.
System freezes during a video change, such as an image scrolling or changing	Video driver could be at fault.	Update the video card drivers.

Symptom	Probable cause	Suggested solution
Video connected to DVI connector, but monitor displays message that Analog connection is disconnected	Button that switches between analog and video was pressed or menu option was changed.	Reset the button or menu choice to digital connection.
Display image is sideways or upside down	Hot-key combination of keys was pressed on a system that enables flipping the image	Check documentation for Hot-key sequence, but it is often Ctrl+Alt+⬆ to return it to the proper orientation.

Sound cards

The following table lists sound card-related problems that you might encounter.

Symptom	Probable cause	Suggested solution
No sound	External speakers not connected or turned off, Windows configured to operate silently.	Connect the speakers or turn them on. Confirm the sound configuration in the Control Panel.
Sound is very low	Volume on speakers is set too low, audio output levels set too low or muted.	Turn up the volume knob on the speakers. Click the speaker icon in the System Tray (right end of Windows taskbar), slide the volume slider up. You might need to uncheck Mute.
Sound is distorted	Volume set too high for speakers, bad driver.	Turn down the volume knob on the speakers. Click the speaker icon in the System Tray and slide the volume slider down. Update the audio card drivers.
No audio captured	Microphone not connected, bad microphone, audio input levels set too low or muted.	Right-click the speaker icon in the System Tray and choose Open Volume Controls. Under Line In, slide the volume slider up. You might need to uncheck Mute.
No audio from CD	CD audio volume set too low or muted, CD audio cable not connected to sound card.	Right-click the speaker icon in the System Tray and choose Open Volume Controls. Under CD Audio, slide the volume slider up. You might need to uncheck Mute. Open PC and confirm that the sound cable from your CD drive is connected to your sound card, and connected properly.

Internal modems

The following table lists modem-related problems that you might encounter.

Symptom	Probable cause	Suggested solution
Modem picks up line and dials, but doesn't connect	Not dialing correct number, remote modem disconnected.	Confirm you are dialing the correct number (try dialing the number with a telephone to confirm you get modem tones from the remote end). Confirm that the remote modem is online and accepting calls.
Modem reports no dial tone detected	Phone line not connected, bad phone line, phone cord connected to wrong port on modem.	Confirm that the modem is correctly connected to the phone jack. Connect a phone to the modem line, pick up the handset. If there's no dial tone, contact your telephone company or technician to troubleshoot the line problem.
Connection drops frequently	Noisy phone line.	Connect a phone to the modem line, pick up the handset, and press a single number. If the line isn't silent, contact your telephone company or technician to troubleshoot the line noise.
Modem connects, but only at low speeds	Noisy phone line, remote modem supports only lower speeds.	Connect a phone to the modem line, pick up the handset, and press a single number. If the line isn't silent, contact your telephone company or technician to troubleshoot the line noise. Confirm that the remote modem supports high speed connections.
Modem doesn't work at all	Modem has failed, drivers not installed.	Try installing another modem. Confirm that the required modem drivers are installed.
Configuration related error messages	COM port conflicts, system resource conflicts.	Use Device Manager to confirm that the COM port used by the modem is available and not assigned to another device. Confirm or resolve resource (IRQs, I/O channels, etc.) conflicts.

Do it!

D-1: Troubleshooting expansion card problems

Here's how

You must set up this lab according to the Troubleshooting Labs Setup section of the Course Setup instructions.

1 One or more expansion card-related problems have been introduced into your lab computer. Troubleshoot these problems to determine their cause.

2 Remedy the problems you have found in your PC to return it to a working state. Solving one problem might reveal the presence of another problem. Troubleshoot and fix all problems that arise.

3 Document the problem(s) you found here:

4 Document the steps you took to fix the problem(s) here:

Updating drivers

Often one of the solutions to hardware problems involves obtaining and installing updated device drivers. As a device is put in use by users, the manufacturer might find that changes need to be made to the drivers due to conflicts, for faulty code, or just to make it function more efficiently.

Searching for device drivers

Although most devices are packaged with drivers, some of the drivers might not be the most up-to-date. Windows might not install the best drivers for your new device if the device is installed with PnP. At some point, you might need to find additional drivers on the Web, most likely from the device manufacturer's Web site.

Most manufacturers offer free downloads of drivers and utilities for their devices. Just determine the name of the manufacturer, and visit the appropriate Web site. Look for a link that offers drivers, support, or downloads. Then download the driver (which is often zipped) to a local hard disk, from where you can install it on the appropriate computer.

Updating device drivers

After you've found an updated device driver, you can install it. In Device Manager, choose to update the driver for a device, and then point the wizard to the location of the new driver.

D-2: Searching for and installing updated drivers

Here's how

1 In Device Manager, pick a device you want to update (maybe one of the devices you installed, or maybe a display adapter). Write down the manufacturer's name and the model of the device.

2 Visit the manufacturer's Web site. (Use a search engine if you have to.) On the Web site, find the link for support or downloads or drivers.

3 Find the drivers for the device you chose. Download them to your computer and save them in My Documents.

4 In Device Manager, right-click the device and choose **Update Driver**. Choose to install the driver from a specific location. Don't search for a driver; choose the driver to install. Complete the wizard, clicking **Have Disk** when prompted. Update the drivers if they are the same version or newer.

5 If necessary, restart the computer. Use Device Manager to verify that the device is working properly.

Unit summary: Expansion cards

Topic A   In this topic, you learned that **video adapters** convert computer data into the signals that are sent to the monitor for display. You learned that **sound cards** produce music, computerized voices, and tones to be played on external, **powered speakers**. You learned about the three popular **riser slot** types—**AMR**, **CNR**, and **ACR**—that are often used for attaching internal modems to motherboards. Finally, you learned how to install each of these expansion devices into desktop computer systems.

Topic B   In this topic, you learned that many components are specific to a model of notebook. You examined how to install and remove **PC Cards** and internal expansion adapters in notebook computers.

Topic C   In this topic, you learned how to install **legacy devices** into PCs. You also learned how to **override Plug and Play settings** to accommodate expansion devices that either don't support Plug and Play or cannot adapt to available system resources.

Topic D   In this topic, you learned that expansion cards can fail for various reasons. You learned how to troubleshoot expansion cards. You also examined common symptoms of failures and the probable causes and suggested solutions.

Review questions

1 Are V.92-compatible modems faster than V.90 modems?

   The bits per second connection speed for both types of modems are the same. V.92 modems feature reduced connection times, that is, the time it takes for them to negotiate the connection parameters with the remote modem is less.

2 Name the typical connectors on a sound card.

   Typically, sound cards provide speaker out, line out, microphone in, line in, and MIDI/game port connectors.

3 List the types of riser card slots that can be used with modems.

   AMR (Audio Modem Riser), CNR (Communications and Networking Riser), and ACR (Advanced Communications Riser) slots.

4 What does the port speed setting for a modem control?

   The port speed setting controls the speed at which communications between the PC and modem proceed.

5 You must connect what to the sound card in order to play audio CDs through your computer's speakers?

   You must connect the CD drive's audio out port to the sound card's CD-in connector.

6 Which MNP class introduced data compression?

   MNP class 5 introduced data compression. Speed improvements of earlier classes were due strictly to protocol efficiencies.

7 Which can show more colors, High color or True color?

   True color shows 16,777,216 colors, whereas High color can show only 65,536 colors.

8 Are the terms baud and bits per second (bps) equivalent?

No, baud is the measure of the number of signal changes per second. Modern modems send more than one bit per signal change. Thus, bits per second is the product of the baud rate times the number of bits sent per signal change.

9 Define refresh rate.

The rate at which the electron gun paints the full screen, measured in hertz (Hz or cycles per second).

10 VGA and newer CRT display technologies use _____ signals, while the older technologies used _____ signals.

digital; analog

11 Typical computer speakers require _____.

an external source of power

12 The cables that you connect a modem to a phone jack feature RJ-45 connectors. True or false?

False. Such cables use an RJ-11 connector.

13 What are the functions of the ADC and DAC components on a sound card?

The ADC is the analog to digital converter, which converts analog sound signals to digital signals. The DAC is the digital to analog converter, which converts digital signals to analog, producing the signals needed by speakers or other analog audio devices.

14 Can you manually assign system resources to all devices?

No. You cannot manually assign system resources to many modern devices. Typically you can assign resources only to legacy devices.

15 What is the best source for driver updates?

The device manufacturer's Web site.

16 What is a softmodem?

A software modem that uses the computer's resources instead of having dedicated hardware.

17 What are the basic troubleshooting steps?

Acquire, Simplify, Implement, and Document (ASID)

18 Which utility can you use to verify a PC Card is properly installed?

Device Manager

19 What is a legacy device?

Legacy devices are older devices that do not support the modern computing standards, such as Plug and Play.

20 How would you typically access a mini PCI card?

Through a panel in the bottom of a laptop.

Independent practice activity

1 Record your video adapter's resolution and color depth settings. Configure your video adapter to display at VGA resolution. Return it to the original resolution and color depth settings.

2 Record the IRQ assignments, as listed by Device Manager. Install a new PnP-compatible adapter. Compare the IRQ assignments to see which devices have kept their previous IRQ assignments and which have been assigned new IRQs. Resolve any conflicts.

3 Connect a microphone to your sound card. Using the Windows Sound Recorder accessory, record and play back a sound (for example, speak into the microphone). Adjust the input and output volumes, as needed, to achieve good sound quality in the recording.

Unit 2
Data storage devices

Unit time: 150 minutes

Complete this unit, and you'll know how to:

A Describe, install, and use hard drives.

B Troubleshoot data storage devices.

Topic A: Hard drives

This topic covers the following CompTIA A+ 220-603 exam objectives.

#	Objective
1.1	**Install, configure, optimize, and upgrade personal computer components**
	• Add, remove, and configure display devices, input devices and adapter cards including basic input and multimedia devices.
2.1	**Identify the fundamental principles of using operating systems**
	• Use command-line functions and utilities to manage Windows 2000, XP Professional and XP Home, including proper syntax and switches, for example:
	• FORMAT
2.1	**Identify the fundamental principles of using operating systems**
	• Identify concepts and procedures for creating, viewing, managing disks, directories and files in Windows 2000, XP Professional and XP Home, for example:
	• Disks (e.g. active, primary, extended and logical partitions)
	• File systems (e.g. FAT 32, NTFS)
	• Locate and use Windows 2000, XP Professional and XP Home utilities and available switches
	• Disk Management tools (e.g. DEFRAG, NTBACKUP, CHKDSK, Format)

Hard disk drives

Explanation

Hard drives are PC components on which data is stored. Hard drives use magnetism to store data. Hard drives are made up of the following parts:

Component	Description
Platters	Platters are the metal or plastic disks on which the magnetic material is coated. Data is recorded in that magnetic material as magnetically polarized regions.
Motor	The motor turns the platters very quickly, typically 7200 revolutions per minute or faster.
Spindle	The spindle is the axis, or central hub, around which the platters spin.
Read/write heads	The heads are the magnetic devices that both read and write data on the platters.
Voice coil actuator	The voice coil actuator is the mechanism that moves the heads very precisely into position over the magnetic tracks written on the platters.

The typical hard drive components are illustrated in Exhibit 2-1.

Exhibit 2-1: The internal components of a hard drive

Hard drive geometry

Data is written by the heads onto the platters as the platters spin beneath the heads. Data is recorded onto both the top and bottom of each platter. A disk drive typically has more than one platter stacked concentrically.

Data is not written in a spiral groove, as with an old phonograph record. Instead, data is written in a series of concentric *tracks*. A *cylinder* is the logical collection of all the tracks at a given distance from the axis.

Each track is divided into *sectors*. Each sector contains identification information at its beginning and end, and contains data in between. Sectors typically hold 512 bytes of data. Sectors are gathered logically into groups called *clusters*. Clusters typically contain between 4 and 64 sectors each.

Files are stored in one or more clusters. Small files leave empty space within the cluster that cannot be used to store other files. Large files will be split and stored in multiple clusters. A table stored on the hard drive tracks the clusters assigned to each file.

Exhibit 2-2 illustrates the geometry of the typical hard drive.

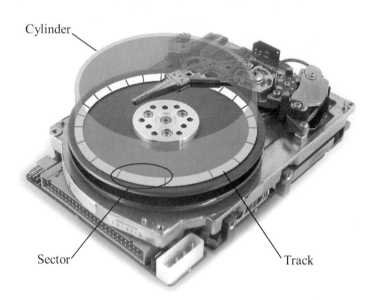

Exhibit 2-2: Hard drive geometry

Heads and head crash

There are approximately 40 microinches in a micron (thousandth of a millimeter). 1/2-microinch equals about 0.0127 microns.

During use, the read/write heads float on a very thin cushion of air about 1/2 of a millionth of an inch—1/2 of a microinch—above the platter. In comparison, a human hair or common dust particle is 2-3000 microinches in diameter.

This makes hard drives susceptible to head crash, a condition in which the heads come into contact with the platter surface. Head crash can cause damage to the heads, platters, or both. Fortunately, modern materials and manufacturing techniques have made head crash less of a concern than with older drives.

When you shut down your PC, the read/write heads are moved by the voice coil actuator into a safe position and safely brought to rest either on the surface or mechanically suspended above it. The heads are said to be parked.

Before Windows and an actual operating system shutdown procedure, you used to have to use a special utility to park the heads on your hard drive. Before shutting off your old DOS PC, you would run the utility to park the heads. Then, you'd turn off the power to your PC. Drives themselves now handle this operating automatically when you shut down Windows.

File systems

The operating system must be able to access and track files stored on the hard drive. The file system is the collection mechanisms that enable these functions. A file system defines such parameters as the minimum and maximum cluster size, how the locations of files are tracked, as well as how files and directories are stored within the actual clusters.

A file system is like a library's card catalog system—every book in the library is represented by a card in a file drawer. Each card lists details about the corresponding book, such as its title and author, as well as describing the location of the book within the library.

Just as a library patron can find any book in the library by looking up its card in the catalog, an operating system can find any file on the hard drive by looking it up in the file system's data structures.

There are two broad families of file systems used with PCs, which are:

- The FAT file system family
- The NTFS file system family

The FAT file system

The File Allocation Table (FAT) file system was originally developed for the DOS operating system. It has since been extended to support the Windows 9x family of operating systems. There are 16-bit and 32-bit versions of the FAT file system, called FAT16 and FAT32, respectively.

The FAT16 file system can store files with names containing up to eight alphanumeric characters and a three letter file extension. FAT16 file names cannot contain spaces or most punctuation characters. This is the file system that was used with DOS, Windows 3.1, and Windows 95.

The FAT32 file system can store files with names containing up to 255 characters with multiple letter extensions. FAT32 file names can contain spaces, but still cannot contain most punctuation characters. This file system is used with Windows 98 and Me, and is supported by Windows 2000 and XP, though it's less common in those operating systems.

The NTFS file system

The Windows NT File System (NTFS) was developed for Windows NT and has since been extended with new features for use with Windows 2000 and Windows XP. NTFS supports larger files, larger volumes, and many more files per volume. NTFS supports file compression and encryption. It also contains structures that make it more resilient and less prone to file loss or corruption.

For small volumes, the FAT32 file system is normally faster. However, for large volumes (over 10 GB), the NTFS file system is much faster. You should use it with Windows 2000 and XP unless you have a compelling reason to use the FAT32 file system.

File system comparison

The following table compares selected features of the FAT16, FAT32, and NTFS file systems.

Feature	FAT16	FAT32	NTFS
File name length	1-8 characters	1-255 characters*	1-255 characters*
File extensions	0-3 characters	0-255 characters*	0-255 characters*
Max. file size	2 GB	4 GB	Limited only by volume size
Max. volume size	2 GB	32 GB	2 TB (2,048 GB)
Max. files per volume	Approx. 6,500	Unlimited	Unlimited
Most often used with	DOS, Windows 3.1, Windows 95	Windows 9x, Me	Windows NT, 2000, and XP
Supports file level security	No	No	Yes
Supports file compression and encryption	No	No	Yes

* FAT32 and NTFS file names are limited to 255 characters overall, which is divided between the file name and extension. For example, you could assign a 200-character file name and a 55-character file extension.

The directory tree

Most PC operating systems use the paradigm of a directory tree to organize files. In this scheme, a disk contains one or more *folders*, also called *directories*. Each folder contains zero or more folders and zero or more files. These folders are arranged in a family tree-like hierarchy collectively called the directory tree.

The *root directory* is the highest level folder on the disk, it's the starting point for the directory tree. The root directory can contain files and folders. With the FAT16 file systems, the root directory could contain a maximum total of 512 files and folders. The FAT32 and NTFS file systems do not have this limitation.

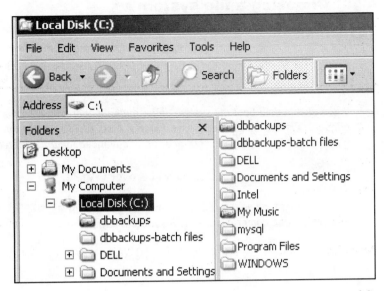

Exhibit 2-3: Windows Explorer identifies the root directory of C: as Local Disk (C:)

A file system table (with the FAT file systems, it's called the file allocation table) stores the names and first cluster of each file and folder contained in the root directory. A marker in each cluster either notes the address of the file's next cluster or marks it as the last cluster in the chain.

Folders other than the root directory are essentially files that contain data about the actual files and folders it contains. The operating system reads these special files and uses the information they contain to display to you the list of files and folders within. There is no limit on how many files and folders that you can store in a folder that's not the root directory.

File organization problems

Files can be divided across multiple clusters on the disk. From a speed perspective, the optimal arrangement would be to have all of a file's clusters located contiguously on the disk. However, as you add and remove files, and change the contents of the files causing them to grow or shrink, files can become fragmented into many clusters spread across discontinuous portions of the disk.

The operating system accesses fragmented files less efficiently than contiguous files. You can use a file defragmentation utility to relocate file clusters and return the disk to a less fragmented state. Using such a utility is sometimes called *defragging* the disk.

Additionally, viruses or poorly-written programs can break the chain of clusters that make up a file. Such a rogue application might change or remove the marker in one cluster that points to the file's next cluster.

You can use a utility like chkdsk to read and test your hard drive's file system for errors. If chkdsk finds errors that it cannot correct, you might end up with a collection of file fragments—it creates a separate file for each lost or disconnected cluster that it finds.

Third-party utilities, such as Norton Disk Doctor, are sometimes better at determining which disconnected clusters belong to which files. You can use these utilities instead of chkdsk to scan your disk for errors, and correct them, too.

Do it!

A-1: Choosing a file system

Exercise

1 Give at least one reason you might choose to use the FAT32 file system rather than NTFS on a Windows XP system.

   If you plan to dual-boot the system under multiple operating systems, you will need to choose a file system each of them supports. Also, FAT32 is faster on small hard drives than NTFS. You might not need security or other advanced features offered by NTFS.

2 List at least two advantages of NTFS over FAT32.

   Answers might include: NTFS is faster for large hard drives. NTFS supports security, encryption, and compression. NTFS supports larger files.

3 When do you think you assign the file system that will be used with the disks in your PC?

   You choose the file system when you first install and set up the hard drive in your PC.

Physical installation

Explanation

Physically installing a disk drive into a PC involves a few steps, which you must perform in the following order:

1 Set jumpers or switches on the drive to provide for drive identification.

2 Install the drive into the PC chassis.

3 If you're installing a SCSI drive, you might need to configure bus termination. The bus must be terminated on both ends. It cannot have extra termination installed in the middle of the chain. You might need to set switches or jumpers, or install or remove terminator blocks to set termination.

4 Connect data and control cables from the drive controller to the drive.

5 Connect the power cable from the PC's power supply to the drive.

Of course, you must shut down your PC and open its case (observing electrical and safety precautions) before you begin these steps. Additional preparation steps are also required after you physically install the drive to make it available to your operating system.

ATA drive identification

With IDE/ATA drives, you can install one or two drives per channel. One drive must be designated as the master, or primary disk. The other is called the slave. With older drives, you set a jumper or DIP switch to specify its role: master, slave, or the only drive in the system. With newer drives, you can set the switch to the cable select position. In this case, the drive detects where it is connected on the cable. Its position defines its role, as shown in Exhibit 2-4.

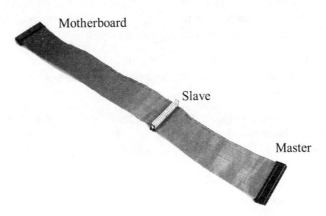

Exhibit 2-4: An ATA cable showing where to connect the master and slave drives

SCSI drive identification

You must assign a unique SCSI device ID number to every device, including the host bus adapter, on the SCSI bus. SCSI IDs begin at 0 and count upward, with higher IDs having a higher priority on the SCSI bus.

Most newer SCSI devices include switches that you can use to set the device's SCSI ID. Older devices provided a block of jumpers that you used to set the SCSI ID. Exhibit 2-5 illustrates a typical switch that you'd use to assign SCSI IDs.

Exhibit 2-5: A switch for assigning the SCSI ID

Chassis installation

You can typically use any available bay for a hard drive. However, one or more smaller, drive-sized bays are typically available for this precise purpose. Make sure to install in a location where the data and power cables can reach.

Most modern drives work equally well mounted horizontally or vertically. Unlike older drives, there's typically no harm in mounting a drive one way and then mounting it in a different orientation later.

As always when you open your PC's case, make sure to shut down the computer and unplug it from the outlet. Follow all the typical static safety precautions, too. Do not bump or jar the drive. They are very sensitive to shocks and you can damage them easily.

Data cable connections

Most drive cables are keyed, that is, their connectors are molded in such a way that you can insert them only the correct way into the connector socket. If you're using an older non-keyed cable, wire 1 in the cable will be marked with a red stripe. Pin 1 on the socket will be labeled, either with a number or a small triangle pointing at the pin. You need to line up the cable so that pin 1 goes into socket 1.

Make sure to connect your IDE drive to the correct connector if you're using cable select to set the master/slave selection for your drive.

You must terminate each end of the SCSI bus. Typically, the HBA includes removable resistors. Modern devices have switch-selectable termination built in: if you need a device to provide termination, then you switch on its terminators. Otherwise, you can leave its terminators turned off.

Power cable connections

Most IDE/ATA and SCSI drives use the large peripheral power connector. This connector has triangular corners so that you can be sure to insert it into the socket correctly. SATA drives use a specialized power connector that looks very different than the peripheral power connector. It is also keyed so that you're sure to connect it properly.

Do it!

A-2:   Physically installing a hard drive

Provide students with a drive to install into their systems.

Students are installing a second drive in their systems.

Here's how	Here's why
1 If necessary, shut down your PC and unplug it from the outlet	You will install an additional hard drive into your system.
2 Following all electrical and ESD precautions, open your PC's case	
3 Set the jumpers or switches, as appropriate, to specify the drive identification	You'll need to set Master/Slave/Single-drive/Cable Select for an IDE drive or the SCSI ID for a SCSI drive.
4 Locate an available drive bay and install the drive	
5 Install the data ribbon cable	Make sure to install the cable in the correct orientation and connect the drive to the correct connector on the cable.
6 Install the power cable	
7 Close the PC's case	
8 Do not turn on your computer	You have physically installed the drive. But, you must prepare it for use with the operating system.

Hard drive preparation

Explanation

Once you have physically installed a hard drive, you must prepare it for use by the operating system. With hard drives, the following steps must be performed separately:

- Low-level format
- Partition the drive
- Format the drive

Low-level formatting

Low-level formatting is the preparation step that divides the disk into tracks and divides each track into sectors. This is a step that must be performed when a drive is brand new. Additionally, with older drives, you occasionally had to re-low-level format your drive to fix read and write errors.

In older hard drives, each track contained the same number of sectors. Hard drives of that era used a stepper motor to move the heads into position, which was a less precise mechanism than modern voice-coil actuators. Over time, the motor might begin to position the heads in a slightly different position than it did when it was new.

When that happened, read and write errors would become more frequent. To solve these problems, you could re-low-level format your drive. Of course, doing so obliterated all of the data on your drive, so you had to carefully back up your data first.

Modern hard drives use complex sector arrangements, such as zoned bit recording (ZBR). With ZBR, more sectors are recorded in the larger outer tracks than in the smaller inner tracks. Modern voice coil actuators are precise and accurately position the heads over the tracks every time.

With modern drives, low-level formatting is not a generic process that could be performed by the operating system. Nowadays, low-level formatting is almost always done by the hard drive manufacturer and never needs redoing.

Partitioning

The first step in hard drive preparation that you will have to do is to *partition* the drive. Partitioning divides the hard drive into one or more *logical drives*, also called *volumes*. Consider a 20 GB drive. You could partition it into two 10 GB drives where each gets its own drive letter. You still have one physical disk drive, but it appears to the operating system to be two drives.

Some users like to create multiple partitions so that they can store different types of information on each. For example, they might store their data on drive D rather than mixing it with Windows and the application files on C.

Partitioning drives was an important consideration with early hard drives and operating systems that could not support large volumes. Without partitioning to create additional volumes, you could not use all of the available space on a hard drive.

Most modern computers and operating systems support enormous volumes. So, you can generally use the entire space of a drive in a single volume. However, you must still partition a hard drive into at least one volume.

Partitioning defines the type of file system that will be used on your hard disk. Different operating systems use different file systems. Currently, the most popular file systems for PCs include NTFS (the Windows NT file systems, used also by Windows 2000 and XP) and FAT32 (the Windows 98 file system).

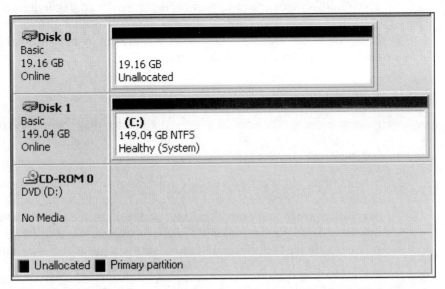

Exhibit 2-6: A new, unpartitioned disk, as shown in Windows Disk Management

Master boot record (MBR)

The first sector on the bootable hard disk is called the master boot record (*MBR*). This sector serves the same purpose as the boot sector on a floppy. The MBR, which is sometimes called the master boot block or partition table, contains partition information and other information used by the computer after the POST test has finished.

Primary and extended partitions

Primary partitions are those partitions that are directly accessed by the operating system as volumes. Under DOS and Windows 9x, you can create a single primary partition on each hard drive. Under Windows NT, 2000, and XP, you can create four primary partitions per drive. Most of the partitions you create will be primary partitions.

You can also create *extended partitions*. Each extended partition contains one or more logical drives, which is what the operating system accesses for file storage. With all of the PC operating systems, you can create a single extended partition, which can contain up to 23 logical drives. In general, you won't create extended partitions unless you need to create a system that boots to both DOS/Windows 9x and Windows NT/2000/XP for which you need multiple volumes.

Partitioning utilities

For DOS and Windows 9x systems, you use the MS-DOS `fdisk` command to partition a hard drive. The version of `fdisk` that was included with Windows 98 could also partition drives for use with the FAT32 and NTFS file system.

The `fdisk` command does not rewrite the MBR if an MBR is present. To force `fdisk` to write a new MBR, you must use the `fdisk /mbr` command.

With Windows 2000 and XP, you can use the Disk Management component of the Computer Management console. From the Start menu, choose Administrative Tools, Computer Management and then from the left pane, select Disk Management. You can use this console component to partition and format new disk drives, as well as manage partition types.

The Disk Management component is designed for adding a drive to a working Windows system. For new drives in new systems, you will need a different method. Most versions of Windows since Windows NT offer you the option of partitioning the hard drive during the operating system installation.

Formatting

Formatting is the final hard disk preparation step that you must perform. This step is sometimes called high-level formatting. With it, you clear out the file system tables and structures to prepare them to store new files.

While formatting is considered a destructive process, you can sometimes recover from accidentally reformatting your hard drive. The contents of the disk clusters are not overwritten when you format the disk. Instead, just the file allocation tables are emptied. Special utilities can painstakingly read every cluster on the disk to recover most of what was stored in the file allocation tables. You will probably lose some files during the recovery. But you will be able to recover most of your data.

For DOS and Windows 95 systems, you use the MS-DOS Format command to format a hard drive partitioned to the FAT16 file system. You can use the Windows 98/Me Format command to format FAT16 and FAT32 partitioned hard drives. Windows NT, 2000, and XP include a command-line utility also named Format that you can use to format FAT32 and NTFS partitioned hard drives. Or, you can use Windows Disk Management, which runs the Format command through the GUI utility.

Do it!

A-3: Partitioning and formatting a hard drive

Here's how	Here's why
1 Boot your PC	(Log in using your RSTADMIN## user account.)
2 Open the Computer Management console	(Click Start and choose All Programs, Administrative Tools, and Computer Management. Alternatively, right-click on My Computer and choose Manage.)
3 In the left pane, select Disk Management	
4 If the new drive is not listed in Disk Management, shut down your PC and use the BIOS setup utility to enable the drive	Depending on your system and other drives already present, you might need to enable the drive controller or drive channel.
5 Right-click on the unpartitioned drive and choose **New Partition...**	

This activity assumes students are running Windows XP.

Students must have installed an additional hard drive or have an unpartitioned drive in their system to complete this activity.

6 Click **Next**

   If necessary, select **Primary partition** and click **Next**

To specify that you're creating a primary partition on the drive.

7 Click **Next**

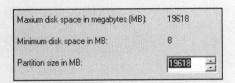

Maxium disk space in megabytes (MB):	19618
Minimum disk space in MB:	8
Partition size in MB:	19618

To accept the default partition size, which typically fills the entire drive.

8 Click **Next**

To accept the default drive letter assignment. (The driver letter may vary, depending on how each computer is configured.)

9 Configure the partition formatting options as shown

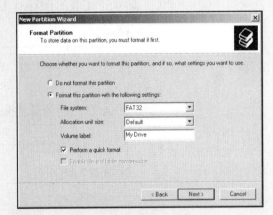

10 Click **Next** and **Finish**

To proceed with partitioning and formatting.

11 Observe the Disk Management window

Your drive is partitioned, formatted, and ready for your use.

12 Right-click My Drive and observe the Mark Partition as Active option

With this option, you can mark the partition as a bootable partition.

13 Record the drive letter of your new drive

Drive letter: _____

14 Do not choose the option, instead choose **Explore**

To open the drive in Windows Explorer. The drive is empty, so no files are listed.

15 Close Windows Explorer

File system type changes

Explanation

With Windows 2000 and Windows XP, you can convert from the FAT or FAT32 file systems to NTFS without losing data. But, you can't convert from NTFS to any other format without losing data. With older operating systems, you cannot change the file system in this way without using special third party utilities.

You must use the command line tool convert.exe to perform this conversion. You cannot do so through Disk Management. You can format a drive with Disk Management in order to change the file system type. However, in doing so, you will destroy any data on the drive.

If your Windows 2000 or Windows XP system has a single drive, the actual file system change will be performed the next time you boot your system. If you have multiple drives, Disk Management can convert the partition without requiring you to restart your PC.

Do it!

A-4: Changing the file system type

Here's how	Here's why
1 Open a command prompt window	(Click Start and choose All Programs, Accessories, Command Prompt.)
2 At the command prompt, enter **convert** *driveletter*: **/FS:NTFS**	
Press (← ENTER)	Substitute the drive letter you recorded in the preceding activity for *driveletter*.
	You are prompted to enter the volume label for your drive to confirm which drive you want to convert.
3 Enter **My Drive** and press (← ENTER)	Determining disk space required for file syst Total disk space: 20089251 KB Free space on volume: 20079408 KB Space required for conversion: 86430 KB Converting file system Conversion complete
4 Close the command prompt window	
5 Observe the drive in Disk Manager	Disk 0 Basic 19.16 GB Online · MY DRIVE (E:) 19.16 GB NTFS Healthy
	It has been converted to NTFS. If this drive had contained any files, your data would have been preserved during the conversion.

Basic and dynamic partitions

The standard type of partition supported by DOS, Windows 9x, as well as newer Windows versions is called a *basic partition*. Most partitions that you create will be basic partitions.

Dynamic partitions are a new type supported by Windows 2000, XP Professional, and Windows Server 2003. With this enhanced partition type, you can make changes to your partitions and the volumes they contain without restarting the operating system. This partition type is most useful in a server environment where downtime must be kept to a minimum.

A-5:   Converting to a dynamic disk

Here's how	Here's why
1 In the left pane, select Disk Management	
2 Right-click **Disk #**, where # is the disk number of your new disk	
Choose **Convert to Dynamic Disk...**	
	With this dialog box, you can select one or more disks to convert to dynamic disks.
Click **Cancel**	To cancel converting the disk to a dynamic disk.
3 Close all open windows	

Topic B: Troubleshooting storage devices

This topic covers the following CompTIA A+ 220-603 exam objectives.

#	Objective

1.2	**Identify tools, diagnostic procedures, and troubleshooting techniques for personal computer components**
	
	• Identify and apply basic diagnostic procedures and troubleshooting techniques, for example:
	   • Identify and analyze the problem/potential problem
	   • Test related components and evaluate results
	   • Identify additional steps to be taken if/when necessary
	   • Document activities and outcomes
	• Recognize and isolate issues with display, peripheral, multimedia, specialty input device and storage

1.3	**Perform preventative maintenance on personal computer components**
	
	• Identify and apply common preventative maintenance techniques for storage devices, for example:
	   • Software tools (e.g., Defrag, CHKDSK)
	   • Cleaning (e.g., optics, tape heads)

2.1	**Identify the fundamental principles of using operating systems** • Locate and use Windows 2000, XP Professional and XP Home utilities and available switches • Disk Management tools (e.g. DEFRAG, NTBACKUP, CHKDSK, Format)
2.2	**Install, configure, optimize and upgrade operating systems** • Identify procedures and utilities used to optimize the performance of Windows 2000, XP Professional and XP Home, for example: • Hard drives (i.e. disk defragmentation)
2.3	**Identify tools, diagnostic procedures and troubleshooting techniques for operating systems** • Use diagnostic utilities and tools to resolve operational problems, for example: • Bootable media

Hard drive maintenance

Explanation

Common problems with hard drives include fragmentation, file system corruption, insufficient space, and damaged or deleted files.

Checking for disk errors

The Check Disk (CHKDSK) tool allows you to scan your disk for bad sectors and file system errors. You should check your drive for errors if you suspect that your drive might be failing or that some sectors have become incapable of properly storing data. To check your hard drive for errors:

1 In My Computer or Windows Explorer, right-click the hard drive you want to check. Choose Properties.

2 Activate the Tools tab.

3 Under Error-checking, click Check Now.

4 Optionally, check Automatically fix file system errors and Scan for and attempt recovery of bad sectors.

5 Click Start.

When you start the Check Disk tool, there are two options:

- Automatically fix file system errors. Select this option to have Windows repair any errors in the file system that it finds during the disk checking process. In order to use this option, all programs must be closed.

- Scan for and attempt recovery of bad sectors. Select this option to have the system find and fix bad sectors and file errors, recovering any information that it can read. Choosing this option also includes the file system fixes that are performed by the Automatically fix file system errors option.

You can also check your disk for errors by running the CHKDSK command, which is the command line version of the utility. You can enter the CHKDSK command from the command line or Run command. CHKDSK also starts automatically when you boot, if the boot process detects a corrupt file allocation table or corrupted files. CHKDSK can be used to check FAT16, FAT32, NTFS, or a combination of these (on a dual-boot computer). When the file system is FAT16 or FAT32, the utility checks the file allocation table, folders, files, disk sectors, and disk allocation units. In NTFS, it checks files, folders, indexes, security descriptors, user files, and disk allocation units.

To run CHKDSK at the command line, enter `chkdsk volume: /f /r`, where `/f` tells CHKDSK to automatically fix errors, and `/r` tells CHKDSK to scan for and attempt to recover information in bad sectors.

Freeing space

You can recover some of the space used by temporary files and the files cached by your Internet browser. Doing so will give you more space for your applications and data files. To recover free space:

1 In My Computer or Windows Explorer, right-click the hard drive you want to check. Choose Properties.

2 On the General tab, click Disk Cleanup.

3 Select the files you want to delete and the actions you want to take and click OK.

4 Optionally, activate the More Options tab to remove Windows components, applications, or system restore points to free more space.

Defragging

Files are stored in sets of clusters on the disk. These clusters can become spread across the drive. Accessing files gets slower and slower as files become more fragmented across the disk. You can speed disk reads and writes by defragmenting, or defragging, the drive.

When you defrag a hard drive, software reads in all the clusters that comprise your files. Then, the software writes those clusters sequentially on the disk. Typically, the defragging utility must read and write files multiple times to arrange all of your various files in the most efficient physical locations on the disk.

To defrag your hard drive:

1 Check your drive for errors before defragging.

2 Free space on your disk before defragging so that you don't have to wait while old or temporary files are defragmented.

3 In My Computer or Windows Explorer, right-click the hard drive you want to defragment. Choose Properties.

4 Activate the Tools tab.

5 Under Defragmentation, click Defragment Now.

6 Click Defragment. (You can instead click Analyze to determine if your drive needs defragmenting.)

You can also defragment your hard disk by using the Defrag utility at the command line. However, it's easier to use the GUI version of Defrag than to run the Defrag utility at the command line. To run Defrag at the command link, enter `defrag volume:`. You can use the optional `-a` parameter to analyze the volume level without defragmenting.

Recovering deleted files

Deleting files under Windows involves two steps: you move the files to the Recycle Bin, then you actually delete the file. You can recover files from the Recycle Bin by selecting the files and clicking Restore. This returns them to their former locations.

When you delete a file in the Recycle Bin, the operating system does not truly erase the file. Instead, it simply marks the file as deleted in the file allocation tables. The space used by the deleted file is now available for other uses.

Using a third-party utility, you can sometimes recover these deleted files. The utility scans the file table for files that are candidates for recovery. Some utilities then scan each file's chain of clusters to determine which files are fully recoverable. Then, you select the files to recover and the utility re-marks the file as not deleted. The name of the file is often altered in the process, typically the first letter of the name is changed or removed.

You should have the file-recovery utility installed before attempting to restore deleted files. Otherwise, as you install the utility, its files will use up the disk space containing the files you're trying to recover.

Diagnostic utilities

Various vendors supply utilities that you can use to diagnose disk troubles, recover data, and optimize the operations of your hard drives. Examples of this sort of utility include Symantec's Norton SystemWorks, Ontrack Data Advisor, Stellar Phoenix, and more.

Do it!

B-1:   Maintaining your hard drive

Here's how	Here's why
1 Check your hard drive for errors	
2 Clean up your disk to remove temporary files	Don't compress the disk or delete application install logs.
3 Defrag your drive	This process can take a considerable amount of time. Your instructor might ask you to cancel the operation before it finishes.

You can ask students to cancel the process after it has run for a minute or two.

Tape and optical drive maintenance

Explanation

Dirt is a major source of problems with optical and tape drives. You should clean the media and read/write systems as recommended by the drive's manufacturer.

Optical disc and drive cleaning

Dirt and scratches on the data storage side of an optical disc can prevent its contents from being read. If this is the case with your discs, you can carefully clean them. Use a soft, lint-free cloth to wipe from the center out—not in circles around the disc. You can use water or gentle soap and water on the cloth to remove stubborn dirt. Don't use household cleaners or abrasives and don't rub too hard or you will damage the disc's surface.

Unless you operate your computer in a very dusty or dirty environment, you should not have to clean the laser lens inside the optical drive. If you decide that you should do so, purchase a drive cleaning kit. Optical drives are built so that they cannot be disassembled. The lasers used inside can be dangerous and manufacturers want to keep you out of harm's way.

Tape head cleaning

Regardless of type, the tape is in direct contact with the read/write heads during any read and write operations. Because of this, any dirt on the tape is quickly transferred to the heads. Also, small bits of magnetic material and tape substrate can "rub off" onto the tape heads.

Tape drive manufacturers normally provide cleaning and maintenance recommendations with their products. You should follow these guidelines, cleaning the heads as often as recommended.

Troubleshooting data storage devices

As a PC technician, you should be familiar with the most common symptoms, probable causes, and suggested "first try" solutions. The following tables list problems, probable causes, and suggested solutions for various data storage device issues you might encounter.

Troubleshooting hard drives

Symptom	Probable cause	Suggested solution
Cannot access drive at all	Cables disconnected, master/slave or SCSI ID conflict, dead drive, drive controller disabled in BIOS.	Confirm that you have all the cables connected fully and properly. Check the master/slave or SCSI settings. Try replacing the drive with a known good drive to see if that drive works in the system. Try the suspect drive in another system to see if it works there. These steps will help you determine if the drive is good or bad. Confirm that the controller is enabled in the BIOS.
Cannot boot from the hard drive	BIOS drive order prevents booting from the hard drive, non-bootable disk, another drive is set to be bootable.	Confirm the boot drive order in the BIOS. Drive not set to be bootable and formatted as bootable disk. Make sure you have not set another drive to be the boot drive, or installed another boot drive into a higher-priority position on the drive chain.
Space on drive doesn't match advertised space	Disk unit misunderstanding, file system limitations, space being used by system recovery programs.	Sometimes the M in MB or the G in GB refers to a decimal measurement (multiples of 1000) while other times it's a binary measurement (multiples of 1024 based on powers of 2). Perhaps you have just misunderstood which units are being used. The FAT32 file system is less efficient with very large drives compared to NTFS. You can also "lose" space when using some sector and cluster size combinations.
Files becoming corrupted	Drive failing, bad data cable, terminator missing.	Try replacing the data cable with a new high-quality cable. Make sure all the connectors are seated fully. Confirm that you have the SCSI chain terminated properly. Use a disk testing utility, such as Windows Check Disk to determine if the drive is failing.
System will boot from hard drive when you do a warm restart, but not from a cold boot	System booting too quickly.	Sometimes the motherboard portions of the boot process can move too quickly for a slower hard drive, which isn't ready when the CPU tries to access it. Use the BIOS setup utility to disable the Quick Boot option and if available, enable the boot delay time option.
Drive letter incorrect	Cables connected incorrectly or master/slave set incorrectly, drive letters reassigned with Windows.	Confirm that you have installed the drive in the correct location on the cable and that you have the master/slave settings configured correctly. Use Windows Disk Manager (part of the Computer Management console) to modify drive letter assignments.
Cannot use the full space of a very large hard drive	The BIOS on your system or your operating system cannot support very large drives.	Install a BIOS update from your motherboard or drive controller manufacturer. Install the BIOS patch included with many extremely large drives. Upgrade to Windows 2000 or XP to use the full capacity of extremely large drives.
Drive not autodetected during boot process	BIOS settings incorrect, bad data cable connection, failing drive.	Confirm that the BIOS settings controlling the disk drive detection are set correctly. Make sure the cables are connected properly and fully seated. Try using a different data cable. Test the drive using a diagnostic utility to confirm that the drive is functioning correctly.

Troubleshooting CD drives

Problem	Probable cause	Suggested solutions
No audio plays from CD	Volume turned down, speakers disconnected, CD drive not connected to sound card.	Make sure you check the volume on both the volume control (in the Windows system tray) and on the speakers. Make sure the speakers are plugged in and turned on. Make sure the CD-to-sound card cable is connected. Check Device Manager to see if a resource conflict is preventing Windows from accessing the drive properly.
CD drive not found	Drive disabled in BIOS, driver problem, wrong drive letter.	Check your system BIOS settings to confirm that the drive is enabled. Make sure you're using the newest driver versions. CD drives often get assigned the last drive letter, but can be assigned other letters. Make sure that the drive is truly not being found rather than just being assigned an unexpected drive letter.
Disc can't be read	Disc scratched or damaged, using a DVD disc in a CD drive.	Treat all optical discs gently and store them inside suitable cases or sleeves. If you must set one down without a case, lay it label side down. Make sure the disc type matches your drive type.
Buffer underrun	This occurs if the buffer empties before you've finished recording.	Enable the buffer underrun protection checkbox in your software, if it's available. Record from an image on disc rather than directly from some other source. Don't run anything else on the computer while recording. Disable virus, screensaver, or other software that might "wake up" and disrupt the CD burning process. Adjust virtual memory settings to prevent swapping.
Write process fails several minutes after starting	On all of the media you insert, the write process stops at the same point.	Try recording at 1X and write from a disc image using disc-at-once writing mode. This could also be due to a bad batch of CDs. Try another package of CDs or another brand of CDs.
Zip files are corrupted when recorded on a SCSI CD-RW drive	Most files have redundant information in them. Compressed files make use of every bit, so any lost information causes a problem.	Check the SCSI cable, connection, and termination for the drive. Also check L2 cache and memory settings for potential problems.
Burned CD-RW disc can't be read on another computer	You can read the CD fine on the computer from which it was burned but not on other players.	Check media compatibility. Some players and CD drives read only pressed CDs or CD-R and not CD-RW discs. With Windows 95/98/Me, you can change the recording mode. Instead of packet-based writes, try recording with No Read Ahead enabled. (In Control Panel, Performance, File System, CD-ROM, set Access Pattern to No Read Ahead.)

Troubleshooting DVD drives

Problem	Probable cause	Suggested solutions
DVD can't be played when two displays are being used	When using a laptop or other system with two displays, the overlay can't be created to play on both devices.	Use only one display when playing video through Windows Media Player. Refer to support.microsoft.com/kb/306713 for more information.
UDF formatted discs can't be read. You might be able to read some of the files, none, or the disc might not even show up in Explorer.	You need to apply the latest Windows XP service pack	Apply the latest Windows XP service pack; make sure recording software is up to date. Refer to support.microsoft.com/kb/321640 for more symptoms, causes, workarounds, and other information.
Cannot play DVD movie	No DVD playback software installed, decoders missing	You must have special software for playing DVD movies on a PC. Make sure you have such a program installed. Movies are encoded in various formats and it's quite possible that you won't have the correct type installed. You might find a suitable decoder at www.free-codecs.com.

Do it!

B-2: Troubleshooting data storage devices

You must set up this lab according to the Troubleshooting Labs Setup section of the Course Setup instructions.

Here's how

1 One or more drive-related problems have been introduced into your lab computer. Troubleshoot these problems to determine their cause.

2 Remedy the problems you have found in your PC to return it to a working state. Solving one problem might reveal the presence of another problem. Troubleshoot and fix any other problems that arise.

3 Document the problem(s) you found here:

4 Document the steps you took to fix the problem(s) here:

Unit summary: Data storage devices

Topic A In this topic, you learned that the components of **hard drives** include the **read/write heads**, **voice coil actuator**, **platters**, **motor**, and **spindle**. You learned that **file systems**, such as **FAT32** and **NTFS**, define how operating systems access the data stored on a drive. You learned that there are three steps to preparing a drive, two of which you must perform. You learned how to physically install a hard drive into a PC, and that there are three steps to preparing a hard drive for use by the operating system: **low-level formatting**, **partitioning**, and (high-level) **formatting**.

Topic B In this topic, you performed basic disk maintenance. You also learned that drives and disks can fail for various reasons. You learned how to troubleshoot these components. You also examined common symptoms of failures and the probable causes and suggested solutions.

Review questions

1 Which disk drive component is made from a metal or plastic disk?

   The platters

2 Tracks are divided into clusters. True or false?

   False. Tracks are divided into sectors. Sectors are grouped into clusters.

3 The NTFS file system is available in 16-bit and 32-bit versions. True or false?

   False. The FAT file system is available in 16-bit and 32-bit versions.

4 What are the four steps to physically installing a hard drive into a PC?

   Configure drive identification options. Install the drive in the PC chassis. Connect the data and control cables to both the controller and the drive. Connect the power cable to the drive.

5 You can configure an IDE drive to be _____, _____, or _____ by using jumpers or switches on the drive.

   Master; slave; cable select

6 You can configure two drives in a single PC to be the master drive. True or false?

   True; however, they must be on separate controller channels.

7 You're installing a drive and find that its data cable is not keyed, though the motherboard connector is keyed. How can you be sure to install the drive cable in the correct orientation?

   Look for pin 1 on the cable and connector. On the cable, it's typically identified by a red stripe running along the edge of the ribbon cable. On the connector, the pin will either be numbered or an arrow will point to pin 1.

8 Hard drive tracks are concentric regions on the platters onto which the data is written via magnetism. True or false?

   True

9 What is the purpose of low-level formatting a hard drive?

   Low-level formatting is the preparation step that divides the disk into tracks and divides each track into sectors. This is a step that must be performed when a drive is brand new.

10 What is head crash and how can you avoid it?

Head crash is when the read/write heads come into contact with the platter surface while the drive is operating. You can avoid head crash by not bumping or jarring your computer and turning it off before moving it.

11 What is the purpose of partitioning a hard drive?

Partitioning divides a drive into one or more logical drives, also called volumes.

12 A voice coil actuator is the disk drive mechanism that

_____.

moves the read/write heads precisely into position over the magnetic tracks recorded on the platters

13 When you defrag your hard drive, what do you do to it?

When you defrag your drive, you rearrange the clusters that comprise each file so that they are contiguous and sequential on the disk.

14 Describe the difference between sectors and clusters.

Sectors are physical division of a track on a platter. A cluster is a logical grouping of one or more sectors.

15 Describe the purpose of the "cable select" setting on an IDE hard drive.

With cable select enabled, the drive will be treated as either the master or slave depending on where it is attached to the interface cable.

16 You have assigned SCSI ID 0 to your hard drive and ID 6 to your CD-ROM drive. Which has a higher priority on the SCSI bus? Are these IDs appropriate for most PC configuration needs?

The CD-ROM has the higher priority—devices with a higher SCSI ID have a higher priority on the bus. Typically, you should configure your hard drive with the highest SCSI ID so that it has the highest priority on the bus.

17 What is the purpose of ZBR?

ZBR, or zoned bit recording, is a technique that writes more sectors in the larger outer tracks of a hard disk platter than on the inner tracks. ZBR permits more data to be stored in a given physical area.

18 You're fixing a customer's PC. The PC won't boot from the hard drive but will boot from a CD. What are some potential sources of this problem?

The boot order in the BIOS is set to boot from the CD before the hard drive or the hard drive is not listed as a bootable device. The partition is not marked active. The active partition doesn't contain a bootable operating system.

19 A customer asks you to install a new 200 GB drive in their system. You find you can't use all of the space on the drive as a single partition. What is a possible cause of this issue and how might you solve it?

The BIOS in some drive controllers cannot support very large partitions. You might be able to work around this by getting a BIOS update from the PC's or drive controller's manufacturer.

20 A customer complains that his system is running slowly. He tells you that the drive light is on all the time, even during simple operations. What might be the cause and solution to this problem?

The hard drive might be fragmented and defragging the partition might help restore normal operation speeds. Alternatively, the drive might be failing or the interface cable might have come loose or become damaged. Back up the PC and then perform further diagnosis to solve a failing drive.

Independent practice activity

1 If you installed a second drive and that drive is still installed, convert that disk to an active disk.

2 Delete the partition on your additional drive.

3 Physically remove the additional drive from your computer.

Unit 3

Printers and scanners

Unit time: 90 minutes

Complete this unit, and you'll know how to:

A Identify printing technologies.

B Install and configure a printer.

C Optimize and troubleshoot a scanner.

Topic A: Printing technologies

This topic covers the following CompTIA A+ 220-603 exam objective.

#	Objective
3.1	**Identify the fundamental principles of using printers and scanners**
	• Describe processes used by printers and scanners including laser, ink dispersion, impact, solid ink and thermal printers.

Printing with a dot-matrix printer

Explanation

If you have access to a dot-matrix printer, it would be helpful to be able to show students the print head, the ribbon, the tractor feed, and if equipped, paper park level and any other features.

Dot-matrix printers have been around as long as personal computers have been available. They aren't as popular as they used to be but still have their place in many companies due to the fact that you can print *multipart forms* with them.

These printers are noisy and slow, especially in comparison to other printers. The noise comes from the impact nature of the print method. *Impact printers*, such as dot-matrix printers, use a mechanical means to press ink from a ribbon onto the page. With a dot-matrix printer, small pins do the pushing. Each character is printed separately, leading to slower output than from other printers.

Print quality on dot-matrix printers is comparable to that produced by a typewriter. One of the main uses of typewriters was typing letters. Thus, the top print quality of a dot-matrix printer is referred to as Near Letter Quality or *NLQ*.

Components

A dot-matrix printer uses a print head that usually contains 9 or 24 pins. The pins are pushed forward in patterns to form letters, numbers, and other shapes. The pins strike an inked ribbon, and the ribbon strikes the paper.

9-pin printers produce low-quality images. Some printers print over the same area after moving the paper slightly to overprint between the first set of dots, thus improving the print quality. 24-pin printers have smaller pins closer together, so they produce a finer image than a 9-pin printer does.

The paper is pulled through the printer using a *tractor feed* or friction. A tractor feed uses a sprocket to mesh with holes in the side of *continuous form* paper. The sprockets turn, pulling the paper through the printer. Friction feed uses single sheets of paper. The roller is held tight against the print head and the paper moves through. Typewriters use friction feed. Most printers have a lever to choose between using the tractor feed or friction feed.

The continuous form paper usually has perforations at 11-inch or 14-inch intervals. This enables the paper to be separated into standard sized pages. It usually has perforations along the side, so that the tractor holes can be removed from the sides of the pages as well. When setting up the paper in the printer, it's therefore necessary to align the top of the page with the print head so that pages don't print across the perforations.

Banners are often printed on dot-matrix printers using continuous feed paper. Banners can be printed on perforated paper, usually without worrying about whether the paper is at the top of the first page. You might also print it on paper that has no perforations between sheets.

Multipart forms are the main use of dot-matrix printers now that other printer types have become more affordable and easier to use. The forms can be preprinted or blank. Preprinted forms require careful alignment so that the print falls in the boxes or on the lines of the forms.

Friction feed is usually used for envelopes and other single sheet papers. Some dot-matrix printers include a paper tray from which single sheets are fed, but more often, you must insert the single sheet, set the lever for friction feed, and print each page one at a time.

Connections

Dot-matrix printers usually have either a serial or parallel interface connection. These printers were the usual choice for users when personal computers were first introduced, when interfaces such as USB, infrared, FireWire, and other more recent interfaces hadn't yet been introduced. It's also rare to find a dot-matrix printer with a built-in network interface. Some printers have both serial and parallel interfaces, so that the user can make a choice.

Options

Dot-matrix printers don't usually have a lot of optional features. However, some have slots for adding font cards, memory, or additional paper feeders so that the paper can easily be switched from single sheet to continuous form paper.

Other impact printers

Other printer types also use an inked ribbon to strike the paper to produce images. These included daisy-wheel printers. These could produce letters only in the font that was on the wheel installed in the printer.

Band printers have the letters, numbers, and symbols repeated multiple times around on a band. The band moves at a high speed and strikes the ribbon when struck by hammers. There are hammers for each column of print on the page. Some band printers combine dot-matrix pins with the hammers for each print column. Additional information on this can be found at:

    techweb.com/encyclopedia/defineterm.jhtml?term=band+printer

Do it!

A-1: Examining the dot-matrix print process

Questions and answers

1 Why do companies use dot-matrix printers?

   To print multipart forms

2 How many pins are in most dot-matrix print heads?

   9 or 24

3 What are the paper feed mechanisms typically used on dot-matrix printers?

   Tractor feed or friction feed

4 In addition to dot-matrix printers, what other impact printers might you encounter?

   Daisy wheel and band printers

Producing images on inkjet printers

Explanation

Inkjet printers, also known as *ink dispersion* printing technology, produce images by forcing ink through tiny nozzles and onto the paper. Each nozzle is approximately 50 to 60 *microns* in diameter. The way the ink is forced through the nozzles falls into one of two basic methods: *thermal bubble* or *piezoelectric bubble*. Exhibit 3-1 shows an example of an inkjet printer.

Exhibit 3-1: An inkjet printer

Thermal bubble technology heats the ink, which vaporizes it, creating a bubble. The bubble protrudes out through the nozzle, and sprays onto the paper. When the bubble bursts, it creates a vacuum which draws more ink from the cartridge into the print head, readying it to create another dot.

Piezoelectric technology creates a bubble with a *piezo crystal* behind each nozzle. An electrical current sent to the crystal causes it to vibrate. When it vibrates inward, it releases ink onto the paper; when it vibrates outward, it pulls ink from the cartridge.

The letters C-Y-M-K are used rather than CYMB so that the B is not misunderstood to mean blue. The K is from the last letter of "black."

Ink cartridges are the reservoirs in which ink for inkjet printers is held. The number of cartridges varies from printer to printer, but most have a black cartridge and then a color-color cartridge with compartments for yellow, cyan, and magenta, often referred to as CYMK (cyan, yellow, magenta, and black). Some printers have separately replaceable cartridges for each of the colors. Some have more colors than these three basic ones. Some inexpensive printers don't have a separate black cartridge. Instead, when black is required, they mix all three colors together to produce a dark color. Exhibit 3-2 shows examples of inkjet cartridges. In this case, there's a single color cartridge that contains the cyan, yellow, and magenta inks. There's a separate black cartridge.

Exhibit 3-2: Inkjet cartridges

Shades of each of the basic colors are often produced using *dithering*, which is also known as *half-tones*. By varying the pattern of dots, as well as the density of the dots, you can make a color appear to be more saturated or darker. Newspapers use this method to print photos.

The print head on an inkjet printer is usually part of the ink cartridge. Since this is the part of a printer that wears out the soonest, having it replaced each time you replace the ink means you always have a good print head. This also makes the cartridges more expensive. If the print head is part of the printer rather than the cartridge, the cartridges are usually less expensive, but after a couple of years, you might notice that the print quality has degraded. Exhibit 3-3 shows the print head on an inkjet cartridge.

Exhibit 3-3: Inkjet cartridge print heads

There are usually between 300 and 600 separate nozzles on a print head, corresponding to a 300 to 600 DPI printer. This is the standard for thermal bubble printers. Piezoelectric printers can print 720 x 720 DPI. Enhancements through the software drivers can raise the DPI by having the print head move fractionally so that dots can be placed between existing dots on the page. Thus, a 600 DPI printer can produce 1200 DPI images and a 720 DPI printer can print images at 1440x720.

The print head moves across the page printing columns of pixels at a time. To increase the resolution, a second pass is made across the page to overwrite between the existing dots. On some printers, printing occurs on both passes across the page—left to right and right to left. On others, it prints only in one direction, and as the stepper motor advances the page, the print head moves back across the page to begin printing the next line.

Visit www.microscopy-uk.org.uk/mag/artjan99/inkjet.html for close-up photos and information about inkjet print cartridges and heads. The page is a bit dated, but it still provides interesting and relevant information about how inkjet print heads work.

Print quality

Inkjet printers were a major improvement over the quality offered by dot-matrix printers. The ink dots could be grouped much closer together than the pins in the dot-matrix printer. The standard against which inkjet printers are compared was originally the laser printer, the output of which was considered very high-quality. This is still true for text output. Now, with advances in inkjet technology, traditional, analog, chemically-produced darkroom photographs have become the standard against which quality is compared.

In addition to purchasing a printer with a higher DPI to ensure high-quality output, your choice of paper on which to print affects the quality of the output. Regular copier paper doesn't produce as clear of an image as specially-coated inkjet paper does. The ink bleeds out on regular paper, creating fuzzy edges to characters and images. Coated inkjet paper has a waxy layer that the ink sits on, thus preventing bleed-out of the ink.

Attempting to print on a shiny surface such as a transparency can also prove difficult if the wrong type of transparency plastic is used. The ink might not dry properly and could smudge on the kind of transparency plastic used to write on with markers. Transparency sheets with a special textured coating allow the ink to adhere and dry properly.

The ink in most inkjet cartridges is water soluble. This can be a problem if your printouts get wet. Being caught in the rain with a poster containing images printed from an inkjet printer can result in the ink running down the page. You can purchase waterproof inks for some inkjet printers.

Inkjet photo printers

Most inkjet printers are designed to be everyday printers for a variety of documents from text to graphics. Printing photos on an inkjet printer can produce some very nice prints, but they don't hold up as long as a traditional, chemically produced dark-room photos do. Special photo paper is required for printing high-quality images from a camera or photos that were scanned in. Printing them on regular paper or even coated inkjet paper results in lower-quality photos. Some printers also enable you to print on non-paper items, such as CDs. Exhibit 3-4 shows an example of a photo printer printing on a CD.

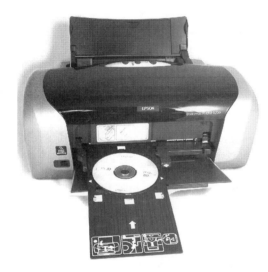

Exhibit 3-4: Printing directly onto a CD

Some printers are designed just for printing photos. These are often small printers that can print 4 x 6-inch or smaller photos on specialty paper.

Paper path

Some inkjet printers have a paper tray behind the printer and pull the paper through the printer on a straight-through paper path. This setup leads to fewer paper jams and is good for heavy paper stock. Exhibit 3-5 shows a straight-through paper path in an inkjet printer.

Exhibit 3-5: Straight-through paper path

Other printers store the paper in a tray below and to the front of the printer then pull the paper up through rollers and under the print head. Printers using this technology pull the paper up through an S-curve or a U-curve. Exhibit 3-6 shows a curved paper path in an inkjet printer.

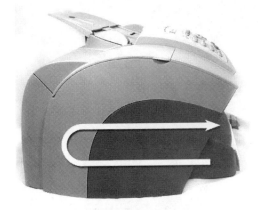

Exhibit 3-6: Curved paper path

Do it!

A-2: Examining how inkjet printers work

Questions and answers

1 What are the two basic methods of ink dispersion in inkjet printers?

   Thermal bubble or piezoelectric bubble

2 List the colors found in a 4-color inkjet printer

   Cyan, yellow, magenta, and black

3 The print head moves across the page and prints columns of pixels. True or false?

   True

4 You can print photos on any paper, but some papers enable you to print higher-quality images than others do. True or false?

   True

5 Describe the paper path for inkjet printers.

   Some printers use a straight-through paper path in which the paper stays the same side up as it's pulled from the paper tray above or behind the printer to the output tray in the lower front of the printer. Other printers use a curved paper path, in which the paper is stored below and to the front of the printer. The paper is pulled up through an S or U curve into the printer. Depending on the printer, the side of the paper that's down in the tray might be the side printed on.

Producing output on a laser printer

Laser printers are the standard level of quality by which other printers are compared. They're able to create high-quality documents in a high-volume printing environment. Most laser printers are black-and-white output devices, but color laser printers are dropping in price to the point where they're worth considering even for home use if you plan to do more printing than an inkjet printer can handle. Exhibit 3-7 shows an example of a laser printer.

Exhibit 3-7: A laser printer

The price on a laser printer is now nearing the price of a good inkjet printer. As with inkjet printers, the manufacturer can sell the printer itself at or below cost. They make up the cost with the consumables. For example, one $100 laser printer requires a replacement toner cartridge that costs $90. A $300 color laser printer from this same manufacturer requires 3 color cartridges and a black cartridge that add up to almost $300. It varies from manufacturer to manufacturer, but on average, you should be able to get at least 1,000 to 1,500 printouts from a cartridge. Check the specifications for the printer you're considering to determine the lifespan of a toner cartridge for that printer.

Laser printers produce images using an *electrophotographic* process. By combining electrostatic charges, toner and laser light, high-quality images are produced, one page at a time. The components in a laser printer include:

- Toner cartridge
- Laser scanning assembly
- Power supplies
- Paper control and transport assembly
- Transfer corona assembly
- Fusing assembly
- Electronic control package

Toner cartridge

An example of a *toner* cartridge is shown in Exhibit 3-8. A toner cartridge contains:

- A hopper filled with toner. Toner is a fine powder composed of plastic, iron, and carbon particles.
- An EP drum covered with photosensitive coating that holds a static charge until exposed to light.
- A blade to remove used toner from the drum.
- A corona charging assembly, which applies a static charge to the drum after an image has been printed.

Exhibit 3-8: Toner cartridge from top and bottom

Laser scanning assembly

The laser scanning assembly contains the following components:

Component	Description
Laser	Shines on the drum and creates an electrostatic image of what's printed. Creates areas of negative charge on the positively charged drum.
Mirror	Reflects the laser beam.
Lens(es)	Focuses the laser beam. Multiple lenses may be used to focus the laser beam on the various areas of the drum: the areas being closer to or farther away from the mirror and laser beam.

Power supplies

A high-voltage power supply (*HVPS*) converts 120 volt, 60 Hz AC current into high-voltage electricity used by the EP process. A DC power supply (*DCPS*) is used to power components that don't require high voltages.

Paper control and transport assembly

Paper is moved through the printer by a series of rollers. Some of the rollers simply guide the paper from one location to another and some rollers function to apply pressure to the printed page to fuse the toner.

Transfer corona assembly

The HVPS applies a high-voltage charge to the corona wire. The wire then charges the paper so that the toner from the drum can be transferred onto the paper as it passes under the drum. After the paper passes the drum, the static charge eliminator strip drains the charges from the paper so that it doesn't adhere to the toner cartridge and create a paper jam.

Fusing assembly

The fusing assembly is composed of rollers and a heating lamp. It applies heat and pressure to adhere the toner permanently to the page.

Electronic control package

The electronic control package is also known as the printer control circuitry or the main logic assembly. This component is responsible for communicating with the internal printer memory, the control panel, and the computer from which the print job is being received.

Laser print process

All laser printers use basically the same process to produce images. Through the use of negative and positive electrostatic charges, a laser writes the image to be printed into the charges, and then negatively charged toner is attracted to the positively charged paper.

Some sources use different terms for the steps or stages of the process, but the most common terminology has been listed here.

Stage	Description
Charging or conditioning	The primary corona wire applies a negative charge of approximately -600 volts to the EP drum.
Writing or exposing	The laser beams reduces the negative charge to about -100 volts on the EP drum in the areas that become the image to be printed.
Developing	Areas of the drum that were written to by the laser attract toner.
Transferring	A positive charge of about + 600 voles is applied to the paper by the transfer corona wire.
Fusing	Pressure and heat set the toner to the paper. A 350°F fusing roller melts the toner, and squeezing the paper through a set of rollers presses the toner into the paper.
Cleaning and erasing	A rubber blade clears the excess toner from the drum. Another corona wire removes the charges from the drum.

Some sources place the cleaning and erasing stage at the beginning of the process. Others place it at the end of the process. In either case, it prepares the drum for receiving and printing the next image.

Do it!

A-3: Examining how laser printers work

Questions and answers

1 Compare the cost of a laser printer to the cost of the consumables.

   They are roughly the same.

2 What process is used by laser printers to produce images?

   Electrophotographic process

3 List the components of a toner cartridge.

   Hopper filled with toner, EP drum covered with photosensitive coating, blade, corona charging assembly

4 List the components of the laser scanning assembly.

   Laser, mirror, and lenses

5 The HVPS converts 120 volt current into high voltage electricity used by the EP process. True or false?

   True

6 List the steps in the laser printing process.

   1. Charging or conditioning

   2. Writing or exposing

   3. Developing

   4. Transferring

   5. Fusing

   6. Cleaning and erasing

Other printers

Explanation

Most corporate and home users use either an inkjet or laser printer. A few still use dot-matrix printers for special requirements or because they never upgraded as newer technologies became available.

There are several other types of printers that you might encounter in your support career. Most of these are too expensive for the casual user, but as prices continue to drop on printer technologies, even these more expensive printer types might become more commonplace.

Most of the printers in this topic are for high-quality production of graphics. They produce a higher resolution image even if the DPI statistics are listed as the same as inkjet or laser printers. Printer resolution refers to addressable dots per inch. Each of these dots can be composed of over 25 dots. This enables a 300 DPI image to appear the same as a 4800 dpi inkjet print.

Solid ink printers

Solid ink printers use sticks of wax that are melted to create the ink for printing. There are usually cyan, magenta, yellow, and black sticks. These are heated to a melting point. The ink is then sprayed onto the drum after being combined to form the various colors in the image. The paper passes over the drum under a roller, and the image is transferred onto the paper.

These printers are environmentally friendly, since they don't produce ozone. Also, the ink itself is nontoxic. The process doesn't use excessive heat as laser printers do.

The output from solid ink printers is very high quality. The ink sticks last approximately 3,000 pages as compared to an average of 1,500 pages for laser printers or 500 to 1,000 pages for ink jet printers.

Dye sublimation printers

Another high quality printer is the *dye sublimation printer*. These are often referred to as dye sub printers. The dye is a solid contained on either a ribbon or a roll. The roll is consecutive pages of cyan, magenta, yellow, and sometimes black.

The term dye sublimation is a bit of a misnomer in most cases. The dye is a solid dye, so that part of the name fits fine. However, the scientific process of *sublimation* refers to a solid being converted to a gas without its becoming a liquid in between. While this does happen on a few of the very high-end printers, in most cases the dye sub printers in actuality use a diffusion process. The *dye diffusion thermal process* is known as D2T.

To transfer the dye from the ribbon or roll, the print head is pushed against the paper by weights or springs. The depth of color is regulated by varying the heat applied. This enables printing without use of either *halftones* or *dithering*, which are required for other printing methods. The transparent dyes are combined for creating colors in a wide variety of 256 shades of each of the colors.

Dye sub printers require special paper. The paper has a special layer to receive the dye. A layer is applied after the image has been created to protect the output from water, UV light, and fingerprints.

Dye sub printers print square dots with higher densities of color in the center and lower density at the edges of each dot. The density varies by the amount of power applied to the print head, thus changing the shade of the color.

Thermal printers

Thermal printers produce output with heat. The image can be creating using:

- Thermal wax transfer
- Direct thermal
- Thermal autochrome

Thermal wax transfer

Thermal wax transfer printers use ink in a wax base. The ink is melted from the transfer ribbon by a heating element in the print head. Separate cyan, yellow, magenta, and black transfer ribbons are used to create the image. The cooled wax becomes a permanent image on the paper. These printers don't require special paper.

Direct thermal

Direct thermal printers use coated paper. A row of heating elements is used to burn dots directly onto the paper. These are monochrome printers.

Thermal autochrome

Thermal autochrome printers use special paper in which cyan, magenta, and yellow pigments are embedded. Each page passes three times under the thermal print head at different temperatures. Each color is processed at a different temperature. UV light sets the colors after each pass so that no more processing of that colors occurs on the subsequent passes under the print head.

Plotters

Plotters are pen-based output devices that create *line images*. Printers create *raster images* as compared to line images. Plotters are typically used to create precision engineering documents from *CAD* applications. A pen in the printer moves side to side on an X-axis as the paper moves up and down on the Y-axis.

A multi-color plotter uses multiple pens to create an image. In most cases, this is a carousel containing 4 to 12 pens, but in some, you need to change the pen to each color as you need it.

Plotters create lines with the pens. Other printers create lines only by spacing the dots very close together. By using a pen, curved lines are smoother than what can be obtained with dots.

Most plotters are used to create engineering documents. Some other industrial uses have replaced the pens with cutting devices. These have been used in the garment industry to cut out fabric from the computer application when it's cut from the fabric rather than printed. The sign industry has also used plotters with cutting devices to cut out signs from an application outputting the sign shape to the material to be cut.

More printer types

Other printers you might encounter are variations on the printer types already discussed. Some of these are designed to create smaller than standard letter-sized output, and some printers produce very large output formats.

Snapshot printers typically produce 4 x 6 inch pictures or 5 x 7 inches pictures. These typically use inkjet or dye sub printing technologies. They often require special paper to get photo-quality prints.

Some of these printers accept media cards from digital cameras allowing users to print directly from the card to the printer without using a computer between the card and the printer.

Some of these printers also include a pop-up screen that enables you to manipulate the picture before printing it. You can perform such editing as cropping and red-eye reduction on such printers.

Large format printers are typically inkjet-based printers. These are often used to create banners and large signs.

Musician Graham Nash was involved in creating the Iris inkjet printer. This was designed to create high quality art prints on a variety of materials. The output was designed to be fade-resistant with UV-protective layers.

Do it!

A-4:   Identifying other printer technologies

Questions and answers

1 What's the base in which solid ink colors are held?

   Wax sticks

2 What features make solid ink printers environmentally friendly?

   They produce no ozone, the ink is non-toxic, and they don't use excessive heat as laser printers do.

3 What base is the ink for a dye sub printer held in?

   A ribbon or a roll.

4 What's another name for the dye diffusion thermal process?

   D2T

5 Dye sub printers require the use of halftones and dithering to create shades of colors. True or false?

   False

6 List three types of thermal printers.

   Thermal wax transfer, direct thermal, and thermal autochrome

7 Why can a plotter make a smoother line than other types of printers?

   A pen is used to draw a line rather than create a line by grouping dots together.

Topic B: Printers

This topic covers the following CompTIA A+ 220-603 exam objectives.

#	Objective
3.2	**Install, configure, optimize and upgrade printers and scanners** • Install and configure printers and scanners • Power and connect the device using network or local port • Install/update the device driver and calibrate the device • Configure options and default settings • Install and configure print drivers (e.g. PCL™, Postscript™ and GDI) • Validate compatibility with OS and applications • Educate user about basic functionality
3.3	**Identify tools, diagnostic procedures and troubleshooting techniques for printers and scanners** • Gather information required to troubleshoot printer/scanner problems • Troubleshoot a print failure (e.g. lack of paper, clear queue, restart print spooler, recycle power on printer, inspect for jams, check for visual indicators)

The Windows print process

Explanation

The *Windows print process* can be broken into three major processes. Each of those processes is composed of several processes in getting the print request from the user to the printer. The three main processes are:

- Client
- Spooler
- Printer

Client processes

The client processes include:

- A print job is sent from an application by a user.
- A graphics device interface (GDI) is called by the application.
- The spooler receives the print job from the GDI.

Spooler processes

The spooler processes include:

- Winspool.drv issues an RPC to Spoolsv.exe. Winspool.drv is on the client side. Spoolsv.exe is on the server side.
- Spoolss.dll, the print router, is called by Spoolsv.exe.
- Localspl.dll routes the print job to either the local print provider or to the remote print server.
- Local print provider locates a print processor capable of handling the job's data type, and then sends the job to the print processor.

- The print processor makes any necessary modification for printing the job.
- The page separator processor receives the print job from the print processor and, if necessary, adds a separator page.
- The job is sent either directly to the appropriate port monitor or to a language monitor and then on to the port monitor. The port monitor is responsible for communications between the PC and the printer. A language monitor is responsible for translating the print job into code the printer understands.

Printer processes

The printer processes include:

- The print spooler sends the job to the printer.
- The print language is translated into information the printer can print.

Do it!

B-1: Examining the Windows printing process

Questions and answers

1 List the three main processes of the Windows print process.

Client, spooler, and printer processes

2 A graphics device interface (GDI) is called by the application. Into which process does this step fall?

Client

3 The print language is translated into information the printer can print. Into which process does this step fall?

Printer

4 The print processor makes any necessary modification for printing the job. Into which process does this step fall?

Spooler

Inkjet printer installation

Explanation
Most printers connect via USB today, so when you connect the printer, Windows automatically detects it and attempts to install the driver for you. Your printer likely comes with a CD-ROM containing drivers and additional software to enhance the printing quality. Exhibit 3-9 shows the bubble alerting you that new hardware was found on your computer.

Exhibit 3-9: New hardware bubble

One useful utility that's usually installed with a printer is a monitor for the ink levels in the cartridges. This helps you know when ink supplies are getting low and need to be replaced. Exhibit 3-10 shows the utility displayed when printing. Notice that it includes information about the print job and about the ink levels in the printer.

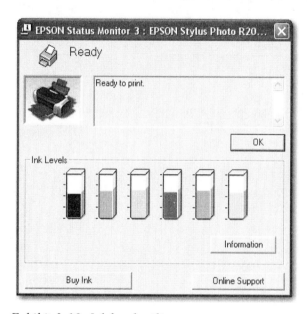

Exhibit 3-10: Ink level utility

While you can purchase kits to refill the cartridges, this usually voids the printer warranty. If you do refill the cartridge, make sure that you get the ink that's right for your printer. Thermal inkjet printers need ink that can withstand high heat. Getting a water-soluble ink for a solvent-based ink printer or vice versa can result in improper application of the ink to the page and create a major mess. Since the print head is contained within most print cartridges, it's recommended that it be refilled only two or three times.

Printer interfaces

Most inkjet printers are connected by USB interfaces today. In supporting inkjet printers, you might encounter some that still use the parallel port interface. Even less likely, you might encounter some with SCSI or serial interfaces. Exhibit 3-11 shows the communications interfaces on an inkjet printer. In this case, there's a parallel and a USB port.

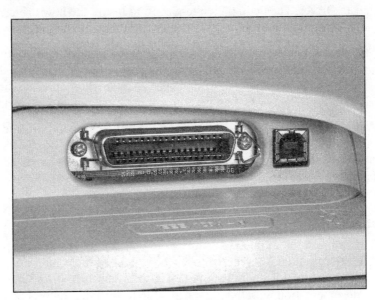

Exhibit 3-11: Communications interfaces on an inkjet printer

Be sure to configure the printer in Windows to use the connection type to which the printer is connected. If it's using SCSI, be sure to assign a unique device ID. If it's using parallel, be sure that you've specified the correct LPT port. If it's using serial, verify that you've specified the correct COM port. Exhibit 3-12 shows Device Manager information for a printer connected to a computer.

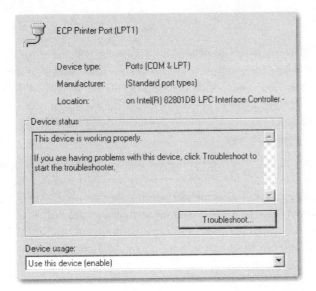

Exhibit 3-12: Port identified for the printer

To install an ink jet printer, connect the printer to a computer using the correct interface, and then plug it in and power it up. If you're connecting it to a Windows computer, Windows will likely recognize you've connected a new device and install drivers for it automatically. If drivers aren't installed automatically, you can do it manually using the materials that shipped with the printer.

To upgrade a device driver, in Device Manager, right-click the printer and choose Update Driver. Then complete the wizard to install the new driver. Alternately, you can use any installation program that comes from the manufacturer.

After the printer is connected and working, you can configure options and calibrate it for best performance. To calibrate a printer, you can print a test page, and then adjust printer settings to ensure the print heads are properly aligned so they produce clear, crisp images. Then print a another test page to verify that it's working properly.

You'll also need to educate the user on the printer's operation, and verify that it works with the user's programs and operating system. You can do this by printing test pages. If possible, leave some documentation with the user to help answer any initial questions that might arise.

Laser printer installation

When a printer is shipped to a store or to you, the toner cartridge needs to be removed. Otherwise, the toner can get all over the insides of the printer and make a huge mess. Therefore, the first step to installing a laser printer is to install the toner cartridge. Check the documentation with the toner cartridge for installation procedures. It usually begins with gently rocking the cartridge from side to side. This distributes the toner, as it likely settled during shipment.

On some printers, the drum and some other components are outside of the cartridge. If this is the case, refer to your documentation for how and where to install them.

Laser printers usually come with chunks of Styrofoam in place of the toner cartridge. Other components might be taped down so that they don't move during shipment. Be sure to remove all of the packing materials and tape before trying to use the printer.

Interfaces

Laser printers are used in a wide variety of situations. These printers have the most widely varied connection types of any printers. Most laser printers have two or more connection interfaces. These include parallel, SCSI, USB, serial, IEEE 1394/FireWire, and wired or wireless Ethernet network connections. Examples of the communications interfaces on a laser printer are shown in Exhibit 3-13.

Exhibit 3-13: Communications interfaces on a laser printer

Some interfaces also include network connections, infrared ports, and wireless connections. A network connection enables the printer to be connected directly to the network without being connected to a computer, such as a print server. Print servers can make multiple printers available to network users. Infrared and other wireless technologies, such as Bluetooth and 801.11, enable users with computers equipped with compatible interfaces to print to the printer without the need to connect the printer and computer physically with a cable.

To install a laser printer, connect the printer to the network or a computer using the correct interface, and then plug it in and power it up. If you're connecting it to a Windows computer, Windows will likely recognize that you've connected a new device and install drivers for it automatically. If drivers aren't installed automatically, you can do it manually using the materials that shipped with the printer.

To upgrade a device driver, in Device Manager right-click the printer and choose Update Driver. Then complete the wizard to install the new driver. Alternately, you can use any installation program that comes from the manufacturer.

After the printer is connected and working, you can configure options and calibrate it for best performance. Then print a test page to verify that it's working properly, and verify it's compatible with any programs or operating systems that are deployed. Also take a few minutes to educate the user about basic printing functionality and leave documentation if it's available.

B-2:   Installing a printer

Here's how	Here's why
1 Connect the power cord to the printer, but don't turn it on	You'll install either an inkjet printer or a laser printer on your computer.
2 Connect the interface cable to the printer	The interface cable will vary based on the connection type the printer uses. Most current printers are USB printers, but some also have parallel or serial ports, and some have SCSI ports.
3 Plug the power cord into an electrical outlet	If possible, this should be on a surge protector strip.
4 Connect the interface cable to the computer	The port will vary based on the connection type the printer is using.
5 Insert paper in the printer	If none is loaded.
Install print cartridges	If they aren't already installed. Refer to the documentation for the printer for the procedure on installing the cartridges.
Turn on the printer	The Found New Hardware wizard displays.
6 Select **Yes, this time only**	You could select the other options, but for classroom purposes, we'll choose this option.
Click **Next**	
7 Click **Next**	To install the software automatically, the default selection.
8 Click **Back**	If the software wasn't found.
9 Select **Install from a list or specific location**	
Click **Next**	
10 Select the appropriate option	If you have the drivers on CD or floppy disk or have downloaded them, select Search for the best driver in these locations, then check the appropriate option. If the driver is included with the operating system, you can choose Don't search. I will choose the driver to install.
Click **Next**	Follow the prompts to finish installing the drivers.
If appropriate, cancel the wizard, then install the software from the appropriate location	Some printers require that you install software from the CD or from a download rather than installing the driver through the Add Hardware wizard.

11	Click **Start**, **Printers and Faxes**	Your newly installed printer should be listed.
12	Right-click the printer	
	Choose **Properties**	
	Click **Print Test Page**	
	Click **OK**	If the test page prints successfully. If it doesn't print, click Troubleshoot and follow the steps to resolve the problem until you can successfully print a test page. If necessary, adjust the print-head alignment.
13	Open Notepad, and print a test page	
14	Click **Start**, right-click **My Computer** and choose **Manage**	To open Computer Management, where you can access Device Manager.
15	In the console tree, select **Device Manager**	To display the computer's devices.
	Find your printer in the list	It might be under Other Devices.
16	Right-click the printer and choose **Update Driver...**	You would use this wizard to upgrade the device driver.
	Click **Cancel**	To close the wizard.
17	Close all open windows and dialog boxes	

Printer options

Explanation

The options and upgrades available for printers vary widely. Some are specific to a certain type of printer. Some apply to all printers. In most cases, you need to purchase options and upgrades from your printer manufacturer, because they're integrated into the printer mechanism. Some options and upgrades are very basic, while others turn a printer into a multifunction device.

Options and upgrades for dot-matrix printers

Dot-matrix printers with both a friction feed and tractor paper feed might have an option called paper park or a similar name. This option enables you to switch between sheet feed single page paper and tractor feed paper without having to unload either from the printer.

Another option on dot-matrix printers is input and output trays. An input tray with multiple sheets of paper is often an option that can be purchased separately or removed, if it was included with the printer. Many dot-matrix printers don't have an output tray—the printed pages just pile up on the table or floor in front of or behind it.

Some dot-matrix printers include a slot in which font cartridges can be installed. This was useful before print jobs sent font details with the print job. This was true on DOS applications and early Windows applications. Documents were printed with the default font on the printer.

Other upgrades include additional paper input and output trays. For printers that use continuous roll paper rather than perforated sheet paper, some manufacturers offer a paper cutter. This enables you to tear off the printout cleanly at the end of the document.

Options and upgrades for inkjet printers

Options for inkjet printers vary by manufacturer. Most printers come bundled with software to enhance the printer's output.

One option offered for a while enabled users to turn their inkjet printer into a scanner. The user removed the ink cartridge from the printer and installed a scan-head in its place. It was slow, but if desk space is at a premium, it offered a good option.

A more recent variation on this idea is the combination printer, scanner, copier, fax device. These devices are popular for home users and home offices. Exhibit 3-14 shows an example of a multifunction printer.

Exhibit 3-14: A multifunction printer

Another option you might encounter is additional paper trays. These allow you to leave the paper in the paper tray and select which tray to feed from when you want to print. Other printers enable you to leave the paper in the paper tray and hand feed a single sheet of paper or an envelope or postcard through an alternate paper path.

Some printers come with holders for printing on smaller media or on unconventional media such as CDs. The sensors often detect a paper jam if you try to feed envelopes or small media through the normal paper path, so these holders enable the sensor to see a full size sheet going through. Exhibit 3-15 shows an example of an add-on for printing CDs with an inkjet printer.

Exhibit 3-15: Printing on a CD

Upgrades for inkjet printers include an auto-duplexer. In most cases, to print two-sided pages with an inkjet printer, you have to determine how the sheet feeds through the printer, and then turn the paper over so that the second side doesn't print upside down or on top of the first page. The duplexer takes care of positioning the pages correctly for the printing of the back side of the page.

A PostScript upgrade kit is available for some printers. This kit enables the user to send PostScript output to the inkjet printer. Most printers don't use such sophisticated language for creating printer output.

Mobile inkjet printers include batteries. This variation on the inkjet printer is popular with those who do a lot of traveling and need to print documents. Options for mobile printers include car adapters that plug into the cigarette lighter, additional batteries, and carrying cases.

A Bluetooth adapter can be plugged into the USB port on the printer. This enables any Bluetooth-compatible device to print wirelessly.

Most inkjet printers aren't designed for high-volume printing, but if you want to share your printer on a network, and you want to connect it directly to the network, some printers have the option of installing an Ethernet card or a print server card. Some other interfaces you might be able to add include FireWire and type B serial ports.

Options and upgrades for laser printers

Laser printers have the most robust selection of options and variations between printers of any printer type. Most laser printers have one or more page description languages—usually PCL and PostScript. Some have proprietary languages instead of or in addition to these.

Laser printers usually have at least one input tray and one output tray. Additional input and output trays are common options that users request as upgrades. One type of output device that makes multiple-page and multiple-copy print jobs easier to identify each complete set, is an offset stacker. This device stacks each set of output either to the left or the right of the output tray.

Laser printers are often connected directly to the network. This requires a network card to be installed in the printer or a network adapter to be connected to one of the existing printer ports. Laser printers often include USB, serial, and parallel ports. They also might include infrared, AppleTalk, Ethernet, or wireless Ethernet ports as well.

To speed up printing large jobs, an internal hard drive can be added to some laser printers. The jobs are spooled to the printer and read directly from the internal hard drive. Large jobs with a great deal of graphics consume large amounts of printer memory. You might need to upgrade the memory in the printer if large jobs start out fine, but end in gobbledygook or have missing sections.

Duplexers might be built into the laser printer or added as an upgrade. This is useful in creating long documents, if both sides of the paper can be used. Some also include collators and stapling options. Some copiers can be connected to the network and used as printers with all of the features of the copier available as printer options.

Options and upgrades for other types of printers

For large format printers that print on continuous roll paper, an automatic take-up reel is very useful. Rather than the paper piling up on the floor, this device rolls the paper onto a spool as it's printed. Another option for some of these printers is a refillable ink tank rather than ink cartridges. In addition, a network card or other interface card can be installed in some large format printers to make it able to connect directly to a network or via other connection types.

Do it!

Provide students with options for their printers.

B-3: Installing printer add-ons and upgrades

Here's how	Here's why
1 Obtain the option or upgrade for your printer	You will install it in this activity.
2 Obtain the manufacturer's documentation for the printer	You will need it for the installation.
3 Install the option or upgrade	According to the manufacturer's instructions.
4 Verify that the option or upgrade is working	(Print a test page, if necessary.)

Maintenance

Explanation

Sometimes just simple maintenance is all that's needed to keep a printer running smoothly. In the following sections, you'll learn how to perform routine maintenance on various types of printers.

Some common maintenance tools will include:

- Cleaning solutions, including alcohol
- Cleaning equipment, including soft clothes and cotton swabs
- Compressed air
- Low-static vacuum
- Screwdrivers, to open compartments
- Extension magnets

Dot matrix printers

Keeping the printer clean helps it last a long time. Paper bits, dust, and other debris can easily get into the printer and cause problems. Compressed air can be sprayed to help remove such contaminants from the printer. Mild household cleaners can be used on the exterior case to keep it clean.

The roller can become sticky, especially if it gets printed on without any paper in the roller. Rubbing alcohol is useful for cleaning this off. Oil the print head or guide only if told to do so in your printer documentation. Otherwise, doing so can clog the workings of the printer.

As with any electronic devices, care should always be taken when working around it. Precautions particular to dot-matrix printers include not becoming entangled with the print feed mechanism. Neckties and hanging jewelry should be secured before leaning over the printer and operating the mechanism.

Inkjet printers

The main thing you need to do to keep an inkjet printer working properly is to change the cartridge when the ink gets low. You usually have a visual warning from either lights on the printer, a software utility, or just poor quality output. Always be sure to use recommended supplies when replacing consumables or parts.

In some cases, you might have to clean the print nozzles and recalibrate the printer. You can do this by simply following manufacturer's instructions, which will have you use the buttons on the printer or a Windows utility. Then print a test page to verify functionality.

You can tell when one of the colors is low; often the output doesn't match the colors on the screen even remotely. For example, the output might all have a pink cast to it if the blue or yellow ink is low, but the red is still going strong.

Color matching is one area that printer manufacturers continue to improve on. The colors used on a monitor are based on a different color scheme (RGB) from that of the printers (CYMK). The results are usually close to what you see on screen but might need to be adjusted a bit when you see the actual output. Some printers come with utilities to adjust the calibration of ink output to match your desired output more closely.

Keeping the inkjet printer's environment properly ventilated helps the printer last longer as well. Adequate ventilation keeps the printer from overheating. Another environmental concern is keeping dust out of the printer. Most inkjet printers have a very open design, which allows dust to gather inside the printer. This can result in stray marks on the paper, the overheating of elements, and other such problems.

When working with inkjet printers, be sure to take certain safety precautions. These include practicing ESD safe practices, keeping dangling jewelry and neckties out of the printer, and handling ink cartridges so as not to damage their print heads. Also, if you're clearing a paper jam, be careful about not damaging the printer, the cartridges, or yourself.

Laser printers

Laser printers generally require more maintenance than inkjet printers. Laser printer maintenance can include:

- Replacing cartridges.
- Cleaning internal components. (Be sure to follow safety procedures.) Follow the manufacturer's guidelines for cleaning components
- Replacing components as recommended by the manufacturer. Often the components will come in a special *maintenance kits* that you can obtain from the manufacturer. Some manufacturers recommend installing maintenance kits after a specified duration or number of printed pages to keep the printer operating smoothly. After installing the maintenance kit, you may have to reset page count. Check with your manufacturer.

When replacing components, take some time to clean out any accumulated toner and paper dust inside the printer. This will prevent the debris from hindering printer operations, and it will keep a clean printing environment. Often manufacturer's maintenance kits will include cleaning materials.

Be sure the printer is well ventilated and situated securely on a flat surface, and keep the printer trays full. Try to use only recommended supplies. Remember to follow appropriate safety precautions when working with the laser printer.

B-4: Performing printer maintenance

Here's how	Here's why
1 Turn off and unplug your printer	You're going to perform some routine maintenance on your printer. Be sure to use only recommended supplies when replacing parts.
Follow necessary safety procedures to prepare to open the printer	
2 Open the printer and remove the ink cartridge or toner cartridge	
Remove any dust or debris in the compartment and on the outside of the printer	Use cleaning solutions as necessary.
3 If you have an inkjet printer, re-install the ink cartridge	
Follow the manufacturer's instruction to clean the print heads	(Plug in the printer if using a Windows-based utility.) This will ensure good-quality output.
4 If you have a laser printer, follow the manufacturer's cleaning and maintenance instructions	This can include removing accumulated toner, paper dust, and cleaning internal components.
5 Close the printer, and plug it in	
6 Ensure the printer has enough paper	
7 Plug in the printer and print a test page	To verify the printer is working properly.
8 Ensure the printer has adequate ventilation and is set on a secure surface	

Provide students with necessary cleaning materials, according to manufacturer's instructions.

Printer configuration and optimization

Explanation

After installing a printer in Windows, you can configure how the printer prints. Some printers enable you to configure how the printer prints using buttons or menus on the printer. Some of the configuration options include setting the defaults for orientation, number of pages, print quality, and printer language among other settings.

Some of the common configuration options include the following options.

Option	Description
Orientation	Portrait (narrow dimension is the top of page) or landscape (wide dimension is the top of the page)
Collation	How the individual pages within a multipage document are printed when you print more than one copy. Collated means entire copies of the document are printed together. Uncollated means that all the copies of page 1 are printed before all the copies of page 2, and so forth.
Copies	Number of copies to print.
Quality	Options for draft, normal, or high quality on some printers. Others offer varying resolutions.
Color	You can specify if the document should print in full color or in black-and-white. There might also be options for color matching software to be used, if such software was installed with your printer.
Order	Some printers allow you to specify whether to print from last page to first or first page to last on multipage print jobs.

Print spool optimization

Another way to optimize printing is to re-configure print spool settings. To configure the print spooler:

1 In Windows 2000, on the Start menu, choose Settings, Printers. In Windows XP, choose Start, Printers and Faxes.

2 Right-click the printer you want to configure and choose Properties. Select the Advanced tab.

By default, documents are spooled and printing is started immediately. In most cases, this is sufficient. But if you have users who often print large documents that have many graphics, you might be able to optimize performance by selecting "Start printing after last page has spooled."

B-5: Optimizing printing

Here's how	Here's why
1 Open Notepad	You'll examine the print options available for your printer.
2 Type some text in Notepad	
3 Choose **File**, **Print...**	
4 Click **Preferences**	The options available will vary based on those offered for your printer.
5 Close all open windows and dialog boxes	Do not save the Notepad document.
6 Click **Start**, and choose **Printers and Faxes**	To open the Printers and Faxes window.
7 Right-click your printer and choose **Properties**	
Activate the Advanced tab	
8 Select **"Start printing after last page has spooled"**	To configure the printer to print only when the entire document you're printing has been spooled. This can optimize printing when a user frequently print large documents with many graphics.
9 Click **OK**	
10 Close all open windows and dialog boxes	

If possible, use different types of printers for different students and have them compare the options available for each.

If the printer has options that can be set on its control panel, have students refer to the documentation and set some of the options.

Basic printer troubleshooting

Explanation

When troubleshooting printer problems, it's best to apply the ASID troubleshooting method.

1 Acquire information about the problem.

- Ask the user what symptoms he or she is experiencing.

- Check the printer to see if it's displaying any error codes. These can including messages on a small LCD screen or a combination of blinking lights. Match error codes to a list of error codes in the manufacturer's documentation. Cycle the power off and then back on to see if the error codes still appear.

- Try to print a test page to see if the symptoms persist.

- Review Windows 2000 and Windows XP error codes, such as those in Event Viewer, or employ downloadable diagnostic utilities, including those provided generically that can diagnose any printer, and those provided by the printer's manufacturer.

- Check the print spooler service to see if it has stopped or stalled. If it has, check Event Viewer for an error code. Restart the spooler service to see if it solves the problem. To restart the service, in Control Panel, open Administrative Tools. Double-click Services, right-click the Spooler Service, and choose Restart.

2 Simplify by removing any non-critical components, shut down unnecessary running programs, disconnect from the Internet or network, and so on. If the problem goes away, its cause lies with one of the components you removed. If not, then you have simplified the system, which will make troubleshooting easier.

3 Implement by identifying probable causes and implementing potential solutions one at a time. Check available reference materials for potential solutions, and check existing service documentation for the printer. Available resources might include manuals and product documentation, Web resources such as the Microsoft Knowledge Base, and manufacturers' Web sites and users' forums. When you define a specific cause, apply the fix. Replace any consumables, and then have the user sign off that the problem has been solved.

4 Document the error symptoms, the components you removed from the computer, and the solutions you tried and whether they were successful. At the end of this process, you must fully document the resolution for later reference. It's just as important to record any significant or obvious solutions that turned out not to be the cause of this problem so that you can avoid dead ends in the future.

Be sure to have your toolkit with you as you troubleshoot printer problems. You may find you need to perform some maintenance, so you'll need all the maintenance tools listed above. You might also want a multi-meter with you in case you have to test the electrical supply.

Dot-matrix issues

Dot-matrix printer print heads wear out after awhile. The ink from the ribbon can clog the tiny pins that make up the print images. The pins can also be bent. Any of these problems usually appear as missing dots on the page. The electromagnet contained in the print head that regulates which pins to push forward can also become damaged. Replacing the print head involves unscrewing it from the guide bar to which it's attached. Sometimes the manufacturer can fix the print head if you send it in. Other times, you come out ahead financially if you just replace the printer.

Poor print quality can simply be that the ribbon needs to be replaced. If all of the ink has been transferred from the ribbon to the paper, the print becomes faint. Each printer takes its own ribbon. The cartridge that the ribbon is contained within varies from printer to printer, and thus they aren't interchangeable.

Since dot-matrix printers are noisy, they're often kept under a padded, sound proofed cover. These sometimes don't have enough ventilation, causing the printer to overheat. The environment in which the printer operates should have adequate ventilation, even if it's in a padded, covered area.

The biggest problem with dot-matrix printers, though, is paper jams. If the paper isn't straight, the perforated sides with the holes can be ripped off and get jammed into the print mechanism. Getting it untangled from the feed mechanism can take some patience, as you work the pieces out without tearing them into smaller bits. If bits of paper or dust are caught under the roller, rolling a thicker paper such as a manila folder through can help push the bits through and clear the paper path.

The following table describes some of the other problems you might encounter when providing support for dot-matrix printers. When supporting a printer, always check for service documentation to see if previous support calls can provide any clues. After you have solved the problem to the best of your ability, and you have verified functionality, have the user verify the printer's functionality and acknowledge completion of the support call.

Item	Description
Printer drivers	If you're encountering problems with the printing of a document and have determined to the best of your ability that there's no physical problem with the printer or between the printer and the computer, then it's time to check that the correct printer driver has been installed. You should also check whether an updated driver is available for the printer. Print test pages as needed.
Error messages	On dot-matrix printers, the error messages are usually shown as blinking lights. Refer to your printer documentation for what the blink pattern indicates.
Memory	Dot-matrix printers rarely have any memory installed in them and instead rely on the print job being stored on the computer. If the drive is filled, this can result in lost jobs. It's also another reason why the printer is slow, as it needs to receive jobs piece by piece from the computer rather than reading from internal memory.
Configuration	There isn't usually much configuration that you can do for a dot-matrix printer, but if it uses font cartridges or other additional features, you might need to configure something on the printer or in software to alert Windows that the feature is available. That isn't usually the case, though. If the feature is available, the printer makes use of it if needed.

Item	Description
Connections	If the printer can't be found, verify that the cable is securely connected to the printer and to the computer. Also, verify that the correct cable is being used. If your printer has both a serial and a parallel connection available, make sure that Windows is trying to access the printer through the correct port. Also, verify that it's trying to access the correct LPT or COM port.
Print quality	Most dot-matrix printers have options on the control panel to set the default print quality. Windows print drivers are usually configured to print high quality as well. If the print quality is poor, check whether the ribbon needs to be replaced. The ink gets used up or dried out after a time.

Inkjet problems

Despite your best efforts to keep your printer clean and in working order, you're likely to encounter problems at some point. Most inkjet printers aren't designed for high volume usage. Therefore, if they're used in a business setting with a high volume of print traffic, you're even more likely to encounter problems.

Cost of consumables

Inkjet printers are inexpensive devices, so it's often more cost effective to replace the printer rather than spend a lot of time trying to figure out how to fix it.

The cartridges included with new printers, especially low-priced models, are often half-full compared to cartridges bought separately.

The cost of ink cartridges can be about the same price as the printer. Manufacturers often sell printers at or below cost, knowing that they'll make up for the loss on the ink cartridges. Manufacturers have moved the print head to the cartridge, so that the cost is borne in the consumables rather than in the initial purchase of the printer.

If an inkjet printer is a high-volume printer, there's a good chance it'll wear out rather quickly. It's usually more cost effective to use a laser printer for high volume. The cost per page for printing with an inkjet printer is roughly 10 times the cost of printing with a laser or dot-matrix printer.

Nothing prints

If nothing prints when you send a print job, there are several reasons this might occur. Verify that the print job is getting to the print queue in Windows. You can do this by double-clicking the icon for the printer in Printers and Faxes. You can also try clearing the queue and sending new print jobs using a basic text editor, such as Notepad.

If there are jobs are listed in the queue, but the printer isn't printing, look for these issues:

- Printer isn't turned on.
- Printer is out of paper.
- Printer isn't connected via the interface cable.
- Ink cartridge(s) are empty or clogged.
- Printer isn't configured for the correct interface.

Poor print quality or stray lines

Poor print quality can be due to a clogged print head, using porous paper that allows the ink to bleed out on the page, or dust in the printer. It can also be that Draft mode was selected on the printer or in Windows through the print driver software.

Stray lines on the page can be due to clogged nozzles, worn print guides, or worn print heads. You might need to print a test pattern and clean or realign the print heads.

Using the incorrect or an incompatible print driver can also result in strange output. The output might not be quite right if it's a driver that's close to what your printer expects, or it might print just garbage if it's completely different from what your printer can interpret.

Paper jams

Humidity affects the paper and how well it moves through the paper path. Paper that's damp from humidity sticks together, and the printer might try to pull several sheets through at once. This often results in part of the image being printed across the tops of several pages, and then the end-of-paper sensor is confused since more than 11.5-inches of paper came through. The printer then begins flashing lights regarding an error.

Laser printer problems

Understanding the laser printing process is useful in helping you determine the cause of problems encountered on laser printers. As with other printer types, the most common problem you're likely to encounter is paper jams. Another common problem is pages that are completely black or completely white when they emerge into the output tray.

Safety issues

Before attempting to work on a laser printer, be aware of some of the environmental factors that exist inside of the printer. The toner can be toxic if inhaled at high levels. Spilled toner is very messy and easily stains skin, clothing, and various plastic or other materials. You should use latex or rubber gloves and possibly a mask over your mouth and nose when working with toner.

In addition, printers contain high voltage power supplies, so you need to take special care when working around them. The fusing assembly also becomes very hot, so if you're working inside the printer, you need to let it cool down a bit so that you don't burn yourself.

Paper jams

The paper path in a laser printer is usually an S-curved path with rollers guiding the paper. If the rollers aren't working properly at one point or another over the course of the paper path, the paper doesn't move along as it should. In some cases, sensors in the printer detect that the paper isn't moving, and an error is issued. Upon opening the printer, you find the paper just sitting there and can easily remove it, but sending another page through results in the same problem.

Other times, no sensor is triggered, but when another sheet of paper comes through the paper path, it encounters the first piece of paper, and since the rollers are only designed to grab one sheet of paper at a time, the second sheet won't fit through, and becomes a crumpled mess.

Another common reason for paper jams is humidity levels. Humidity levels above 50% may result in pages that stick together. Humidity levels below 25% results in paper with static, and as you know from the laser printer process, static electricity is used to create images. Try to keep the paper in its wrapper in a controlled environment until you're ready to use it. This helps keep the paper from being too wet or too dry.

Another static problem you might encounter is that the corona wire is damaged or worn out. If this is the case, the paper isn't discharged and can stick to the drum, causing a paper jam.

All or nothing

Sometimes, you send a print job to the printer, and nothing ever makes it into the printer. It just sits in the queue waiting for the printer. You look at the printer, and it appears to be ready to accept print jobs. This could be due to a problem with the cable or, if it's connected directly to a network, with the network cable or NIC.

If the page comes out all black or all white, obviously you have a problem. If the page comes out blank, look for a problem with the toner cartridge, a broken corona wire, or a non-working HVPS.

Toner cartridge problems are usually either an empty toner cartridge or one that needs to be rocked. You can often get more life out of a cartridge that the printer says is empty just by redistributing the toner within the cartridge. The system also thinks there is no toner if the strips of sealing tape aren't removed before the cartridge is installed. Even if no error message is issued for this problem, no toner is released either, and the result is a blank page. If the HVPS isn't working, then the charging and discharging corona wires aren't properly charged, and the toner isn't sticking to the paper as it should.

If the page comes out completely black, the drum isn't being charged, so the toner sticks to it everywhere instead of just where the image should be created. This is usually the result of a broken corona wire or a faulty HVPS.

Partial prints and smudges

If the image prints but parts of it are missing, light, or indistinct, the problem could be anywhere along the print path. Missing or light portions of the output are most often due to low toner. Gently rocking the toner cartridge end to end can redistribute the toner that's left and get you some more life from the cartridge before it needs to be replaced.

Indistinct images (or those that appear as though the camera was out of focus) are often the result of a faulty transfer corona wire or HVPS problem. If the proper charges aren't being applied to the drum or the paper, the image isn't properly formed and transferred from the drum to the paper. Cleaning or replacing the corona wire might fix this problem. If not, check that the HVPS is outputting the required high voltages.

If the page comes out, but the output flakes off or smudges when you touch it, the fuser isn't doing its job. Toner that isn't melted into the paper through the heat and pressure of the fuser assembly results in this problem. Replacing the fuser assembly fixes the problem, which could be uneven rollers or a blown halogen lamp.

Using a deeply textured paper can result in improperly fused toner as well. If the heat and the pressure can't be properly applied to the image, the toner isn't fused to the paper.

Repeating marks and stray marks

If you find repeating horizontal or vertical black marks on the page, look to the problem being related to dirty rollers or a scratched drum. A continuous mark is usually the result of a scratch on the drum, whereas marks that repeat at a specific interval are usually the result of dirty rollers. Refer to the support Web site for your printer. They might have a description of the distance between marks to help you identify which roller or rollers are affecting the output. Cleaning the rollers usually resolves this problem. If not, you might need to replace them. If the problem is the drum, replace the cartridge or the drum if it's a separate unit.

If you're supporting older laser printers, you might also encounter repeating white areas. This is usually the result of a dirty corona wire. Clean the corona wire to see if the problem is resolved.

Stray marks are usually the result of dirt, loose toner, or a damaged drum. Clean out the printer using a special vacuum cleaner designed for laser printers. A regular vacuum can affect the charges within the printer and shouldn't be used. Laser printer vacuums are designed to be non-static producing.

A bad formatter board could also cause wavy output or random stray dots on the page. The *formatter board* in the printer takes care of taking the computer output and interpreting it into commands that the printer can use to create your output.

Another problem that could be described as ghost images is the result of the previous image not being totally removed from the drum. You might see the entire image ghosted, or just some areas that show up as stray marks on the current page. Check that the cleaning blade and the erase lamp are working properly.

Garbage prints

You go to the printer expecting to see your output—a spreadsheet or a letter, perhaps—but instead, you find several pages with a few characters at the top of each page: some letters and numbers, and possibly some characters from the extended ASCII character set.

If it hasn't happened to you yet, it's either because you haven't used a laser printer or you've been incredibly careful about making sure you had the correct print driver, and you haven't encountered a printer with a damaged formatter board.

This problem is usually the result of using an incorrect or incompatible printer driver. The printer needs to be able to translate the document you want printed into the correct codes to create the desired output. There are two common languages used to do this: *PCL* and *PostScript*.

PCL is the printer control language used in HP laser jet printers. It's also been licensed to other printer manufacturers. PostScript is a page description language. These are two distinct languages, and if the printer has been configured to use one or the other of these, and the driver isn't correctly installed, you won't get the desired output.

Most printers can automatically switch back and forth between PCL and PostScript. This ability requires having the printer configured to do so and using a print driver that can do so as well.

Another possible problem occurs if you have upgraded the firmware and its code is incompatible with the printer. This could result in a printer printing garbage or just not working at all.

Do it!

B-6:   Troubleshooting printer problems

Here's how	Here's why
1 Determine if you can successfully print a document from Notepad.	One or more problems were introduced into your system. You need to resolve the problem(s).
2 Determine if you can successfully print a Test Page	From the Printer Properties page.
3 Determine if the print quality of the page is acceptable	You might need to perform some printer maintenance to resolve print quality problems.
4 Document the problem(s)	*Answers will vary based on the problem(s) that were introduced into the system.*
5 Take the appropriate steps to resolve the problem(s) you encountered	
6 Document the solution to the problem(s)	*Answers will vary based on the problem(s) that were introduced into the system and the steps students took to resolve the problem(s).*
7 Test the system	To verify that the problem(s) were completely resolved.

Topic C: Scanners

This topic covers the following CompTIA A+ 220-603 exam objectives.

#	Objective
3.1	**3.1 Identify the fundamental principles of using printers and scanners** • Describe processes used by printers and scanners including laser, ink dispersion, impact, solid ink and thermal printers.
3.2	**Install, configure, optimize and upgrade printers and scanners** • Install and configure printers and scanners • Power and connect the device using network or local port • Install/update the device driver and calibrate the device • Configure options and default settings • Validate compatibility with OS and applications • Educate user about basic functionality • Optimize scanner performance for example: resolution, file format and default settings
3.3	**3.3 Identify tools, diagnostic procedures and troubleshooting techniques for printers and scanners** • Gather information required to troubleshoot printer/scanner problems

Explanation

Scanners convert pictures or text to digital data. Scanners can be standalone devices or part of a multifunction printer device. Multifunction devices usually include printer, scanner, fax, and copier functions.

Most standalone scanners are flatbed scanners. You place the document or picture to be scanned on a glass surface under a cover. This is works much like an office copier machine. Exhibit 3-16 shows an example of a flatbed scanner.

Exhibit 3-16: Flatbed scanner

Multi-function scanners usually are sheet-feed scanners in which you insert a piece of paper in a paper feeder on the printer. Some have a flat bed for scanning. Exhibit 3-17 shows an example of a multifunction device with a scan feature.

Exhibit 3-17: Multifunction sheet-feed scanner

If you're supporting older equipment, you might also encounter hand-held scanners. These devices are dragged across the paper as the device scans the page. A user had to take care to drag early hand-held scanners at a constant rate or the resulting image would be distorted. Later models used gears or other sensors to match the scanning rate to the drag rate so that you didn't have to be so precise when dragging it.

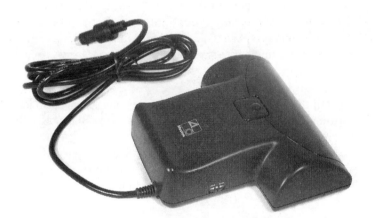

Exhibit 3-18: Hand-held scanner

Many scanners support the TWAIN standard, as do many imaging applications. For example, if your scanner supports TWAIN, you can use features within Adobe Photoshop, Ulead PhotoImpact, and a lot of other applications to control your scanner. Incidentally, TWAIN is not an acronym but is drawn from the phrase "never the twain shall meet." That sentiment reflected the difficulty at the time of connecting computers and scanners, which TWAIN was supposed to ease.

Most scanners also come with specific software to work with the scanner. Such software is typically more full-featured than that provided through the TWAIN interface.

When installing a scanner, be sure it's located on a firm, flat surface in a well ventilated area.

Connections

Scanners used to be either slow parallel port devices or SCSI devices that were temperamental and not easily configured. Current offerings are mostly USB or FireWire devices that are plug-and-play compatible.

After making the connection, plug in the scanner. You're likely to be prompted to install the appropriate drivers for your scanner. Alternatively, your scanner might want you to install software that ships with the scanner and then connect the scanner to your computer. Check the documentation to determine the proper procedure for connecting the scanner you're using.

To update the device driver, in Device Manager right-click the scanner and choose Update Driver, and then complete the wizard to update the driver. You can also use the manufacturer's installation program to install a new driver. After the scanner is attached, you can configure the features described above, scan a test page to ensure the scanner is working, and give the users the basics about its operation.

Do it!

C-1: Connecting a scanner

Here's how	Here's why
1 Determine the connection type for the scanner	You'll connect a scanner to your computer.
2 Locate a cable that's compatible with the scanner connection	It's likely a USB, SCSI, FireWire, or parallel port connection.
3 Connect the scanner to the computer	Using the appropriate cable.
4 Connect the scanner to the power outlet	
5 Install the software to create scanned images	If the scanner also includes OCR software, you can install that as well.
6 Scan a picture	You can open your manual to a page with an exhibit and scan that, if you don't have another picture to scan.

Have various students scan the same picture at different resolutions or using various file formats, so that they can compare the results.

Scanner troubleshooting

When troubleshooting scanner problems, it's best to apply the same ASID troubleshooting method you used to troubleshoot printers.

1   Acquire information about the problem.

- Ask the user what symptoms he or she is experiencing with the scanner.
- Check the scanner is displaying any error codes.
- Try to scan a test page to see if the symptoms persist.
- Review any error codes in Windows 2000 or Windows XP.

2   Simplify by removing any non-critical components, shut down unnecessary programs, disconnect from the Internet or network, and so on.

3   Implement by identifying probable causes and implementing potential solutions one at a time. Check available reference materials for potential solutions, and check existing service documentation for the scanner.

4   Document the error symptoms, the components you removed from the computer, and the solutions you tried and whether they were successful.

Be sure to have appropriate tools with you, including a multi-meter, cleaning solutions and materials, and a test pattern to scan.

C-2:   Troubleshooting scanner problems

Here's how	Here's why
1 Determine if you can successfully scan a test page	One or more problems were introduced into your system. You need to resolve the problem or problems.
2 Determine if the quality of the output is acceptable	
3 Document the problem or problems	*Answers will vary based on the problem(s) that were introduced into the system.*
4 Take the appropriate steps to resolve the problem(s) you encountered	
5 Document the solution to the problem(s)	*Answers will vary based on the problem(s) that were introduced into the system and the steps students took to resolve the problem(s).*
6 Ensure the printer has adequate ventilation and is set on a secure surface	To permit successful operation.
7 Test the system	To verify that the problem(s) were completely resolved.

Scanner optimization

Explanation

The functions available in a scanner's software will vary but usually include features that allow you to configure the following items:

Feature	Description
Image type	Sets to grayscale, color, or line art.
Scan mode	Sets to high-speed or high-quality.
Scan resolution	Sets the DPI to be used for the scanned image.
Scaling	Specifies whether the image is the same size as the original or is enlarged or reduced from the size of the original.
Destination	Sends to a file (converting it from an analog image to a digital file) or directly to a printer (where the scanner functions as a component in a copier).
Image control	Inverts the image (swap black and white, also referred to as a negative image), enables color balancing, controls the brightness and contrast of the image, rotates the image, mirrors the image.
Preview features	Zoom in and out on the scan area without affecting the scanned image, preview what the scanner will output. Preview area usually has a feature to select a specific area of the scanned image to scan to the file or printer.
Scan	Performs the scan in which the image is scanned and the output is sent to the destination configured in the software.

When scanning pictures, you want to set the image type to color for color pictures, the scan mode to high quality, and a resolution that matches the printer or screen resolution where the image will output. Pictures produce very large files when you set the resolution to a high setting, so be prepared to have enough room to save the picture. If you're going to e-mail the picture, keep the resolution as low as you can while still having a useable picture; otherwise, the person you're sending the file to might not be able to receive it if their mail provider has a limit on the size of attachments.

Scanning text using basic scanning software produces a graphics image of the page of text. To scan text in that can be edited and searched, you need to install *optical character recognition (OCR)* software. OCR software uses a recognition engine to interpret the text. OCR has gotten quite accurate at picking up and interpreting typewritten text. Handwritten text is very difficult for it to read. If you use OCR, you want to review the text carefully to determine whether the text was properly interpreted.

Do it!

C-3:   Optimizing scanners

Here's how	Here's why
1 Follow the manufacturer's instructions to access the scanner settings	This might require using the buttons on the scanner or opening a Windows-based utility.
2 Optimize the scanner settings to produce high-quality output for color pictures	(Based on available settings and manufacturer's recommendation.) This might require adjusting settings such as resolution.
3 Choose an output type	This is the type of file created by the scanner.
4 Readjust scanner settings to optimize for speed when scanning documents	This generally means image quality won't be as great.
5 Close all open windows	

Unit summary: Printers and scanners

Topic A

In this topic, you learned about **dot-matrix printers**. You learned that these slow, noisy **impact printers** are good for printing **multipart forms**. You also learned that dot-matrix print heads typically have **9** or **24 pins** and that the paper can be moved through the printer using **tractor** or **friction feed** mechanisms. You also learned about **inkjet printers**. You learned that they force ink through 50 to 60 micron nozzles using **thermal bubble** or **piezoelectric** technology. You learned that cyan, yellow, magenta, and black (**CYMK**) inks are used to create the images. Next, you learned about **laser printers**. You learned that laser printers are becoming quite affordable, but that the consumables cost as much as the printer did in some cases. You learned that laser printers use the **electrophotographic process** to produce images. You identified the **components that make up a laser printer**, and you listed the stages involved in the **laser print process**. Finally, you learned about other types of printers, including **solid ink**, **thermal**, and **dye sublimation** printers. You also examined the use of **plotters**, **snapshot printers**, and **large format printers**.

Topic B

In this topic, you examined the Windows print process and the components that include the **spooler**. Then you installed a printer and learned how to upgrade printer drivers. You installed printer **add-ons** and **upgrades**, and you performed maintenance on a printer. You also optimized printer settings, and learned to troubleshoot printer problems.

Topic C

In this topic, you learned about **scanners**. You learned that scanners are used to convert pictures or text into digital data. You examined scanner types including **flatbed**, **multi-function**, and **hand-held scanners**, and you learned how to optimize scanners.

Review questions

1 What's the print quality of dot-matrix printers compared to?

Typewriter output

2 How are characters produced on a dot-matrix printer?

The pins are pushed forward in patterns to form letters, numbers, and other shapes. The pins strike an inked ribbon, and the ribbon strikes the paper.

3 What paper feed mechanisms are employed by dot-matrix printers?

Tractor feed and friction feed

4 What's a potential problem when attempting to soundproof impact printers?

Overheating due to inadequate ventilation.

5 Explain how thermal bubble technology works.

Thermal bubble technology heats the ink, which vaporizes it, creating a bubble. The bubble protrudes out through the nozzle and sprays onto the paper. When the bubble bursts, it creates a vacuum, which draws more ink from the cartridge into the print head, ready to create another dot.

6 Explain how piezoelectric bubble technology works.

Piezoelectric technology creates a bubble with a piezo crystal behind each nozzle. An electrical current sent to the crystal causes it to vibrate. When it vibrates inward, it releases ink onto the paper. When it vibrates outward, it pulls ink from the cartridge.

7 The print head for inkjet printers is usually part of the ink cartridge. True or false?

True

8 How do inkjet printers raise the DPI above what it's physically configured to produce?

Through software enhancements that move the print head fractionally to place dots between existing printed dots.

9 What's inkjet output quality compared against?

Laser printers for text and chemically created darkroom photographs for images.

10 Laser printers combine electrostatic charges, toner, and laser light to produce high-quality images one page at time. True or false?

True

11 What's the function of the fusing assembly in a laser printer?

It applies heat and pressure to adhere the toner permanently to the page.

12 What are some reasons for paper jams in laser printers?

Rollers are worn or not working properly, paper is too humid, or a corona wire is damaged or worn.

13 Why might 'garbage' be printed on a laser printer instead of your document?

An incorrect print driver, a damaged formatter board, or use of the wrong print language.

14 Solid ink printers need the ink changed about every 500 pages. True or false?

False

15 How are shades of color produced in dye sublimation printers?

The depth of color is regulated by varying the heat applied. The transparent dyes are combined for creating colors in a wide variety of 256 shades of each of the colors.

16 Which thermal printer uses paper with colors embedded in it?

A Direct thermal

B Thermal autochrome

C Thermal wax transfer

D Dye sub

17 Windows printers can be configured only at the printer rather than through the print driver or software. True or false?

False

18 Inkjet printers can't print PostScript. True or false?

False. Some can be upgraded with a PostScript upgrade kit.

19 How can adding memory and a hard drive to a printer speed up printing?

Print jobs are read from within the printer without having to communicate over the slower communications cable connecting the printer to the computer.

20 Scanners typically are connected via serial ports. True or false?

False

Independent practice activity

1 Try to print a test page from the printer.

2 Examine the output, if any, to determine if it's acceptable quality.

3 Document any problems you encountered along with the steps you took to resolve the problem.

Unit 4

Operating system management

Unit time: 210 minutes

Complete this unit, and you'll know how to:

A Manage directories and files.

B Monitor and manage the operating system.

C Use Event Viewer to monitor events on the computer.

D Manage the Registry.

E Optimize virtual memory.

Topic A: Managing directories and files

This topic covers the following CompTIA A+ 220-603 exam objectives.

#	Objective
2.1	**Identify the fundamental principles of using operating systems** • Use command-line functions and utilities to manage Windows 2000, XP Professional and XP Home, including proper syntax and switches, for example: • CMD • HELP • DIR • ATTRIB • EDIT • COPY • XCOPY • MD / CD / RD **Identify concepts and procedures for creating, viewing, and managing disks, directories and files in Windows 2000, XP Professional and XP Home, for example:** • Directory structures (e.g. create folders, navigate directory structures) • Files (e.g. creation, extensions, attributes and permissions) **Locate and use Windows 2000, XP Professional and XP Home utilities and available switches** • System Management Tools • CMD • File Management Tools (e.g. Windows Explorer, ATTRIB.EXE)
2.2	**Install, configure, optimize and upgrade operating systems** • Identify procedures and utilities used to optimize the performance of Windows 2000, XP Professional and XP Home, for example: • Temporary files

Command-line utility

Explanation

Windows 2000 Professional and all Windows XP versions include a program that provides communication between the user and the operating system in a non-graphical user interface. You use this utility to enter character-based commands to run applications and other utilities. You can access the MS-DOS command-line interpreter, command.com, by:

 Cmd.exe is covered in CompTIA A+ Certification: Essentials.

- Clicking Start and choosing All Programs, Accessories, Command Prompt.
- Clicking Start and choosing Run. In the Open box, enter `command` or `cmd`.

The command-line utility is a helpful tool to use when performing management tasks. You can combine multiple commands into one batch or script file that are all run at once. You have the option of running the commands locally or remotely.

Directory structures

Hard disks are divided into usable storage space through *partitions*. Depending on the operating system used and the maximum hard disk size it supports, a hard disk can be configured as a single large partition or multiple smaller partitions. In Microsoft operating systems, each partition is assigned a drive letter and is considered the *root* of the directory structure for that partition.

Underneath the root directory, information is organized through the use of *directories* (also called *folders*). You can use directories to divide your files into logical categories, as shown in Exhibit 4-1, making information easier to find and use.

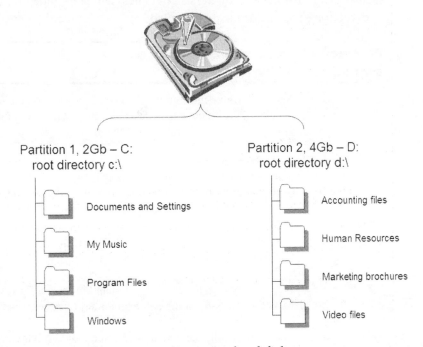

Exhibit 4-1: Directory structure on a hard disk

Navigation

To navigate the directory structure on your hard disk, you can use MS-DOS commands from the command line or use Windows Explorer in any version of Windows.

MS-DOS navigation commands include:

- `command/cmd` — Starts an instance of the MS-DOS command interpreter, Command.com.
- `dir` — Displays a list of the current or specified directory's files and subdirectories.
- `chdir/cd` — Changes the current directory to the specified directory.

Command/cmd

To use this command, you can enter it in either of two ways:

```
command
cmd
```

Optional parameters and switches include those shown below and described in the following table.

```
command drive:path device /e:nnnn /p /c string /msg
```

In syntax statements such as this, information that you must supply for a parameter (such as *path*) is indicated by italics. Switches, which provide options for controlling the execution of a command, are preceded by the "/" symbol (as in /p).

Parameter/ switch	Description
drive:path	Specifies where the command.com file is stored on the hard disk. If no path is specified, the command searches the current directory and any directories listed in the system's PATH statement.
device	Specifies an alternative device you want to use to enter MS-DOS commands. Valid values for the *device* parameter are prn, lpt1, lpt2, lpt3, con, aux, com1, com2, com3, and com4.
/e:*nnnn*	Specifies the environment size, where *nnnn* is the number of bytes. Valid values for *nnnn* are from 160 to 32768. If the /e:*nnnn* value is not specified, the default value of 256 is used.
/p	Is used only with the shell command in the config.sys file. This switch makes a new copy of the command interpreter permanent.
/c *string*	Specifies that the command interpreter should run the command stated in the string value and then stop.
/msg	Specifies that all error messages be stored in memory. This switch must be used with the /p switch.

Dir

The syntax of dir is:

```
dir
```

Optional parameters and switches include those shown below and described in the following table:

```
dir drive:path filename /p /w /a:attributes /o:sortorder /s ▶
/b /l
```

Parameter/ switch	Description
drive:path	Specifies the drive and directory for which you want to see a listing. If none is specified, the command lists the contents of the current directory.
filename	Specifies a particular file or group of files for which you want to see a listing. For example: `dir *.exe` will show all executable files.
/p	Displays the listing one screen at a time. To advance to the next screen of listings, you can press any key.
/w	Displays the listing in wide format instead of as a single-column list.
/a:*attributes*	Specifies which directories and files you want displayed according to their attributes. Valid attribute values include:

h	hidden files
-h	non-hidden files
s	system files
-s	non-system files
d	directories
-d	files only (not directories)
a	files ready for archiving
-a	files that have not changed since the last archive
r	read-only files
-r	non-read-only files

Parameter/ switch	Description
/o:*sortorder*	Controls the order in which the `dir` command displays the results. Valid *sortorder* values include:

n	alphabetical order by name
-n	reverse alphabetical order by name
e	alphabetical order by file extension
-e	reverse alphabetical order by extension
d	chronological by date and time, oldest to newest
-d	chronological by date and time, newest to oldest
s	by size, smallest to largest
-s	by size, largest to smallest
g	grouped directories, then files
-g	grouped files, then directories

Parameter/ switch	Description
/s	Lists every occurrence of a specified file in the specified directory and its subdirectories.
/b	Lists each directory name or file name, with one per line. No heading information or summary is displayed with this switch. The /b switch overrides the /w switch.
/l	Displays unsorted directory names and file names in lowercase.

You can use the wildcard characters ? and * to display a subset of directories and files. For example, `dir *.txt` displays all files with the .txt extension; `dir 200?.txt` displays all files that contain 200 with any final character and the .txt extension, such as 2000.txt, 2001.txt, 2002.txt, and so on.

Chdir/cd

To use this command, you can enter it in either of two ways:

```
chdir
cd
```

Each command displays the name of the current drive and directory.

Optional parameters include:

- `chdir drive:path` (or `cd drive:path`) — Changes the current drive and directory to the one specified.
- `chdir..` (or `cd..`) — Changes the current directory to its parent directory.
- `chdir \` (or `cd \`) — Changes the current directory to the root directory of the current drive.

Windows Explorer

If necessary, remind students that directories are called folders in Windows Explorer.

To navigate the directory structure by using Windows Explorer:

1 Click Start and choose All Programs, Accessories, Windows Explorer.

The left pane in Windows Explorer is the navigation pane; the right pane is the details pane.

2 In the navigation pane, click the plus sign (+) next to a drive or folder to expand the tree and view the subfolders in that drive or folder.

3 Select a drive or subfolder in the navigation pane to view its contents (subfolders and files) in the details pane.

Help

You can obtain general information regarding available command-line commands by entering the following at the command line:

```
help
```

You can get command specific help by entering the following at the command line:

```
command /?
```

Substitute the name of the command you want to get help on.

Do it!

A-1:   Using the command prompt

This material is covered in CompTIA A+ Certification: Essentials.

Here's how	Here's why
1 If necessary, log on to Windows XP	
2 Click **Start** and choose **Run...**	You could also choose Command Prompt from the Start menu, but for this activity, you'll run the MS-DOS cmd command.
In the Open box, type **cmd** and then press ⏎ ENTER	To open a Command Prompt window.
3 Type **help** and press ⏎ ENTER	The operating system returns a list of available commands and a brief description of each.
4 Type **dir /?** and press ⏎ ENTER	Use the help information returned to determine the answer to the following question.
5 What would be the result of the following command?	*A list of all .exe files in c:\windows\system32, one screen at a time, in reverse alphabetical order.*
`dir c:\windows\system32\*.exe /p /o:-n`	
At the command prompt, type the above command and press ⏎ ENTER	To display a directory listing of all executable files in the Windows directory on your C: drive. Notice that only the first screenful of files is displayed, and that the file names are in reverse alphabetical order.
6 Press SPACEBAR	To display the next screenful of files.
Continue to press SPACEBAR	Until you reach the end of the directory listing.

A-2: Navigating a directory tree

Here's how	Here's why
A Command Prompt window is open.	
1 What command would you use to change from the current directory to the root of drive C:?	*Use either of the following:* • `chdir \` • `cd \`
Enter the command	
2 What command would you use to change from the root of C: to C:\Windows\Temp?	*Use either of the following:* • `chdir c:\windows\temp` • `cd c:\windows\temp`
Enter the command	
3 What command would you use to navigate to the parent directory?	*Use either of the following:* • `chdir ..` • `cd ..`
Enter the command	
4 Change the directory to C:\Documents and Settings\RSTADMIN##	
5 Minimize the Command Prompt window	
6 Click **Start** and choose **All Programs, Accessories, Windows Explorer**	
Observe the Folders pane	This is also called the navigation pane; you can use it to move around in the directory structure on your computer.
7 Expand My Computer	
Expand Local Disk (C:)	
Expand WINDOWS	
Select **Temp**	The contents of the Temp folder are displayed in the details pane.
8 Display the contents of the following folder:	Use the navigation pane.
C:\Documents and Settings\RSTADMIN##\Start Menu\Programs	
9 Minimize Windows Explorer	

Creating directories

Explanation

As with navigating the directory structure, you can create directories at the command prompt or through Windows Explorer.

To create a directory at the command prompt, you use the `mkdir/md` command. The syntax is:

```
mkdir drive:path
md drive:path
```

Parameter	Description
`drive`	Specifies the drive on which you want to create the directory.
`path`	Specifies the name and location of the new directory. The maximum length of any single path from the root directory is 63 characters, including backslashes (\).

To create a directory in Windows Explorer:

1 In the navigation pane, select the drive or folder where you want to create the new folder.
2 Choose File, New, Folder.
3 Type the name of the new folder.
4 Press Enter.

When you create a directory in Windows Explorer, the maximum depth of the folder structure is limited by the maximum number of allowable characters in a file path, which is 255. This total number of characters includes the characters representing the drive, plus any file extensions.

Spaces in MS-DOS commands

The Windows operating systems use different command interpreters to process commands at a command prompt. When you're entering MS-DOS commands that include space characters, they are processed differently depending on the version of Windows you're using:

- In Windows 95 and Windows 98, command.com does not allow spaces.
- In Windows NT Workstation and later versions of Windows, cmd.exe treats the spaces as delimiters and processes the command by treating each word after the command as a separate parameter.

To force the command interpreter to recognize the spaces, you should enclose in quotation marks any file or folder names that include spaces.

For example, the command:

```
md c:\my business files
```

is invalid in Windows 95 and 98. In Windows NT Workstation, Windows 2000 Professional, Windows XP Professional, and Windows XP Home Edition, that command would create three directories: c:\my, c:\business, and c:\files.

To create a single directory called "my business files," you need to enter:

```
md "c:\my business files"
```

Do it!

A-3: Creating directories

Here's how	Here's why

1 Maximize the Command Prompt window

A Command Prompt window is minimized on the taskbar.

2 What command would you use to create a directory called **Marketing** at the root of your C: drive?

md c:\marketing

Enter the command

3 What command would you use to view only directories at the root of your C: drive?

dir c:\ /a:d

Enter the command

```
Directory of c:\

11/16/2005  09:21 AM    <DIR>          Dell
11/16/2005  12:12 PM    <DIR>          Documents and Settings
11/16/2005  09:25 AM    <DIR>          drvrtmp
11/16/2005  12:23 PM    <DIR>          marketing
11/16/2005  09:21 AM    <DIR>          Program Files
11/16/2005  11:55 AM    <DIR>          RECYCLER
11/16/2005  09:45 AM    <DIR>          Student Data
11/16/2005  09:19 AM    <DIR>          System Volume Information
11/16/2005  11:52 AM    <DIR>          WINDOWS
               0 File(s)              0 bytes
               9 Dir(s)   2,208,841,728 bytes free
```

To verify that the Marketing directory was created successfully. Your screen should look similar to the one shown here.

4 Minimize the Command Prompt window

Maximize Windows Explorer

A Windows Explorer window is minimized on the taskbar.

5 In the navigation pane, select **My Documents**

Choose **File**, **New**, **Folder**

Type **Business Correspondence**

To replace the words "New Folder," which are selected.

Press ⏎ ENTER

6 Minimize Windows Explorer

Copying directories

Explanation

You can use the MS-DOS `copy` or `xcopy` commands and Windows Explorer to copy directories and their contents. The `copy` command copies one or more files to another location. The `xcopy` command copies files (not including hidden and system files), directories, and subdirectories.

Copy

The syntax for the `copy` command is:

```
copy source destination
```

Parameter	Description
source	Specifies the location and name of the file you want to copy. The source can consist of a drive letter and colon, a directory name, a file name, or any combination of these items.
destination	Specifies the location and name of the file to which you want to copy. The destination can consist of a drive letter and colon, a directory name, a file name, or any combination of these items.

Optional parameters and switches for the `copy` command include those shown below and described in the following table:

```
copy /a/b source /a/b + source /a/b + … destination /a/b /v
```

Parameter/ switch	Description
/a	Indicates that the file is an ASCII text file.
	When the /a switch precedes a list of file names, the switch applies to all file names that follow it, until /b is encountered. When the /a switch follows a file name, the switch applies to the file preceding it and to all files that follow it, until /b is encountered.
/b	Indicates a binary file. The binary file switch works the same as the /a switch.
+	Allows you to list multiple files to copy.
/v	Verifies that the new files are written successfully.

Xcopy

The syntax for the xcopy command is:

```
xcopy source destination
```

Parameter	Description
source	Specifies the location and names of the files you want to copy. The source must include either a drive or a path.
destination	Specifies the destination of the files you want to copy. The destination can consist of a drive letter and colon, a directory name, a file name, or any combination of these items.

Optional parameters and switches for the xcopy command include those shown below and described in the following table:

```
xcopy source destination /a/m /d:date /p /s /e /v /w
```

Parameter/ switch	Description
/a	Copies only source files that have the archive file attribute set.
/m	Copies source files that have the archive file attribute set. The /m switch turns off the archive file attribute.
/d:*date*	Copies only source files modified on or after the date you specify.
/p	Prompts you to confirm the creation of each destination file.
/s	Copies directories and subdirectories unless they are empty. Without the /s switch, xcopy works within a single directory.
/e	Copies subdirectories even if they are empty.
/v	Verifies each file as it's written to make sure it's identical to the source file.
/w	Displays the message "Press any key to begin copying file(s)." You must respond before the copy process begins.

Windows Explorer

To copy a directory and its contents in Windows Explorer:

1 In the navigation pane, select the directory you want to copy. To select multiple directories, hold down the Ctrl key and select each directory.
2 Choose Edit, Copy.
3 In the navigation pane, select the location that you want the directory and its contents to be copied to.
4 Choose Edit, Paste.

Do it!

A-4:   Copying a directory and its contents

Here's how	Here's why
A Command Prompt window is minimized on the taskbar.	
1 Maximize the Command Prompt window	
2 Change the directory to C:\Windows\System32\Drivers	(Enter cd \Windows\System32\Drivers.) This directory contains a folder named etc.
What command would you use to copy the etc folder and its contents to the root of C: and verify that the files were copied correctly?	*xcopy etc c:\etc\ /v*
Enter the command	
Dir c: /a:d *Dir c:\etc*	
3 Verify the etc directory and its files were copied to C:\	(Use the dir command.)
4 If the folder C:\Windows\System32\Drivers\etc contained subfolders that you wanted to copy with the files, even if the subfolders were empty, what command would you use?	*First, change directories:* *cd \windows\system32\drivers* *Then enter the xcopy command:* *xcopy etc c:\etc\ /e /v*
5 Minimize the Command Prompt window	
A Windows Explorer window is minimized on the taskbar.	
Maximize Windows Explorer	
6 In the navigation pane, select **Business Correspondence**	
Choose **Edit**, **Copy**	
Students may need to choose View, Refresh to see the Marketing folder.	
In the navigation pane, under Local Disk (C:), select **Marketing**	
Choose **Edit**, **Paste**	The original folder remains in My Documents. A copy of the folder has been created as a subfolder of Marketing.

7 In the navigation pane, under Local Disk (C:), select the **etc** folder

Choose **Edit**, **Cut**

In the navigation pane, under Local Disk (C:), select **Marketing**

Choose **Edit**, **Paste**   The original folder and its contents are deleted from the root of C:\. A copy has been created as a subfolder of Marketing.

8 Minimize Windows Explorer

Removing directories

Explanation

You can remove a directory by using the MS-DOS `rmdir/rd` command, the `deltree` command, or Windows Explorer.

Rmdir/rd

Before you can delete a directory by using `rmdir/rd` in MS-DOS, you must delete any files and subdirectories in that directory. The directory must be empty except for the "." and ".." symbols and must not contain any hidden or system files. If the directory contains hidden or system files, you must use the `attrib` command to remove the hidden and system attributes from the files first.

The syntax for the `rmdir/rd` command is:

```
rmdir drive:path
rd drive:path
```

The `drive:path` parameter specifies the location and name of the directory you want to delete.

You cannot use `rmdir/rd` to delete the current directory. You must change to another directory.

Deltree

The `deltree` command, which was introduced with Windows NT, is an external command available in MS-DOS versions 6.0 and later. Using `deltree`, you can delete a directory and all of its subdirectories and files, including hidden and system files. Unlike with `rmdir/rd`, the directory does not need to be empty.

The syntax of the `deltree` command is:

```
deltree drive:path
```

The `drive:path` parameter specifies the location and name of the directory you want to delete.

Optional parameters and switches for the `deltree` command include:

```
deltree /y drive:path drive:path
```

Parameter/ switch	Description
/y	Deletes the directory and its contents without prompting the user for confirmation.
drive:path	Enables you to specify multiple directories to delete.

Windows Explorer

To remove a directory and its contents by using Windows Explorer:

1 Select the folder you want to remove. (You can use either pane in Windows Explorer.)
2 Choose File, Delete.
3 Click Yes to confirm moving the folder and all its contents to the Recycle Bin.

Do it!

A-5: Removing directories

Here's how	Here's why
A Command Prompt window is minimized to the taskbar.	
1 Maximize the Command Prompt window	
2 How would you delete the etc folder and its contents by using MS-DOS commands?	*To remove the contents of the etc folder:* **deltree c:\marketing\etc** *To remove the directory:* **rd c:\marketing\etc**
3 What command would you use to delete the C:\Marketing\Business Correspondence folder?	*Because the Business Correspondence folder is empty, you can use:* **rd c:\marketing\"business correspondence"** *You need to enclose "business correspondence" in quotation marks so the command interpreter will recognize the space.*
Enter the command	
Dir c:\marketing	4 Verify the Business Correspondence folder is deleted
A Windows Explorer window is minimized to the taskbar.	5 Maximize Windows Explorer
6 In the navigation pane, under C:\Marketing, select **etc**	You could also use the details pane.
Choose **File**, **Delete**	
Click **Yes**	To confirm that you want to move the folder and all its contents to the Recycle Bin.
7 Close Windows Explorer	

Text files

Explanation

You can create a text file by using the MS-DOS `edit` command or a Windows GUI text-editing application such as Notepad.

To create a text file in edit:

1 At the MS-DOS prompt, type `edit` and press Enter.
2 Enter the desired text.
3 If your mouse driver is loaded and functional, you can use your mouse to choose File, Save As. Otherwise, press Alt, F, A.
4 To change the current directory, press Alt+D.
5 Use the arrow keys and Enter to navigate to the desired directory.
6 To move the cursor to the File Name text box, press Alt+N.
7 In the File Name box, type a file name, including the extension.
8 Press the Tab key several times to highlight the OK button, and then press Enter.
9 Press Alt, F, X to exit the edit program.

To create a text file by using the Windows GUI text editor, Notepad:

1 Click Start and choose All Programs, Accessories, Notepad.
2 Enter the desired text.
3 Choose File, Save As.
4 From the Save in list, select the desired directory.
5 In the File name box, type a name for your file.
6 Verify that Text Documents (*.txt) is selected in the Save as type box.
7 Click Save.
8 Choose File, Exit.

A-6: Creating a text file

Here's how	Here's why
1 Enter **edit**	To start the MS-DOS text editor. Because you ran the edit command from within a Command Prompt window, your mouse driver is loaded and available. However, you'll use keyboard shortcuts to choose menu items in this activity.
2 Type **This is my first text file created with the MS-DOS text editor.**	
3 Press (ALT)	The menu bar is highlighted. The menu choices are shown with their keyboard shortcuts in white.
Press (F)	To display the File menu. The keyboard shortcuts for File menu items are also displayed in white.
Press (A)	To open the Save As dialog box.
4 Press (ALT) + (D)	(While holding down Alt, press D.) To move the cursor to the Directories box.
Press (↓) several times to highlight My Documents	My Documents is added to the File Name box.
Press (ALT) + (N)	To move the cursor back to the File Name box.
Press (END)	To move to the end of the File Name box, leaving "My Documents\" typed in the box.
5 Type **My Text File.txt**	
Observe the buttons at the bottom of the Save As box	OK is highlighted.
Press (↵ ENTER)	To activate the OK button and save the file as My Text File in the My Documents folder.
6 Press (ALT), (F), (X)	(In sequence, not simultaneously.) To close the text editor window.
Minimize the Command Prompt window	
7 Click **Start** and choose **All Programs**, **Accessories**, **Notepad**	You will use the Windows GUI text editor, Notepad, to create a text file.

8 Type **This is my first text file created with the Windows GUI text editor, Notepad.**

9 Choose **File**, **Save As...**

Observe the Save in box   By default, Windows XP saves your documents in the My Documents folder.

In the File name box, enter **My GUI Text File**

Observe the Save as type box   By default, Notepad saves your files as .txt files.

Click **Save**

10 Choose **File**, **Exit**   To exit Notepad.

File attributes

Explanation

Files can have different attributes assigned to them. File attributes tell the operating system and applications how files should be used. The following attributes can be assigned:

Attribute	Description
Read-only	Is assigned to prevent inadvertent changes to a file. MS-DOS commands will not allow you to change a read-only file. Some Windows applications will allow it, although they might prompt you first, letting you know that you are changing a read-only file.
Hidden	Hides the file from view in the default list display of the MS-DOS `dir` command and in Windows Explorer.
System	Indicates that the file is used by the operating system and should not be altered or removed.
Archive	Indicates whether the file has been modified since a backup. The MS-DOS `backup`, `restore`, and `xcopy` commands use this attribute.

You can use the MS-DOS `attrib` command to remove or assign any of these attributes. If a file has a system or hidden attribute assigned, that attribute must be removed before you can change any other attribute for the file. The `attrib` command will recognize wildcards (`?` and `*`) in file names.

The syntax for the `attrib` command is:

```
attrib
```

Optional parameters and switches include those shown below and described in the following table:

```
attrib +r|-r +a|-a +s|-s +h|-h drive:path\filename /s
```

Parameter/switch	Description
+r	Assigns the read-only attribute.
-r	Removes the read-only attribute.
+a	Assigns the archive attribute.
-a	Removes the archive attribute.
+s	Sets the file as a system file.
-s	Clears the system file attribute.
+h	Assigns the hidden-file attribute.
-h	Removes the hidden-file attribute.
/s	Applies the command to all files in the current directory and its subdirectories.

Do it!

A-7:   Modifying file attributes

Here's how	Here's why

A Command Prompt window is minimized to the taskbar.

1 Maximize the Command Prompt window

2 Change the directory to C:\

3 Type **attrib** and press [↵ ENTER]

```
C:\>attrib
A            C:\AUTOEXEC.BAT
    SH       C:\boot.ini
A            C:\CONFIG.SYS
A   SHR      C:\IO.SYS
A   SHR      C:\MSDOS.SYS
A   SHR      C:\NTDETECT.COM
A   SHR      C:\ntldr
A   SH       C:\pagefile.sys
```

A designates the archive attribute; S, the system file attribute; H, the hidden attribute; and R, the read-only attribute.

4 What command would you use to add the hidden attribute to autoexec.bat?

`attrib +h c:\autoexec.bat`

5 Enter **dir**

To verify that you can see autoexec.bat in the directory listing.

6 Add the hidden attribute to autoexec.bat

7 Enter **dir**

To verify that autoexec.bat is not listed.

Editing text files

Explanation

You can edit the contents of a file by using the MS-DOS `edit` command or a text editing application such as Notepad.

To edit a text file by using the `edit` command:

1 At the MS-DOS prompt, type `edit` *drive:\path\filename* and press Enter.
2 Modify the text as needed.
3 If your mouse driver is loaded and functional, you can use your mouse to choose File, Save. Otherwise, press Alt, F, S.
4 Press Alt, F, X to exit the edit program.

To edit a text file in Notepad:

1 Click Start and choose All Programs, Accessories, Notepad.
2 Choose File, Open.
3 In the Look in list, navigate to the folder containing the text file.
4 In the file list, select the desired file.
5 Click Open.
6 Modify the text.
7 Save the file and then exit the program.

Do it!

A-8: Editing a text file

A Command Prompt window is open.

Students can press the up arrow to scroll through previous commands. They can then edit a command to save the effort of having to re-type a long command.

Here's how	Here's why

1 Enter the following command:
 	
`edit "C:\Documents and Settings\RSTAdmin##\My Documents\▶`
`My Text File.txt"`	

	The text file opens in the MS-DOS text editor.
2 Press [END]	To move the cursor to the end of the sentence.
3 Press [SPACEBAR]	
Type **I have edited this file using edit.**	The text continues on one line. The MS-DOS text editor does not have the word-wrap feature that's included in GUI text editors like Notepad.
4 Press [ALT], [F], [S]	To save the changes in your file.
5 Press [ALT], [F], [X]	To exit the text editor.
6 Close the Command Prompt window	
7 Open Windows Explorer	
Right-click **My GUI Text File** and choose **Open**	
8 Press [CTRL] + [END]	To move the cursor to the end of the text in the file.
9 Press [SPACEBAR]	
10 Type **I have edited this file using Notepad.**	
11 Choose **Format, Word Wrap**	To enable the Word Wrap feature of Notepad.
12 Choose **File, Save**	To save the changes.
Choose **File, Exit**	To close Notepad.

Temporary files

Many applications use temporary files to keep track of changes in your files as you work on them. When you save a file and close the application, the temporary files should be deleted automatically. However, sometimes an application shuts down unexpectedly or is not programmed correctly to remove its temporary files. Periodically, you should search for and delete temporary files. This will keep the space on your hard disk available for permanent files.

File names for temporary files typically begin with a tilde (~) or end in .tmp. You can delete temporary files by using the MS-DOS `del` command or Windows Explorer. The procedure given here for using Windows Explorer includes a step to reboot the computer to verify that you have not deleted any necessary system files. This is safer than deleting the files from MS-DOS. However, it can be more convenient to delete the files in MS-DOS if you create a batch file to do the work for you and then schedule the batch file to run at set times.

Del

The syntax of the `del` command is

```
del drive:path\filename
```

where `drive:path\filename` specifies the location and name of the file you want to delete.

You can use wildcards with the `del` command to quickly remove temporary files:

```
del drive:path\*.tmp
del drive:path\~*
```

Optionally, you can add the `/p` switch to display the name of each file being deleted and prompt you to confirm that the file should be deleted.

```
del drive:path\filename /p
```

Undelete

After you have deleted a file by using the `del` command, you can retrieve it by using the MS-DOS `undelete` command as long as no other files have been created or changed on the hard disk.

The syntax of the `undelete` command is

```
undelete drive:path\filename
```

where `drive:path\filename` specifies the location and name of the file you want to undelete.

Point out the "|" symbol, which indicates mutually exclusive switches.

Optional switches include those shown below and described in the following table.

```
undelete drive:path\filename /list|/all /dos|/dt
```

When switches are separated by the "|" symbol (as with /list|/all), you can use one switch or the other, but not both.

Switch	Description
/list	Lists the deleted files that can be recovered, but does not actually undelete them. The /dt and /dos switches control the list displayed.
/all	Recovers all deleted files available without prompting for confirmation on each file.
/dos	Recovers only those files that are internally listed as deleted by MS-DOS and prompts you for confirmation on each file.
/dt	Recovers only those files deleted by the MS-DOS mirror command and prompts you for confirmation on each file.

Removing temporary files in Windows Explorer

To remove temporary files by using Windows Explorer:

1 Click Start and choose Search.
2 Under "What do you want to search for," click "All files and folders."
3 In the "All or part of the file name" box, type *.tmp.
4 Click Search.
5 In the details pane, select all files. (They should all be .tmp files.)
6 Right-click the selected files and choose Delete.
7 Click Yes to send the items to the Recycle Bin. If prompted, click Yes to confirm each file deletion.
8 Click "Start a new search" and then click "All files and folders."
9 In the "All or part of the file name" box, type ~* (tilde and an asterisk).
10 Click Search.
11 In the details pane, select all files.
12 Right-click the selected files and choose Delete. If prompted, click Yes to confirm each file deletion.
13 Close the Search Results dialog box.
14 Restart the computer to verify that you have not inadvertently deleted any required Windows system files.
15 After the computer successfully restarts and you have logged in (if necessary), open the Recycle Bin.
16 Under Recycle Bin Tasks, click Empty the Recycle Bin, and then click Yes to confirm the deletion.
17 Close the Recycle Bin.

If you inadvertently deleted a Windows system file, you will need to use the system recovery tools provided with your version of Windows to restore the file from the Recycle Bin. On FAT16 partitions, you can boot to MS-DOS and move the files by using MS-DOS commands.

Renaming a file

If you are uncomfortable with deleting a file in MS-DOS, you can rename the file by using the MS-DOS `rename/ren` command. Test your system to see if the file was required. If it was not a critical file, you can then delete the renamed file. If it was required, you can use `rename/ren` to change the file name back to the original and restore the file.

The syntax for the `rename/ren` command is:

```
rename drive:path\filename1 filename2
ren drive:path\filename1 filename2
```

Parameter	Description
`drive:path\filename1`	Specifies the location and name of the file you want to rename.
`filename2`	Specifies the new name for the file. You cannot specify a new location for the renamed file. If you want to rename the file and move it, you must use separate commands.

Do it!

A-9: Managing temporary files

Here's how	Here's why
1 From the C:\Student Data\ folder for this unit, copy the following files to C:\Windows\Temp: Temporary File.tmp Second Temporary File.tmp Third Temporary File.tmp	Use Windows Explorer.
2 Click **Start** and choose **All Programs**, **Accessories**, **Command Prompt**	You will search for and delete temporary files from MS-DOS, then from within the Windows GUI.
3 What command would you use to find all .tmp files in C:\Windows\Temp?	*dir c:\windows\temp*.tmp*
Enter the command	Your results should include the following files: Temporary File.tmp Second Temporary File.tmp Third Temporary File.tmp
4 What command would you use to delete all .tmp files from C:\Windows\Temp?	*del c:\windows\temp*.tmp*
Enter the command	

Students can use the up arrow to scroll to this previously entered command.

5   What command would you use to verify that all .tmp files have been deleted from C:\Windows\Temp?

dir c:\windows\temp*.tmp

Enter the command

You should receive the message: File Not Found.

6   Close the Command Prompt window

7   From the C:\Student Data\ folder for this unit, copy the following files to C:\Windows\Temp:

Use Windows Explorer.

~TEMP.txt
~2TEMP.txt
~3TEMP.txt

8   Click **Start** and choose **Search**

Under What do you want to search for?, click **All files and folders**

In the "All or part of the file name" box, type **~***

To search for all files that begin with a tilde (~).

Click **Search**

Name	In Folder
~2TEMP.txt	C:\Data\Unit_02
~3TEMP.txt	C:\Data\Unit_02
~TEMP.txt	C:\Data\Unit_02
~2TEMP.txt	C:\WINDOWS\Temp
~3TEMP.txt	C:\WINDOWS\Temp
~TEMP.txt	C:\WINDOWS\Temp

You may have additional temporary files on your computer that begin with ~.

9   Select the three ~ files in C:\Windows\Temp

Click ~2TEMP.txt, hold the Shift key, and click ~TEMP.txt.

Choose **File, Delete**

Click **Yes**

To confirm that you want to send all three files to the Recycle Bin.

Close the Search Results window

Topic B: System monitoring and management

This topic covers the following CompTIA A+ 220-603 exam objectives.

#	Objective
2.1	**Identify the fundamental principles of using operating systems** • Locate and use Windows 2000, XP Professional and XP Home utilities and available switches • System Management Tools – Device and Task Manager
2.2	**Install, configure, optimize and upgrade operating systems** • Identify procedures and utilities used to optimize the performance of Windows 2000, XP Professional and XP Home, for example: • Services • Startup • Applications
2.3	**Identify tools, diagnostic procedures and troubleshooting techniques for operating systems** • Recognize and resolve common error messages and codes, for example: • Startup (e.g. device/service failed to start, device/program in registry not found) • Windows • Use diagnostic utilities and tools to resolve operational problems, for example: • Task and Device Manager

Explanation

There are many utilities included with Windows 2000 Professional, Windows XP Professional, and Windows XP Home Edition that you can use to perform system management and monitoring tasks. Some of these utilities are graphical user interface tools, some are command-line tools, and some can be used both in the GUI and at the command-line.

Windows Diagnostics

The basics of Windows Diagnostics in the GUI is covered in CompTIA A+ Certification: Essentials.

As an IT Technician, in order to manage or maintain the operating system, you must be able to determine exactly what you have on the system. Windows 2000 Professional and the Windows XP operating systems include a utility that collects and reports information about the configuration of the specified computer. You can use this tool from within Windows or from a command-line with switches.

System Information dialog box

To open Windows Diagnostic from within Windows, click Start and choose All Programs, Accessories, System Tools, System Information. The System Information dialog box as shown in Exhibit 4-2 opens.

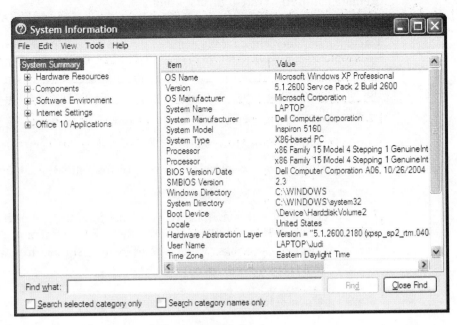

Exhibit 4-2: The System Information dialog box

The System information dialog box displays system summary information plus detailed information in the following categories:

- Hardware resources
- Components
- Software Environment
- Internet Settings

Remote computer system information

You can display the statistics of a remote computer by choosing View, Remote Computer and then entering the name of the computer. For you to run msinfo32 to report on a remote computer, the remote computer must have Windows Management Instrumentation (WMI) installed. This is a Windows component that is installed by default. You must also have appropriate privileges to view system information on a remote computer.

Command-line system information

To run MSINFO32 at the command prompt or from the Run dialog box, enter:

```
path\msinfo32
```

To retain command-line functionality, you must enter the full path of the msinfo32 command. If you don't, it will simply open the default System Information dialog box. The parameters and switches available to use with msinfo32 from the command line are described in the following table:

Parameter/switch	Description
/pch	Opens System Information in History view.
/report:filename.ext	Sends the system information to a file called filename in the current directory. You must specify the extension as .txt.
/computer:computername	Reports on the specified remote computer. You can specify the remote computer by UNC name, IP address, or FQDN (fully qualified domain name).
/category:categoryname	Launches System Information with the specified category selected.
/categories:categorylist	Displays information in only the specified category list.
/showcategories	Displays the list of categories.

The ver command

The ver command is a command-line utility that displays the version of MS-DOS or Windows running on the computer. It is available in all client versions of Windows.

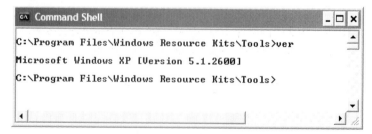

Exhibit 4-3: The ver command on Windows XP

Do it!

B-1: Running Windows diagnostics

Here's how	Here's why
1 Click **Start** and choose **All Programs**, **Accessories**, **System Tools**, **System Information**	
Maximize the System Information dialog box	
Observe the Summary information	The details pane shows general information about the configuration of your computer.
2 Expand Hardware Resources	
	To view the categories listed under hardware resources.

Describe to students what they are seeing in each subcategory.

Select each subcategory and observe the information it reports	
3 Expand Components	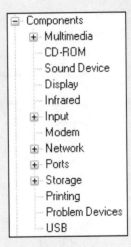
	To view the categories listed.

Describe to students what they are seeing in each subcategory.

Select each subcategory and observe the information it reports	If necessary, expand any subcategories that contain additional categories.

4 Expand Software Environment

To view the categories listed.

Describe to students what they are seeing in each subcategory.

Select each subcategory and observe the information it reports

5 Expand Internet Settings, Internet Explorer

To view the categories listed.

Describe to students what they are seeing in each subcategory.

Select each subcategory and observe the information it reports

If necessary, expand any subcategories that contain additional categories.

6 Close the System Information dialog box

7 Open a Command Prompt window

Type **ver** and press ⏎ ENTER

```
C:\Program Files\Windows Resource Kits\Tools>ver
Microsoft Windows XP [Version 5.1.2600]
```

The version of Windows you are using is reported at the command line.

(Leave the Command Prompt window open for the next activity.)

Do it!

B-2:   Running msinfo32 from a command line

Here's how	Here's why
1 What msinfo32 command would you use to send a report to a file called RSTADMIN##.txt?	*"c:\program files\common files\▶ microsoft shared\msinfo▶ msinfo32.exe" /report:RSTADMIN##.txt*
Enter the command	(Where ## is your student number.)
2 Switch to Windows and open Windows Explorer	
Navigate to C:\Documents and Settings\RSTADMIN##	The command saved the file in the current directory in the Command Prompt window.
3 Open **RSTADMIN##.txt**	It might take a minute or two for msinfo32 to scan the system and create the file.
4 Choose **Edit, Find...**	
In the Find what box, enter **Protocol**	You can use the Search feature to find information you are looking for.
Click **Find Next**	
Click **Find Next** until all instances of Protocol are found, then click **OK**	
Click **Cancel**, and close Notepad	

⚠️ *There are no spaces after the continuation symbol (▶) in the command.*

Make sure students use quotes around the path name because of the spaces.

Task Manager

Explanation

Ctrl+Shift+Esc will also open Task Manager in some Windows operating systems.

Task Manager is a Windows GUI utility that provides information on processes that are running on your computer. A version of Task Manager is available in all Windows operating systems discussed in this course—Windows 2000 Professional and both Windows XP versions.

In all Windows operating systems, you can open Task Manager by pressing Ctrl+Alt+Delete. Depending on the operating system, either Task Manager or the Windows Security dialog box will open. If necessary, in the Security dialog box, click Task Manager. You can also open Task Manager by right-clicking an empty space in the taskbar and choosing Task Manager.

The basics of Task Manager are covered in CompTIA A+ Certification: Essentials.

Windows 2000/XP

In Windows 2000 Professional, Windows XP Professional, Windows XP Home Edition, and Windows XP Media Center, Task Manager has three tabs you can use to troubleshoot problems and monitor your system:

Tab	Use to
Application	Determine the status of applications running on your computer. You can end an application, switch to a running application, or start an application.
Processes	Display information about the processes that are running on your computer. Each process entry displays the name of the executable file, the name of the account running the application (this might be a system service account), the process's percentage of CPU usage, and the amount of memory (in KB) the process is using. You can end processes from this tab as well.
Performance	Display a dynamic representation of the most common performance indicators for your computer. You will see graphs for CPU and page-file usage; summary totals for the number of handles, threads, and processes running; and totals, in KB, for physical, kernel, and commit charge memory.

In Windows XP, Task Manager has two additional tabs:

Tab	Use to
Networking	Display a dynamic graphical representation of your current network utilization. For each network adapter installed, Task Manager lists the percentage of network utilization, the link speed of the connection, and the state of the connection.
Users	Display user names and status of any users currently logged on. You can log users off or disconnect them from this tab. The Users tab is available on Windows XP computers that are not members of a domain and that have Fast User Switching enabled.

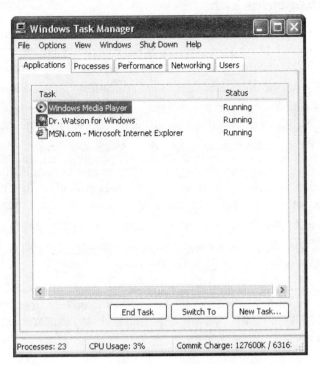

Exhibit 4-4: Task Manager in Windows XP Professional

The Applications tab

Explanation

You can use the Applications tab in Task Manager to end a running application. This is helpful when general protection faults (GPFs) have occurred and applications aren't responding to keyboard or mouse input. To end a running application:

1 On the Applications tab, select the application you want to end.
2 Click End Task.
3 If the application is still not responding, a dialog box is displayed, telling you that the application is not responding. Click End Task.

You can also use the Applications tab to switch to another application. For example, if an application is running but is running in the background or does not have a taskbar button displayed, you can open Task Manager to switch to the application.

1 On the Applications tab, select the application you want to switch to.
2 Click Switch To. This minimizes Task Manager and places the selected application on top of the desktop.

You can start a new instance of an application from within Task Manager. This is helpful if the explorer.exe process has stopped and you have lost your Start menu, taskbar, and desktop items. Creating a new task to start explorer.exe will fix the problem. To do so:

1 On the Applications tab, click New Task.
2 In the Open box, type (or browse to navigate to) the desired executable file.
3 Click OK.

Do it!

B-3: Managing applications

Task Manager should be open.

Here's how	Here's why
1 Right-click an empty spot on the taskbar and choose Task Manager	
2 On the Applications tab, select **RSTADMIN##** and click **Switch To**	Task Manager minimizes to the taskbar, and the Windows Explorer window is now active.
3 On the taskbar, click **Windows Task Manager**	
4 Select **Command Prompt**	If this application experienced a GPF, its status would be "Not responding."
5 Click **End Task**	To end the Command Prompt application.
6 Click **New Task**	
In the Open box, type **notepad** and then click **OK**	Another instance of Notepad runs, and it's listed on the Applications tab.

The Processes tab

Explanation

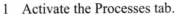

The Processes tab is helpful when you need to determine if a running process is overwhelming the processor and slowing the system down.

1 Activate the Processes tab.

2 As you complete tasks on the computer, observe the CPU column. You should see the number spike as each process takes processor time, and then the number should return to normal.

If a process has a high percentage of CPU usage that doesn't return to normal, you might have to end the process.

3 Select the name of the executable file for the process that is overwhelming the CPU.

4 Click End Process.

5 A warning box states that terminating the process can cause undesirable results. Click Yes to end the process.

Do it!

B-4: Ending a process

Here's how	Here's why
1 Activate the Processes tab	
2 Click **Mem Usage**	(The column heading.) To sort the list of processes by memory consumption.
3 Click **Image Name**	(The column heading.) To sort the list of processes by name.
4 Select **notepad.exe**	
Click **End Process**	
Click **Yes**	Notepad closes, and its executable file is removed from the processes list.

Mem Usage is a column heading.

The Performance tab

Explanation

You can use the Performance tab to monitor your computer's performance, using the most common indicators. The indicators are described in the following table.

Item	Description
CPU Usage	This graph shows the percentage of time the processor is working. If your computer is running slowly, this graph will display a higher percentage.
CPU Usage History	This graph shows how busy the CPU has been over time. The value selected for Update Speed (off the View menu) determines how often this graph is updated. You can set updates to occur twice per second (High), once every two seconds (Normal), once every four seconds (Low), or not at all (Paused). You can press F5 to update a paused graph.
PF Usage	This graph shows the amount of the page file's capacity being used by the computer. If this graph shows that your page file is near the maximum, you should increase the page file's size.
Page File Usage History	This graph shows the percentage of the page file's size used over time. The value selected for Update Speed (off the View menu) determines how often this graph is updated.
Totals	This section shows the dynamic totals for the number of handles, threads, and processes running.
Physical Memory (K)	This section shows the total amount of physical memory installed on your computer. "Available" is the amount of free memory available. "System Cache" shows the amount of current physical memory being used to map pages of open files.
Commit Charge (K)	Commit Charge is the amount of memory allocated to programs and the operating system. This number includes virtual memory, so the value listed under Peak might exceed the actual physical memory installed. The Total value is the same as in the Page File Usage History graph.
Kernel Memory (K)	Kernel Memory is used by the operating system kernel and device drivers. "Paged" is memory that can be copied to the page file to free up physical memory for the operating system to use. "Non-paged" is memory that won't be paged out.
Summary data	This data is displayed along the bottom of the tab. It shows the current number of processes, the current CPU usage percentage, and current amount of commit-charge memory being used, compared to the maximum available.

TIPS
On multiprocessor systems, there is one graph per CPU. On Pentiums with a dual-core configuration, Task Manager shows two graphs.

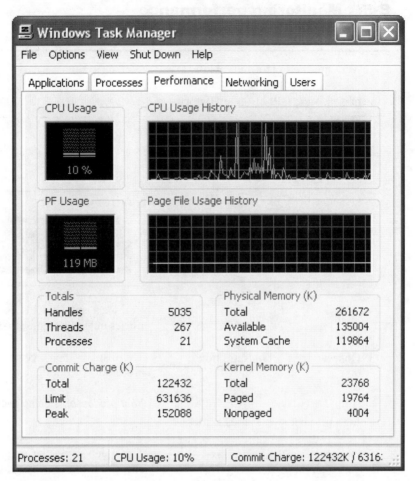

Exhibit 4-5: The Performance tab of Task Manager in Windows XP Professional

B-5: Monitoring performance

Here's how	Here's why
Task Manager should be open.	
1 Activate the Performance tab	
Observe the CPU Usage History graph	
2 From the Start menu, open **My Documents**	
Observe the CPU Usage History graph	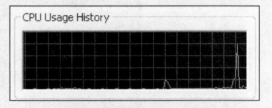
	You see a spike in CPU usage as the processor carries out your request to open My Documents.
3 Observe the CPU Usage box	This displays the percentage of time the processor is working.
4 If the CPU Usage box displays a high number, what does it mean?	*Your processor is being overworked.*
5 Observe the PF Usage box	This graph shows the amount of the page file's capacity being used by the computer.
6 If the PF Usage box displays a number very close to the page file's maximum size, what should you do?	*Increase the size of the page file.*
7 Observe the Physical Memory box	This box shows the amount of RAM installed, the amount of free memory available, and the amount of current physical memory being used to map pages of open files.
8 If the Available memory was very low and the System Cache was very high, compared to the amount listed under Total, what would be your concern?	*That you do not have enough physical memory (RAM) installed in the computer. Your computer is having to page too much data to the hard disk.*

Task Manager should be open.

The Networking tab

Explanation

You can use the data displayed on the Networking tab in Task Manager to quickly see how much of your computer's network bandwidth you're using.

If you have multiple network interface cards (NICs) installed on the computer, the chart displays a combination of the network traffic for all NICs. The summary information at the bottom of the tab displays information about multiple NICs individually, allowing you to compare the traffic on each one.

You can change the columns displayed in the summary area for each NIC by choosing View, Select Columns. Exhibit 4-6 shows the choices available. Information on each of these choices is available on Microsoft's Web site at: http://www.microsoft.com/resources/documentation/windows/xp/all/proddocs/en-us/taskman_whats_there_w.mspx.

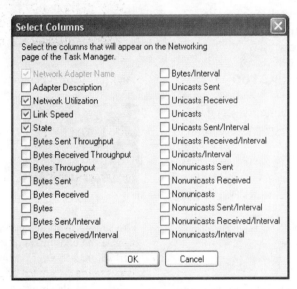

Exhibit 4-6: Data types that can be displayed under the Networking graph.

Do it!

B-6: Monitoring network utilization

Here's how	Here's why
1 Activate the Networking tab	
2 Move Task Manager to the lower-right corner of your screen	You will view the network utilization data as you work with the My Computer window.
3 On the taskbar, click **My Documents**	Task Manager remains on top. My Computer is active behind the Task Manager window.
4 Under Other Places, click **My Network Places** Under Network Tasks, click **View workgroup computers** Double-click **RST00**	Your instructor's computer.
5 In Task Manager, observe the Local Area Connection graph	 You see small spikes in network traffic as you browse the computers in your workgroup and then connect to your partner's computer.
6 Observe the box below the graph	It shows details about your NIC.

Have students maximize My Computer if necessary.

Adapter Name	Network Utilization	Link Speed	State
Local Area Connection	0 %	100 Mbps	Operational

7 Close all open windows except Task Manager	Right-click each button on the taskbar and choose Close.

The Users tab

You can use the Users tab in Task Manager to monitor the users logged onto the computer and to disconnect them, log them off, or send them a message. The columns on the Users tab include:

Item	Description
User	Lists the user names of people logged onto this computer.
ID	Shows a numeric ID assigned to identify the user session on the computer.
Status	Indicates the current status of the user session: Active or Disconnected.
Client Name	If applicable, indicates the name of the computer using the session.
Session	Displays the session name. (You'll need to scroll to the right to view this column.)

Do it!

B-7:   Managing users

Task Manager should be open.

Here's how	Here's why
1 Activate the Users tab	
2 Observe the data on the Users tab	It shows that you are the only user logged into your computer. You can see that your user account is active.
3 Select your user account and click **Logoff**	To log off.
Click **Yes**	To confirm you want to log off.
4 Log back on as your RSTADMIN## user	

Services

When it comes to optimizing and securing your computer, one of the first things you can do is disable any unnecessary components, such as services. When a service is unnecessarily installed or is no longer used, you should disable it. Running unnecessary services consumes additional resources, such as memory and CPU, and adds overhead to the system. If you are having a problem with a component on a computer, you can look to see if the service is running.

The Services MMC

You use the Services MMC, shown in Exhibit 4-7, to configure a variety of settings relating to how services function and respond to potential problems.

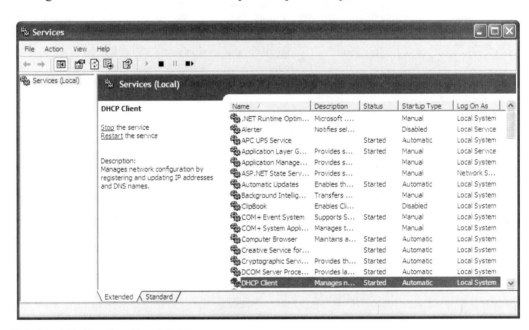

Exhibit 4-7: The Services MMC

The properties of a service include four different configuration tabs, as follows:

- **General** — Displays the service's name, description and the path to the executable file, startup parameters, and buttons allowing you to start, stop, pause, and resume a service.
- **Log On** — Allows you to specify the user name that a service will run as, along with the hardware profiles for which the service is enabled.
- **Recovery** — Allows you to configure the computer's response when a service fails, including different actions depending on the number of failures. It allows you to specify a program that the operating system should run when a service failure occurs.
- **Dependencies** — Specifies the services that a service depends on to function correctly, as well as the services that depend on this service to function.

Before you stop or disable a service, check to see if you are running any necessary services that depend on the service you want to disable. You use the Dependencies tab in the properties view of the service to determine this. Exhibit 4-8 illustrates the Dependencies tab of the DHCP Client service.

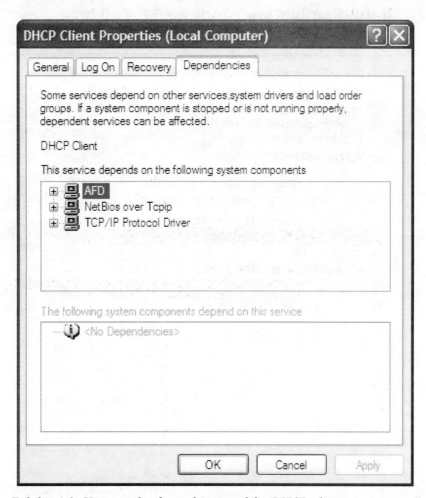

Exhibit 4-8: Viewing the dependencies of the DHCP client service

Do it!

B-8: Configuring Windows XP services

Here's how	Here's why
1 Click **Start** and choose **Control Panel**	
2 Click **Performance and Maintenance**, and then **Administrative Tools**	
Double-click **Services**	
3 Right-click **Remote Desktop Help Session Manager**	
Choose **Properties**	

You might have to expand the width of the Name column.

Service name: RDSessMgr

Display name: Remote Desktop Help Session Manager

Description: Manages and controls Remote Assistance. If this service is stopped, Remote Assistance will be

Path to executable:
C:\WINDOWS\system32\sessmgr.exe

Startup type: Manual

Service status: Stopped

[Start] [Stop] [Pause] [Resume]

You can specify the start parameters that apply when you start the service from here.

Start parameters:

This service manages the Remote Assistance feature. It is currently stopped and will not start unless you manually start it.

Here's how	Here's why
4 From the Startup type list, select **Automatic**	This sets the Remote Desktop Help Session Manager service to start automatically the next time the computer restarts.
5 Click **Apply**	
Click **Start**	This manually starts the Remote Desktop Help Session Manager service.

6 Activate the Log On tab

This displays the properties of the account under which the Remote Desktop Help Session Manager service runs.

7 Activate the Recovery tab

8 From the First failure list, select **Restart the Service**

From the Second failure list, select **Run a Program**

In the Program box, enter **cmd.exe**

This causes the Command Prompt program to start in the event that the Remote Desktop Help Session Manager services fails for a second time.

9 Active the Dependencies tab

Observe the list of services that
the Remote Desktop Help Session
Manager service depends on

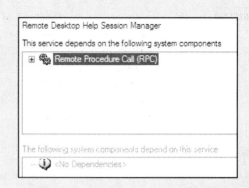

The service depends on the Remote Procedure
Call (RPC) service. A problem with RPC could
cause problems with this service. There are no
services that depend on Remote Desktop Help
Session Manager.

10 Click **OK**

To close the dialog box. The Remote Desktop
Help Session Manager service now shows as
started.

11 Right-click **Remote Desktop
Help Session Manager**

Choose **Stop**

To manually stop the Remote Desktop Help
Session Manager service. Remember that the
startup type is set to automatic, so it will startup
up again automatically the next time the
computer restarts.

12 Close all open windows

The Startup program group

Explanation

Many different types of applications, such as work productivity, network connectivity, entertainment, and operating system support, can be installed on your Windows 2000 Professional, Windows XP Professional, or Windows XP Home Edition computer. When they are installed on the computer, some applications are programmed to start up automatically, or to start up some of their components automatically, when you log in to Windows. You will find these applications or application components in your Startup program group, as shown in Exhibit 4-9.

Exhibit 4-9: The Startup program group

Users can add applications to the Startup group manually by dragging and dropping items or by using Windows Explorer to copy and paste. Sometimes the addition is intentional, sometimes it is inadvertent and the addition can cause problems with startup. To edit the Startup program group, you can drag and drop items on or off the Start menu. You can also right-click Start and choose Open All Users. Use Windows Explorer to copy and remove items.

Microsoft installed software

The Windows XP Help and Support Center contains a tool called My Computer Information, which collects and displays a list of Microsoft registered software on the local Windows XP computer. This list contains the name of the Microsoft software application and its registered product identification number.

My Computer Information - Software
Refresh screen

Software	
Microsoft Registered Software	**Product Identification (PID)**
Windows	76487-oem-0011903-00102
Office	54187-760-8309215-17346
Microsoft Reference	
Microsoft Interactive Training	22404-oem-0000007-00000

Startup Program Group	
Software	**Install Date**
MPFExe	Wednesday, March 02, 2005
OASCInt	Unknown
QuickTime Task	Monday, January 30, 2006
iTunesHelper	Tuesday, December 20, 2005
Auto EPSON Stylus CX5400 on jkhome (Copy 1)	Unknown
MSKDetectorExe	Saturday, April 02, 2005
MSKAGENTEXE	Saturday, April 02, 2005
dla	Monday, February 28, 2005
EPSON Stylus CX5400	Unknown

Exhibit 4-10: The My Computer Information tool displaying software information

The My Computer Information tool for software also lists the applications that are part of the Startup program group. The list of applications in the Startup program group can provide you with insight into system startup behavior, for example, if a user calls to complain that their system has slowed to a crawl during startup the past two days, you can view this list to see if there is an application installed within the past two days that might be causing the new slow startup behavior. You'll notice that comparing the Start menu Startup group shown in Exhibit 4-9 and the My Computer Information tool in Exhibit 4-10, more items are reported in the My Computer Information tool.

The Dr. Watson utility is covered in the CompTIA A+ Certification: Essentials.

There is also a list detailing Windows Watson Crash information. Dr. Watson is a debugger included with many Microsoft Windows products. If Dr. Watson is running when a Windows application crashes, it creates a report containing technical information that can help determine what caused the application to crash. This information is typically most helpful to application developers and not computer support personnel. Summary information, such as date, time and description, from the Dr. Watson log files is listed in the My Computer Information — Software tool.

Do it!

B-9: Managing the Startup program group

Here's how	Here's why
1 Click **Start** and choose **All Programs, Startup**	To display the list of applications that run automatically at startup. You can drag and drop items on and off this menu.
2 Close the Start menu	

3 Right-click **Start** and choose **Explore All Users**

In the navigation pane, expand **Programs**

Select **Startup**

This shows the startup program group items that apply to all users who log on to this computer. You can add or delete items from this window just like any other file management window.

4 In the navigation pane, collapse **All Users**

Expand your **RSTADMIN##** user

In the navigation pane, expand **Start Menu**, **Programs**

Select **Startup**

Each user of the computer can have unique startup items in addition to those applied to all users.

5 Close Windows Explorer

6 Click **Start** and choose **Help and Support**

The Help and Support Center is where you access the tools to view your computer information.

7 Under Pick a Task, click **Use Tools to view your computer information and diagnose problems**

Use **Tools** to view your computer information and diagnose problems

8 Under Tools, click **My Computer Information**

In the details pane, click **View a list of Microsoft software installed on this computer**

You can use this information to resolve problems and to create inventory records.

9 Read the list of Microsoft Registered Software

Windows is listed along with its product identification number.

10 Read the list of software in the Startup Program Group

This list will vary depending on the configuration of your computer. The install date for each software item is listed next to it.

11 Close the Help and Support Center

Error reporting

Explanation

 The error reporting feature is covered inCompTIA A+ Certification: Essentials.

In Windows XP operating system versions, when an illegal operation or other error occurs in a program, such as Microsoft Word, the program stops working. You can elect to report system and program errors to Microsoft. This reporting system allows Microsoft to track and address operating system, Windows component, and program errors.

You can configure error reporting to send only specified information. For example, if you want to report only system errors, you can specify that reports be generated only for the operating system. The same is true for Windows components, such as Windows Explorer or Internet Explorer, and for programs, such as Microsoft Word, installed on your computer. Your organization might decide to disable this error reporting for users' computers. To access the Error Reporting dialog box:

1   Right-click My Computer on the Start menu.

2   Choose Properties.

3   Activate the Advanced tab.

4   Click Error Reporting.

Within the Error Reporting dialog box, you have the following options:

- Disable error reporting: Windows XP won't generate error reports.
- Notify me when critical errors occur: Notify you if a critical error occurs, even if you have disabled error reporting.
- Enable error reporting: Windows XP will generate error reports.
- Windows operating system: Reports errors in the Windows XP operating system.
- Programs: Report errors in application programs.
- Choose Programs: Specify which programs to include or exclude from reporting.
- Clicking the Choose Program button: Opens the Choose Programs dialog box.

From the Choose Programs dialog box, you have the following options:

- All programs: Report errors in all programs.
- All programs in this list: Include all programs from Microsoft, all Windows programs, or individual programs in error reporting.
- Programs from Microsoft: Check to include all programs from Microsoft.
- Windows components: Windows XP operating system components.
- Do not report errors for these programs: Exclude individual programs from error reporting.
- Add button: Add programs to include/exclude from the respective list.
- Remove button: Remove programs to include/exclude from the respective list.

Do it!

B-10: Disabling error reporting

Here's how	Here's why
1 Click **Start** and right-click **My Computer**	
Choose **Properties**	
2 Activate the Advanced tab	
3 Click **Error Reporting**	
4 Select **Disable error reporting**	
Click **OK** twice	

Do it!

B-11: Enabling error reporting for specific programs

Here's how	Here's why
1 Click **Start** and right-click **My Computer**	
Choose **Properties**	
2 Activate the Advanced tab	
3 Click **Error Reporting**	
4 Select **Enable error reporting**	
5 Click **Choose Programs**	
6 Select **All programs in this list**	
Clear **Programs from Microsoft**	To disable error reporting for all programs from Microsoft.
7 Click **Add**	
Click **Browse**	
8 Navigate to select **C:\Program Files\NetMeeting\Conf**	
Click **Open**	To enable reporting errors occurring only in NetMeeting
9 Click **OK** four times	

Topic C: Event Viewer

This topic covers the following CompTIA A+ 220-603 exam objectives.

#	Objective
3.1	**Identify the fundamental principles of operating systems** • Locate and use Windows 2000, XP Professional and XP Home utilities and available switches • System Management Tools – Event Viewer
3.3	**Identify tools, diagnostic procedures and troubleshooting techniques for operating systems** • Recognize and resolve common error messages and codes, for example: • Event Viewer • Use diagnostic utilities and tools to resolve operational problems, for example: • Event Viewer

Explanation

Event Viewer is a Windows GUI utility that enables you to monitor events that occur on your system. The events that are recorded can help you determine the cause of problems you're having with a particular application, a component of the operating system, or a suspected security breach. On workstation computers, Event Viewer events are divided into the following categories:

Item	Contains
Application	Errors logged by individual applications. The types of errors an application logs in Event Viewer is determined by the application's developers and might vary considerably among applications and vendors.
Security	Errors relating to the security of your Windows NT Workstation, Windows 2000 Professional, Windows XP Professional, or Windows XP Home Edition computer. For security events to be logged by the operating system, you must establish an audit policy.
System	Errors reported by Windows system components. The operating system determines which components report errors to the Event Viewer log.

Additional categories are available in Microsoft's Server operating systems.

Event Viewer is available in Windows 2000 Professional, and all Windows XP versions; you can access it through the Administrative Tools in Control Panel. Event Viewer is also a System Tools component of the Computer Management console. Each of the three event categories displays the following header information pertaining to each recorded event:

Item	Description
Type	The type of event that is recorded: Error, Warning, Information, Success Audit (Security Log only), or Failure Audit (Security Log only).
Date	The date the event was recorded.
Time	The time the event was recorded.
Source	The program, system component, or individual component of a large program that recorded the event.
Category	A classification of events, typically used by the Security log.
Event	An ID that identifies the type of event. Event IDs are coded into the operating system and individual applications and can be used by product support personnel to troubleshoot problems.
User	The name of the user who was logged on when the event was recorded. Many components run under a system account, so you might see SYSTEM in this column, even if a user is physically logged on when the event occurs.
Computer	The name of the computer where the event occurred.

Event types

There are five types of events:

Type	Records
Error	A significant problem; for example, a service fails to start.
Warning	An event that is not a significant or immediate problem but could become a significant problem in the future; for example, disk space is running low.
Information	The successful operation of a task; for example, a network driver loads successfully.
Success Audit (Security Log only)	A successful security event; for example, a user logs on successfully.
Failure Audit (Security Log only)	An unsuccessful security event; for example, a user attempts to log on, but fails to submit proper credentials.

Double-clicking an individual event opens an Event Properties dialog box with a description of the event. You can use the arrow buttons to view information about the previous (up arrow) or next (down arrow) event.

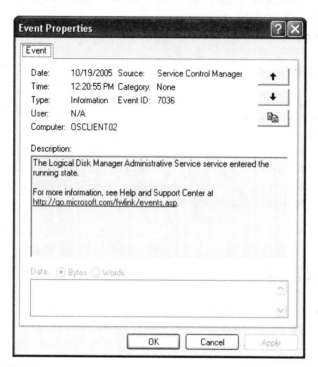

Exhibit 4-11: An Event Properties dialog box in Windows XP

Do it!

C-1: Viewing the event logs

Here's how	Here's why
1 Click **Start** and right-click **My Computer**	
Choose **Manage**	Event Viewer is part of the Computer Management console.
2 Under System Tools, expand Event Viewer	
	(Click the + sign.) The three Event Viewer categories are listed.
3 Select **Application**	
Observe the Type, Date, Time, Source, Category, Event, User and Computer columns	The events are listed from the most recent to the oldest, by default.
Double-click the first event	Description: The Windows Security Center Service has started. For more information, see Help and Support Center at http://go.microsoft.com/fwlink/events.asp.
	To open the Event Properties dialog box, which provides a more detailed description of the event. The description of your first event will vary from the one shown.
4 Click [↓]	To move to the next event in the Application log.
Click **Cancel**	To return to the Application log.
5 Select **Security**	You do not have an audit policy configured, so no security events have been recorded.
Select **System**	To view the events recorded by the operating system and its components.

Events on remote computers

Explanation

You can change the focus of Event Viewer from the local computer to a remote computer on which you have administrative privileges. This allows you to begin troubleshooting a computer problem without needing to physically visit the computer.

To monitor events on a remote computer:

1. In the console tree of Event Viewer or the Computer Management console, select the top object.
2. Choose Action, Connect to another computer.
3. In the Another computer box, enter the name or IP address of the computer you want to monitor.
4. Click OK.
5. If prompted, enter credentials with administrative privileges on the remote computer.

Do it!

C-2: Viewing the event logs of a remote computer

Assign each student a partner to work with.

Here's how	Here's why
1 In the console tree, select **Computer Management (Local)**	You will change the focus of your Computer Management console to your partner's computer.
Choose **Action**, **Connect to another computer...**	To open the Select Computer dialog box.
Enter **RST##**	(Where ## is your partner's assigned student number.) You can also browse to select your partner's computer or enter his or her IP address.
Click **OK**	To close the Select Computer dialog box.
2 Expand System Tools, Event Viewer	You currently do not have administrative permissions on your partner's computer and are denied access to the details in Event Viewer. To view the logs on a remote computer, you must access the computer using an administrative account.
Click **OK**	
3 Choose **Action**, **Connect to another computer...**	Computer Management (RST##) must be selected in order for the command to be available from the Action menu.
Select **Local computer: (the computer this console is running on)**	To reconnect to your own computer.
Click **OK**	

Event display

Explanation

Using the View menu, you can sort and filter the display of events in each event log. You can also search for events that meet particular criteria. These features are helpful in quickly narrowing down a full event log to only certain events.

Sorting events

By default, events are listed from the newest to the oldest, by date and time, but you can easily change the sort order. For example, if you're having a problem with DNS, you can sort by Source to group together all the entries reported by the DNS server, regardless of when the events occurred or what type they are.

You can change the sort order by clicking any column heading. A single click on the column heading sorts the events in ascending order (an up-arrow appears next to the column heading, as shown in Exhibit 4-12). A second click on the column heading sorts events in descending order (a down-arrow appears in the column heading). To return the view to the default, choose View, Newest First.

Up arrow shows that the
log is sorted in ascending
order by Source

| Application   147 event(s) | | | | |
Type	Date	Time	Source	Category
⊗ Error	10/19/2005	3:23:36 PM	Application Hang	(101)
⊗ Error	10/19/2005	3:21:10 PM	Application Hang	(101)
⊗ Error	10/19/2005	3:20:54 PM	Application Hang	(101)
ⓘ Information	10/7/2005	12:08:09 PM	COM+	(113)
ⓘ Information	10/7/2005	12:08:09 PM	COM+	(113)
ⓘ Information	10/7/2005	12:08:09 PM	COM+	(113)
ⓘ Information	10/7/2005	12:08:09 PM	COM+	(113)
ⓘ Information	10/19/2005	11:45:41 …	ESENT	General
ⓘ Information	10/19/2005	11:45:41 …	ESENT	General
ⓘ Information	10/19/2005	11:40:40 …	ESENT	General
ⓘ Information	10/19/2005	11:40:40 …	ESENT	General
ⓘ Information	10/19/2005	11:33:51 …	ESENT	General
ⓘ Information	10/19/2005	11:33:51 …	ESENT	General
ⓘ Information	10/19/2005	11:28:50 …	ESENT	General

Exhibit 4-12: An Application log sorted by Source

Filtering events

To display only certain events, you can apply a filter to the view. Here's how:

1   In the console tree of Event Viewer, select the log whose events you want to filter.

2   Choose View, Filter to open the Application Properties dialog box, with the Filter tab active.

3   Check and clear event types as desired.

4   Select filter criteria as needed from each of the following areas:

- Event source
- Category
- Event ID
- User
- Computer
- From
- To

5   Click OK.

Point out the different components of the filter and the results to students.

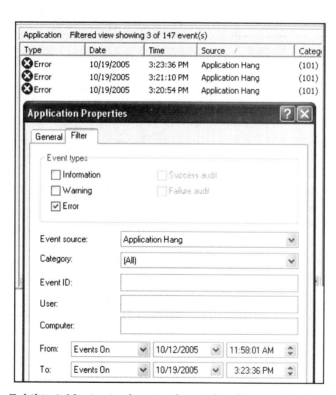

Exhibit 4-13: An Application log with a filter applied

To remove the filter from the log display, choose View, All Records.

If you filter events instead of sorting them, you can then use the Event Properties dialog box to navigate between the details of only the events that meet your filtering criteria.

Searching for events

In Event Viewer, you can search for particular events based on:

- Event type
- Event source
- Category
- Event ID
- User
- Computer
- Description
- A combination of the above

You can search up or down from the current event in the selected log. The Restore Defaults button in the Find dialog box resets the search criteria to the default settings.

The Search capabilities do not group events of interest together as sorting does, but they do allow you greater flexibility in applying multiple criteria to select only those events of interest to you.

C-3: Controlling the display of an event log

Here's how	Here's why
1 With System Tools, Event Viewer, expanded and Application selected, click **Source**	(Click the Source column heading in the details pane.) To group events according to the application that reported them.
Click **Category**	(Click the Category column heading.) To group events by category.
Choose **View**, **Newest First**	To return the list to its default order.
2 Choose **View**, **Filter...**	To open the Application Properties dialog box, with the Filter tab active.
Under Event types, uncheck **Information**, **Success audit**, and **Failure audit**	To display only Warning and Error messages.
3 Open the Event source list	You can choose to display events from just one source.
Choose **Application**	
Observe the Event types check boxes	They were reset to the default when you selected an event source.
4 Open the Category list	With an event source selected, you can further refine your filter to show events from just one category.
Close the Category list	
Observe the Event ID, User, and Computer boxes	You can enter values in these boxes to further refine your filter.
Open and observe the From and To lists	You can show only events that occur within a specified date range.
5 Click **Restore Defaults**	
Under Event types, uncheck **Information**, **Success audit**, and **Failure audit**	
Click **OK**	If your computer has any Error or Warning events in the Application log, they are listed.
6 Choose **View**, **All Records**	To remove the filter.

Managing event log files

Explanation

Each event log is set to take up a maximum of 512 KB; when the maximum file size is reached, the log will overwrite events older than 7 days. If a log is excessively long, you can manually clear it at any time. Before you clear the log or before it begins to overwrite events itself, you can save it as a log file, or as a text or comma-delimited file, to review later.

Event log files can be reopened and viewed in Event Viewer. Text files can be opened in text editors or word processing applications. Comma-delimited files can be opened in spreadsheet or flat-file database applications.

To save a log as a file:

1   In the console tree, right-click the event log you want to save and choose Save Log File As.

2   Navigate to the location where you want to save the file.

3   Enter a file name.

4   From the Save as type list, select one of the following:

- Event Log (*.evt)
- Text (Tab delimited) (*.txt)
- CSV (Comma delimited) (*.csv)

5   Click Save.

To clear an event log:

1   In the console tree, right-click the event log you want to clear and choose Clear all Events.

2   You are prompted to save the events in the log before clearing them. Click Yes to save the events before clearing the log; click No to clear the log without saving the events.

To open a saved event log in Event Viewer:

1   Choose Action, Open Log File.

2   Navigate to select the desired file.

3   From the Log Type list, select the log's type: Application, Security, or System.

4   If desired, enter a Display Name.

5   Click Open.

The saved event log is listed below the current log files in Event Viewer.

If you're having a persistent problem with a computer, you can save daily log files. You can then reopen them together in Event Viewer and compare them to see if you notice any patterns emerging that might point you to the source of the problem.

C-4: Clearing an event log

The Application log should be selected in the console tree in the Computer Management console.

Here's how	Here's why
1 Choose **Action**, **Clear all Events**	To clear the events out of your Application log. You are prompted to save the current contents of the log file before clearing it.
2 Click **Yes**	
In the File name box, enter **RST## AppLog**	Where ## is your assigned student number.
Open the Save as type list	You can save this file as a tab-delimited text file, a comma-delimited file, or an event log file.
Select **Text (Tab delimited) (*.txt)**	
Click **Save**	The Application log is cleared of all recorded events.
3 Open **My Documents**	
Open **RST## AppLog**	The information is saved in a text file. The columns are separated by tabs.
Close Notepad and My Documents	

Event log options

You can overwrite the default maximum log size of 512 KB, as well as change how events are overwritten if the log file reaches its maximum.

- The range for the maximum log size is 64 KB to 4194240 KB. The size-box spinners will increase or decrease the value in increments of 64 KB.
- Your options for overwriting events are:
  — To allow the system to overwrite events on an as-needed basis (called "wrapping the log")
  — To overwrite events that are older than a specified number of days between 1 and 365
  — Not to overwrite events

The "Do not overwrite events" option requires that an administrator regularly clear the log manually. This setting is preferred on high-security and monitored systems. Note that if the log file reaches its maximum setting and the administrator has not cleared the log, the system will shut down to prevent events from being lost.

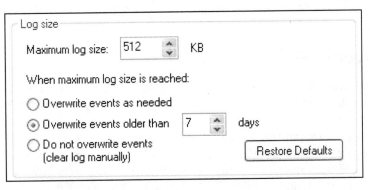

Exhibit 4-14: Log size properties

C-5: Changing event log options

Here's how	Here's why
1 In Computer Management with Application selected, choose **Action**, **Properties**	
2 In the Maximum log size box, use the spinner controls to set the size at **1024**	The range for the maximum log size is 64 KB to 4194240 KB. The size-box spinners will increase or decrease the value in increments of 64 KB.
3 Under "When maximum log size is reached," select **Overwrite events as needed**	To allow the system to overwrite events on an as-needed basis.
Click **OK**	
4 Close Computer Management	

Topic D: The Registry

This topic covers the following CompTIA A+ 220-603 exam objectives.

#	Objective
3.1	**Identify the fundamental principles of using operating systems**
	• Locate and use Windows 2000, XP Professional and XP Home utilities and available switches
	• System Management Tools
	– REGEDIT.EXE
	– REGEDT32.EXE
3.3	**Identify tools, diagnostic procedures and troubleshooting techniques for operating systems**
	• Recognize and resolve common error messages and codes, for example:
	• Registry

Overview of the Registry

Explanation

Registry basics is covered in CompTIA A+ Certification: Essentials.

The *Registry* is a hierarchical database created during the installation of Windows. The Registry contains binary files that hold system configuration information about all aspects of a Windows computer, including security settings, user profiles, installed applications, attached hardware, and system properties. In Windows 2000/XP, the Registry is stored in files called *hives* in the \%systemroot%\System32\Config folder. (The \%systemroom%\ folder is the folder in which Windows is installed. In Windows 2000, by default this folder is C:\Winnt. In Windows XP, the folder is C:\Windows.)

Registry keys

The Registry is divided into sections called *keys*. Each key contains *subkeys*, which in turn contain other subkeys and specific *values*, which define a specific Windows setting. The following table describes each Registry key.

Registry key	Description
HKEY_CLASSES_ROOT	Contains file association data that Windows uses to start the correct program when you open a file from within Windows Explorer or My Computer.
HKEY_CURRENT_USER	Holds the user data for the user who's currently logged on to the computer.
HKEY_LOCAL_MACHINE	Contains all non-user-specific configuration information.
HKEY_USERS	Holds user-specific configuration information for the user accounts on the computer.
HKEY_CURRENT_CONFIG	Maintains hardware profile data.

Registry editors

Registry files are binary files, so you can't edit them directly in a text editor, such as Notepad. You can edit Registry files indirectly by using the Control Panel applets or Device Manager. Changes made there, and in other Properties dialog boxes in Windows, are kept in the Registry.

You can also edit the Registry directly by using one of the Registry editors: regedit.exe or regedt32.exe. (Both tools are called Registry Editor.) Windows 9x/Me provides the regedit.exe utility. Windows 2000 provides both regedit.exe—for its superior search capabilities—and regedt32.exe—a more powerful editing tool. Windows XP combines the two tools into one, pictured in Exhibit 4-15, so you get Regedit whether you start Regedit or Regedt32. If, for some reason, you have to edit the Registry in aWindows operating system other than Windows XP, you might find yourself using Regedit to find a particular key or value, and using Regedt32 to actually edit the settings.

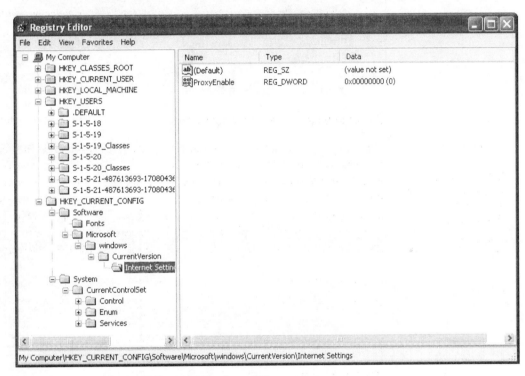

Exhibit 4-15: Registry Editor in Windows XP

To open Regedit or Regedt32, click Start, choose Run, type "regedit" or "regedt32" and click OK. In the navigation (left) pane of the Registry Editor, you can select specific keys or subkeys to display their contents in the details (right) pane.

Although you can edit the Registry directly, you probably shouldn't. If you make a mistake while editing the Registry, you could find yourself with a computer that doesn't work the way you expect it to, or worse, a computer that doesn't work at all. When you're configuring Windows operating systems, you'll find there's very little reason to edit the Registry directly.

D-1: Viewing Registry information

Here's how	Here's why
1 Click **Start**, choose **Run...**, and enter **regedit**	To open the Registry Editor. You're going to view the Registry files in the Registry Editor. Although you probably won't need to configure the Registry directly very often, it's important to know what the Registry files look like and how the data is arranged.
2 Observe the keys in the left pane	The five Registry keys are listed.
3 Expand HKEY_CURRENT_USER	To display its subkeys.
4 Expand Control Panel, Appearance, and select **Schemes**	
Observe the settings in the right pane	These are the same schemes you could set by using the Display applet in the Control Panel. Each scheme is represented here.
5 In the right pane, double-click **Brick**	

	To display the configuration data. If you had to edit this setting manually, you could do it in this dialog box.
6 Click **Cancel**	To close the Edit Binary Value dialog box.

7 Scroll down in the navigation pane and select **Mouse**

In the right pane, double-click **ActiveWindowTracking**

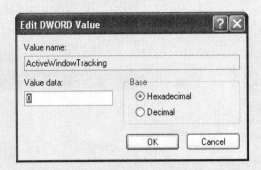

To see another type of data. This value is a hexadecimal value. The field is set to 0, which means that this feature is turned off.

8 Click **Cancel**

To close the dialog box.

Registry searches

Explanation

To search for Registry entries, open Regedit and choose Edit, Find. This opens the Find dialog box, shown in Exhibit 4-16. In the Find What box, enter the text string you want to search for. Then, under "Look at," check Keys, Values, Data, or any combination of the three. (All three are selected by default.) To start the search, click Find Next.

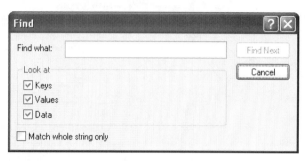

Exhibit 4-16: The Find dialog box

Do it!

D-2:   Searching the Registry

Here's how	Here's why
1 In the Registry Editor, choose **Edit**, **Find...**	To open the Find dialog box. When you have to edit the Registry directly, it can be difficult to find the settings you need. You can use the Find feature to easily find settings by using full setting names or just keywords.
2 In the Find what box, enter **mouse**	To search for all occurrences of the keyword "mouse."
Leave the other options checked	To search through keys, values, and data.
3 Click **Find Next**	To find the first occurrence of "mouse."
4 Press (F3)	To find the next occurrence.
5 Continue pressing (F3)	To find each occurrence of "mouse." You'll see this keyword appear in many different keys in the Registry.

Students don't need to find all instances.

Registry corruption and backups

Explanation

Registry corruption is an uncommon but very real problem that can render a computer inoperable. Registry corruption can happen for a number of reasons, including power failures, corrupted Registry files, hard disk errors, or mistakes made while editing the Registry directly. When the Registry is corrupted, you'll usually see an error message telling you that Windows can't start, and the message will point to one or more of the files associated with the Registry. A corrupted Registry usually means that you'll have to reinstall the operating system unless you've made a backup of the Registry.

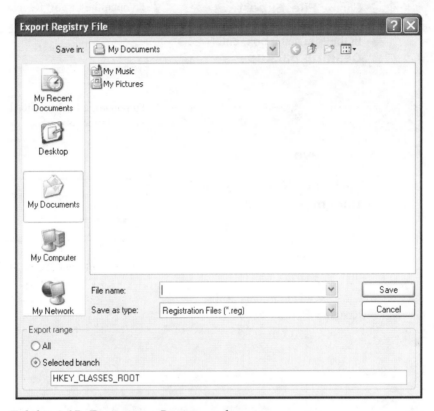

Exhibit 4-17: Exporting a Registry value

One of the fastest and easiest ways to create a backup of a single subkey or value is to export it from the Registry Editor. (If you have to back up a full Registry key, it's better to back up the entire Registry.) To export a portion of the Registry or the entire Registry:

1 Open Regedit.
2 Choose File, Export.
   This opens the Export Registry File dialog box, shown in Exhibit 4-17.
3 Select an option to back up all the keys or just a selected subkey or value.
4 Save the file with a suitable name, in a secure location.
   Keep in mind that a full backup can run several megabytes.

You can also back up the entire Registry by using Emergency Repair Disks (ERDs) in Windows 2000 and Windows XP, or by backing up the System State data in both operating systems.

To restore the Registry or the portion you backed up, double-click the .reg file you created. This will install the information in the correct location in the Registry.

Do it!

D-3: Backing up Registry files

Here's how	Here's why
1 In Registry Editor, under HKEY_CURRENT_USER, select **Desktop**	To prepare to export these settings. You can use the Export feature to back up Registry settings before you make any changes. You can then restore the settings if you make any mistakes or decide to undo your changes.
2 Choose **File**, **Export...**	To open the Export Registry File dialog box.
3 In the File name box, enter **Desktop backup**	File name: Desktop backup Save as type: Registration Files (*.reg) To name the backup file. The file will be saved in My Documents.
4 Click **Save**	
5 Click **Start** and choose **My Documents**	Desktop backup.reg Registration Entries 7 KB To verify that the backup file was created.
6 Close My Documents and Registry Editor	

Topic E: Virtual memory

This topic covers the following CompTIA A+ 220-603 exam objective.

#	Objective
2.2	**Install, configure, optimize and upgrade operating systems** • Identify procedures and utilities used to optimize the performance of Windows 2000, XP Professional and XP Home, for example: • Virtual memory

Virtual memory and page files

Explanation

Windows operating systems use a memory-management scheme called *virtual memory*. Virtual memory is actually hard disk space that's used to deceive applications into "thinking" that there's more RAM available than is physically installed in the computer.

With virtual memory, Windows swaps data back and forth between actual RAM and a file called a *page file* or *swap file*. If an application calls for data it thinks is in RAM, but that Windows has temporarily placed in a page file on the hard disk, Windows' Virtual Memory Manager will pull that data back into RAM for the application to access.

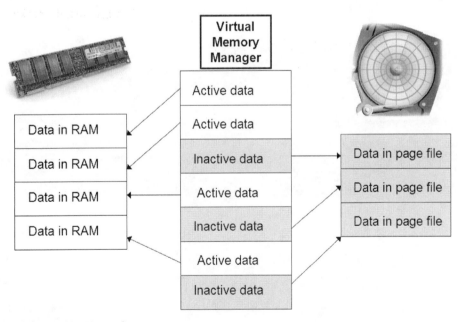

Exhibit 4-18: Virtual memory

Caches

A *cache* is a temporary storage area. A *disk cache* is either a reserved area of RAM or a special area of the hard disk where a copy of the most recently accessed data and adjacent data is stored for fast access. RAM can be viewed as a cache for data that is initially loaded from the hard disk.

Do it!

E-1: Displaying virtual memory settings

Here's how	Here's why
1 Click **Start** and choose **Control Panel**	
Click **Performance and Maintenance**	
Click **System**	To open the System Properties dialog box.
Activate the Advanced tab	
Under Performance, click **Settings**	To open the Performance Options dialog box.
2 Activate the Advanced tab	
Observe the Memory usage box	It shows that the computer is set to use a greater share of memory to optimize program performance.
Observe the Virtual memory box	It shows the total page file size for all drives.

TIPS✔ *You can open the System Properties dialog box by right-clicking on My Computer and choosing Properties.*

Optimizing the page file

Explanation

By default, Windows places the page file on the boot partition, where the operating system is installed. The page file's size is initially determined by the amount of physical RAM installed. To provide the best performance, Windows can automatically increase or decrease the size of the page file based on system memory requirements and available hard disk space. However, you also can manually override these settings and establish minimum and maximum values in megabytes.

To determine the size of the page file, Microsoft recommends multiplying the amount of physical RAM by 1.5; the maximum recommended size is 4095 MB. You can also place a page file on a different hard disk from the boot partition to optimize performance. When the page file is stored on the boot partition, Windows has to perform disk input/output (I/O) processes on both the system directory and the page file. Moving the page file to a different hard disk allows Windows to handle multiple I/O requests more quickly.

Do it!

E-2: Optimizing virtual memory

The Performance Options dialog box is open.

Here's how	Here's why
1 On the Advanced tab, under Virtual memory, click **Change**	You're going to configure Windows to manage the size of the page file.
2 Select **System managed size**	
3 Click **Set** Click **OK**	
4 Click **OK**	To verify that you need to restart your computer.
5 Click **OK** twice	To close the Performance Options and System Properties dialog boxes.
6 Click **Yes**	To restart your computer.
Log on as **RSTADMIN##**	

Unit summary: Operating system management

Topic A   In this topic, you learned how to manage directories and files using both the **command-line utility** and the Windows Explorer GUI. You learned how to **navigate** the directory structure; **create**, **copy**, and **delete** files and directories; and alter **file attributes**. In addition, you learned how to remove **temporary files** from your system to create space and improve operating system performance.

Topic B   In this topic, you learned how to monitor and manage the operating system using tools such as **Windows Diagnostics**, **Task Manager**, and **Computer Management — Services**. You ran Windows Diagnostics from both the GUI and command-line interfaces. You used Task Manager to manage applications and users, end a process, and monitor both performance and network utilization. You started, stopped, and changed startup options for the services running on your computer. You also learned how to identify startup items and how to manage those items using the **Startup Program Group** and the **My Computer Information** tool in the **Windows XP Help and Support Center**.

Topic C   In this topic, you used **Event Viewer** to monitor events on the computer. You worked with the three different logs—**Application**, **Security**, and **System**—on both local and remote computers. You learned how to **sort**, **filter**, and **search** through events in the log. In addition, you learned how to manage the **Event log files** and change their options.

Topic D   In this topic, you learned the differences between the two Registry management tools—**regedit.exe** and **regedt32.exe**. You used regedit.exe to manage the Registry. You learned how to **search** the Registry to find information. In addition, you learned how to **back up** the Registry files in order to recover from a Registry problem.

Topic E   In this topic you learned about **virtual memory**. You used Windows to configure virtual memory to optimize its performance.

Review questions

1 Hard disks are divided into usable storage space through _____.

A files

B folders

C directories

D partitions

2 You organize information under the root of a hard disk partition by using _____.

A files

B folders

C directories

D partitions

3 Which command-line command is used to change the current directory?

A `dir`

B `cd`

C `md`

D `rd`

4 What `dir` command would you use to view all hidden files in C:\Windows\System32 in alphabetical order, by extension, across multiple columns?

dir c:\windows\system32 /w /a:h /o:e

5 When you're creating a directory in Windows Explorer, what is the maximum depth of the folder structure?

A 63 characters

B 254 characters

C 255 characters

D Unlimited

6 What is the difference between the command-line commands `copy` and `xcopy`?

The copy command copies one or more files to another location. The xcopy command copies files (not including hidden and system files), directories, and subdirectories.

7 When you're using the `msinfo32` command at a command prompt, what happens if you don't enter the full path?

It does not retain its command-line functionality and simply opens the System Information dialog box.

8 Which is the GUI utility that provides information on processes that are running on your computer?

A Event Viewer

B Task Manager

C System Monitor

D Windows Diagnostic

9 Which are the two additional tabs that are available in the Windows XP versions of Task Manager?

A Applications

B Networking

C Performance

D Processes

E Users

10 Which tab in Task Manager can you use to end an application that has experienced a general protection fault and isn't responding to keyboard or mouse input?

A Applications

B Networking

C Performance

D Processes

E Users

11 Which tab in Task Manager can you use to determine if an application is overloading the CPU?

A Applications

B Networking

C Performance

D Processes

12 Which area of the Performance tab in Task Manager is helpful in determining if you need to increase the size of your page file?

A Commit Memory

B CPU Usage

C PF Usage

D Physical Memory

13 If you believe an unauthorized person might be accessing a computer after hours, which Event Viewer log would you monitor?

Security

14 Which two event types are used only in the Security log?

A Error

B Warning

C Information

D Success Audit

E Failure Audit

15 You can use Event Viewer to view the events recorded on another computer. True or false?

True. You can view events on a remote computer as long as you have administrative rights on that computer.

16 In Event Viewer, what is the difference between sorting a view and filtering a view?

When you sort a view, it groups all events displayed in ascending or descending order by the column you clicked on. When you filter a view, it displays only those events that meet your selected criteria.

17 Which are valid file formats for saving an event log as a file?

A .xls

B .csv

C .evt

D .doc

E .txt

18 Where are the Registry files located in Windows XP?

In the \%systemroot%\System32\Config folder

19 Which Registry key contains file association data for application startup?

A HKEY_CLASSES_ROOT

B HKEY_CURRENT_USER

C HKEY_DYN_DATA

D HKEY_CURRENT_CONFIG

20 Which Registry key is not found in Windows XP operating system versions?

A HKEY_CLASSES_ROOT

B HKEY_CURRENT_USER

C HKEY_DYN_DATA

D HKEY_CURRENT_CONFIG

Independent practice activity

In this activity, you will practice monitoring and managing your Windows XP operating system.

1 View events recorded on your computer by the operating system.

2 Sort the events by type.

3 Create a filter to display just Warning and Error system events.

4 Return the display to all system events.

5 Save the events recorded in your System log to an Event file called SYSTEM## where ## is your assigned student number.

6 Clear all events from the System log without saving them in a file.

7 View the SYSTEM## event log file in Event Viewer.

8 Display only Error messages in the Saved System Log.

9 Close Event Viewer.

10 Run Notepad and Internet Explorer.

11 Open Task Manager.

12 Use the Applications tab to end Notepad.

13 Find the process for Internet Explorer and end it.

14 End the explorer.exe process.

15 Use the Applications tab to start a new task for explorer.exe.

16 Close Task Manager.

17 What `msinfo32` command would you use to open System Information in History view?

"C:\Program Files\Common Files\Microsoft Shared\Msinfo\msinfo32.exe" /pch

Enter the command.

18 Select each category and observe the changes listed. Use the "View changes Since" list to select a longer history view.

19 Close all open windows.

20 Use Regedit to create a backup of each of the five keys in the Registry. Save the files in the My Documents folder.

Unit 5

OS maintenance and troubleshooting

Unit time: 180 minutes

Complete this unit, and you'll know how to:

A Perform operating system maintenance tasks.

B Troubleshoot operating system problems.

Topic A: Operating system maintenance

This topic covers the following CompTIA A+ 220-603 exam objectives.

#	Objective
2.1	**Identify the fundamental principles of operating systems** • Locate and use Windows 2000, XP Professional and XP Home utilities and available switches • System Management Tools • System Restore
2.4	**Perform preventative maintenance for operating systems** • Perform preventative maintenance on Windows 2000, XP Professional and XP Home including software and Windows updates (e.g. service packs)

Maintenance tasks

Explanation

The best troubleshooting technique you can employ in your organization is preventing problems from occurring in the first place by maintaining your operating system properly. By keeping the operating system up to date and backed up, you can prevent many known problems from affecting your organization's computers and be able to recover data successfully should there be a problem.

Backup

Microsoft operating systems include a backup utility you can use to create copies of your files so that, in the event of a system failure, you can recover your data. On a bootable computer, you should back up any critical data before you begin attempting to troubleshoot any problems.

Windows Backup

Windows Backup is a GUI utility you can use to:

- Archive selected files and folders on your hard disk in another location, including on removable storage devices.
- Restore the archived files and folders to your hard disk.
- Make a copy of your computer's system state, which includes:
  — The Registry
  — Boot files
  — The COM+ class registration database
  — The IIS metadirectory
  — Windows File Protection system files
- Copy your computer's system partition, boot partition, and files needed to start up the system.

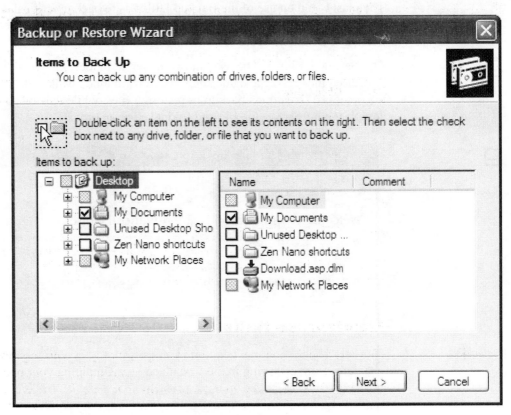

Exhibit 5-1: The Backup Utility in Windows XP

The most common use of the Backup Utility is to back up critical data and operating system files to ensure that recovery is possible in the event that files are accidentally deleted or a disaster occurs.

The Backup Utility can be used in two different modes, known as Wizard mode and Advanced mode. As the name suggests, Wizard mode walks you step by step through the process of creating a backup or restoring files, while Advanced mode provides complete control over the file and folder selection process.

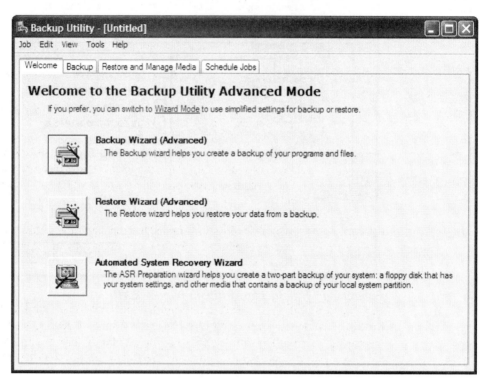

Exhibit 5-2: The Backup Utility in Advanced Mode

Backup types

The Windows Backup Utility supports five types of backups, described in the following table.

Copy backups can be used between normal and incremental backups without affecting their settings.

Type	Backup description
Copy	All selected files, but doesn't clear the archive attribute, which shows that the file has been backed up.
Daily	All selected files that have been modified the day of the daily backup. The archive attribute isn't cleared.
Differential	The selected files that have been created or modified since the last normal or incremental backup. It doesn't clear the archive attribute. Differential backups require that you have the most recent normal backup in addition to the differential backup, if you want to restore files.
Incremental	The selected files that have been created or modified since the last normal or incremental backup. An incremental backup clears the archive attribute. Incremental backups require that you have the most recent normal backup in addition to the incremental backup if you want to restore files.
Normal	All selected files. A normal backup clears the archive attribute. With a normal backup, you need only the most recent copy of the backup file to restore from backup.

The Backup Utility (accessible through System Tools) is installed with Windows 2000 Professional and Windows XP Professional. Windows XP Home Edition and Media Center include the Backup Utility, but you need to install it manually. From the Windows XP Home Edition or Media Center installation CD-ROM, navigate to ValueAdd\Msft\Ntbackup and double-click Ntbackup.msi.

You can also run the command-line utility Ntbackup to back up files and folders. If you just run Ntbackup at the command line, the Backup or Restore Wizard starts. Most likely you're going to use Ntbackup only in a *batch file*, which is one used to automate administrative tasks.

Do it!

A-1:   Backing up files using Wizard mode

Here's how	Here's why
1 If necessary, log on to your computer as **RSTADMIN##** with a password of **Pa$$321**	
2 From the C:\Student Data folder for this unit, copy **Backup.doc** to My Documents	
Close My Documents	
3 Click **Start** and choose **All Programs**, **Accessories**, **System Tools**, **Backup**	
Click **Next**	
4 Verify that "Back up files and settings" is selected	
Click **Next**	
5 Verify that My documents and settings is selected	
Click **Next**	
6 Next to Choose a place to save your backup list, click **Browse**	
Click **Cancel**	
7 Browse to select the root of D: and click **Save**	
8 In the Type a name for this backup box, enter **RSTADMIN## Backup**	
Click **Next**	You can use the Advanced button to: • Select a different backup type. • Set verification, compression, and shadow copy options. • Append to or replace the existing backup. • Schedule the backup to run at a later time.
Click **Finish**	

9 In the Backup Progress box, click **Report**

After the backup is complete. The report looks similar to the one shown here.

```
Backup Status
Operation: Backup
Active backup destination: File
Media name: "User02 Backup.bkf created 10/14/2005 at 3:04 PM"

Backup (via shadow copy) of "C: "
Backup set #1 on media #1
Backup description: "Set created 10/14/2005 at 3:04 PM"
Media name: "User02 Backup.bkf created 10/14/2005 at 3:04 PM"

Backup Type: Normal

Backup started on 10/14/2005 at 3:04 PM.
Backup completed on 10/14/2005 at 3:04 PM.
Directories: 71
Files: 166
Bytes: 17,620,382
Time:  7 seconds
```

Close Notepad

Click **Close**

Restore

Explanation

If files are erased, are overwritten, or become inaccessible because of a disk problem, you can restore them from the backup. However, because of incompatibilities among various versions of the Backup Utility, you need to restore by using the same version you used to create the backup. For example, if you created the backup by using MS-DOS's `msbackup` or a third-party utility, you can't restore by using the Windows XP Restore Wizard.

Do it!

A-2: Restoring information from a backup

Here's how	Here's why
1 Open My Documents	
Delete **Backup.doc**	
Close My Documents	
Empty the Recycle Bin	
2 Start Backup	
Click **Next**	
3 Select **Restore files and settings**	
Click **Next**	
4 In the Items to restore list, double-click **File**	
Expand RSTADMIN## Backup.bkf	
Check **C:**	
Click **Next**	The Restore Wizard gives you a summary of the settings. You can click Advanced to change them.
5 Click **Finish**	Restore creates a system restore point and then restores the files.
View the report	One file was restored.
Close Notepad and the Restore Progress dialog box	
6 Open My Documents and verify that Backup.doc was restored	
Close My Documents	

Scheduling backups

Explanation

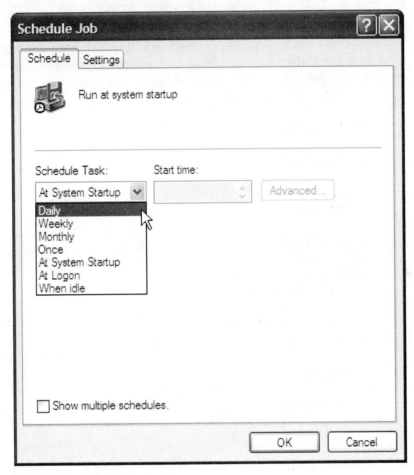

Once you've decided how often, when, and with what methods backups should be made, the Backup utility allows you to schedule them. Backups can be scheduled:

- Daily
- Weekly
- Monthly
- At predefined times
- On predefined days

Exhibit 5-3 illustrates the Schedule Job dialog box from the Advanced settings of the Backup and Restore Wizard.

Exhibit 5-3: Scheduling backups

Backing up and restoring System State data

Explanation

Besides the ability to back up normal data files and folders, the Backup Utility also allows you to backup what's referred to as System State data. This includes the following elements and conditions:

- Registry (always)
- COM+ Class Registration database (always)
- Boot files (always)
- IIS Metadirectory (if IIS is installed)
- System files (always)

For added security, you should also back up these components as part of your standard backup schedule. In the event of a system startup failure, the most common solution is to restore the System State data.

Notice that one limitation of the Backup Utility is that you can't back up individual components of the System State data. Third-party backup applications, such as Veritas Backup Exec, often allow individual component backups.

Do it!

A-3:   **Backing up System State data**

Here's how	Here's why
1 Open Backup	
2 Click **Advanced Mode**	
3 Activate the Backup tab	
4 Under My Computer, select and then check **System State**	
Observe the individual items in the details pane	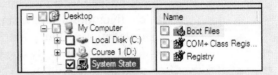
	They're grayed out. You can't pick and choose which system components to back up using this utility.
5 In the Backup media or file name box, enter **d:\systemstate.bkf**	
6 Click **Start Backup**	
In the Backup Job Information dialog box, click **Start Backup**	
7 After the Backup process is complete, click **Close**	
8 Open **My Computer**, **D:**	
Right-click **systemstate.bkf** and choose **Properties**	
From the General tab, observe the size of this file	This gives you a sense of how large a System State backup of your system is.
9 Close all open windows and dialog boxes	

System Restore

Explanation

System Restore is also covered in CompTIA A+ Certification: Essentials.

The System Restore utility in Windows XP Professional, Windows XP Home Edition, and Windows XP Media Center, creates snapshots of your computer's configuration. There are three types of snapshots:

- **System checkpoints** — Created automatically when Windows XP detects the beginning of a request to make a system configuration change.
- **Manual restore points** — Manually created by a user using the System Restore utility.
- **Installation restore points** — Created automatically when certain programs are installed.

Using the System Restore utility, you can restore your computer to a previous configuration with the settings recorded in a system checkpoint, manual restore point, or installation restore point. This selection is helpful in recovering a system that isn't functioning properly due to newly installed hardware or software or updated configuration settings. The restore process might also help you recover from a virus or worm that's infected your computer. Before you begin troubleshooting, you can create a System Restore point, so you can return the computer to its original state, if your troubleshooting solutions cause larger or additional problems.

Restoring the system

Before using System Restore to undo a change, if the change involved a hardware device, first try using Driver Rollback. It reverses fewer system changes. If Driver Rollback doesn't solve the problem, then revert the system to a restore point.

To restore the system from a restore point:

1. Click Start and choose All Programs, Accessories, System Tools, System Restore.
2. If necessary, select Restore my computer to an earlier time.
3. Click Next.
4. Select the date and time and the specific restore point, as shown in Exhibit 5-4.

   When selecting a restore point, select a point as close to the present as possible, so as few changes in the system as possible are lost.
5. Click Next twice.

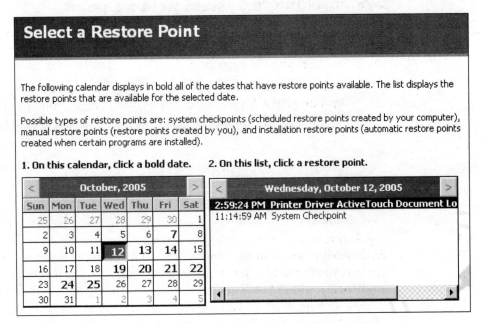

Exhibit 5-4: System Restore selection in Windows XP Professional.

Windows XP reboots and restores the system state to the settings saved in the restore point. Changes in user data aren't affected, but any installation or configuration changes made after the restore point are lost.

Be aware that System Restore doesn't replace the process of uninstalling a program. To remove the files installed by a program completely, Microsoft recommends that you remove the program by using the Add or Remove Programs utility or the program's own uninstall program.

Booting to a system restore point

If the Windows GUI won't load during normal startup, use the Advanced startup options to boot into Safe mode. You're prompted to go directly to System Restore or boot into Safe mode. Choose to boot directly to System Restore.

ConfigSafe

You can also purchase a third-party utility snapshot, utility such as ConfigSafe. ConfigSafe takes a snapshot of your computer's configuration, including:

- Configuration files (win.ini, system.ini, autexec.bat, config.sys)
- System changes
- Drives
- Directories
- Registry
- Windows desktop

You can use the ConfigSafe snapshot to restore your system to a previously working configuration. ConfigSafe is compatible with Windows 95, Windows 98, Windows Me, Windows NT, Windows 2000, and Windows XP.

A-4: Creating a System Restore point

Here's how	Here's why
1 Click **Start** and choose **All Programs**, **Accessories**, **System Tools**, **System Restore**	You'll create a restore point. It's a good idea to create a restore point before you begin making changes to troubleshoot a problem. If you implement a change that makes the problem worse, you can use System Restore to return the computer to its pre-troubleshooting state.
2 Select **Create a restore point**	
Click **Next**	
3 In the Restore point description box, enter **Pre-troubleshooting restore point**	
Click **Create**	New restore point: Tuesday, May 30, 2006 3:25:07 PM Pre-troubleshooting restore point
	Your restore point is created.
4 Click **Home**	

Do it!

A-5: Booting to System Restore

Here's how	Here's why
1 Select **Restore my computer to an earlier time** and click **Next**	Dates that have restore points available are displayed in bold on the calendar. If a particular date has multiple restore points, they're listed when you select that date. Often, if a user makes changes that cause a problem with the computer, you can use System Restore to undo the changes.
2 Select the most recent restore point and then click **Next** twice	Windows XP shuts down and restarts. The System Restore utility restores settings.
3 Log in as RSTADMIN##	The Restoration Complete dialog box shows that your computer has been successfully restored to your selected restore point.
4 Click **OK**	
5 Click **Start** and choose **All Programs**, **Accessories**, **System Tools**, **System Restore**	
Observe the task choices	To begin, select the task that you want to perform: ⦿ Restore my computer to an earlier time ◯ Create a restore point ◯ Undo my last restoration You restored your computer by using a system restore point, so you now have the ability to reverse that change. You can undo the last system restoration.
Click **Cancel**	

Windows service packs

Explanation

Microsoft periodically releases *service packs* for its Windows 2000/XP operating systems. Service packs contain several types of files:

- **Hotfixes** — Fix errors in the operating system code.
- **Security patches** — Remove security vulnerabilities in the operating system.
- **Updates** — Enhance the current operating system and some of its features, making it easier to use or adding functionality.

Service packs are free and downloadable from Microsoft's Web site. If for some reason you don't want to download the service pack, you can usually order it on CD-ROM for a small fee.

Service packs contain hotfixes, security patches, and updates, most of which are geared toward creating a more secure computing environment. The following table describes some of the feature enhancements SP2 adds to Windows XP Professional:

Feature	Description
Internet Explorer pop-up blocker	Blocks annoying pop-up windows when you're browsing the Web in Internet Explorer.
Internet Explorer Add-on Manager	Used to manage programs that have been installed as add-ons to Internet Explorer, such as Sun Java Consoles, the Google toolbar, and instant messaging programs like Yahoo! and AOL Instant Messenger.
Internet Explorer Information Bar	Provides information about sites you're visiting and any events that occur as you move from one Web page to another.
Internet Explorer download monitor	Warns you about potential hazards when you're downloading files. You can open the file, save it to hard disk, or discontinue the download.
Outlook Express updates	Provide enhanced security by protecting your computer from spammers and dangerous attachments.
Windows Security Center	Provides a central location for managing important security settings, including the Windows Firewall, Automatic Updates, and virus protection.
Windows Firewall updates	Provide a more secure and easily managed firewall.
Automatic Updates enhancements	Make it easier to stay current with Windows updates and security patches.
Windows Media Player 9	Lets you enjoy multimedia on the Web without sacrificing security.
Bluetooth support	Allows you to connect Bluetooth-enabled keyboards, PDAs, and cell phones.

You should install or reinstall any service packs as soon as possible after installing, upgrading to, or restoring Windows 2000 or Windows XP. Remember to check with your organization to see if the service packs are stored locally. This saves the time of downloading them from Microsoft's site. Be sure there's enough free disk space on the computer for the service pack files, and always back up important files on your computer before you begin installation.

Do it!

A-6: Installing a Windows XP service pack

Here's how
Provide students with the path to the installation file and the necessary user credentials. *It might be faster to have students copy the installation file to their computers and run setup locally.*	1 Follow your instructor's directions to locate the Windows XP Service Pack 2 network installation file. 2 Follow your instructor's directions to run the executable file. 3 Accept the license agreement and all the defaults. Complete the installation wizard, and restart the computer when prompted. When the computer restarts, select Not right now, and click Next. Log back on to the computer.

Windows Update

Explanation

You should install any hotfixes that were released after the current service pack. Microsoft maintains a Web site called Windows Update at http://update.microsoft.com that you can access to scan your Windows 2000 Professional or Windows XP computer for missing operating system hotfixes. To access the Windows Update site:

1 Choose Start, All Programs, Windows Update; or open Internet Explorer and choose Tools, Windows Update.

2 The Windows Update site scans your computer for the latest Windows Update software. You might be prompted to install Windows Update software that can scan your computer for the latest updates.

3 You have two choices from the main Windows Update page:

- Express — Scans your computer for critical updates only (the High Priority category). You can review the critical updates prior to installing them.

- Custom — Scans your computer for updates in three categories (High Priority, Software, and Hardware) and allows you to choose which updates you want to install.

4 Review the updates available and select the ones you want to install.

5 Click Install.

Some updates must be installed separately from all other updates and require a reboot after they're installed.

6 You might be prompted to restart your computer.

Office updates

Microsoft also maintains a Web site for updates to its Microsoft Office products at http://office.microsoft.com/officeupdate. If your organization uses Office, you should check for updates to these products. If you reinstall Office on a computer you're troubleshooting, you should also reapply any updates. The update engine on the Office Update Web site works in the same manner as the Windows Update web site.

Do it!

A-7:   Using Windows Update to install hotfixes

Here's how	Here's why
1 Click **Start** and choose **All Programs**, **Windows Update**	(You can also open Internet Explorer and choose Tools, Windows Update.) The Windows Update site scans your computer for the latest Windows Update software.
2 If prompted, install the Windows Update software	
3 Click **Express**	To scan your computer for critical updates.
Download and install any updates to Windows software and restart, when prompted	You might have to install some Windows Update components before the update process can continue.
4 Log on and access the Windows Update site again	You're going to scan for updates now that any necessary software has been installed.
Click **Express**	To scan again for critical updates.
5 Click Continue, if prompted	To validate your version of Windows.
6 If any critical updates are found, review them and then click **Install**	Depending on the updates found, you might need to install some updates separately from others.
7 If prompted, restart your computer	

Depending on your activation status, you might not be able to continue.

Automatic Updates for Windows XP

Explanation

To guarantee that you have the most recent operating system version, Windows XP is configured to scan automatically for and download updates from the Microsoft Update Web site. By default, Windows XP notifies you when an update has been downloaded and is ready for installation. You can change the default notification setting, if desired. To do so, run the Automatic Update Setup Wizard by clicking the icon in the Notification area or opening the Windows Security Center (click Start and choose All Programs, Accessories, System Tools, Security Center; under Manage Security Settings For, click Automatic Updates).

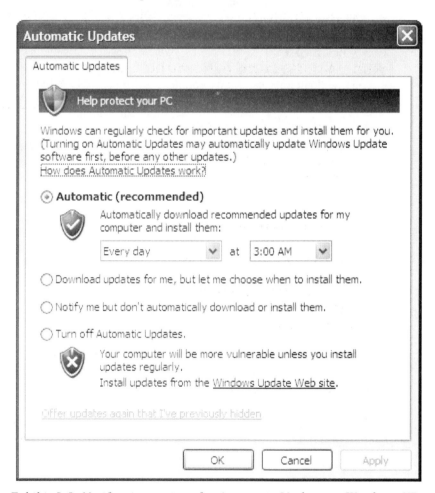

Exhibit 5-5: Notification options for Automatic Updates in Windows XP.

You have the following notification options available:

- Automatic — This choice automatically scans the computer for updates at the set time, downloads them to your computer, and then installs them.

- Download updates for me — This choice automatically scans the computer for updates, downloads them to your computer, but then prompts you that they need to be installed.

- Notify me — This choice automatically scans the computer for updates, but doesn't download them. It prompts you that updates are available for you to download and install.

- Turn off Automatic Updates — This choice disables the Automatic Updates feature.

Do it!

A-8: Configuring Automatic Updates

Here's how	Here's why
1 Click **Start** and choose **All Programs, Accessories, System Tools, Security Center**	
2 Under Manage security settings for, click **Automatic Updates**	
3 Examine the available options	
4 Select **Notify me but don't automatically download or install them.**	
5 Click **OK**	
6 Close Security Center	
7 Observe the system tray	You'll be notified that there are updates ready for your computer. This may take a few seconds.

Topic B: Operating system troubleshooting

This topic covers the following CompTIA A+ 220-603 exam objectives.

#	Objective
2.1	**Identify the fundamental principles of operating systems**
	• Locate and use Windows 2000, XP Professional and XP Home utilities and available switches
	• System Management Tools
	• MSCONFIG.EXE
	• Remote Desktop
2.3	**Identify tools, diagnostic procedures and troubleshooting techniques for operating systems**
	• Recognize and resolve common operational problems, for example:
	• Auto-restart errors
	• Bluescreen errors
	• Device drivers failure (input/output devices)
	• Application install, start or load failure
	• Recognize and resolve common error messages and codes, for example:
	• Boot (e.g. invalid boot disk, inaccessible boot devices, missing NTLDR)
	• Startup (e.g. device/service has failed to start, device/program references in registry not found)
	• Use diagnostic utilities and tools to resolve operational problems, for example:
	• Bootable media
	• Startup modes (e.g. safe mode, safe mode with command prompt or networking, step-by-step/single step mode)
	• MSCONFIG
	• Recovery CD / Recovery partition
	• Remote Desktop Connection and Assistance
	• System File Checker (SFC)

Computer startup problems

Explanation

 Computer startup problems are covered in CompTIA A+ Certification: Essentials.

There are operating system problems, which you need to troubleshoot, that manifest themselves as symptoms during computer startup. These errors can be grouped into three categories:

- Boot errors — The computer system doesn't boot successfully.
- Operating System Startup errors — The computer system boots successfully, but reports an error message when loading the operating system.
- Operating System Load errors — The computer successfully boots, but the operating system interface doesn't load properly.

Boot errors

To resolve boot errors, you need access to your computer system BIOS or CMOS, a boot disk, and disk-based utilities. You can follow the troubleshooting techniques described in the following table to identify and resolve boot errors.

Boot error	Cause	Resolution
Invalid boot or non-system disk error	A floppy or CD-ROM that isn't bootable is in a bootable drive.	Check for a disk in the floppy or CD-ROM drive.
	The system BIOS or CMOS is not configured properly to boot to the hard disk.	Verify that system BIOS or CMOS boot-order settings are correct.
	The hard disk drive doesn't have the Windows boot files on it.	Depending on the OS, boot from your emergency repair disk, your Windows installation CD-ROM, or your restore CD.
	The hard disk drive isn't connected properly.	If the computer was moved recently or if the hard drive was just installed, check that the hard disk is properly connected to the computer.
	The hard disk is bad.	If the previous solutions fail to resolve the problem, the hard disk drive might be bad and need to be replaced.
Inaccessible boot device	The system BIOS or CMOS is not configured properly to boot to the hard disk.	Verify that system BIOS or CMOS boot-order settings are correct.
	The hard disk drive isn't connected properly.	If the computer was moved recently or if the hard drive was just installed, check that the hard disk is properly connected to the computer.
	The motherboard was recently changed, or you moved the Windows system disk to another computer with a different motherboard.	Reinstall Windows to fix the Registry entries and drivers for the mass storage controller hardware. You might be able to use a Microsoft generic driver until you can find the proper driver.
	The hard disk is bad.	If the previous solutions fail to resolve the problem, the hard disk drive might be bad and might need to be replaced.
NTLDR is missing or Couldn't find NTLDR	A floppy or CD-ROM that isn't bootable is in a bootable drive.	Check for a disk in the floppy or CD-ROM drive.
	The system BIOS or CMOS isn't configured properly to boot to the hard disk.	Verify that system BIOS or CMOS boot-order settings are correct.

Boot error	Cause	Resolution
	The boot.ini file is configured incorrectly.	View the contents of boot.ini. Edit, if necessary.
	The Ntldr file is missing or corrupt.	Copy the Ntldr file from the Windows installation CD-ROM, a Windows boot disk, or another computer. If other Windows files are missing or corrupt, you might have to reinstall the operating system to resolve the problem.
	The hard disk drive isn't connected properly.	If the computer was moved recently or if the hard drive was just installed, check that the hard disk is properly connected to the computer.
	There's a corrupt boot sector or MBR.	There might be a virus. Use your virus removal software.
	You're trying to upgrade from FAT32 to a Windows version that doesn't support FAT32.	Boot into the previous version of the operating system, back up data, and complete a fresh installation of the new operating system.
	The hard disk is bad.	If the previous solutions fail to resolve the problem, the hard disk drive might be bad and need to be replaced.
Bad or missing Command interpreter	A floppy or CD-ROM that isn't bootable is in a bootable drive.	Check for a disk in the floppy or CD-ROM drive.
	The system BIOS or CMOS isn't configured properly to boot to the hard disk.	Verify that system BIOS or CMOS boot-order settings are correct.
	The command.com, msdos.sys, io.sys, or drvspace file was deleted, was renamed, or has become corrupt.	Boot the computer by using a boot disk. Replace the missing or corrupt file.
	The hard disk is bad.	If the previous solutions fail to resolve the problem, the hard disk drive might be bad and might need to be replaced.

Startup errors

To identify and resolve startup errors, you can use troubleshooting techniques described in the following table:

Startup message	Cause	Resolution
Error in CONFIG.SYS line ##	There's a problem with the specified line in the config.sys file.	View the specified line in config.sys. Look for typing errors or calls to files that don't exist. Edit as necessary to resolve the problem.
Himem.sys not loaded	The himem.sys file is missing or corrupt.	Copy a new version of himem.sys to the hard disk. Verify that the reference to himem.sys is correct in config.sys.
	There's a problem with physical memory.	If the above solution fails to solve the problem, your physical memory might be bad and need to be replaced. Himem.sys runs a check on RAM and can't do so, if a RAM chip is bad.
Missing or corrupt Himem.sys	The himem.sys file is missing or corrupt.	Copy a new version of himem.sys to the hard disk. Verify that the reference to himem.sys is correct in config.sys.
	There's a problem with physical memory.	If the above solution fails to solve the problem, your physical memory might be bad and need to be replaced. Himem.sys runs a check on RAM and can't do so if a RAM chip is bad.
Device/service has failed to start	Windows is trying to load a device or service that won't load properly.	Check the Event Viewer logs to determine which device or service failed to load. Check the installation or configuration of the device (by using Device Manager) or service (by using the Services MMC). Reinstall the device or service if necessary.

Operating system load errors

Common operating system load errors and troubleshooting techniques include the following:

Error	Cause	Resolution
Failure to start GUI	Explorer.exe is missing or corrupt.	Copy Explorer.exe from the Windows installation CD-ROM, a Windows boot disk, or another computer. If other Windows files are missing or corrupt, you might have to reinstall the operating system to resolve the problem.
Windows Protection Error—illegal operation	An application asks the operating system to process an operation that the OS doesn't recognize.	Illegal-operation messages typically have an error code or something else you can use to research the exact cause and resolution of the specific error.
	Outdated device drivers need to be updated.	If the device driver is being loaded by the operating system at Startup, try to boot into Safe Mode and roll back or update the driver.
		If the illegal operation causes a general protection fault (GPF), you might need to reboot the computer.
		An incorrect or corrupt device driver can also cause an auto-restart error, where the computer reboots automatically when it tries to load the driver. Once you identify the driver causing the problem, you need to replace it.
User-modified settings cause improper operation at startup	The user has changed a system setting that causes the computer to hang at startup.	If available, boot using one of the Startup modes to reverse the changes. On Windows XP computers, roll back to a System Restore point.
Application install, start or load failure	An attempt is made to install or start an application that isn't compatible with the operating system.	Research the application to see if a patch is available that allows it to run on your operating system. You might need to upgrade the application to one whose coding functions according to the application rules of your operating system.
Device/program reference in registry not found	The operating system is attempting to load a device or program whose information isn't found in the Registry.	Reinstall the device or program to attempt to update the Registry with the correct information.

Remind students that a general protection fault (GPF) is also referred to a the blue screen of death (BSOD).

System lockups

When applications compete for the same memory space, a conflict can occur. Memory conflicts can cause an application or your entire system to stop responding. This situation is called a *system lockup*. There are two types of system lockups:

- **Soft lockup** — The computer stops responding, but the mouse and keyboard continue to function properly.
- **Hard lockup** — The computer stops responding, and the mouse and the keyboard aren't functioning. (Pressing the Num Lock, Caps Lock, or Scroll Lock key doesn't light up the indicator LEDs on the keyboard.)

Additional reasons that a computer might stop responding include the following:

- Too many programs are running simultaneously.
- There isn't enough memory to support the running programs.
- The computer is infected with a virus.
- Data is too fragmented on the hard drive.
- Software is corrupt or misconfigured.
- A hardware device driver is corrupt.
- A hardware device has failed.
- There's a power management or screen saver problem.
- Operating temperatures and humidity levels are improper.

Recovering from a soft lockup

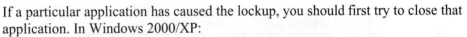

If a particular application has caused the lockup, you should first try to close that application. In Windows 2000/XP:

1 Press Ctrl+Alt+Delete to open the Windows Task Manager. (If your mouse is functioning, you can also right-click the taskbar and choose Task Manager.)
2 Activate the Applications tab.
3 Observe the Status column.
4 Select the application whose status is listed as "Not responding."
5 Click End Task.
6 If prompted, click End Task again.

Any data that hasn't been saved when you shut down an application through the End Task button is lost. Some applications use temporary files and might be able to recover some of the data.

Recovering from a hard lockup

With a hard lockup, when you press Ctrl+Alt+Delete, nothing happens. If you can't close a nonresponsive application by using Task Manager, you might have to force a system shutdown. On most computers, you do this by pressing and holding the power button until the system turns off. (Pressing Ctrl+Alt+Delete repeatedly might cause the system to restart, but if it doesn't, you have to shut down the system by pressing and holding down the power button.) A forced shutdown isn't preferred, because Windows can't save any settings, but sometimes it's the only option.

General protection faults

A *general protection fault* (GPF) occurs when one application tries to access memory that's being used by another application or that's invalid. A GPF can cause a single application to crash or can force a reboot of Windows. GPFs are sometimes referred to as the *blue screen of death (BSOD)*, because they cause Windows to shut down immediately and improperly and display a blue screen with an error message. The computer must then be powered off and back on.

To resolve persistent GPFs, try the following:

- Remove all Terminate and Stay Resident programs (TSRs).
- Delete all program temporary files.
- Use ScanDisk to scan your hard disk for errors.
- Defragment your hard disk.
- Verify that your computer has more than 200 MB of available hard disk space.
- Uninstall or reinstall any recently installed software or hardware.
- If your computer uses an external cache, disable it through the computer's CMOS.
- Disable power management features and screen savers.
- Attempt to reinstall your operating system, or repair system files.
- Have your computer's RAM tested to determine if it's bad.

Do it!

B-1: Troubleshooting operating system startup errors

Questions and answers

Although this material is covered in CompTIA A+ Certification: Essentials, the troubleshooting problems in this activity are different from the ones in the prerequisite course.

1 You recently installed a new hard disk in a user's computer. You installed Windows XP Professional, the needed applications, and then copied over the user's data. The computer was functioning just fine in your office. You delivered it to the user's office and, when you started it up, you receive the message, "NTLDR is missing." What do you suspect might be the likely cause?

When you connected the new hard disk, the connections weren't made tightly. When you transported the computer from one place to the other, the connections loosened just enough to prevent the hard disk from functioning.

2 If your first solution doesn't resolve the problem, what's another likely cause of the "Missing NTLDR" message?

- *When installing applications or moving over the user's data, you left a floppy or CD-ROM that isn't bootable in a bootable drive.*

3 You're installing Windows XP on a computer for a user. When you start Windows XP, it loads the desktop, but then you receive a Windows Protection Error—illegal operation. Each time you restart the computer, the same thing happens. What do you suspect is the problem and how could you resolve it?

   The computer might be using an outdated device driver for a device on the computer that loads during startup, or the computer contains a device that isn't compatible with Windows XP.

   - *Boot into Safe mode:*

     – *Check the Event Logs to see if an error was recorded about a device or service not starting.*

     – *Check Device Manager to see if there's a warning or error icon next to a device.*

     – *Run the Windows XP compatibility wizard to determine if there's a device that's installed on the computer that isn't supported.*

   - *Use Device Manager's Update Driver Wizard to fix a device driver problem.*

4 A user calls the Help desk and tells you that he is working in Word and can't get it to take any input from the keyboard or mouse. What should you ask him?

   "Can you switch to the desktop or another application where the mouse or keyboard will work?"

5 If the user tells you that s/he can switch to the desktop by right-clicking the taskbar and choosing Show the Desktop, what would you recommend?

   A soft lockup is occurring. The user should right-click the taskbar and choose Task Manager. On the Applications tab, select Word Not Responding and click End Task twice. Close Task Manager. The user can then reopen Word and use its automatic recovery feature to recover some of the data that was lost at the time of the lockup.

6 If the user tells you that the mouse isn't responding, what would you recommend?

   Ask the user to press Ctrl+Alt+Delete to see if the keyboard is functioning and if Task Manager opens. If the keyboard is functioning, the user can end the Word application in Task Manager.

7 If the user tells you that s/he's pressed Ctrl+Alt+Delete several times and there's no response, what do you recommend?

   The system is probably in a hard lockup and must be restarted by pressing and holding the computer's power button until it cycles off. The user can then use the power button to restart the computer, and then reopen Word and use its automatic recovery feature.

Startup modes

Explanation

Startup modes are covered in CompTIA A+ Certification: Essentials.

Each Windows operating system includes alternative startup modes you can use to diagnose and fix startup problems or driver and application failures. To access the menu for the startup modes, boot the computer and press F8 after you hear your computer's startup beep. You should press F8 during the first few moments of the boot process—before the Windows logo/splash screen is displayed.

Startup mode	Description
Safe mode	Boots the computer with a minimum configuration, such as mouse, keyboard, and standard VGA device drivers. Can be used to solve problems with a new hardware installation or problems caused by user settings.
Safe mode with networking	Boots the computer with a minimum configuration, plus networking devices and drivers. Use Safe mode with networking when files that you need to resolve problems, such as your installation or driver files, are on stored on the network.
Safe mode with command prompt	If Safe mode doesn't load the operating system, you can try this startup mode to get a command prompt. You can then use your MS-DOS-based utilities to troubleshoot and resolve startup problems.
Enable boot logging	The operating system loads normally. All files used during the boot process are recorded in a file called Ntbtlog.txt. If you're having a problem with a device, you can check Ntbtlog.txt to see which devices loaded successfully and which didn't.
Enable VGA mode	Boots the operating system using a generic VGA display driver. You can use this mode to correct improper video or display settings or to fix a nonfunctioning video driver.
Last Known Good Configuration	Uses the boot settings stored in the Registry from the last successful boot. If the system was configured incorrectly, you can use this option to reverse all system setting changes made after the last successful boot.
Debugging mode	Allows you to move system boot logs via a serial port from a failing computer to another computer for evaluation. This option sends the boot information to the serial port.
Start Windows normally	Boots the computer as if you hadn't entered the Advanced boot options menu.

TIPS ✔ *Boot logging is most effective if you have a copy of ntbtlog.txt that recorded a non-problematic startup.*

Boot.ini switches

You can add switches to your boot.ini file to change the startup configuration of Windows 2000 Professional and Windows XP. These switches were originally designed for use on Windows NT systems. Some of the more commonly used switches are described in the following table:

Switch	Description
/basevideo	Loads the Windows GUI with a display of 640×480, 16-color VGA mode. Use this switch if the wrong video resolution or refresh rate is set.
/baudrate=####	Use to debug a modem. Typically for modem debugging, #### is set to 9600. The default baud rate is 19,200, if not set.
/crashdebug	If you're having problems with a COM port, use this switch to enable the COM port for debugging in case Windows NT crashes. When Windows NT Workstation is running in this mode, the COM port is available for normal use, but if Windows NT Workstation crashes, the port is converted to a debug port for remote troubleshooting.
/debug	Enables the COM port for kernel debugging. While Windows NT Workstation is running in this mode, the COM port can't be used for normal use.
/debugport=com#	Changes the default debugging port from COM1 to another specified COM port.
/maxmem=##	Specifies the amount of memory Windows NT Workstation detects and uses at startup. You can use this switch to check for bad memory chips. Never set maxmem to less than 12.
/noserialmice:com#	Disables the mouse-port check for the specified COM port. If no COM port is specified, the mouse is disabled on all COM ports. (Not available in Windows 2000 Professional and Windows XP.)
/sos	During Windows NT Workstation startup, the progress dots are replaced by a list of the individual drivers that are loaded.
/win95	Loads the bootsec.dos file. NTLDR uses this file to boot to Windows 95 instead of to Windows NT Workstation 4.0. (Not available in Windows 2000 Professional and Windows XP.)
/win95dos	Loads the bootsec.w40 file. NTLDR uses this file to boot to MS-DOS instead of to Windows NT Workstation 4.0. (Not available in Windows 2000 Professional and Windows XP.)

Do it!

B-2: Booting the computer in various startup modes

Although this material is covered in *CompTIA A+ Certification: Essentials*, the startup mode in this activity is different from the one in the prerequisite course.

Here's how	Here's why
1 A user has changed the display driver, and now the screen is blank. How can you fix the problem?	*Boot into Safe mode, which loads a generic VGA display driver. Change the display driver and reboot the computer normally.*
2 If you keep a copy of all drivers on a file server on your network, which startup mode must you use to access the driver?	*Safe mode with networking.*
3 Click **Start** and choose **Turn Off Computer**	You'll boot the computer into Safe mode with networking for troubleshooting a problem, such as replacing an incorrect device driver from a network location.
Click **Restart**	Make sure you watch the computer screen carefully so you know when to press F8 in the next step.
4 After the Windows shutdown screen disappears and the black startup screen displays, press `F8`	You might need to press it more than once to get the correct timing to display the operating system start menu.
If necessary, press `F8` again	To display the Windows Advanced Options Menu.
Observe the menu choices	
Press `↓` four times	To select Safe mode with networking.
Press `↵ ENTER`	
Press `↵ ENTER`	To select Microsoft Windows XP Professional from the operating system start menu. You can see the list of files and drivers loaded during Safe-mode with networking startup.
5 Click **Administrator**	
In the Type your password box, enter **Pa$$321** and then click the white arrow	To log on as an administrator. The Administrator user has a wider range of permissions to troubleshoot a computer problem than a regular user.
6 Click **Yes**	To begin working in Safe mode.
Observe the desktop	It appears with a plain black background with white Safe-mode text in all four corners.

When the highlight gets to the end of the list, it scrolls to the top again.

7 Open **Windows Explorer**

   Expand My Computer

You have access to local disks in Safe mode and Safe mode with networking.

   Expand My Network Places, Entire Network, and select **Microsoft Windows Network**

You're able to browse the network because Safe mode with networking loads networking drivers. If you don't need to access files on the network, you should boot into Safe mode, so that the networking drivers don't load.

   Click **OK**

8 Close Windows Explorer

You can make any changes on the local system to solve your problem. If there were a display driver problem, you could right-click the desktop and choose Properties. Activate the Settings tab. Make the desired changes and then reboot the computer normally.

9 Restart the computer in Safe Mode with Command Prompt

If booting the computer into Safe mode doesn't load the GUI, you can use the Safe Mode with Command Prompt and use command-line tools to fix the problem.

   Log on as **Administrator** with a password of **Pa$$321**

You have access to a Command Prompt window.

   Enter **shutdown –s**

To shut down the computer from the command prompt.

You receive a message that the system is shutting down. A timer shows you how long until the system shuts down. The computer powers off.

10 Turn the computer on, boot Windows XP normally, and log on as RSTADMIN##

System Configuration Utility

Explanation

The System Configuration Utility is covered in CompTIA A+ Certification: Essentials.

Using the System Configuration Utility, also called Msconfig, you can view, disable, and enable services and software that run at startup. Msconfig.exe is included with Windows XP. You can use the Windows XP version on a Windows 2000 Professional computer.

The System Configuration Utility, as shown in Exhibit 5-6, makes it easier to resolve startup issues with your operating system. In this utility, you check and clear check boxes to enable or disable startup configuration options, as opposed to using a text editor to edit startup files manually. Using the check boxes, you can quickly make configuration changes to test solutions to a startup problem.

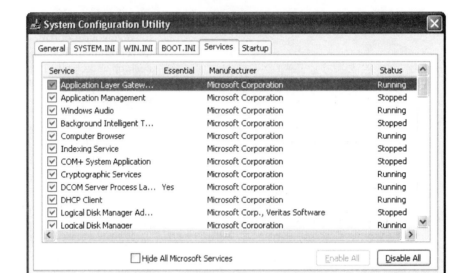

Exhibit 5-6: The Services page of the System Configuration Utility in Windows XP Professional

To start the System Configuration Utility, click Start, choose Run, type msconfig, and click OK.

Startup modes for troubleshooting

The General tab of the System Configuration Utility allows you to start the computer in any of three modes when troubleshooting:

- **Normal Startup** — Loads all device drivers and services.
- **Diagnostic Startup** — Loads only basic devices and services.
- **Selective Startup** — Loads only the files and services you select. In Windows XP, the choices are:
  - System.ini
  - Win.ini
  - System services
  - Startup items
  - Choice of boot.ini file

To prevent individual lines or items in a specific configuration file from loading, activate the tab for the desired configuration file and clear the check box next to the line or item that you don't want to load.

When you're done troubleshooting, you need to verify that all of the configuration files and all of the items that are listed in those files are loaded. Then activate the General tab and select Normal Startup.

Do it!

B-3: Using the System Configuration Utility

Here's how	Here's why
1 Click **Start** and choose **Run...** Enter **msconfig** and click **OK**	You'll see how you can use the System Configuration utility to troubleshoot startup problems with Windows XP.
2 Observe the General tab	Startup Selection ◉ Normal Startup - load all device drivers and services ○ Diagnostic Startup - load basic devices and services only ○ Selective Startup ☑ Process SYSTEM.INI File ☑ Process WIN.INI File ☑ Load System Services ☑ Load Startup Items ◉ Use Original BOOT.INI ○ Use Modified BOOT.INI
	You can use this tab to boot into a diagnostic mode without having to use the F8 key.
Select **Diagnostic Startup**	To load just basic devices and services.
Click **OK**	
3 Click **Restart**	The computer boots into a diagnostic mode without your having to press F8 at startup.
Log on as RSTADMIN##	A message states that you've configured Windows to start in a special diagnostic mode.

4 Click **OK**	The System Configuration Utility is open. You must switch back to Normal Startup after you're done troubleshooting.
5 Select **Normal Startup**	To load all device drivers and services.
Click **OK**	
When prompted, restart the computer and log in as RSTADMIN##	
6 Run msconfig	
7 Activate the SYSTEM.INI tab	Each item listed corresponds with a line in the system.ini configuration file. Enabling and disabling lines by using this interface decreases the chances of typing errors.
Expand [drivers] and [386enh]	
	You can enable and disable items in system.ini. You can also add new items.
8 Click **Start** and choose **Run...**	You'll compare the contents of the SYSTEM.INI tab with the lines in the system.ini file.
In the Open box, enter **notepad ▶ c:\windows\system.ini**	To open the system.ini file in Notepad.
Click **OK**	
9 Compare the contents of the system.ini file in Notepad with the contents of the SYSTEM.INI tab in the System Configuration Utility	
Close Notepad	

10 With **; for 16-bit app support** selected, click **Disable**

With **;msconfig; for 16-bit app support** selected, click **Enable**

11 Activate the WIN.INI tab

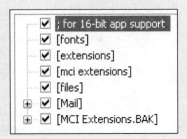

On this tab, you can enable and disable lines in the win.ini file. You can also add new items.

12 Activate the BOOT.INI tab

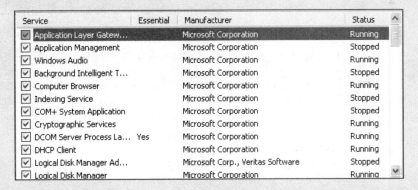

You use this tab to enable boot.ini switches, such as /SAFEBOOT. You can also check your boot path.

13 Activate the Services tab

Service	Essential	Manufacturer	Status
Application Layer Gatew...		Microsoft Corporation	Running
Application Management		Microsoft Corporation	Stopped
Windows Audio		Microsoft Corporation	Running
Background Intelligent T...		Microsoft Corporation	Stopped
Computer Browser		Microsoft Corporation	Running
Indexing Service		Microsoft Corporation	Stopped
COM+ System Application		Microsoft Corporation	Stopped
Cryptographic Services		Microsoft Corporation	Running
DCOM Server Process La...	Yes	Microsoft Corporation	Running
DHCP Client		Microsoft Corporation	Running
Logical Disk Manager Ad...		Microsoft Corp., Veritas Software	Stopped
Logical Disk Manager		Microsoft Corporation	Running

Here you can enable and disable individual services. The status of each service is listed, so you can see which services are running or stopped, as shown here.

14 Activate the Startup tab

You can disable items in your Startup group.

15 Click **OK**

To close System Configuration Utility and save changes.

When prompted, restart the computer and log in as RSTADMIN##

Bootable media

Explanation

There are also various bootable media that you can use to boot a computer that's experiencing startup problems.

- **Startup disks** — In all Microsoft systems, you can create a startup disk (also called a boot disk) that you can use to boot the computer to an operating system, if it won't boot from the hard disk.

- **Emergency Repair Disks** — An Emergency Repair Disk (ERD), available in Windows 2000 Professional, contains basic files that you can use to restore your computer to a bootable state, if your Registry is damaged or if the operating system is on an NTFS partition that isn't successfully booting.

- **Automated System Recovery** — In Windows XP Professional, you can use the Automated System Recover (ASR) to recover from a system failure caused by problems with the system/boot volume, such as Registry corruption.

- **Recovery CDs** — Many computer manufacturers ship their computers with recovery CDs. You can use these CDs to reinstall the computer to the state it was when it was shipped to you.

Startup disks

Startup or boot disks are useful tools for troubleshooting boot problems. You should create a startup or boot disk for each of your operating systems before there's a problem.

MS-DOS startup disk

Using Windows Explorer in Windows XP, you can create an MS-DOS startup disk that can be used to boot into MS-DOS mode, giving you an A: prompt. This bootable disk is sometimes needed when you're following a BIOS manufacturer's procedure to update (or flash) the BIOS. The disk can be useful if the computer doesn't boot, the hard drive is formatted as FAT, and you need to access the drive to recover or replace files.

To create an MS-DOS startup disk:

1. Insert a floppy disk in your computer's disk drive.
2. Open Windows Explorer.
3. Expand My Computer.
4. Right-click 3 ½ Floppy (A:) and choose Format.
5. Check "Create an MS-DOS startup disk."
6. Click Start and click OK.
7. When the format process is finished, click OK.
8. Click Close.

You can also create an MS-DOS boot disk in MS-DOS:

1. Boot to MS-DOS.
2. Insert a floppy disk in your computer's disk drive.
3. Enter `format a: /s`
   This command formats the disk and copies the basic MS-DOS system files to it.
4. Press Enter twice.
5. Enter N.

This procedure copies io.sys, msdos.sys, command.com, and drvspace.bin to the disk. You can use the `copy` command to copy the following MS-DOS external commands to your disk. These commands are helpful to have on your MS-DOS boot disk for troubleshooting:

- Fdisk.exe
- Format.com
- Edit.com and Qbasic.exe
- Xcopy.exe
- Attrib.exe

To help you access additional computer resources, such as the CD-ROM drive, your internal network, and memory, you might also want to consider putting these additional files on your disk:

- MS-DOS drivers for your CD-ROM drive
- MS-DOS drivers for your NIC
- Himem.sys
- Emm386.exe
- Mem.exe
- Memmaker.exe

Windows 2000/XP startup disk

Windows 2000/XP startup disks are covered in CompTIA A+ Certification: Essentials.

You can create a startup disk for Windows 2000 Professional and any Windows XP version. You can use this startup disk to access an NTFS or FAT drive when trying to recover from the following startup problems:

- The startup sector is corrupt.
- The MBR is corrupt.
- Your computer has been infected by a virus or worm.
- NTLDR or Ntdetect.com is missing or corrupt.
- The Ntstartupdd.sys driver is incorrect.

Unlike the MS-DOS startup disk, which holds the MS-DOS operating system, a Windows 2000/XP startup disk holds a few key operating system files—just enough to get the operating system up and pointed to the remainder of the files on your hard disk. To use a Windows 2000 startup disk, you must be able to access the \WINNT or \WINDOWS folder on your hard disk.

To create a Windows 2000/XP startup disk:

1 Insert a floppy disk in your computer's disk drive.

2 Open Windows Explorer.

3 Expand My Computer.

4 Right-click 3 ½ Floppy (A:) and choose Format. (You must format the disk by using the GUI—this modifies the boot sector of the disk so the system can run the boot files.)

5 Copy the following files from C:\WINNT or C:\ to the startup disk:

- NTLDR
- Ntdetect.com
- Boot.ini

If present, copy:

- Bootsect.dos
- Ntbootdd.sys

Do it!

B-4:   Creating an MS-DOS startup disk

Students created a Windows XP startup disk in CompTIA A+ Certification: Essentials.

Here's how	Here's why
1 Insert a disk in your computer's floppy drive	You'll create an MS-DOS startup disk. If the files become corrupt or damaged, you can use a startup disk to boot the computer, use MS-DOS commands to repair the problem.
2 Open Windows Explorer Expand My Computer	
3 Right-click **3 ½ Floppy (A:)** and choose **Format...**	
4 Check "Create an MS-DOS startup disk"	
5 Click **Start** and click **OK**	To format the disk.
Click **OK**	To acknowledge the Format Complete message.
Click **Close**	
6 With your 3.5" disk in drive A:, click **Start** and choose **Turn Off Computer**	
Click **Restart**	Watch the light on your floppy disk drive as the computer restarts. Your computer boots from the files on the floppy disk and then loads the MS-DOS operating system from the floppy disk. You have an A: prompt and could access FAT drives on the computer.
7 Remove the disk from drive A: Restart the computer and log back on as RSTADMIN##	

Recovery Console

Explanation

Recovery Console is covered in CompTIA A+ Certification: Essentials.

The Windows Recovery Console can help you recover when your Windows 2000 Professional or Windows XP computer doesn't start properly or at all. Using the Recovery Console, you can access FAT, FAT32, and NTFS volumes from a command line without the Windows GUI. You can then:

- Repair the boot sector.
- Replace missing or corrupt operating system files.
- Create and format partitions.
- Enable or disable services or devices.

When you're working with the command line in the Recovery Console, you have access to only these folders:

- The root folder
- The *%systemroot%* folder and the subfolders of the Windows XP or Windows 2000 Professional installation you selected when loading the Recovery Console
- The Cmdcons folder
- Removable media drives, such as CD-ROM and DVD drives

Windows 2000 Professional

To run the Recovery Console in Windows 2000 Professional:

1 Boot your computer using your Windows 2000 Professional installation CD-ROM.
2 When prompted to install Windows 2000 Professional, press Enter.
3 Press R and then press C.
4 Select the desired Windows 2000 installation.
5 Enter the administrator recovery password.
6 Use the command prompt to implement recovery solutions. (You can type Help at the command prompt to view the available commands.)
7 When finished, remove the Windows 2000 Professional CD-ROM.
8 Type Exit and press Enter. The system reboots normally.

Windows XP

To run the Recovery Console in Windows XP:

1 Boot your computer using your Windows XP installation CD-ROM.
2 On the Welcome to Setup screen, press R.
3 If necessary, select the desired Windows installation.
4 Enter the administrator recovery password.
5 Use the command prompt to implement recovery solutions. (You can type Help at the command prompt to view the available commands.)
6 When finished, remove the Windows XP CD-ROM.
7 Type Exit and press Enter. The system reboots normally.

B-5: Running the Recovery Console

Here's how	Here's why
1 Insert the Windows XP installation CD into your computer's CD-ROM drive	In this activity, you'll boot into the Recovery Console. Your computer has been configured to boot from the floppy drive, the CD-ROM drive, and then the hard drive.
2 Click **Start** and choose **Turn Off Computer** Click **Turn Off**	
3 Turn the computer on	
4 When you see the message, "Press any key to boot from CD," press SPACEBAR	Windows Setup begins. It detects that you have a current installation of Windows XP Professional on the computer.
5 When you see the "Welcome to Setup" screen, press R	To start the Recovery Console.
Type **1** and press ENTER	To select the first installation of Windows XP.
For the Administrator password, type **Pa$$321** and press ENTER	You're at the C:\Windows prompt. You now have access to the FAT, FAT32, and NTFS volumes from the command line. You can use command-line utilities to repair the boot sector, replace missing or corrupt operating system files, create and format partitions, or enable or disable services or devices.
6 Type **Exit** and press ENTER	To exit the Recovery Console and restart Windows. When prompted, don't boot from CD.
7 Log in as RSTADMIN##	
8 Remove the Windows XP installation CD	If the Windows XP installation CD autostarts before you get a chance to remove it, close the window and then remove the CD from the drive.

Emergency Repair Disks

Explanation

 ERD and ASR are covered in CompTIA A+ Certification: Essentials.

An Emergency Repair Disk (ERD) contains basic system configuration files that you can use to restore your computer to a bootable state, if your Registry is damaged or if the operating system is on an NTFS partition that isn't successfully booting. When you create an ERD, basic system configuration information from the Registry is placed on the disk and in the *%systemroot%*Repair folder on the hard disk. An ERD isn't bootable, but when it's used with the Windows installation CD-ROM, it allows you to boot a nonfunctioning computer and restore critical system files and information from the Registry. An ERD can help you:

- Inspect and repair the boot sector.
- Inspect and repair the startup environment.
- Verify Windows 2000 system files and replace missing or damaged files.

Whenever you make configuration changes on your computer—such as installing new software, changing software configuration, changing the network configuration, changing hardware, or installing operating system updates—you should update your ERD and repair information. Note that the ERD isn't a substitute for a full Registry backup.

In Windows XP Professional, the emergency repair feature is called Automated System Recovery (ASR). There''is no equivalent feature in other Windows XP versions.

Windows 2000 Professional ERD

To create an Emergency Repair Disk in Windows 2000 Professional:

1. Click Start and choose Programs, Accessories, System Tools, Backup.
2. Choose Tools, Create an Emergency Repair Disk.
3. Insert a floppy disk in the disk drive.
4. Check "Also back up the registry to the repair directory."
5. Click OK twice.
6. Close Backup.

Contents of the Windows 2000 ERD include:

File	Description
Autoexec.nt	Initializes the MS-DOS environment.
Config.nt	Initializes the MS-DOS environment.
Setup.log	Contains cyclical redundancy check information for core Windows 2000 Professional files.

The Windows 2000 ERD doesn't include Registry information. If you choose to back up the Registry also, the ERD creation process creates a *%systemroot%*Repair\RegBack directory on your hard disk and places the Registry files in there.

To use the Emergency Repair process:

1. Boot your computer using your Windows 2000 Professional installation CD-ROM.
2. When prompted to install Windows 2000 Professional, press Enter.

3　Press R twice.

4　Select the desired repair option: Fast or Manual.

The Fast option repairs system files, boot sector problems, and Registry hives and has no user interaction.

The Manual option allows you to choose any of the following:

- Inspect Setup Environment
- Verify Windows 2000 System Files
- Inspect Boot Sector

5　Press Enter to use the Emergency Repair Diskette.

6　Insert the Emergency Repair Diskette and press Enter.

7　If prompted, enter the Windows 2000 Professional installation CD-ROM.

8　When prompted, remove the ERD.

9　After the files have been repaired, reboot the operating system.

Automated System Recovery

In Windows XP Professional, you can use the Automated System Recovery Wizard to create a backup of your system partition and a floppy disk containing critical system settings. You can then use ASR to recover from a system failure caused by problems with the system/boot volume, such as Registry corruption. When you recover from a system failure by using ASR, it:

1　Restores the disk configurations.

2　Formats your system and boot volumes.

3　Installs a bare-bones version of Windows.

4　Runs Backup to rebuild your system and boot volumes from your ASR backup set.

ASR should be used as your last attempt to recover a system, after you try other recovery methods, such as the Last Known Good Configuration. ASR formats your system and boot volumes and doesn't restore user data. The ASR backup files don't include user data—you need to reinstate user data from another backup source.

To create an ASR recovery set:

1　Format a floppy disk.

2　Click Start and choose All Programs, Accessories, System Tools, Windows Backup.

3　Click Advanced Mode.

4　Click Automated System Recovery Wizard and click Next.

5　In the "Backup media or file name" box, enter the location for your backup.

6　Click Next and then click Finish.

7　When prompted, insert the formatted floppy disk and click OK.

8　When prompted, remove the disk, label it "ASR" with the computer name, date, and time, and click OK.

9　Click Close.

10　Close Backup.

Automated System Recovery isn't available in Windows XP Home Edition or Media Center.

To use your ASR recovery set to resolve a system failure:

1 Boot the computer using your Windows XP installation CD-ROM.

2 If you have a third-party driver for the backup storage device, press F6 to install the driver.

3 When prompted to perform an ASR, press F2. (Watch the screen carefully for this prompt; it doesn't stay on the screen very long.)

4 When prompted, insert the ASR floppy disk.

5 When prompted, specify the location of your ASR backup set.

6 When the ASR is complete, log on.

Recovery CDs

Many computer manufacturers ship their computers with recovery CDs. These CDs contain a restore program to reinstall the computer to the state it was in when it was shipped to the customer. If you want to return the computer to its original state, you can boot to the recovery CD and follow the prompts in the manufacturer's restore program. Typically, a recovery CD program:

- Repartitions and formats the hard disk.

- Reinstalls the operating system.

- Installs any manufacturers' drivers for the computer's hardware.

- Installs any software shipped with the computer.

Do it!

B-6: Creating an ASR set

Students have a formatted NTFS simple volume. Its capacity is at least 4 GB. If students don't have this volume, have them create it before completing this activity. Also, you might need to delete any files currently on the volume.

Here's how	Here's why
1 Insert a 3.5" disk in your floppy disk drive Format the disk	
2 Click **Start** and choose **All Programs, Accessories, System Tools, Backup** Click **Advanced Mode**	
3 Click	To start the Automated System Recovery Preparation Wizard.
4 Click **Next**	

If students' drive isn't D:, tell them the correct drive letter.

5   In the "Backup media or file name" box, enter
     D:\RST## ASR

    Click **Next**

    Click **Finish**

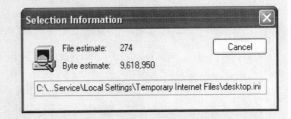

The Selection Information box displays. When the automated file selection for the ASR backup is complete, Backup runs.

6   When prompted for the 1.44 MB formatted disk, verify that it's in drive A: and click **OK**

    Remove the disk and label it "ASR"

    Click **OK**

7   Click **Close**

    Close the Backup Utility

8   Insert the ASR disk in drive A:

    Use Windows Explorer to view the contents of the ASR disk

It contains three files.

    Open the Setup file

It contains detailed information about the configuration of your computer.

    Close all open windows

    Remove the ASR disk from the disk drive

System File Checker

When you install some programs, they attempt to overwrite Windows system files. Such overwriting can cause problems down the line when the operating system or another program attempts to access those files. Protecting system files prevents problems with applications and the operating system. Fortunately, a feature called *Windows File Protection (WFP)* prevents application installations from replacing critical Windows system files.

To verify that you have the original protected system files, you can use the command-line tool called System File Checker to scan all protected files to verify their versions. If System File Checker discovers that a protected file has been overwritten, it retrieves the correct version of the file from the cache folder (the folder that holds needed system files) or the Windows CD-ROM and replaces the incorrect file.

To use the System File Checker to scan all protected system files, open a Command Prompt window and enter `sfc /scannow`. If prompted, insert the Windows XP CD-ROM and complete the scan. You can also use the `/scanonce` switch to scan once at the next reboot and the `/scanboot` switch to scan at every boot. For help with the System File Checker syntax, at a command prompt, enter `sfc /?`.

Do it!

B-7:   Using System File Checker

Here's how	Here's why
1 Click **Start**, and choose **Run**	
2 Type **cmd** and press (← ENTER)	To open a Command Prompt window.
3 At the command prompt, enter **sfc /scannow**	To verify that the protected operating system files are the originals.
4 After the scan is complete, enter **sfc /scanonce**	To schedule a scan for the next system restart.
5 Restart your computer and log on as Administrator	
6 Observe the scan as System File Checker scans your system files again	To see what the scan at reboot looks like. If you schedule a scan for a reboot, you need to inform users to expect to see this progress dialog box.

Students shouldn't be prompted for the Windows XP installation files unless System File Checker has found a file that has been modified from the original version.

Remote Desktop on Windows XP Professional

Explanation

You can use Remote Desktop to administer remote Windows XP Professional computers. Using Remote Desktop, you can access MMC, Control Panel, network configuration tools, and most other tools remotely. For troubleshooting purposes, this tool allows you to:

- Access most configuration settings remotely.
- Diagnose problems and test solutions.
- Access Windows XP computers worldwide.
- Perform batch jobs.
- Perform remote computer application and operating system upgrades.

Before you can remotely administer a computer, you need to enable Remote Desktop locally on that computer. It's installed by default on a Windows XP Professional systems, but it isn't enabled. For security purposes, you must be an administrator on the local computer to enable Remote Desktop. You need administrative privileges to perform most troubleshooting tasks you would use a remote connection for, or at least enough privileges to perform the task.

Do it!

B-8: Enabling Remote Desktop

Here's how	Here's why
1 Click **Start**	You'll enable the Remote Desktop through the System Properties dialog box
Right-click **My Computer**	
Choose **Properties**	
2 Activate the Remote tab	
3 Check **Allow users to connect remotely to this computer**	Only users with Administrative privileges can enable this feature.
Click **OK**	
4 Click **Start** and choose **Control Panel**	You need to add your partner's user account to your local computer's security accounts management (SAM) database. This allows your partner rights to your computer. In a domain environment, you could use domain accounts instead of adding the user individually to the local computer's SAM.
Click **User Accounts**	
Click **Create a new account**	
5 In the "Type a name for this account" box, enter **RSTADMIN##**	(Where ## is your partner's assigned user number.)
Verify Computer administrator is selected and click **Create Account**	
6 Click **RSTADMIN##**	You'll set a password for your partner's user account on your computer.
Click **Create a password**	
In the "Type a new password" and "Type the new password again to confirm" boxes, enter **Pa$$321**	
Click **Create Password**	
7 Close User Accounts and Control Panel	

8 Open System Properties and activate the Remote tab	You must specify which users can access the computer remotely.
Click **Select Remote Users**	
Click **Add...**	
Enter **RSTADMIN##**	(Where RSTADMIN## is your partner's student number.)
Click **OK** three times	

Connecting remotely

Explanation

You can connect to a Windows XP Professional computer with Remote Desktop enabled from any Windows computer with the Remote Desktop Connection tool installed. This tool is installed by default on all Windows XP versions and is available to download from Microsoft's Download Web site for Windows 2000 Professional.

When you connect to the remote computer, the console of the remote computer is locked, preventing anyone from working on it while the remote connection is established. The Remote Desktop feature redirects output to the remote computer; all applications run locally on the remote computer.

Do it!

B-9:   Making a Remote Desktop connection

Tell students that they'll work with a partner in this activity.

Here's how	Here's why
1 At one partner's computer, click **Start** and choose **All Programs**, **Accessories**, **Communications**, **Remote Desktop Connection**	
2 In the Computer box, enter the name of your partner's computer	(ITTADMIN##.)
In the User name box, enter **RSTADMIN##**	(Where ## is your assigned user number.)
3 Click **Connect**	
4 In the User name box, verify that your RSTADMIN## user is listed	
In the Password box, type **Pa$$321**	
Click **OK**	
If prompted, click **Yes**	To log off your partner.
	Notice that the console on the remote computer is now locked.
5 Experiment with your rights on the remote computer	Access Device Manager, the System Configuration utility, and other tools you'd use to troubleshoot a problem. Do NOT make any changes that would prevent your partner's computer from functioning.
6 Click **Start** and choose **Log Off**	
Click **Log Off**	To close the remote connection to your partner's computer.
At the remote computer console, log back on locally	
7 Switch roles with your partner and repeat the activity	

Remote Assistance

Explanation

Remote
*Assistance is covered
in CompTIA A+
Certification:
Essentials.*

The *Remote Assistance* tool provides a means for a user to ask a user at another computer for help with a computer problem. Remote Assistance allows the helping user to view the other user's desktop and, where policy permits, to take control of their system temporarily to resolve problems. Both users should be running Microsoft Windows XP (any version) for this tool to work. Where the computers are members of a domain, a security policy might be in place that prevents a second user from taking control of the first computer's keyboard and mouse.

Invitations

A Windows XP user can solicit help from another Windows XP user by initiating a Remote Assistance invitation in one of the following ways:

- MSN buddy list: Invitation is delivered through Windows Messenger Service accounts.

- E-mail invitation: An attachment in the message is used to initiate the session.

- File invitation: A file saved as a Microsoft Remote Control Incident starts the process.

Exhibit 5-7: The Remote Assistance tool provides three methods for initiating the invitation

The most popular method is file invitation.

File invitations

You might be familiar with the terms Microsoft uses when discussing Remote Assistant—expert and novice. An expert is a computer-savvy colleague, and a novice is a person who desires help from the expert. The process in which a novice asks an expert to view the desktop on the novice's computer using a file invitation is this:

1 Invite a Friend — The novice launches Help and Support from the Start menu. Under "Ask for assistance," select "Invite a friend to connect to your computer with Remote Assistance." The novice can invite a friend, the expert, to connect to his or her computer with Remote Assistance by selecting Invite someone to help you.

2 Save the Invitation — The novice selects "Save invitation to a file (Advanced)."

3 Specify the User — The novice enters the name to appear on the invitation. The default user name is acceptable, continue to the next dialog box and confirm the password. It's recommended that you provide a password. The novice must communicate the password to the expert.

4 Connect to the Share — The novice connects to the shared Invitations folder on the expert's computer. Select SaveInvitation to save the invitation request file on the expert's computer in the Invitations folder.

5 Process the Invitation — The expert locates the invitation file in the Invitations folder and selects the file to initiate the connection to the novice's computer. A message appears on the novice's computer. The novice indicates readiness to permit the expert to connect by selecting Yes.

The expert responds to the action of the novice. The expert is then asked to type the password that was furnished by the novice. After typing the password, the expert can view the novice's screen and chat with the novice. As a security precaution, the expert must request permission of the novice to take control from the novice's desktop.

Do it!

B-10: Using Remote Assistance

Partner two students together for this activity.

Here's how	Here's why
1 At the expert's computer, click **Start**, and then choose **My Documents**	You'll work with a partner in this activity. One of you will be the expert; the other the novice.
Under File and Folder Tasks, click **Make a new folder**	
Name the folder **Invitations**	
2 At the expert's computer, right-click **Invitations** and choose **Sharing and Security...**	
Select **Share this folder on the network**	
3 At the novice's computer, click **Start**, and then choose **Help and Support**	
Under Ask for assistance, click **Invite a friend to connect to your computer with Remote Assistance**	
Click **Invite someone to help you**	At this point, you could choose to send someone a Windows Messenger message (this requires Microsoft Passport accounts), send an e-mail message, or use a file invitation.
Click **Save invitation as a file (Advanced)**	
4 At the novice's computer, click **Continue**	To accept the default user name and invitation expiration time of one hour.
In the Type password and Confirm password boxes, enter **Pa$$321**	
Click **Save Invitation**	

5 At the novice's computer, click
   My Network

   Double-click **Entire Network**

   Double-click **Microsoft
   Windows Network**

   Double-click **TechSupport**

   Double-click **RST##**   (Where ## is your partner's student number.)

   Double-click **Invitations**

   Click **Save**   Notice that the View status of all my invitations
                                             has changed from (0) to (1).

6 At the expert's computer, double-
   click **Invitations**

   RAInvitation
   Microsoft Remote Assistance I...
   1 KB

                                             To open your invitations folder. The Microsoft
                                             Remote Assistance Invitation from your partner
                                             displays.

   Double-click **RAInvitation**

   In the Password box, enter **Pa$$321**

   Click **Yes**   To connect to your partner's computer. You
                                             must wait until your partner accepts the
                                             connection.

7 At the novice's computer, click   To accept the connection from your partner.
   Yes

8 At the expert's computer, in   You'll see your partner's smaller Remote
   Message Entry, enter **What can**   Assistance dialog box on screen; make sure
   I help you with?   you're using the Message Entry area in your
                                             larger Remote Assistance window.

   Click   The message appears in the Chat History area on
        Send   both computers.

9 At the novice's computer, in Message
   Entry, type **I can't change my**
   screen saver to 30 seconds

   Click
        Send

10 At the expert's computer, click 	The novice user is prompted to allow you to take control of the novice's computer.
11 At the novice's computer, click **Yes**	The expert user is presented with a dialog box acknowledging his or her control of the partner's computer. The novice can watch as the expert controls his or her computer.
12 At the expert's computer, click **OK** In the Remote Assistance window, scroll down so you can see the Start menu and a portion of the blank desktop on your partner's computer Right-click the desktop and choose **Properties** Activate the Screen Saver tab In the Wait box, enter **30** Click **OK**	To close your partner's Display Properties dialog box.
13 At the novice's computer, in the Message Entry box, enter **Thank you** and click	
Click	Both the expert and novice receive messages telling them the session is over.
14 Click **OK** on both computers	
15 At both computers, close Remote Assistance and any other open windows	

If time allows, have students reverse roles and complete the activity again.

Unit summary: OS maintenance and troubleshooting

Topic A

In this topic, you learned how to perform operating system **maintenance** tasks that can help prevent problems from occurring with your Windows 2000 Professional and Windows XP computers. These tasks include **backing up** and **restoring** data, manually and on a schedule; creating a **system restore point** and restoring to a restore point; installing Windows **service packs** and **hotfixes**; and configuring Windows XP computers for **automatic updates**.

Topic B

In this topic, you learned how to use Windows 2000 Professional and Windows XP **troubleshooting tools** to identify and resolve operating system problems. You identified the symptoms, causes, and resolutions of common **startup errors**. The troubleshooting tools you learned how to use include: **startup modes**, the **System Configuration Utility**, MS-DOS and Windows 2000/XP **startup disks**, the **Recovery Console**, and **Automated System Recovery**. You also learned how to manage and troubleshoot problems remotely using the **Remote Desktop** feature and the **Remote Assistance** feature.

Review questions

1 When you use Windows Backup to back up System State Data, which files are backed up?

- *The Registry*
- *Boot files*
- *The COM+ class registration database*
- *The IIS metadirectory*
- *Windows File Protection system files*

2 What are the two different modes you can run in the Windows Backup in?
Wizard mode and Advanced mode.

3 Which backup type requires that you have the most recent normal backup in addition to this backup, if you want to restore files? (Check all the apply.)

A Copy.

B Daily.

C Differential.

D Incremental.

E Normal.

4 At what intervals can you schedule backups?

- *Daily*

- *Weekly*

- *Monthly*

- *At predefined times*

- *On predefined days*

5 True or False? A limitation of the Windows Backup utility is that you can't back up individual components of the System State data.

True. To back up individual components of the System State data, you need to use a third-party utility such as Veritas Backup Exec.

6 Which type of restore points are created when Windows XP detects the beginning of a request to make a system configuration change?

A System checkpoints.

B Manual restore points.

C Installation restore points.

D Automatic checkpoints.

7 Can you use System Restore to uninstall a program?

System Restore doesn't replace the process of uninstalling a program. To remove the files installed by a program completely, Microsoft recommends that you remove the program by using the Add or Remove Programs utility or the program's own uninstall program.

8 Which types of files in a service pack are included to enhance the current operating system and some of its features, making it easier to use or adding functionality?

A Hotfixes.

B Security patches.

C Updates.

9 Which Windows Update mode scans your computer for updates in three categories—High Priority, Software, and Hardware?

A Express.

B Security.

C Custom.

D Manual

10 What's the URL of the Windows Update site?

http://update.microsoft.com

11 Which notification option for Windows XP's Automatic Updates automatically scans the computer for updates but doesn't download them?

   A Automatic.

   B Download updates for me.

   C Notify me.

   D Turn off Automatic Updates.

12 Which type of errors presents as the computer system booting successfully but reports an error message when loading the operating system?

   A Boot errors.

   B Operating system startup errors.

   C Operating system load errors.

   D Hardware errors.

13 A floppy or CD-ROM that isn't bootable in a bootable drive can cause which boot error(s)?

   A Invalid boot or non-system disk error.

   B Inaccessible boot device.

   C NTLDR is missing or Couldn't find NTLDR.

   D Bad or missing Command interpreter.

14 A problem with physical memory can cause which operating system startup error(s)?

   A Error in CONFIG.SYS line ##.

   B Himem.sys not loaded.

   C Missing or corrupt Himem.sys.

   D Device/service has failed to start.

15 An outdated device driver that needs to be updated can cause which operating system load error(s)?

   A Failure to start GUI.

   B Windows Protection Error—illegal operation.

   C User-modified settings cause improper operation at startup.

   D Application install, start or load failure.

16 If you're having problems with a device, which startup mode can you use to record all files used during the boot process in a file called Ntbtlog.txt?

Enable boot logging.

17 Which switch can you add to your boot.ini file to replace the progress with a list of the individual drivers that are loaded?

A /basevideo.

B /crashdebug.

C /debug.

D /sos.

18 In the System Configuration Utility, which mode can you use to load only basic devices and services while troubleshooting a problem?

A Normal.

B Diagnostic.

C Selective.

D Debug.

19 Which bootable media can you use to return your computer to the state it was in when it was shipped to you by the manufacturer?

A Windows Startup disk.

B Emergency Repair Disk (ERD).

C Automated System Recovery Disk (ASR).

D Recovery CD.

20 If you're running Windows XP, when might you need an MS-DOS startup disk?

You might need an MS-DOS startup disk when you're following a BIOS manufacturer's procedure to update (or flash) the BIOS.

Independent practice activity

In this practice activity, you'll complete an automated system recovery. You must have a tape drive available for backup. If you back up the data to your hard disk, as you did during the activity units, you won't be able to complete the ASR.

1 Use Advanced Mode of the Backup utility to complete a backup of the user data on your computer to a tape drive. Be sure to include the C:\Student Data folder in your backup.

2 Prepare an ASR recovery set, backing up to the tape drive.

3 Initiate the ASR.

4 When prompted, complete the ASR.

5 Verify that Windows XP Professional has been successfully restored.

6 Use Advanced Mode of the Backup utility and the backup on your tape drive to restore the user data, including the C:\Student Data folder.

7 Enable Remote Desktop connections for your computer.

8 Create an administrative user account that your partner will use to establish a remote connection to your computer.

9 One partner at a time, connect remotely to your partner's computer and run Windows Update to install the latest fixes to the operating system. When the first partner is done, switch roles.

10 At both computers, remove your partner's administrative user account from your local security accounts database.

Unit 6

Networking

Unit time: 210 minutes

Complete this unit, and you'll know how to:

A Configure a LAN connection.

B Share resources on a network.

C Create an Internet connection.

D Implement network protection strategies.

E Troubleshoot network connection problems.

Topic A: Networking configuration

This topic covers the following CompTIA A+ 220-603 exam objectives.

#	Objective
4.1	**Identify the fundamental principles of networks**
	• Identify names, purposes and characteristics of basic network protocols and terminologies for example:
	• TCP/IP (e.g., gateway, subnet mask, DNS, WINS, static and automatic address assignment)
	• IPX/SPX (NWLink)
	• NETBEUI/NETBIOS
	• DNS
4.2	**Install, configure, optimize and upgrade networks**
	• Establish network connectivity and share network resources

Network types

Explanation

 Network types were covered in CompTIA A+ Certification: Essentials.

There are two basic types of networks a CompTIA A+ technician will encounter:

- **Peer-to-peer network** — This type of network, as illustrated in Exhibit 6-1, usually consists of several client computers that are connected to a network for simple file and printer sharing in a small office or home office. Each computer has a network card, which is connected to the network by a network cable or a wireless network card. All the communication is among the client computers. There are often fewer than a dozen users and computers. When accessing one computer from another, you must have an account on the computer you want to access.

Exhibit 6-1: A peer-to-peer network

- **Client/server network** — In this type of network, as illustrated in Exhibit 6-2, computers called *servers* hold data and provide a wealth of services that users can share. Most of the communication is between the client computers and the servers. Client/server networks usually have at least one server with a central database of user accounts that are used to authenticate users. (In Windows, this server is called a *domain controller*.) On this type of network, users can log on and use whatever resources their user accounts allow them to use without needing an account for each computer. (Networks without a domain controller require separate user accounts for each computer; such a setup isn't easy to manage or maintain). There are often dozens, hundreds, or thousands of users. Such a network can span a building, an office park, a country, or the globe. Client computers are connected to the network via network card and network cable or a wireless connection.

Exhibit 6-2: A client/server network

Network operating systems

A *Network Operating System* manages LAN resources. Windows 2000 is a series of operating systems, each designed for a particular size computer and computing needs. Windows 2000 Server is a network operating system, while Windows 2000 Professional is appropriate as a client operating system, just as Windows XP Professional is.

Windows Server 2003 comes in many editions, each designed to meet certain needs with specific system requirements. Both the Standard and Enterprise Editions of Windows Server 2003 come with a built-in firewall. The four Windows Server 2003 operating systems editions are:

- Windows Server 2003, Standard Edition
- Windows Server 2003, Enterprise Edition
- Windows Server 2003, Datacenter Edition
- Windows Server 2003, Web Edition

A Windows 2000 Server or Windows Server 2003 domain uses one or more domain controllers that replicate the database among themselves. In other words, the database is stored on all domain controllers instead of on only one. This type of configuration is useful for organizations that need to keep things running in the event of a domain controller failure. Users might be unaware of a domain controller failure, because they can still continue using their computers and network resources. Windows 2000 Server and Windows Server 2003 keep lists of network resources in a database called Active Directory.

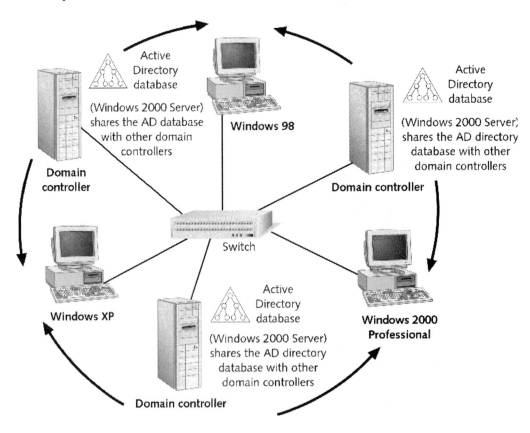

Exhibit 6-3: A Windows 2000 Server domain

Active Directory is a centralized system that controls computer and user configuration settings, security settings, and access to resources on a LAN. It uses a hierarchical organization that provides the administrator with a single place for all system administration, including user and computer configuration and management. Active Directory follows the client/server model and allows users to access network resources from any computer on the network. The Windows 2000 Server Active Directory management console GUI is nearly identical to the one found in Windows Server 2003, but it lacks some management features and tools.

Novell NetWare

NetWare by Novell, Inc. (www.novell.com) was, for many years, the tried-and-true, industry-accepted solution to LAN management. In versions of NetWare up to 5.0, the default protocol is a suite of protocols collectively called IPX/SPX, which is also supported by Windows 2000 Professional and all Windows XP versions. The IPX portion of the protocol is responsible for routing, and the SPX portion of the protocol manages error checking, similar to the way TCP manages error checking and IP manages routing on a TCP/IP network. NetWare versions 5.0 and higher use the TCP/IP protocol suite by default, though they continue to support IPX/SPX. If hosts on a NetWare network require access to the Internet, the network must use TCP/IP to do that. NetWare supports both protocols running on the network.

NetWare is installed on the server that controls the LAN, and each computer connected to the LAN must run a NetWare client to interact with the server and provide a logon screen when the user first accesses the network. Windows operating systems all include a NetWare client, but you might still have to install the NetWare client software in some situations.

UNIX and Linux

Until recently, UNIX was the only reliable option for an NOS that provided services over the Internet. TCP/IP was born in a UNIX environment, and for a long time, to think of OS for the Internet was to think UNIX. UNIX also can support a LAN as a file and database server, managing user accounts and access privileges. UNIX was also the first, and still is the most popular, NOS for midsize servers responsible for supporting thin clients. Java was developed in a UNIX environment to support thin clients served by a UNIX computer. The first Web servers used UNIX. It's also the accepted mainstay for the firewall market. Many popular firewall applications (SunScreen, BorderWare, Checkpoint) were originally designed to be used on a UNIX platform.

UNIX isn't an easy operating system to learn. Even though it does offer a GUI interface, a system administrator can't fully perform his or her job without a working knowledge of a somewhat cryptic command-line shell. Installing UNIX and installing hardware devices on a UNIX system require expertise far beyond that of a casual user.

Several hardware manufacturers offer their own versions of UNIX. IBM's UNIX is called AIX. Sun's UNIX is named Solaris. Compaq has a version of UNIX named Tru64 UNIX. Hewlett-Packard's UNIX version is called HP-UX.

Linux is quickly becoming a viable option as a NOS. Red Hat, Inc. (www.redhat.com) sells an impressive version of Linux that has proven to be competitive as an NOS for Internet services.

Network services

For smooth operations and ease of manageability on client/server networks, servers provide a variety of network services. These services enable users to share files, communicate with one another via e-mail, share printers, compile information in centralized databases, and access the Internet. The following table describes some important network services.

Service	Description
Dynamic Host Configuration Protocol (DHCP)	DHCP assigns numerical addresses to computers in the network. These addresses, called *IP addresses*, are used to identify each computer uniquely and are needed for computers to communicate on the network using TCP/IP. This network service is hosted on a server called a *DHCP server*. Administrators use DHCP so they don't have to manage address assignments manually, which can get complicated on networks with thousands of computers.
Domain Name Service (DNS)	DNS translates computer names, called *host names* or *DNS names*, into IP addresses on a local area network (LAN) and on the Internet. DNS servers maintain a database that contains name-to-address mappings. It's DNS that enables you to enter "www.yahoo.com" instead of having to remember a numerical address such as 216.109.118.75. The process of translating a familiar name into an IP address is called *name resolution*.
Windows Internet Naming Service (WINS)	WINS is similar to DNS, but it translates IP addresses into simpler computer names, such as "Computer100," which are called *NetBIOS names*. WINS was widely used in earlier Microsoft networks, but with Windows 2000, Microsoft came to rely more on DNS, because DNS provides more flexibility in naming computers in large networks.
Authentication	Servers that provide authentication services are used to restrict access to the network and other computers and the services they offer. In Windows networking, servers that provide authentication are called *domain controllers*. Windows domain controllers run Windows NT Server 4.0, Windows 2000 Server, or Windows Server 2003.
Internet access	Some servers act as a gateway between an organization's private LAN and the Internet, funneling communication between computers on the network and those on the Internet. Some servers and devices protect the network from malicious activity on the Internet; these are called *firewalls*.
File sharing	Some servers just store files or databases that are accessed by network users. These servers' only function is to hold data and make it available to users across the network.
Printing	Printers can be connected to the network if they have networking capability and a network card built in. Printers without that capability must be connected to a computer that offers the printer's services to network users.

Client operating systems

On a LAN, each personal computer must have an operating system that's capable of interfacing with a *network interface card (NIC)*, also called a network adapter, and the resources available on the network. A NIC is the hardware device inside a computer that works with the client OS to provide access to a network. Personal computer OS options include all Windows XP versions, Windows 2000 Professional, Windows NT Workstation, Windows 98, Mac OS, and Linux, which can all function as client operating systems.

Windows 9x and Windows Me

Windows 95, Windows 98, and *Windows Me* are older client operating systems that are still used on many home computers. Windows 9x is backwards compatible with MS-DOS, Windows 3.x, and older (legacy) hardware devices. Some devices that are found on newer computers might not function correctly under Windows 9x. You can look at the speed and configuration of a computer to decide whether to install Windows 9x or Windows Me. Slower systems like an Intel Pentium II 350 MHz would run Windows 9x perfectly.

Windows 9x and Windows Me support network access and can be used in a peer-to-peer or client/server network. Using the OSes, you can give others on the network access to files and folders on your hard drive (or even the entire hard drive) and to a printer that's directly connected to your computer. For this feature, file and printer sharing must be installed and individual files, folders, and printers must be shared. Windows 9x users on a LAN might not be able to access shared resources, such as files on Windows 2000 or Windows XP computers. This can happen if Windows 2000 or Windows XP computers are configured to use NTFS. NTFS is a newer technology that is used to manage files and folders on a hard drive. It offers greater stability and security than older file systems used in Windows 9x and Windows Me.

Windows NT Workstation, Windows 2000 Professional, and Windows XP

Microsoft has sold many client operating systems over the years. One of the oldest that's still in use is Windows NT. It offers two operating systems, *Windows NT Workstation* and *Windows NT Server.* By the late 1990s, Windows NT Workstation was widely used by many small and large businesses. It worked well in a peer-to-peer network or in a client/server network.

However, by today's standards, Windows NT Workstation is often difficult to set up and to configure device drivers, because Windows NT Workstation doesn't use the Device Manager graphical user interface. Windows NT Workstation also lacks plug-and-play capabilities. Plug-and-play is used to install drivers automatically for new devices that are added to a computer. Occasional computer problems were common as software vendors struggled for many years to write stable programs for Windows NT Workstation.

Microsoft ended its support for its Windows NT product line in January 2005. However, many businesses had already upgraded their Windows NT Workstation computers to Windows 2000 Professional.

The Windows 2000 OS family has four different operating systems, depending on your needs: Windows 2000 Professional, Windows 2000 Server, Windows 2000 Advanced Server, and Windows 2000 Datacenter Server. Of these four, Windows 2000 Professional is appropriate for use as a client OS. Windows 2000 Professional was based on the technology used in Windows NT but offers better support for devices than Windows NT.

It's more reliable than Windows NT Workstation and offers a user-friendly interface. Some businesses have already upgraded their computers to Windows XP, although others still use Windows 2000 Professional.

Windows XP comes in four different operating systems: *Windows XP Professional*, *Windows XP Home Edition*, *Windows XP Media Center*, and *Windows XP 64-Bit Edition*. Windows XP is very similar to Windows 2000 Professional but offers much wider support for devices, such as printers, NICs, USB devices, and others. The Windows XP default Start menu is very different from any previous Microsoft operating system and offers instant access to frequently used programs. Windows XP also offers a Classic View Start menu that's nearly identical to the one found in Windows 2000 Professional. Windows XP Home Edition and Media Center have a user interface that's identical to Windows XP Professional, but that lacks some networking features found in Windows XP Professional. As its name implies, Windows XP Home Edition is meant for home users. Windows XP Home Edition and Media Center computers can't be used on a client/server network where the NOS is Windows Server 2003, Windows 2000 Server, or Windows NT Server. However, Windows Home Edition and Media Center are useful on small, peer-to-peer networks. Windows XP Home Edition and Media Center are designed to replace Windows 9x, Windows Me, Windows NT Workstation, and Windows 2000 Professional that still exist in many homes and small offices. Windows XP Professional is designed to replace older operating systems used in medium to large offices. Windows 64-Bit Edition is similar to Windows XP but has been optimized for newer, 64-bit processors. It's intended for people who use highly technical software applications.

When considering whether to use Windows 2000 Professional or a Windows XP version on a computer, verify that all the hardware and software already installed on the computer is compatible with the new operating system. For hardware, check the Hardware Compatibility List (HCL) on the Microsoft Web site, www.microsoft.com/hcl. If your specific hardware isn't listed, you most likely can't successfully install Windows 2000 Professional or Windows XP on the system without contacting the hardware manufacturer directly for updated drivers.

Linux

There was a time when UNIX wasn't considered a viable option as a personal computer OS, but that changed in 1991 when Linux was invented. Linus Torvalds created Linux with the help of volunteers from all over the world. Linux was designed as a scaled-down version of UNIX. It's free, although companies offering Linux charge a price for the documentation, technical support, and add-on modules. Linux is small enough to fit and run on a computer that's 10 years old, yet it has network capabilities similar to a full-fledged commercial version of UNIX. For a time, Linux was considered only a training tool for learning UNIX, because it could be installed on an inexpensive, low-end computer and easily used in a training environment or at home. Linux is no longer considered just a training tool and is rapidly gaining acceptance as an operating system of choice in certain situations.

Linux is an excellent NOS to use in a small company environment with low-volume traffic for intranet services. It can be used as the OS for a Web server or proxy server for a LAN. Apache Web Server, a popular Web server application, is often used on a UNIX or Linux platform. Even though Linux generally isn't considered an appropriate OS for the kind of high-volume traffic that UNIX is known to handle, several high-traffic Web sites now run successfully using Apache Web Server on a Linux platform. As a result, the industry's perception of Linux is quickly changing.

Linux's popularity is also growing. Apple, Computer Associates, Compaq, Corel, Dell, Hewlett-Packard, IBM, Informix, Intel, Lotus, NAI, Netscape, Novell, Oracle, SAP, and Sybase are among the companies that have recently provided support for their products using the Linux OS.

The largest drawbacks to using Linux in a corporate environment don't so much entail the technical strength of the OS but the support and standards surrounding it, lack of application software written for it, and lack of experienced technical support people.

Linux is very different from Windows. To evaluate Linux as an operating system, you need to understand the difference between an operating system kernel and an operating system shell. The operating system kernel is the part of the operating system that interfaces with the hardware (including the NIC) that accesses the network. The user or applications software can't command the kernel directly but must go through a command interface called the shell. Applications software must also interface (communicate) with the OS through the shell and, in most cases, can't access the hardware directly. The Linux kernel is considered a much more stable operating system kernel than the Windows kernel, which results in fewer Linux crashes than Windows crashes in comparable situations.

Linux and UNIX use a command-line shell as the default shell. On newer versions of Red Hat Linux, the user can load a GUI shell similar to the Windows user interface. Linux isn't as popular an operating system for personal computers as Windows. It can be difficult to install, because the software responsible for communicating with Linux to interface hardware devices (called drivers) isn't as readily available for Linux as it is for Windows, and the installation can sometimes be very complex. Even so, many applications are being written for Linux, and GUI shells are becoming standard.

Macintosh operating system

Several versions of the Macintosh operating system (Mac OS) are available for Macintosh computers, the latest being *Mac OS X* (ten). OS X provides easy access to the Internet and allows any Macintosh computer to become a Web server for a small network. The Mac OS has an excellent icon-driven interface, and it's easy to learn and use. Many applications exist for the Mac OS to create and edit graphics, build Web sites, and manage multimedia devices.

The Mac OS uses a suite of networking protocols called *AppleTalk* but also supports the networking protocol suite TCP/IP. Thus, it can access the Internet and other TCP/IP networks. Mac OS X supports TCP/IP networking out of the box and can communicate with Windows computers on any TCP/IP network.

Do it!

A-1: Discussing network models

Questions	Answers
1 How are client/server networks different from peer-to-peer networks?	*Client/server networks have servers in addition to client computers. Client/server networks are also usually larger and offer more services than peer-to-peer networks.*
2 Why would a company want to implement a client/server network?	*A company would implement a client/server network if it has resources (files, printers, databases, Internet access) it wants to share among a large number of employees.*
3 What kind of company would implement a peer-to-peer network?	*A small company that wanted to share files or a printer among a small number of client computers.*

Network interface card (NIC)

A network interface card (NIC) is an adapter card that plugs into one of the expansion slots that all PCs have on their motherboards, or it attaches to the computer through an external port, such as a USB 2.0 port. The NIC has one or more ports built into it that are used to connect the NIC and its computer to a network using a cable that plugs into the port or wireless radio waves. A NIC can support Ethernet, token ring, or FDDI network architecture, but only one of the three. It may have ports that can accept more than one type of cable connection. For example, an Ethernet card might have connectors for both coax and twisted-pair with a BNC connector and/or DB-15 DIX connector for coax cables and an RJ-45 connector for twisted-pair cables.

The function of the NIC is to send and receive information from the system bus in parallel and to send and receive information from the network in series. The NIC also converts the data that it receives from the system into a signal that's appropriate to the network. For an Ethernet card, this means converting the data from the 5-volt signal used on the computer's motherboard into the voltage used by twisted-pair cables. The component on the NIC that makes this conversion is a transceiver. An Ethernet card may have more than one transceiver to convert data into the appropriate voltage for various types of cable connectors, which are wired into the NIC. Such cards are called combo cards. A combo card is shown in Exhibit 6-4. Exhibit 6-5 shows other examples of NICs.

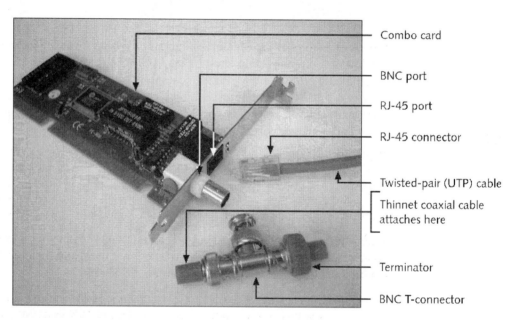

Exhibit 6-4: An Ethernet combo NIC

a. FDDI   b. Token Ring

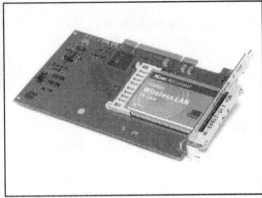

c. Ethernet   d. Wireless

Exhibit 6-5: Examples of Network Interface Cards (NICs)

NICs have built-in identifying addresses coded into them by the manufacturers. These codes are used by the network to identify the computer (node) using the card. These addresses are called *media access control (MAC) addresses*, physical or adapter addresses, or Ethernet addresses. They consist of 6-byte (48-bit) hexadecimal codes, which are unique for each card. Part of the address contains the manufacturer identifier, and the rest is a unique number. No two NICs have the same identifying code.

When selecting a NIC, it's critical to match it with the network architecture to which it connects, the specific type of cable connection it uses, and the type of slot in the computer (PCI or ISA) in which it's installed.

All internal cards for desktop systems are PCI cards at this point. If you're supporting older equipment, you might encounter some ISA or EISA cards in which you need to configure the IRA, DMA, and I/O addresses. A utility from the manufacturer is used to configure the settings on such cards.

Do it!

A-2: Installing a NIC

You can have students install a second NIC.

Here's how	Here's why
1 Shut down the computer	You'll remove and then reinstall the NIC in your computer.
Unplug the computer from its power source	Many components, including network cards continue to receive power even if the computer isn't turned on, so it's best practice to unplug the computer in addition to turning it off.
2 Remove the case	To access the slots on the motherboard.
3 Remove the cable from network card	Unless you're using a wireless adapter, in which case there's no cable.
Remove the network card	If it's a desktop computer, you probably need to unscrew it from the chassis. If it's a laptop computer, you need to eject it from the PC Card slot.
4 Install the NIC into the slot	Be sure it's fully seated into the slot.
Attach the NIC to the case	If there's no screw, just be sure that the card is fully seated in the slot.
5 Replace the case	
6 Plug the computer into the power source	
7 Connect the network cable to the network card	Unless you're using a wireless adapter, in which case there's no cable.
8 Turn on the computer	
9 If prompted to install drivers, follow the prompts to do so	
10 Remove the NIC	To leave just the original NIC in your computer.

Network protocols

Explanation

In addition to one or more operating systems, a network also requires a network protocol, so all computers on the network can communicate. Network *protocols* are the languages that computers, servers, and network devices use to communicate with each other. Protocols send data across the network in units called *packets*. To communicate, all computers, including the NOS on the server, must use the same network protocol. The selected network protocol must be supported by every operating system on the network. The following table lists some common network protocols that you can use in Windows networks.

Protocol	Description
Transmission Control Protocol/Internet Protocol (TCP/IP)	A routable, nonproprietary protocol that's the predominant Windows network protocol. It's supported by all versions of Windows and most other non-Microsoft operating systems. TCP/IP is also the protocol of the Internet.
Internetwork Packet Exchange/Sequenced Packet Exchange (IPX/SPX)	A routable, proprietary protocol that was the native protocol in early versions of Novell NetWare. Later versions of NetWare supported TCP/IP as the native protocol. Windows computers can connect to IPX/SPX networks and NetWare servers by using Microsoft's version of IPX/SPX, called NWLink. To share files and printers on a NetWare server, you must install the Microsoft Client for NetWare.
AppleTalk	A routable network protocol supported by Apple Macintosh computers. Windows NT and Windows 2000 support AppleTalk. Mac OS X (10.2 and later) supports TCP/IP and can connect to Windows networks without requiring AppleTalk support. AppleTalk computers are called *nodes* and can be configured as part of *zones* for sharing resources. Each node on a network must be configured with a unique network address.
NetBEUI	A non-routable, proprietary Microsoft protocol that's supported in Windows 9x/Me, Windows NT, and Windows 2000. NetBEUI uses Network Basic Input/Output System (NetBIOS) services to communicate with other computers on a network. (NetBIOS helps with computer names and some basic communication services.) Although it isn't technically supported in Windows XP, you can install NetBEUI by manually copying files from the installation CD-ROM. What's nice about NetBEUI is that it has no settings to configure. You install the protocol, connect the computer to the network, and it just works. The drawback is that it isn't routable, so it can't pass from one network segment to another. This means it can't be used for remote access or any communication outside a single segment.

To view the network protocols that are supported by Windows XP:

1 Click Start and choose Control Panel.

2 In Category View, click Network and Internet Connections.

3 Click Network Connections. The network devices installed on your computer are listed. If a NIC is installed, you see a Local Area Connection icon.

4 Right-click the Local Area Connection icon, and choose Properties.

5 Click Install.

6 Select Protocol and click Add. The Select Network Protocol displays the three network protocols supported by Windows XP: Microsoft TCP/IP version 6; Network Monitor Driver, and NWLink IPX/SPX/NetBIOS Compatible Transport Protocol.

7 Click Cancel three times.

TCP/IP provides the LAN with access to the Internet. Sometimes, however, a network must support more than one network protocol, because each protocol is used for a different purpose. For example, if the NOS on the server is Novell NetWare 5.0 or below, the client computer must have the NWLink IPX/SPX/NetBIOS Compatible Transport protocol installed. Installing this protocol in Windows XP actually installs the IPX/SPX protocol and the NetBIOS protocol. The IPX/SPX protocol is used to route and check data for errors. The NetBIOS protocol allows one application to communicate with another application on the same LAN. It isn't unusual for computers on a LAN to use several different protocols, each for a different purpose.

Do it!

A-3: Viewing installed network protocols

Here's how	Here's why
1 Click **Start**, and choose **Control Panel**	
2 Click **Network and Internet Connections**	
Click **Network Connections**	
Right-click **Local Area Connection**, and choose **Properties**	This connection uses the following items: ☑ 🖳 Client for Microsoft Networks ☑ 🖳 File and Printer Sharing for Microsoft Networks ☑ 🖳 QoS Packet Scheduler ☑ ⌐ Internet Protocol (TCP/IP) TCP/IP is the only protocol installed on the computer for network communication.
3 Click **Cancel**	
Close the Network Connections window	

TCP/IP configuration

Explanation

TCP/IP is the network protocol in just about every organization, so it's important to know how to configure TCP/IP on client computers. Basic TCP/IP configuration consists of the IP address and subnet mask, examples of which are shown in Exhibit 6-6.

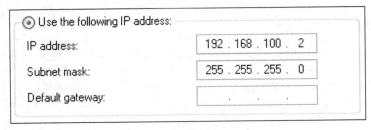

Exhibit 6-6: IP address and subnet mask

IP addresses

Each computer on a TCP/IP network is assigned a unique numerical address called an IP address. An IP address is like a house number or a cell phone number. It's used to provide a unique identification that distinguishes the computer it's assigned to from all other computers. Without an IP address, a computer can't communicate on a network using TCP/IP.

IP addresses consist of four one-, two-, or three-digit numbers separated by periods, like this: 192.168.115.231. You must have all four parts of the number for the IP address to be complete. Part of the IP address defines the network address, also known as the *subnet*; the other part of the IP address defines the computer address. Taken together, the two parts uniquely identify a computer, much like an area code and phone number identify a specific phone. In the example 192.168.115.231, the network portion of the address (the area code) is 192.168.115, and the computer address (the phone number) is 231.

IP addresses can be assigned manually in the Windows GUI, or they can be assigned automatically by DHCP. When you assign an IP address manually, you enter it in a dialog box. A manually assigned IP address is called a *static IP address*.

When you use DHCP, you tell the computer to ask the DHCP server for an address. The DHCP server sends the address to the computer and keeps track of all addresses it has assigned to all computers, so there are no conflicts. The computer then uses that address as its IP address.

Windows 2000 and Windows XP computers can assign themselves IP addresses by using *Automatic Private IP Addressing* (APIPA). They assign themselves IP addresses in the range of 169.254.0.0 to 169.254.255.255, if they haven't been assigned an IP address manually, and there's no DHCP server on the network. APIPA is a great feature for a small network, because the computers just assign themselves IP addresses, and you don't have to worry about doing it manually or setting up a DHCP server.

Subnet masks

The *subnet mask* is a number that looks something like an IP address. Its function is to separate the IP address into the network address and the computer address so that routers and other network devices know where to send data packets. A subnet mask often looks like this: 255.255.255.0. This example would be the default subnet mask for the IP address example in the preceding section; this subnet mask would tell other computers and routers that 192.168.115 is the network address and 231 is the computer address.

Subnet masks can get very complicated, but as a CompTIA A+ technician, you don't have to worry about figuring them out. You just need to assign the appropriate subnet masks, which the network administrator or engineer provides, and you need to verify that a computer has been assigned the correct subnet mask if you're troubleshooting networking errors.

The DHCP process

If a computer is configured to use DHCP, when it starts up, it broadcasts a request across the network for a DHCP server. A DHCP server responds with an offer of an IP address and associated TCP/IP properties. The computer then uses this data to configure TCP/IP. If the computer can't get an IP address from a DHCP server, it has no IP address, or, if it's a Windows Me/2000/XP computer, it assigns itself an APIPA address.

The IP address is assigned or *leased* to the computer for a specified duration—anywhere from a few hours to a few days, depending on how the DHCP server is configured by the network administrator. If you need to update IP addressing information, you can remove the DHCP address that's been assigned to you and then manually send a request to the DHCP server for another IP address. This procedure, which you'll see later, is called *release and renew*.

IP address assignments

To assign an IP address or configure a computer to use DHCP:

1 In Windows 2000/XP, right-click My Network Places and choose Properties.
2 Right-click Local Area Connection and choose Properties.
3 Double-click Internet Protocol (TCP/IP).
4 Choose to use DHCP or assign an IP address manually.

Do it!

A-4: Configuring an IP address and subnet mask

Here's how	Here's why
Have a range of private IP addresses ready for students to use.		

Here's how	Here's why
1 Click **Start**	
Right-click **My Network Places** and choose **Properties**	To open the Network Connections window. You're going to assign a static IP address.
2 Right-click **Local Area Connection** and choose **Properties**	To open the Local Area Connections Properties dialog box.
3 From the list of components, select **Internet Protocol** and then click **Properties**	To open the Internet Protocol (TCP/IP) Properties dialog box.
4 What's your current IP address?	*It isn't displayed. Currently your computer has been assigned an IP address by a DHCP server.*
5 Select **Use the following IP address**	
In the IP address box, enter the IP address supplied by your instructor	IP address: 192 . 168 . 100 . 185 Subnet mask: . . . Default gateway: . . . To assign a static IP address to your computer.
6 Press TAB	192 . 168 . 100 . 185 255 . 255 . 255 . 0 To enter a default subnet mask. You can change the subnet mask if necessary. Leave the dialog box open for the next activity.

Additional TCP/IP properties

Explanation

The following table lists some of the other TCP/IP properties you can configure. Keep in mind that these properties can also be assigned by using a DHCP server—a method that provides greater ease and flexibility when managing a large network.

Property	Description
Default gateway (gateway)	This is the IP address of the server on the subnet that forwards packets to other subnets. You need to configure a default gateway, if the computer needs to communicate with other subnets or with the Internet.
DNS server address	This is the IP address of the DNS server. The DNS server helps the client computer find other computers on the internal network or on the Internet. The DNS server might be on the LAN, or it might be maintained by the Internet service provider. There could be multiple DNS server addresses.
WINS server address	This is the IP address of the WINS server on the network. There could be multiple WINS server addresses. You see WINS used mostly in older Windows networks.

Computer names

All Windows computers have names. They can be simple and easy to remember, such as Computer1, or they can be more complex, such as cca-xp-89-444-00A.organization.int. Each organization determines its own computer naming scheme, with the understanding that computer names on the same network must be unique.

There are two types of computer names: NetBIOS names and DNS names. NetBIOS names look like this:

- Computer10
- Andy
- MyComputer
- Client1
- XPComp
- rco-313-00-A

DNS host names include a NetBIOS-type computer name plus the *DNS suffix* of the DNS domain of which the computer is a member. DNS host names typically look like this:

- computer10.class.internal
- support.microsoft.com
- www.course.com
- client100.local.mycompany.class

In these examples, the host names are computer10, support, www, and client100. The DNS suffixes are class.internal, microsoft.com, course.com, and local.mycompany.class.

You won't be responsible for creating names, but you might be responsible for assigning names and DNS suffixes to computers from a list you've been given. You might also find that computers with identical names on the same network are causing errors that prevent users from accessing the network. Understanding some naming basics is important.

Do it!

A-5: Configuring additional TCP/IP properties

Here's how	Here's why
1 In the Internet Protocol (TCP/IP) Properties dialog box, press `TAB`	To move to the Default gateway box. You're going to continue configuring TCP/IP manually, so you can connect to the Internet.
Enter the default gateway supplied by your instructor	Default gateway: 192 . 168 . 100 . 1
2 In the Preferred DNS server box, enter the IP address supplied by your instructor	Preferred DNS server: 204 . 127 . 202 . 4
3 Click **Advanced**	To open the Advanced TCP/IP Settings dialog box.
4 Observe the IP Settings tab	You can enter additional IP addressing information here.
5 Activate the DNS tab	DNS server addresses, in order of use: 204.127.202.4
	The IP address you entered earlier is displayed. You can enter multiple DNS server addresses, if necessary. You can also configure the DNS suffix here.
6 Activate the WINS tab	You can configure the WINS client here.
7 Activate the Options tab	You can configure TCP/IP port filtering here.
8 Click **Cancel**	To close the Advanced TCP/IP Settings dialog box.
9 Click **OK**, and click **Close** to close the Local Area Connection Properties dialog box	To close open dialog boxes and assign the IP addressing information you entered.
Close the Network Connections window	
10 Open Internet Explorer and access a Web page	To verify that you have network connectivity using the manually assigned IP address.
11 Close Internet Explorer	

Be prepared with at least a default gateway and DNS server address. Provide other settings necessary for Internet access.

Be sure to use the DNS server configured on the classroom domain controller.

Windows workgroups and domains

Explanation

Windows computers can be grouped into workgroups and domains. *Workgroups* are just groups of computers that share the same workgroup name. It's more of a means for organizing computers than it is a membership in anything. However, a domain is different. A *domain* is a secure group of computers, printers, and other devices that share a *directory service:* a common database of accounts. Membership in a domain is special: it gives you access to a wide variety of network resources that might not be available to just anybody.

Computers that are joined to a domain as members can be administered through domain administrative accounts and can be configured to allow access through domain user accounts. This makes it easier to share resources, because accounts are kept in a central location. Otherwise, you'd have to maintain accounts on each separate computer. As a CompTIA A+ technician, you don't have to set up or manage domains, but you do need to know how to join a computer to a domain, log on to a domain, and recognize when a problem with a domain logon might be causing an error that prevents a user from accessing network resources, such as a file server or e-mail.

Joining a workgroup or domain

To join a computer to a workgroup or domain, you need to obtain the workgroup name or the domain's NetBIOS name or DNS name from the network administrator. You also need to be sure that all the DNS properties have been correctly configured.

- In Windows 2000, right-click My Computer and choose Properties. On the Network Identification tab, click Properties, and enter the workgroup or domain name.
- In Windows XP, right-click My Computer and choose Properties. On the Computer Name tab, click Change, and enter the workgroup or domain name.

When joining or exiting a domain, you're required to enter a user name and password with sufficient privileges to perform the action—typically user credentials of a domain administrator. Be sure to have the user name and password handy before you begin this process. You don't need a special user account just to switch workgroups.

Do it!

A-6:   Joining a Windows domain

Here's how	Here's why
1 Click **Start**, right-click **My Computer** and choose **Properties**	To open the System Properties dialog box. You can join a computer to a domain at any time, either during Windows installation or after installation is complete.
2 On the Computer Name tab, click **Change**	To open the Computer Name Changes dialog box.
3 Select **Domain** and enter **RSTDOMAIN.CLASS**	To join the classroom domain, which has the full DNS name RSTDOMAIN.CLASS.
Click **OK**	

4 Enter the user name
   Administrator and the
   password **Pa$$321**

   Click **OK**

5 Click **OK** twice

6 Click **OK**   To close the System Properties dialog box.

7 Click **Yes**   To restart the computer.

8 Observe the new logon dialog box   This is the logon dialog box you use in
                                         Windows XP when the computer is a member of
                                         a domain. This logon method is more secure
                                         than the default Windows XP logon screen.

9 Press ⌈ CTRL ⌉ + ⌈ ALT ⌉ + ⌈ DELETE ⌉

   Type the user name
   Administrator and the
   password **Pa$$321**

   Click **Options**

   From the Log on to list, select   This is the NetBIOS name of the classroom
   RSTDOMAIN   domain.

   Click **OK**   To log on to your computer as the domain
                                         administrator for the RSTDOMAIN.CLASS
                                         domain. While the user name is the same, the
                                         actual user account is different, with different
                                         rights and privileges on the computer and in the
                                         domain. (You're still an administrator of the
                                         computer in front of you.)

Do it!

A-7: Viewing network resources

Here's how	Here's why
1 Click **Start**, and choose **My Computer**	
2 Under Other Places, click **My Network Places**	
Under Other Places, click **Entire Network**	
In the details pane, double-click **Microsoft Windows Network**	RSTDOMAIN is the classroom Active Directory domain.
In the details pane, double-click **RSTDOMAIN**	Each student computer is listed with a computer icon and the label RST##. The classroom server is listed with a computer icon and the label RSTSRV.
3 View the network resources on the RSTSRV computer	
4 Close the RSTSRV window	

NWLink

Applications on NetWare servers that are running IPX/SPX aren't available to a Windows computer unless that computer has the NWLink IPX/SPX protocol installed. Typically, NetWare servers running NetWare version 4 or older are running IPX/SPX, but you might find servers with later versions of NetWare running that protocol, too. IPX/SPX requires three configuration settings:

- **External network number** — The number assigned to the network as configured on the NetWare servers. Windows detects this number automatically.

- **Internal network number** — The unique number that identifies the computer on the network. Windows detects this number, too.

- **Frame type** — The type of format used to package and send data on the network. There are three types—802.2, 802.3, and 802.5—which Windows attempts to detect in that order. Windows assigns the correct frame type, even if there are multiple frame types configured on the network. When multiple frame types are in use, Windows assigns 802.2, but you need to assign the other manually.

To install NWLink:

1 In Windows 2000/XP, open the Properties dialog for the Local Area Connection.
2 Click Install.
3 Select Protocol.
4 Select NWLink IPX/SPX/NetBIOS Compatible Transport Protocol.

To configure NWLink, select it as you would TCP/IP and click Properties.

Many times, if a user can't connect to an older NetWare network, the frame type is incorrectly set or isn't being detected correctly by Windows. To fix the problem, go into the Properties of the NWLink protocol and set the correct frame type.

Do it!

A-8: Installing and configuring NWLink

Here's how	Here's why
1 Open Control Panel	You're going to install NWLink, which you can use to communicate on an IPX/SPX network.
2 Click **Network and Internet Connections**	
Click **Network Connections**	To open the Network Connections window.
3 Right-click **Local Area Connection** and choose **Properties**	
4 Click **Install...** and double-click **Protocol**	To open the Select Network Protocol dialog box.
5 Select **NWLink IPX/SPX/NetBIOS Compatible Transport Protocol**	To install NWLink.
Click **OK**	
6 Observe NWLink in the list of components	This connection uses the following items: ☑ NWLink NetBIOS ☑ NWLink IPX/SPX/NetBIOS Compatible Transport Prot ☑ Internet Protocol (TCP/IP)
7 Double-click **NWLink IPX/SPX/NetBIOS Compatible Transport Protocol**	
8 Observe the Internet network number box	Internal network number: 00000000
	The number is an eight-digit hexadecimal number, currently set to zero.

9 From the Frame type list, select
Ethernet 802.2

In the Network number box, enter
000E0011

To set a frame type.

Frame type:	Ethernet 802.2
Network number:	000E0011

To configure a network number. (There isn't an
actual IPX/SPX network in the classroom, but
you can practice.)

10 Click **OK** and click **Close**

Close the Network Connections
window

Topic B: Resource sharing

This topic covers the following CompTIA A+ 220-603 exam objectives.

#	Objective
4.2	**Install, configure, optimize and upgrade networks**
	• Establish network connectivity and share network resources
5.1	**Identify the fundamental principles of security**
	• Identify the names, purposes, and characteristics of access control and permissions
	• Permission levels, types (e.g., file systems and shared) and actions (e.g., read, write, change and execute)

Resource sharing

Explanation

You'll be hard-pressed to find a Windows network where users aren't sharing resources of some kind, whether it's spreadsheets and Word documents or the best printer in the office. As a CompTIA A+ technician, you need to know how to share files and printers, and you need to know how to troubleshoot errors users encounter when trying to share and access shared resources.

Network client software

You can share and access shared folders in all versions of Windows, as long as the necessary components are installed. To share folders and printers, you need *File and Printer Sharing for Microsoft Networks*. To connect to a shared folder or printer, you need the *Client for Microsoft Networks*. You can see both of these components in Exhibit 6-7. If you want to access files or printers on a NetWare server, you need the Microsoft Client for NetWare Networks.

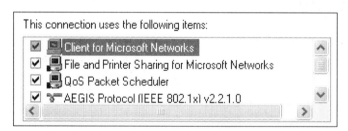

Exhibit 6-7: Components for file sharing

File and folder sharing

File sharing is already accessible in Windows 2000/XP. In Windows XP, you might have to disable Simple File Sharing, which is enabled by default on computers installed into workgroups, to have greater control over NTFS permissions. To disable Simple File Sharing:

1 In My Computer, choose Tools, Folder Options.
2 On the View tab, uncheck "Use simple file sharing."
3 Click OK.

To share a file or folder on a Windows computer:

1   In Windows Explorer, right-click the file or folder and choose Properties.

2   On the Sharing tab, enable sharing.

3   Enter a share name, if you don't want to use the default share name. (Sharing folders is easier to manage than sharing files.)

4   Click OK.

Do it!

B-1:   Sharing a folder

If Simple File Sharing hasn't been disabled, have students disable it now. The Windows Firewall should be configured to allow file and printer sharing.

Here's how	Here's why
1 Open My Computer	You're going to create and share a folder—pretty common practice in offices that need to share information among many people.
2 On drive C:, create a folder named **NNShare**	☐ ALShare
	Enter your initials instead of "NN."
3 Right-click the new folder and choose **Sharing and Security...**	To open the folder's Properties dialog box with the Sharing tab activated.
4 Select **Share this folder**	◉ Share this folder Share name: ALShare
Leave the default share name	
5 Click **OK**	
6 Observe the folder's icon	☐ ALShare
	The hand indicates that the folder is shared.

NTFS permissions

Explanation

Files and folders located on NTFS partitions or volumes can be secured through the use of NTFS permissions. NTFS permissions can't be applied to files or folders that reside on partitions formatted using the FAT or FAT32 file systems.

It's important to understand the various NTFS file and directory permissions that are available, as well as how they're applied.

- NTFS permissions are configured via the Security tab, which is accessed by right-clicking any file or folder and clicking Properties.

- NTFS permissions are cumulative. If a user is a member of multiple groups that have different permissions, the final permission is the sum of all permissions.

- Permissions that are explicitly denied always override those that are allowed. For example, if the Mark Manore user account is explicitly denied Write on a folder through an individual or group permission assignment, this overrides any permissions that Mark may have been allowed via other group memberships.

- NTFS folder permissions are inherited by child folders and files, unless otherwise specified.

- NTFS permissions can be set at a file level, as well as at a folder level.

Exhibit 6-8 shows the standard NTFS permissions available for a folder.

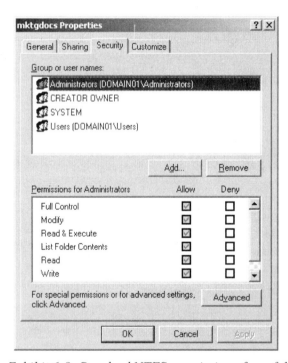

Exhibit 6-8: Standard NTFS permissions for a folder

The following table lists the standard NTFS permissions.

NTFS permission	Capabilities
Full Control	Allows the user to make any changes to the file or folder.
Modify	Gives full permissions except the permission to delete subfolders and files, change permissions, and take ownership.
Read and Execute	Gives permissions to traverse folders, list folders, read attributes and extended attributes, read permissions, and synchronize; these permissions are inherited by both files and folders.
List Folder Contents	Same as Read and Execute permissions, except that the permissions are inherited only by folders and not by files; visible only on folders.
Read	Same as Read and Execute, except without the permission to traverse folder; inherited by files and folders.
Write	Gives permissions to create files and folders, write attributes and extended attributes, read permissions, and synchronize.
Special Permissions	Used to designate that a user has been allowed or denied one or more of the more granular special permissions configured in the Advanced section of the security settings.

Note: When assigning shared folder or NTFS permissions to users and groups, never grant them a higher level of access than they actually require. For example, if users need to be able only to read (but not change) files, the Read permission is sufficient. Granting users too liberal a level of access can result in files being accidentally or purposely deleted, changed, etc.

Enabling the Security tab

By default, the Security tab of the Properties dialog box isn't visible with Windows XP Professional. It's inaccessible entirely in Windows XP Home. To enable the tab in Windows XP Professional:

1   Open Windows Explorer.
2   Choose Tools, Folder Options.
3   Activate the View tab.
4   Clear the checkbox beside Use simple file sharing.
5   Click OK.

Share permissions

There's a similar set of permissions to NTFS that you can set to control access to resources you share on the network. These permissions, called *share permissions*, are described in the following table:

Share permission	Users with this permission can...
Read	Connect to the folder, open the folder, open files within the folder, and run applications inside the folder.
Change	Connect to the folder, open the folder, open files inside the folder, run applications inside the folder, and create, delete, and modify files and subfolders inside the shared folder.
Full control	Do anything with any of the files, applications, or subfolders inside the folder, and create anything inside the folder.

In Windows 2000/XP, you assign share permissions in much the same way you assign NTFS permissions. As you can see in Exhibit 6-9, they look much the same as NTFS permissions. (There are no NTFS permissions on Windows 2000/XP drives that are formatted as FAT or FAT32.)

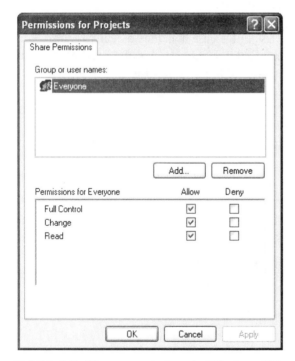

Exhibit 6-9: Share permissions in Windows XP

To set share permissions:

1   Right-click a file or folder and choose Properties.
2   On the Sharing tab, click Permissions.
3   Select the user account you want to configure, and assign the necessary permissions.
4   Click Add to add users, if they aren't already in the list.

If you're a member of a domain, you can choose to search the domain for user accounts to add to the list.

Effective permissions

When you combine share permissions with NTFS permissions, the resulting set is called the *effective permissions*. When a user tries to access a share from across the network, Windows checks to see if the user has been granted share and NTFS permissions to the share. (Windows also checks to see if a group the user belongs to has been granted share and NTFS permissions.) If a user hasn't been granted share permissions, then the user can't access the share from across the network. If a user has both share and NTFS permissions, Windows assigns the most restrictive permissions to that user.

For example, if the user has been assigned Full Control share permissions and Read NTFS permissions, the user has Read permissions to the shared folder. If the user has Read share permissions and Full Control NTFS permissions, then the user still has Read permissions to the shared folder.

Remember that a permission that has been denied in Windows 2000/XP overrides any permission that has been allowed.

B-2: Setting access permissions

Here's how	Here's why
1 Right-click **NNShare** and choose **Sharing and Security...**	To open the folder's Properties dialog box with the Sharing tab active. You're going to secure your shared folder by restricting access to it.
2 On the Sharing tab, click **Permissions**	To open the Permissions dialog box. The group Everyone has Full Control share permissions by default.
3 Click **Add**	To open the Select Users, Computers, or Groups dialog box.
4 In the "Enter the object names to select" box, type **Domain Users**	Enter the object names to select (examples): Domain Users
Click **OK**	To assign the Domain Users group share permissions to the folder on your computer.
5 Under "Group or user names," select **Domain Users**	In the Permissions dialog box.
In the Permissions for Domain Users list, under Allow, check **Change**	Permissions for Domain Users — Allow — Deny Full Control ☐ ☐ Change ☑ ☐ Read ☑ ☐
6 Select the group **Everyone** and click **Remove**	
7 Click **OK**	To close the Permissions dialog box and return to the folder's Properties dialog box.
8 Activate the Security tab	You're going to assign Domain Users NTFS permissions.
9 Click **Add** and enter **Domain Users**	
Click **OK**	
10 Select **Domain Users**	
In the permissions list, under Allow, check **Full Control**	Permissions for Domain Users — Allow — Deny Full Control ☑ ☐ Modify ☑ ☐ Read & Execute ☑ ☐ List Folder Contents ☑ ☐ Read ☑ ☐ Write ☑ ☐
Click **OK** and close all open windows	

TIPS ✔ *Students can click Check Names to verify that they entered a valid name before clicking OK..*

11 Which users have access to your shared folder?

The Domain Users group has access to your shared folder.

What effective permissions do members of that group have? Why?

Members of that group have Change permissions, even though they've been assigned Full Control NTFS permissions. The reason is that the most restrictive permissions are the effective permissions.

Connecting to shares

You can connect to a share by using Network Neighborhood or My Network Places to browse to the computer that holds the share, or you can click Start, choose Run, and enter the Universal Naming Convention (UNC) path to the share. The format for the UNC is `\\computername\sharename`.

Do it!

B-3:   Connecting to a shared folder

Here's how	Here's why
1 Talk to your partner and find out his or her computer name	You're going to use a UNC path to connect to another student's shared folder. This is the most direct way to connect to a Windows share over the network.
2 Click **Start** and choose **Run...**	
3 Enter **\\computername**	Where *computername* is the name of your computer. Share names and computer names are not case-sensitive.
4 Click **OK**	To access your partner's computer.
5 Observe the shared folder	It's listed with the Printers and Faxes folder and the Scheduled Tasks folder. Note the name of the share.
6 Close the window	
7 Click **Start** and choose **Run...** Enter **\\computername\share**	(Where *computername* is the name of your computer, and *share* is the name of the share.) To connect to the share directly. You weren't prompted for a user name and password, because you're using the domain Administrator account, which has privileges to the shared folder. (The account is a member of Domain Users.)
8 Close the window	

Assign students to work in pairs. If you have an odd number of students, have one student work with you. Make sure students know their computer names.

Shared printers

Explanation

You share printers much the same way you share folders. To share a printer, right-click it and choose Properties. On the Sharing tab, choose to share the printer, and add a share name, if you don't want to use the default share name. Users can print to a shared printer but can't manage (pause, delete) print jobs by default. For that, you need to assign users additional permissions.

To connect to a shared printer, browse to the computer with the shared printer through Network Neighborhood or My Network Places. You can then drag the shared printer to your desktop or right-click the printer and choose Connect.

Do it!

B-4: Sharing a printer

Students should have printer drivers installed. (The printer drivers make it appear as if a printer is installed, even if one isn't attached to the computer.) If students don't have a printer installed, have them install one now.

Here's how	Here's why
1 Click **Start** and choose **Printers and Faxes**	You're going to share a printer—a fairly common occurrence in offices with a limited number of printers. Not every user is going to have a printer attached to his or her computer; in fact, none might because they might all use a print server.
2 Right-click an installed printer and choose **Sharing...**	
3 Select **Share this printer** and leave the default share name	The printer share name is limited to 8 characters by default for backward compatibility with older applications.
4 Click **OK**	The printer icon has a hand on it.
5 Close all open windows	

Do it!

B-5: Connecting to a shared printer

Here's how
1 Work with your partner to connect to exchange printer information.
2 Connect by using the UNC path to your partner's computer. (Hint: Use the Add Printer Wizard.)
3 Use My Network Places to find the computer in the RSTDOMAIN domain.
4 Close all open windows when you're done.

Installing NetWare client software

Explanation

If you want to connect to a Novell NetWare server and use its file and print resources, you must install the Microsoft Client for NetWare Networks, just as you need the Client for Microsoft Networks to connect to resources on a Windows computer.

In Windows 2000/XP:

1 In the Properties dialog box for the local area connection, on the General tab, click Install.

2 Select Client, and then select the NetWare client.

3 After restarting, you're prompted for a server or NDS context. Enter them now or later in the Novell client's properties.

Do it!

B-6: Installing the NetWare client

Here's how	Here's why
1 In Control Panel, click **Network and Internet Connections** Click **Network Connections**	You're going to install the Client Service for NetWare. This client software enables you to connect to a NetWare file and printer server.
2 Right-click **Local Area Connection** and choose **Properties**	
3 Click **Install** and double-click **Client**	To open the Select Network Client dialog box.
4 Verify that Client Service for NetWare is selected, and click **OK**	
5 Click **Yes**	To restart your computer.
6 Log back on to the RSTDOMAIN domain as **Administrator** with a password of **Pa$$321**	
7 In the Select NetWare Logon dialog box, click **OK**	You don't have a NetWare server or NDS context on the network. You can configure these settings at any time by opening the Properties dialog box for the client service.

Topic C: Internet connectivity

This topic covers the following CompTIA A+ 220-603 exam objective.

#	Objective
4.1	**Identify the fundamental principles of networks**

- Identify names, purposes and characteristics of basic network protocols and terminologies, for example:

  - ISP
  - SMTP
  - IMAP
  - HTML
  - HTTP

  - HTTPS
  - SSL
  - Telnet
  - FTP
  - DNS

- Identify names, purposes and characteristics of technologies for establishing connectivity, for example:

  - Dial-up networking
  - Broadband (e.g. DSL, cable, satellite)
  - ISDN Networking
  - Wireless
  - LAN/WAN

Internet technologies

Explanation

In today's world, the Internet is business, and business is the Internet. There's hardly an organization around that doesn't have an Internet presence, and most (if not all) organizations nowadays connect to the Internet in some way, even if it's just to send and receive e-mail. Most organizations use the Internet for much more, and as a CompTIA A+ technician, you're responsible for configuring and troubleshooting user Internet access.

Basic terminology

Although there's some overlap between networking concepts and Internet concepts and terminology (after all, the Internet is just a huge TCP/IP network), there are some terms worth highlighting for prospective CompTIA A+ technicians. The following table explains these terms:

Term	Description
Internet service provider (ISP)	A company that sells Internet access to an organization. An ISP provides the connection to the Internet and might also provide other services, such as server space for a company to host a Web site or store data files.
E-mail	A form of electronic communication where text messages are sent and received from computers, personal digital assistants (PDAs), or cell phones. E-mail clients, such as Outlook or Eudora, are used to create, send, and receive e-mail. E-mail messages are processed through e-mail servers, such as Microsoft Exchange or Lotus Domino, within each organization or ISP.
	There are three e-mail protocols:
	• **Post Office Protocol** (POP) — Used to retrieve e-mail from an e-mail server. Used with SMTP, although POP version 3 (POP3) can be used without SMTP.
	• **Internet Message Access Protocol** (IMAP) — Used to retrieve e-mail from an e-mail server. Used with SMTP, although IMAP4 can be used without SMTP.
	• **Simple Mail Transfer Protocol** (SMTP) — Used to send e-mail to an e-mail server. Used with POP or IMAP.
Hypertext Markup Language (HTML)	Used to format Web pages for transfer and display in Web browsers, such as Internet Explorer or Firefox.
DNS	Domain Name Service is the service that maps names to IP addresses. DNS makes it easy to use familiar names rather than unfamiliar IP addresses.
World Wide Web	The collection of computers and servers used to store and share information on the Internet in the form of Web pages. The Web isn't synonymous with the Internet. The Internet is the vast, global network of computers, of which the Web is just one part, one way of communicating. Other services and means of communicating on the Internet include e-mail, newsgroups, and instant messaging.

A good way to remember that SMTP is used to send messages is the mnemonic "Send Mail To People."

Internet protocols

The following table describes some of the protocols that are used on the Internet:

Protocol	Description
TCP/IP	The protocol of the Internet.
Hypertext Transfer Protocol (HTTP)	The protocol used to make Web requests and download Web pages over TCP/IP.
Secure Sockets Layer (SSL)	A public-key/private-key encryption protocol used to transmit data securely across the Internet over TCP/IP. Web sites that require SSL begin with https://, rather than the usual http://. When you connect using SSL, the connection itself is secure, and so is any data transferred across the connection.
Secure HTTP (S-HTTP)	Another protocol used to secure Internet transmissions. Whereas SSL secures a connection between two computers, S-HTTP secures the individual data packets themselves.
Telnet	A terminal emulation protocol used over TCP/IP networks. You can use Telnet to connect to a remote server across the Internet. You can then enter commands on your computer, and the commands are executed as if you were entering them into the server directly. Telnet is used mainly for remote management of servers and other devices, such as routers.
File Transfer Protocol (FTP)	FTP is used to transfer files to and from an FTP server over a TCP/IP network.

ISP connection technologies

A local area network has much less need for data throughput than does a national backbone. Lying between these two extremes on the spectrum are many types of systems that require varying degrees of bandwidth. Exhibit 6-10 illustrates various types of networks and their bandwidths.

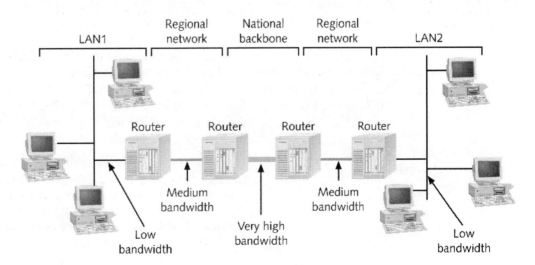

Exhibit 6-10: The Internet infrastructure

Regular telephone lines

Regular telephone lines, one of the most common ways to connect to an ISP, require an internal or external modem. A modem converts the computer's digital data (data made up of zeros and ones) to analog data (a continuous and infinite number of variations of frequencies) that can be communicated over telephone lines. As data travels from the computer to the modem, it's converted from digital to analog. On the receiving end, as it travels from the modem to the computer, it's converted from analog back to digital.

Use this slide to explain the concepts pertaining to Internet connections over regular phone lines.

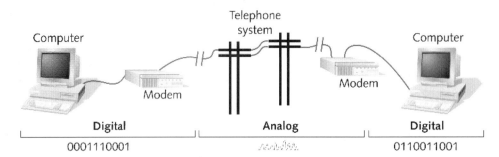

Exhibit 6-11: Communication via PSTN

When data packets are traveling over telephone lines, the Data Link layer protocol used is *PPP (Point-to-Point Protocol)* or *SLIP (Serial Line Internet Protocol)*. PPP most often is used to transmit TCP/IP packets from a computer connected to an ISP or intranet access point by telephone line. PPP encloses a TCP/IP packet within its own header and trailer information. This header and trailer information is used only while the packet travels on the telephone line. After it's off the line, the PPP header and trailer information is stripped from the packet before it continues over the network. The TCP/IP frame is enclosed in the PPP header and trailer and then presented to the modem for delivery over telephone lines to a modem on the receiving end. The modem on the receiving end passes the packet to the PPP utility, which removes the PPP header and trailer information before sending the packet on its way.

An earlier version of a line protocol is SLIP, which also supports a TCP/IP network but seldom is used today. SLIP doesn't support authentication or other security features, including encrypted passwords.

The telephone system is carrying analog data from modem to modem, which seldom occurs on actual systems. The data is only analog from a customer's telephone or modem to the telephone company's central office, where it's converted to digital until it reaches the central office of the recipient. If the recipient is an ISP that's using regular telephone lines to connect to its customers, the data is converted to analog for the final leg of its journey from the ISP's central office to the ISP modem. Because of the standards used by the telephone companies to convert from digital to analog or analog to digital, the fastest possible transmission over telephone lines is 56 Kbps (56,000 bits per second), although speeds this fast are rarely attained, even when both the user and the ISP are using 56K modems. New technology has opened the way for faster and more advanced methods of communication.

Cable modem

Cable modem communication uses cable lines that already exist in millions of households in the United States. Just as with cable TV, cable modems are always connected. A cable modem is an example of *broadband media*. Broadband refers to any type of networking media that carries more than one type of transmission. With a cable modem, the TV signal to your television and the data signals to your computer share the same cable.

Cable television lines are analog. A cable modem converts your computer's digital signals to analog before sending data out on the cable television line and also converts incoming data (from the television cable or the telephone line) from analog to digital. Cable modems primarily use a technology called DOCSIS (data over cable service interface specifications).

Unlike a telephone line, which creates a single, point-to-point connection between your house and the telephone company facilities, a cable coming to your home doesn't provide a single point-to-point connection. Instead, a cable establishes a *point-to-multipoint* connection, whereby the signal from the cable company is sent to multiple destinations. Your connection is one of many in the neighborhood that all tie to a single backbone cable coming into the neighborhood. For this reason, you can see degradation in service if many people are using cable modems in your area and are competing for the same bandwidth.

Another disadvantage of cable modems is the lack of security between you and the cable company ISP, because many users are sharing this connection with you. For this reason, if you use a cable modem, you might want to use a personal firewall to protect your computer from hackers.

When you lease cable modem service, you are most likely also agreeing to use the cable modem company as your ISP. The cost for cable modem service including ISP cost is in the range of $20 to $60 per month.

PPPoE (Point-to-Point Protocol over Ethernet)

When you set up either a cable or DSL connection for your computer, you need to use a converter box that sits between your computer and the DSL line or TV cable line. For cable modems, the converter box is called the cable modem, and for DSL, the box is called the DSL converter box. (Sometimes, a router is used in place of a DSL converter box.) This device connects to your computer using an Ethernet cable that plugs into an Ethernet NIC in your computer, as shown in Exhibit 6-12. The PPPoE protocol carries the data packets over this short Ethernet link from your computer to a broadband connection.

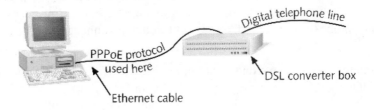

Exhibit 6-12: PPPoE

PPPoE (Point-to-Point Protocol over Ethernet) is a protocol that adapts PPP to work with Ethernet. PPPoE describes how the computer is to interact with the converter box or modem when the two are connected by an Ethernet cable connected to an Ethernet network card in the computer. PPPoE gives the user the security and authentication that's offered with PPP. PPPoE also sets standards for networks to connect to the Internet via DSL modems and other high-speed access services.

ISDN

ISDN (Integrated Services Digital Network) is a technology developed in the 1980s that uses regular telephone lines and is accessed by a dial-up connection. ISDN is actually an early implementation of DSL. For home use, an ISDN line is fully digital and consists of two channels, or telephone circuits, on a single pair of wires called B channels and a slower channel used for control signals, called a D channel. Each B channel can support speeds up to 64,000 bps. The two lines can be combined so that, effectively, data travels at 128,000 bps, which is about three to five times the speed of regular telephone lines.

ISDN requires an ISDN converter box that provides an Ethernet connection to the computer, or you can use an ISDN card installed inside the computer. ISDN is expensive for home and small business Internet connections and is being replaced by DSL, which is a faster and less expensive solution for Internet access.

DSL

The telephone industry has developed several similar technologies that collectively are called DSL (Digital Subscriber Line). DSL is fast data transmission technology, which is affordable for home use and offers a direct connection rather than a dial-up. It's a broadband technology that uses ordinary copper telephone lines and a range of frequencies on the copper wire that aren't used by voice, making it possible for you to use the same telephone line for voice and DSL at the same time. The voice portion of the telephone line requires a dial-up as normal, but the DSL part of the line is always connected.

Because DSL uses regular telephone lines, it's point-to-point. That means you don't need to be concerned that you're competing with others in your area for bandwidth, as is the case with cable modems. The cost of a DSL line varies greatly, from $35 to $85 per month, depending on your location.

Satellite

People who live in remote areas and want high-speed Internet connections are often limited in their choices. DSL and cable modems might not work where they live, but satellite access is available from almost anywhere. Technology is even being developed to use satellites to offer Internet access on commercial airlines. Customers can use their own laptops to connect to the Internet through a connection at their seats to a satellite dish in the airplane.

A satellite dish mounts on top of your house or office building and communicates with a satellite that's used for communication by an ISP offering the satellite service. Originally, satellite access was only one-way. Data was sent to the users via satellite, but data transmitted from the users to the servers was sent over the telephone lines. This was usually acceptable because, for normal Internet use, the amount of data transmitted from the client is small when compared with what's sent from servers to the client.

A computer using this system connects to a satellite modem, which connects to a satellite dish on the house. The computer also is connected to the ISP by telephone line.

When a request is made to a Web site, the request is sent through the telephone line. The ISP receives the request and then sends the response through the satellite.

New technology allows data to be transmitted both ways over the satellite so that telephone line connections aren't needed. An external satellite modem providing two-way transmission has two interface cards each with a cable connection, one for sending and one for receiving data. The modem box connects to the computer using either an Ethernet connection to a NIC installed in the computer or a USB port, which is a standard port on most computers. Data in both directions is transmitted via satellite. For remote users, this often eliminates a long-distance telephone call.

Several companies offer satellite Internet access. The average setup cost is around $600 with monthly fees starting at $60.

Wireless

The term "wireless" refers to several technologies and systems that don't use cables for communication, including public radio, cellular telephones, one-way paging, satellite, infrared, Bluetooth, and private, proprietary radio. Because of the expense and the concern that increasing the use of wireless might affect our health, airplane control systems, pacemakers, and other similar things, wireless isn't as popular as wired data transmission. Wireless is an important technology for mobile devices and for Internet access in remote locations where other methods aren't an option.

For Internet access, two popular applications of wireless are:

- Fixed-point wireless, sometimes called Wireless Local Loop (WLL)
- Mobile wireless

With fixed-point wireless, an antenna sits on your house or office building and communicates with a base station antenna. With mobile wireless, a wireless modem connects to a laptop computer and communicates with a grid of transmitters spread over a wide geographical area. This grid is called a wireless WAN.

Use this slide to explain Wireless WAN concepts.

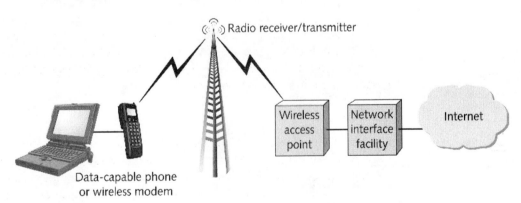

Exhibit 6-13: Wireless WAN

C-1: Identifying Internet technologies

Questions and answers

1 Which of the following is the protocol of the Internet?

    A   HTTP

    B   TCP/IP

    C   HTTPS

    D   SSL

2 Which of the following protocols retrieve e-mail messages from an e-mail server? (Choose all that apply.)

    A   IMAP4

    B   SMTP

    C   POP3

    D   HTTP

3 Which of the following protocols send e-mail messages to e-mail servers? (Choose all that apply.)

    A   IMAP4

    B   IMAP

    C   POP3

    D   SMTP

4 Which protocol secures connections between two computers?

    A   SSL

    B   TCP/IP

    C   FTP

    D   Telnet

5 Which connectivity technology uses digital telephone lines exclusively?

    A   DSL

    B   ISDN

    C   WLL

    D   Cable

6 What are two ways of making a wireless connection to the Internet?

First, a user can connect to a wireless hotspot in a building, provided by a business, such as a coffee shop or airport, or a hotspot provided by a municipality. Second, a user can connect to the Internet by using a cellular telephone network.

7 Why might you use Telnet to connect to a remote server? Give an example.

To administer that server from another location, for example, from home or from a branch office.

8 What's the difference between HTML and HTTP?

HTML is a coding language used to format Web pages. HTTP is the protocol used to connect to a Web site and download a Web page.

9 How does TCP/IP relate to other protocols, such as SSL and HTTP?

These other protocols run on top of the TCP/IP network.

Do it!

C-2: Selecting a connection technology

Exercises

Discuss with students why they feel their answer is the best choice in each scenario.

1 For each user, select the appropriate connection technology.

Susan is a salesperson who travels extensively. She needs to be able to send and receive communication to the home office and clients while in transit. What's Susan's best choice for connection technology?

Wireless. Many locations, such as coffee houses, airport terminals, and other public buildings, have wireless access points that Susan could use to connect to her company's LAN through the Internet.

James is an architect who works out of his home in the Adirondack mountains. James must send and receive large CAD drawings to/from clients and builders. What's James' best choice for connection technology?

Because of James' remote location, he's probably too far away to connect via cable or DSL lines. Dial-up service using PSTN would likely be terribly slow uploading and downloading the CAD drawings. Although it might be more expensive, James' best bet would be satellite service with transfer speeds that are the same for uploading and downloading.

Grace lives next to James in the Adirondacks. She's retired and uses e-mail to communicate with her children and grandchildren all over the country. Sometimes they send her digital pictures attached to the e-mail messages so she can see the grandchildren. She occasionally uses her Web browser to look up information. What's Grace's best choice for connection technology?

Grace's livelihood doesn't rely on her Internet connection. She doesn't send large files and receives picture files occasionally. An inexpensive dial-up service using the phone lines already connected to Grace's house would serve her needs just fine.

WAN bandwidth technologies

Explanation

Faster WAN technologies are used to connect a small ISP or large business to a regional ISP and a regional ISP to an Internet backbone. These technologies include:

- T lines and E lines
- X.25 and frame relay
- ATM
- Mesh topology

T lines and E lines

The first successful system that supported digitized voiced transmission was introduced in the 1960s and called a T-carrier. A T-carrier works with a leased digital communications line provided through a common carrier, such as BellSouth or AT&T. Although it was originally intended for voice, the line also works with data. The system has become a popular choice for Internet access for larger companies. The leased lines are permanent connections that use multiplexing, a process of dividing a single channel into multiple channels that can be used to carry voice, data, video, or other signals. Several variations of T-carrier lines are available; the most popular are T1 and T3 lines.

- For a T1 line, multiplexing allows the line to carry 24 channels, and each channel is capable of transmitting 64 Kbps. Therefore, a 24-channel T1 line can transmit a total of 1.544 Mbps. If a T1 is used for voice only, it can support 24 separate telephone lines, one for each channel.
- A T3 line can carry 672 channels, giving it a throughput of 44.736 Mbps.

T1 and T3 lines can be used by a business to support both voice and data, with some channels allocated to voice and others to data.

The E-carrier is the European equivalent of the American T-carrier. The E-carrier is a digital transmission format devised by ITU at www.itu.int. An E1 line can transmit data at a rate of 2.048 Mbps, and an E3 line can work at speeds of 34.368 Mbps.

Both T-carriers and E-carriers use four wires, two for receiving and two for sending. Originally, copper wires were used (telephone wiring), but digital signals require a clearer connection, so shielded twisted-pair wiring is preferred. The carriers need repeaters that can regenerate the signal every 6,000 feet. Businesses with multiple T1 lines generally use coaxial, fiber-optic, or microwave cabling, a high-end, high-performance cabling that can support microwave frequencies. With T3, microwave or fiber-optic cabling is required.

A fractional T1 line is an option for organizations that don't need a full T1 line. The fractional T1 allows businesses to lease some of the channels of a T1 line rather than leasing all 24 channels. This arrangement is also good for businesses that expect to grow into a T1 line eventually. Because each T1 channel has a throughput of 64 Kbps, a fractional T1 can be leased in 64-Kbps increments.

X.25 and frame relay

Both X.25 and frame relay are packet-switching communication protocols designed for long-distance data transmission rather than the circuit-switching technology used by the telephone system. Packet-switching technology divides data into packets and sends each packet separately. It's the technology used by the Internet. Each packet might be sent on a different path. This technology works well, because it can use the bandwidth more efficiently.

Frame relay is based on X.25, but it's a digital version, whereas X.25 is an analog technology. Because frame relay is digital, it can support higher throughput of up to 1.544 Mbps, compared with X.25, which supports up to 56 Kbps. X.25 was popular for about 20 years and was the most common packet-switching technology used on WANs. Frame relay, which was standardized in 1984, has largely replaced X.25.

Both X.25 and frame relay use a PVC (permanent virtual circuit). PVC is a permanent, logical connection between two nodes. PVCs aren't dedicated lines, like the T-carriers. Rather, when you lease a PVC, you specify the nodes (two endpoints) and the amount of bandwidth required, but the carrier reserves the right to send the data along any number of paths between the two stationary endpoints. You then share the bandwidth with other users who lease the X.25 or frame relay circuit.

The biggest advantage of X.25 and frame relay is that you have to pay only for the amount of bandwidth you require. Frame relay is also less expensive than newer technologies, and it has worldwide standards already established. Because both X.25 and frame relay use shared lines, throughput decreases as traffic increases.

Circuits for X.25 aren't readily available in North America, but frame relay circuits can be found easily. International businesses that communicate overseas might use frame relay to connect offices.

ATM

ATM (Asynchronous Transfer Mode) is a very fast network technology that can be used with LANs, as well as WANs. It uses fixed-length packets, called cells, to transmit data, voice, video, and frame relay traffic. Each cell is 53 bytes, 48 bytes of data plus a 5-byte header. The header contains the information necessary to route the packet. Because all the packets used by ATM are 53 bytes, it's easy to determine the number of packets and the traffic flow, which helps utilize bandwidth.

ATMs also use virtual circuits, meaning that the two endpoints are stationary, but the paths between these two endpoints can change. They can use either PVCs or SVCs. SVCs (switched virtual circuits) are logical, point-to-point connections that depend on the ATM to decide the best path to send the data. The routes are determined before the data is even sent. In contrast, an Ethernet network transmits the data before determining the route it takes. The routers and switches are responsible for deciding the paths.

ATMs achieve a throughput of 622 Mbps, which makes them popular for large LANs, because they're faster than Ethernet at 100 Mbps. An ATM network works best with fiber-optic cable, so that it can attain high throughput, but it also works with coaxial or twisted-pair cable.

Mesh topology

A mesh network topology is highly reliable and is used when the network reliability is critical and can justify the added expense. A mesh topology provides multiple point-to-point links between routers in a wide area network, giving more than one choice on how data can travel from router to router. In a mesh topology, a router searches out multiple paths and determines the best path to take. Routers can make these decisions based on how busy a network is, how many hops are between two remote networks, how much bandwidth is available, and the cost of using a network. A mesh topology offers added security, because routers can have their own dedicated line connections. A mesh topology also offers added reliability, because there's more than one option between routers, and if one router fails, the WAN can still function. On the other hand, a mesh topology can be rather expensive, as added network cards and cabling are required. It's sometimes used on an ATM LAN or WAN.

Do it!

C-3: Discussing WAN bandwidth technologies

Questions	Answers
1 What's the difference between a T line and an E line?	*T lines are available in North America. E lines are the European equivalent of T lines.*
2 How often is a repeater needed on a T line?	*T carriers need repeaters that can regenerate the signal every 6,000 feet.*
3 What's a fractional T1 line?	*A fractional T1 line allows businesses that don't need the complete bandwidth of a full 24-channel T1 line to lease just some of the channels.*
4 What's packet-switching technology?	*Packet-switching technology divides data into packets and sends each packet separately. Each packet might be sent on a different path thus using the bandwidth more efficiently.*
5 Name two packet-switching technologies.	*X.25 and frame relay*
6 What's ATM?	*ATM (Asynchronous Transfer Mode) is a very fast network technology that can be used with LANs, as well as WANs. It uses fixed-length packets, called cells, to transmit data, voice, video, and frame relay traffic.*
7 What's a benefit of ATM?	*ATM uses virtual circuits where the two endpoints are stationary, but the paths between these two endpoints can change so that it can decide the best path to send the data before the data is even sent.*
8 What are the benefits of mesh topology?	*A mesh topology provides multiple point-to-point links between routers in a wide area network, giving more than one choice on how data can travel from router to router. It also offers added reliability, because there's more than one option between routers, and if one router fails, the WAN can still function.*

Internet connections

Explanation

CompTIA A+ technicians are generally asked to configure and troubleshoot two types of user Internet connections: those made from the workplace and those made from a remote location, typically a user's home. It's important to note that CompTIA A+ technicians typically aren't responsible for connecting an entire LAN to the Internet or troubleshooting that connection. That task is left to network administrators and engineers. Your job is to ensure that users can connect to the Internet from their Windows computers. Any network configuration beyond the desktop is left to other individuals.

LAN Internet connections

In a workplace or office, a user connects through the organization's LAN. A connection through the LAN requires a valid network connection, and that requires, at a minimum, a working network card, an IP address, and a subnet mask. In addition, you need to add the IP address of a *gateway*, which is generally the server or router that connects the LAN to the Internet. In larger networks, the gateway might just be a router on the same network segment that eventually forwards the packets to the Internet gateway. You might also need to add the IP addresses of one or more DNS servers.

In all Windows operating systems, to configure TCP/IP settings, open the TCP/IP properties of the network connection, or configure the computer to use DHCP and make sure the necessary information is configured on the DHCP server. Exhibit 6-14 shows TCP/IP properties configured for Internet access through a LAN.

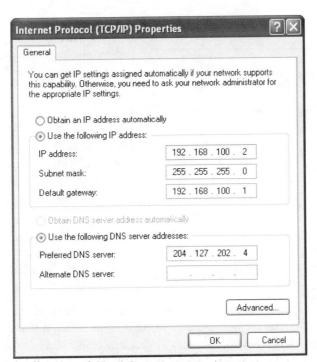

Exhibit 6-14: TCP/IP connection properties for access through a LAN

If you're connecting users to a wireless LAN, you need the necessary wireless information, such as the name of the wireless network and any passwords or encryption keys used to secure wireless access.

Network address translation

If the hosts on a network using private IP addresses need to access the Internet, a problem arises, because private IP addresses aren't allowed on the Internet. The solution is to use *NAT (Network Address Translation)*, which uses a single public IP address to access the Internet on behalf of all hosts on the network using other IP addresses.

When a computer on the network tries to access the Internet, it must go through a server, router, or other device that substitutes its own IP address for that of the computer requesting the information. Because the device is standing in proxy for the other hosts that want Internet access, it's called a *proxy server*. A proxy server has at least two NICs installed. One card connects to the LAN, and the other card connects to a cable modem and on to the ISP and the Internet. The proxy server software on this server must be told which NIC is to be used to access the Internet and which card accesses the LAN.

Use this slide to explain proxy server concepts.

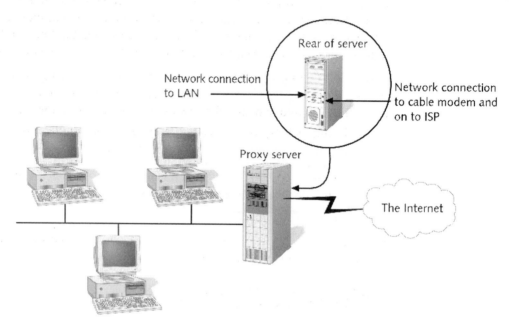

Exhibit 6-15: A proxy server

When NAT is used, it appears to all computers on the Internet that all Internet activity traffic is coming from the proxy server rather than from individual hosts on the network. This increases security to the network, because an outside computer on the Internet views the entire network (with potentially thousands of hosts attached) as a single host device. Therefore, the network appears, from the outside, as a less attractive target for potential hackers.

Another way a proxy server can increase security on the network is to examine traffic passing in and out of the network and reject communication that it determines can pose a security risk. When a proxy server or other device is used to protect a network by filtering traffic in this way, it's called a firewall. A firewall limits the traffic between the Internet and a network to secure the private network. The proxy server itself can be the firewall, when it's configured to filter the traffic passing through it. Or, if the proxy server is installed on a computer inside the network, the firewall can be a router that's between the proxy server and the Internet, which also filters traffic.

A proxy server has another advantage, if your network is accessing the Internet through an ISP that charges you additional fees for each IP address it has assigned to you at any one time. In this situation, a network could use a proxy server to provide access to the

Internet for all its computers, using only a single IP address, which was assigned by the ISP to the proxy server when it first connected to the ISP. This solution is becoming a common money-saving practice for small home and business networks.

For more information on NATs, search for RFC 3022 at www.rfc-editor.org.

In addition to optional firewalls, most proxy servers come with caching systems. The cache holds data in case it's requested later and is used to speed up Internet and intranet access to Web servers. When a user on a network with a proxy server requests a Web page from the Internet, the request first goes to the proxy server. If the proxy server is also acting as a firewall, the proxy server filters the request to ensure that it doesn't break any security standards. Next, if the proxy server has a cache, it looks in the cache to see if the request can be handled without accessing the Internet. If it doesn't find the requested Web page, it sends the query over the Internet, using its own IP address instead of that of the requesting computer. When the proxy server receives the Web page, it passes it on to the computer.

Windows 2000 Professional and all Windows XP versions offer a NAT service called Microsoft *Internet Connection Sharing (ICS)*. In ICS, two or more computers on a home network can share the same IP address when accessing the Internet. Under ICS, one computer acts as the proxy server for other computers on the home network.

Proxy server settings on the client can be configured manually or automatically through DHCP, depending on network setup. To configure proxy server settings, if the settings are configured automatically for network clients, do the following:

1   In Internet Explorer, open the Internet Options dialog box

2   On the Connections tab, click LAN Settings.

3   Under Proxy server, check "Use a proxy server for your LAN."

4   Enter the IP address of the proxy sever.

5   Click OK.

The location in other browsers might vary. Exhibit 6-16 shows Internet Explorer configured with proxy server information.

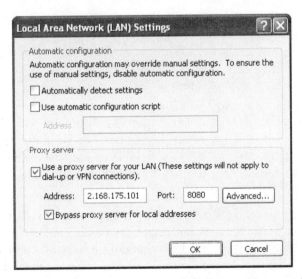

Exhibit 6-16: Proxy server information in Internet Explorer

Do it!

C-4: Configuring a browser to use a proxy server

Here's how	Here's why
1 Your computer is receiving a private IP address from the DHCP server. How's your computer able to access the Internet?	*The classroom is connected to a NAT device or is using a proxy server.*
2 Open Internet Explorer	
Choose **Tools**, **Internet Options...**	
Activate the Connections tab	
Click **LAN Settings**	
3 Check **Use a proxy server for your LAN (These settings will not apply to dial-up or VPN connections).**	If you have a single proxy server, you enter its address and port here.
Click **Advanced**	Windows XP allows you to set proxy servers for HTTP, Secure (HTTPS), FTP, Gopher, and Socks.
4 Click **Cancel** three times	
5 Close Internet Explorer	

Topic D: Network protection

This topic covers the following CompTIA A+ 220-603 exam objectives.

#	Objective
4.3	**Identify tools, diagnostic procedures and troubleshooting techniques for networks**
	• Diagnose and troubleshoot basic network issues for example:
	• Firewall configuration
5.2	**Install, configure, optimizing and upgrade security**
	• Install and configure hardware, software, wireless and data security, for example:
	• Authentication technologies
	• Software firewalls
	• Wireless client configuration
	• Unused wireless connections
5.3	**Identify tools, diagnostic procedures and troubleshooting techniques for security issues**
	• Diagnose and troubleshoot software and data security issues, for example:
	• Software firewall issues
	• Wireless client configuration issues

Firewalls

Explanation

One of the most important things to do when setting up a computer, a server, or a local area network is to install a firewall. A *firewall* is software or hardware used to control information that's sent and received from outside the network. The firewall resides on the network's gateway, which is the connection point between the internal network and outside communication. The firewall ensures that all communication is received from outside users and computers that are legitimate. A firewall can be installed on several different types of gateways, including a router, server, or computer. Firewalls can be used to help prevent DoS attacks and infections from viruses, worms, or Trojan horses.

Various types of firewalls can function in several ways:

- Firewalls can filter data packets, examining the destination IP address or source IP address or the type of protocol used by the packet (for example, TCP or UDP).

- Firewalls can filter ports so that outside clients can't communicate with inside services listening at these ports.

- Firewalls can filter applications, such as FTP, so that users inside the firewall can't use this service over the Internet.

- Some firewalls can filter information, such as inappropriate Web content for children or employees.

In addition, some firewalls can set alarms, when suspicious activities happen, and track this activity in log files. Several variations of firewalls are available, from personal firewalls to protect a single computer up to expensive firewall solutions for large corporations. When selecting a firewall, know what's being filtered, how it's filtered, and what options the firewall offers.

Hardware firewall

A good firewall solution is a hardware firewall that stands between a LAN and the Internet (see Exhibit 6-17). A hardware firewall is ideal for a home network consisting of two or more computers, because it protects the entire network. For most home and small-office LANs that connect to the Internet through a single cable modem or DSL converter, a broadband router is used as a hardware firewall. You can buy a broadband router with enough ports to connect several computers and perhaps a network printer to it. Some broadband routers also serve double duty as a wireless access point to the network, DHCP server, and proxy server. The broadband router connects directly to the cable modem or DSL converter. Note that some DSL devices are also broadband routers and include embedded firewall firmware.

Use this slide to explain hardware firewall concepts.

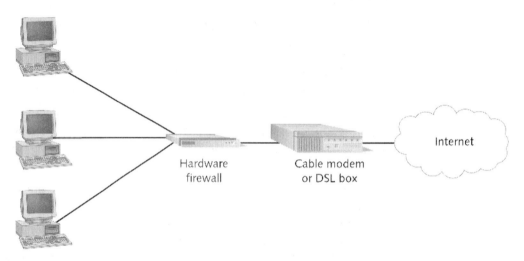

Exhibit 6-17: A hardware firewall

Software firewall

When a home or business computer has an "always on" connection to the Internet, such as a cable modem or DSL, it's a good idea to install a software firewall in addition to a hardware firewall. Firewall software can be installed on a computer connected directly to the Internet. For a local area network, you can install firewall software on each computer on the LAN. The firewall also requests permission from the user prior to allowing any programs access to the Internet. All open ports are blocked, as are any probes from Web sites.

With Service Pack 2 for Windows XP, Microsoft included the security enhancement Windows Firewall. Unlike most firewalls, Windows Firewall can be configured to block only incoming network traffic on your computer. All outgoing network traffic is allowed to travel, unrestricted, from your computer to its destination.

Windows Firewall offers many new features, such as allowing incoming network connections based upon software or services running on a user's computer and the ability to block network connections based upon its source—the Internet, your local area network, or a specific range of IP addresses. By default, Windows Firewall turns on when Service Pack 2 is installed.

Proxy server

When a proxy server is acting as a firewall, it can filter traffic in both directions. It can filter traffic that's coming into the network from outside computers, and it can filter traffic that's leaving the network. One way to filter incoming traffic is to limit communication from the outside to specific ports on the inside of the private network. Some firewalls maintain a list of ports to which they prevent access.

Firewalls filter outgoing traffic through a variety of methods. One method is to examine the IP address of the destination Web site against a list of either allowed addresses or forbidden addresses.

Port and packet filters

When a firewall filters ports, it prevents software on the outside from using certain ports on the network, even though those ports have services listening to them. For example, if you have an intranet Web site that's to be used only by your employees inside the network, you can set your firewall to filter port 80. Those on the intranet can access your Web server using port 80 as normal, but those outside can't reach your Web server.

When a router also acts as a firewall, it can be called a screening router. Sometimes, screening routers can use a technique called *stateful inspection*. The router keeps track of all TCP sessions currently made and allows only those packets to pass that have been requested inside the network for these open sessions.

Sometimes, a problem arises when you want to allow certain ports to be accessed but others to be filtered or to allow packets that aren't a part of a current TCP session, such as when there's a videoconference. Employees on the inside of your firewall need to participate in a videoconference on the Internet, but when you tell your firewall software to allow these ports needed for the conference to be exposed to the Internet or to allow certain type of packets but not others, sometimes the firewall software doesn't respond properly. In this case, some system administrators temporarily "drop their shields" and remove port and packet filtering altogether, so the conference can take place. During these times, the network is vulnerable to an attack.

Windows Security Center

A secure computer is more important than ever in protecting against data and identity theft, so Microsoft decided to make it easy for Windows users to manage the most important security settings in one place. Windows Security Center, as shown in Exhibit 6-18, is a new feature added to Windows XP when you install Service Pack 2 (SP2). From this central location, you can manage Windows Firewall, Automatic Updates, and any antivirus software you have installed on the computer. To open Security Center, click Start, choose Control Panel, and click Security Center. (If you're working in Classic View, double-click Security Center in the Control Panel.)

Exhibit 6-18: Security Center in Windows XP

Windows Firewall

Windows Firewall (known as Internet Connection Firewall before SP2) is turned on by default. If a user is experiencing problems sending or receiving data, the problem could be that the current firewall settings are preventing the communication from passing through. You might need to allow a specific type of communication—that's prohibited by default—to pass through the firewall. When you need to configure Windows Firewall, open the Windows Security Center. Under Manage Security Settings For, click Windows Firewall to open the Windows Firewall dialog box, as shown in Exhibit 6-19.

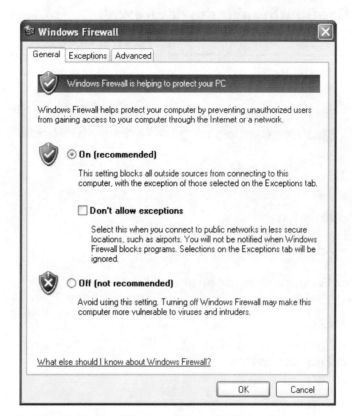

Exhibit 6-19: The Windows Firewall dialog box

You can use this dialog box to turn the firewall on and off, and you can use the Exceptions tab to allow or deny specific types of network communication. The Settings on the Advanced tab let you configure firewall protection for multiple network connections, manage the log file, and configure Internet Control Message Protocol (ICMP) settings. If users are having difficulty accessing Web sites, you should check the firewall settings.

Do it!

D-1: Configuring Windows Firewall

Here's how	Here's why
1 Open Control Panel	You're going to configure the firewall to allow communication through Windows Messenger, Microsoft's instant messaging client software.
Click **Security Center**	To open the Windows Security Center.
2 Under "Manage security settings for," click **Windows Firewall**	To open the Windows Firewall dialog box.
3 Activate the Exceptions tab	
4 Click **Add Program**	
5 Select **Windows Messenger** and click **OK**	To add Windows Messenger to the list of exceptions. You'll see that it's been added to the list and the box has been checked.
6 In the Programs and Services list, select **File and Printer Sharing**	You'll configure specific ports.
7 Click **Edit**	
With TCP 139 selected, click **Change scope**	
Choose **My network (subnet) only**	To close the port to any traffic that isn't on the subnet.
Click **OK**	
8 Click **OK** three times, and close Security Center and Control Panel	

Wireless standards

Explanation

Ever since the first wireless transmissions took place over a century ago, there has been a push to manage the public airwaves responsibly. During that time, frequency bands have been divided up to accommodate the various user categories such as the military, broadcasters, and amateur radio operators. One of the issues with the current wireless technology is that it's a broadcast signal. This means a wireless device advertises its presence, making it easy for an intruder to pick up and monitor. In order to prevent this from happening, standards were developed and implemented. The WLAN solution provided by Windows XP and Windows Server 2003 is based on IEEE standards 802.1x and 802.11.

802.1x standard

The *802.1x standard* is a port-based, authentication framework for access to Ethernet networks. Although this standard is designed for wired Ethernet networks, it applies to 802.11 WLANs. This port-based network access control uses the physical characteristics of the switched LAN infrastructure to authenticate devices attached to a LAN port. It requires three roles in the authentication process:

- A device requesting access
- An authenticator
- An authentication server

802.1x allows scalability in wireless LANs by incorporating centralized authentication of wireless users or stations. The standard allows multiple authentication algorithms and is an open standard.

802.11 standard

The *IEEE 802.11 standard* specifies a technology that operates in the 2.4 through 2.5GHz band. Wireless networks operate according to the specifications of the IEEE 802.11 standards. The IEEE 802.11 standards are defined at the Data Link layer of the Open Systems Interconnection (OSI) model. In this standard, there are two different ways to configure a network: ad-hoc and infrastructure. In the ad-hoc network, computers are brought together to form a network on the fly. The 802.11 standard also places specifications on the parameters of both the physical and medium access control (MAC) layers of the network.

The 802.11 standard defines an *access point (AP)* as a device that functions as a transparent bridge between the wireless clients and the existing wired network. The access point contains at least one interface to connect to the existing wired network and transmitting equipment to connect with the wireless clients. It also contains IEEE 802.1D bridging software, to act as a bridge between wireless and wired data-link layers.

The current and future WLAN standards under 802.11 are:

Standard	Description
802.11a	Ratified in 1999, 802.11a uses Orthagonal Frequency Division Multiplexing (OFDM). OFDM offers significant performance benefits compared with the more traditional spread-spectrum systems. OFDM is a modulation technique for transmitting large amounts of digital data over radio waves. Capacity per channel is 54Mbps with real throughput at about 31Mpbs. It operates at a frequency of 5GHz, which supports 8 overlapping channels.
802.11b	Ratified in 1999, 802.11b is one of the most popularly used 802.1x technologies. Uses Direct Sequence Spread Spectrum (DSSS). Capacity per channel is 11Mbps with real throughput at about 6Mpbs. It operates at a frequency of 2.4GHz, which supports 3 nonoverlapping channels.
802.11c	Pertains to the operation of bridge connections. Was moved to the 802.1 standards set.
802.11d	Ratified in 2001, 802.11d aims to produce versions of 802.11b that are compatible with other frequencies so it can be used in countries where the 2.4GHz band isn't available.
802.11e	Not yet ratified, 802.11e will add Quality of Service (QoS) capabilities to 802.11 networks. It uses a Time Division Multiple Access (TDMA) scheme and adds extra error correction.
802.11F	Ratified in 2003, 802.11F improves the handover mechanism in 802.11, so that users can maintain a connection while roaming. It's aimed at giving network users the same roaming freedom that cell phone users have.
802.11g	Ratified in 2003, 802.11g is a combination of 802.11a and 802.11b. It can use either Direct Sequence Spread Spectrum (DSSS) or Orthagonal Frequency Division Multiplexing (OFDM). Capacity per channel is 54Mbps with real throughput at about 12Mpbs. It operates at a frequency of 2.4GHz. 802.11g is also a popularly used 802.11 technology.
802.11h	Ratified in 2003, 802.11h attempts to improve on 802.11a by adding better control over radio channel selection and transmission power.
802.11i	Ratified in 2004, 802.11i deals with security. This is an entirely new standard based on the Advanced Encryption Standard (AES). This standard has a feature called Robust Security Network (RSN), which defines two security methodologies. The first is for legacy-based hardware using RC4, and the second one is for new hardware based on AES.
802.11j	Ratified in 2004, 802.11j allows 802.11a and HiperLAN2 networks to coexist in the same airwaves. 802.11j made changes to the 5GHz signaling capabilities to support Japan regulatory requirements.

Standard	Description
802.11k	A WLAN management system, currently in progress.
802.11l	This letter was skipped by the IEEE governing board to avoid confusion with 802.11i.
802.11m	This contains maintenance of the 802.11 family documentation.
802.11n	Currently in progress, 802.11n is a 100+ Mbps standard.

While devices that support the 802.11a standard are generally incompatible with those that support 802.11b, some devices are equipped to support either 802.11a or 802.11b. The newest standard, 802.11g, allows 802.11b and 802.11g devices to operate together on the same network. This standard was created specifically for backwards compatibility with the 802.11b standard.

WLAN security

Given all of the benefits, the security drawbacks with WLANs would need to be fairly severe to undermine their appeal. Wireless devices present a whole new set of threats that network administrators are unaware of. The most obvious risks concerning wireless networks are theft and rogue devices. Most cell phones, text pagers, PDAs, and wireless network cards are small enough that they can be easily lost or stolen. Since they're simple to conceal and contain valuable information about a company, they've become favorite targets of intruders. Wireless LANs can be subject to session hijacking and man-in-the-middle attacks. Additional risks remain, because anyone can purchase an access point and set it up.

WLAN security problems

Wireless access points, when set up right out of the box, have no security configured. They broadcast their presence—in essence saying, "Hey, my name is xxx, here I am!" The free availability of 802.11 network audit tools, such as Airsnort and NetStumbler, means that breaking into wireless networks configured with weak security is quite easy. These tools can be used to check wireless security by identifying unauthorized clients or access points, as well as verifying encryption usage. There are tools available in the form of management software. To eliminate existing 802.11 shortcomings and to help improve the image of wireless technology on the market, the *Institute of Electronic and Electric Engineers (IEEE)*, together with the *Wireless Ethernet Compatibility Alliance (WECA)*, proposed standards for significantly improved user authentication and media access control mechanisms.

Additional risks associated with wireless networks include:

- 802.1x transmissions generate detectable radio-frequency traffic in all directions. Persons wishing to intercept the data transmitted over the network might use many solutions to increase the distance over which detection is possible, including the use of metal tubes such, as a Pringles container or a large tomato juice can.

- Without the use of an encryption standard of some type, data is passed in clear text form. Even though technologies, such as Wired Equivalent Privacy (WEP), encrypt the data, they still lack good security, and a determined listener can easily obtain enough traffic data in order to calculate the encryption key in use.

- The authentication mechanism is one-way, so it's easy for an intruder to wait until authentication is completed and then generate a signal to the client that tricks the client into thinking that it has been disconnected from the access point. Meanwhile, the intruder begins to send data traffic to the server pretending to be the original client.

- The client connection request is a one-way open broadcast. This gives an intruder the opportunity to act as an access point to the client and act as a client to the real network access point. This allows an intruder to watch all data transactions between the client and access point, then modify, insert, or delete packets at will.

- A popular pastime is wardriving. *Wardriving* involves driving around with a laptop system configured to listen for open wireless access points. Several Web sites provide detailed information locating unsecured networks. These sites provide locations, sometimes on city maps for the convenience of others looking for open access links to the Internet. This is an attractive method not to only capture data from networks, but also to connect to someone else's network, use their bandwidth, and pay nothing for it.

- *War chalking* is the process of marking buildings, curbs, and other landmarks indicating the presence of an available access point and its connection details by utilizing a set of symbols and shorthand.

WLAN security solutions

Wireless security comes in two major varieties today:

- Wired Equivalent Privacy (WEP)
- Wi-Fi Protected Access (WPA)

Both include methods to encrypt wireless traffic between wireless clients and APs. WEP has been included in 802.11–based products for some time and includes a strategy for restricting network access and encrypting network traffic based upon a shared key. A company can protect itself from security threats by:

- Enabling WEP—Nearly all Wi-Fi certified products ship with basic encryption capabilities (40-bit key WEP). However, it isn't enabled by default. When you enable WEP, it's designed to provide the same level of security as your wired LAN.

- Changing default access point administration passwords—Many devices right out of the box don't have a password set on the Administrator account. Programs, such as AirSnort, identify the manufacturer based on the MAC address, so if you change only the SSID, chances are that an informed hacker can easily gain access.

- Changing default Service Set Identifiers (SSIDs)—Don't change the SSID to reflect your company's main names, divisions, products, or address. This makes you an easy target. If a SSID name is enticing enough, it might attract hackers.

- Disabling broadcast SSID—Broadcast SSID is enabled by default. This means it will accept any SSID. When you disable this feature, the SSID configured in the client must match the SSID of the access point.

- Separating the wireless network from the wired network—Consider using an additional level of authentication, such as RADIUS, before you permit an association with your access points. The wireless clients can be separated so the connections not only use RADIUS authentication but are also logged.

- Putting the wireless network in an Internet access-only zone or a Demilitarized Zone (DMZ)—Place your wireless access points in a DMZ and have your wireless users tunnel into your network using a VPN. This requires extra effort on your part to set up a VLAN for your DMZ, but this solution adds a layer of encryption and authentication that makes your wireless network secure enough for sensitive data.

- Disabling DHCP within the WLAN to keep a tighter control over users—Assign static IP addresses to your wireless clients. This creates more administrative overhead to manage, but it makes it harder to access your network.

- Enabling MAC address filtering on access points to limit unauthorized wireless NICs—Many access points allow you to control access based on the MAC address of the NIC attempting to associate with it. If the MAC address of the wireless client's NIC isn't in the access point's table, access is denied. Although there are ways of spoofing a MAC address, it takes an additional level of sophistication.

As a network administrator, you should periodically survey your site using a tool, such as NetStumbler or AirSnort, to see if any rogue access points are installed on the network. You should also determine if there are any unused wireless connections and remove or disable them. In addition, take a notebook equipped with a wireless sniffer installed and an external antenna outside your office building. Check to see what information inside your building can be accessed by someone parked in the parking lot or across the street.

D-2: Identifying the technology used to implement WLANs

Questions and answers

1 You work for a company that supplies parts to several automobile dealerships on a daily basis. Each part is assigned an ID, and that ID is bar coded on the shelf where it's stocked. Currently, as each item is pulled for delivery, it's taken to one of the three central computers and scanned to update the inventory database. Can wireless networking benefit your organization?

Yes, implementing wireless networking would allow personnel to scan the bar code on the shelf with a handheld wireless device, as each item is pulled from stock. One of the benefits of wireless networking is that inventory taking is more convenient, because personnel can freely walk around the warehouse or organization.

2 Match the 802.11 standard with its description.

A. 802.11a

B. 802.11b

C. 802.11F

D. 802.11g

E. 802.11i

It can use either DSSS or OFDM and operates at a frequency of 2.4GHz.

D.

Uses Direct Sequence Spread Spectrum (DSSS) operating at a frequency of 2.4GHz, which supports 3 non-overlapping channels.

B.

Uses the OFDM modulation technique for transmitting large amounts of digital data over radio waves. It operates at a frequency of 5GHz, which supports 8 overlapping channels.

A.

A standard based on the Advanced Encryption Standard (AES). It includes a feature called Robust Security Network (RSN), which defines two security methodologies: the first is for legacy-based hardware using RC4, and the second one is for new hardware based on AES.

E.

Allows users to maintain a connection while roaming.

C.

3 What are the two technologies you can use to secure your wireless networks?

Wired Equivalent Privacy (WEP) and Wi-Fi Protected Access (WPA)

4 You've recently been hired as a consultant to evaluate Outlander Spices wireless network security. What items should you check in evaluating their security practices?

- *Is WEP enabled on their wireless devices? If not, enable WEP.*

- *Have they changed the default administrator passwords on their wireless access points? If not, change the default administrative passwords on the devices using a complex password.*

- *Are they still using the default Service Set Identifiers (SSIDs) on their WAPs? If they are, change the SSIDs, but don't use meaningful names, such as division or department names.*

- *Are they still broadcasting SSIDs? If so, disable broadcast SSID, so the client SSID and the WAP SSID match.*

- *Are they using RADIUS to add authentication to their WAP? If not, consider setting up a RADIUS server to authenticate the wireless connections with the WAP.*

- *Is the wireless network in a DMZ? If not, consider setting up an Internet-only zone and placing the wireless network in it to add a layer of encryption and authentication that makes the wireless network secure enough for sensitive data.*

- *Are wireless clients getting their IP addresses assigned statically or dynamically from a DHCP server? If the wireless clients are using DHCP, change to static IP addresses for wireless clients.*

- *Are MAC filters in place? If not, enable MAC address filtering on access points to prevent unauthorized wireless NICs from accessing the network.*

Wireless access point configuration

Explanation

After you've installed your wireless access point, you need to configure it. To configure your wireless access point properly for secure connections, you should:

- Enable WEP
- Alter the wireless access point's factory settings
- Use MAC filters
- Enable 802.1x
- Use Wi-Fi Protected Access mode

Enabling WEP

WEP encrypts data across the wireless network using a network key that can be automatically provided for clients. WEP encryption uses a shared- secret key and the RC4 encryption algorithm. The access point (AP), and all stations that connect to it, must use the same shared key. For each packet of data sent in either direction, the transmitter combines the contents of the packet with a checksum of the packet. Once you've created a wireless network policy in Group Policy, you can configure WEP to enable:

- Data encryption (WEP-enabled)
- Network authentication (Shared mode)
- Provide the key automatically

If available, use 128-bit WEP and change the keys frequently. The WEP standard doesn't provide for any way to change keys automatically. As a result, you can only rekey an AP and its stations manually, unless the access points can provide dynamic WEP keys, and wireless clients can support dynamic WEP keys.

Alter wireless access point factory settings

In addition to enabling WEP on the wireless access point, you should also change the WAP's default settings. WAPs broadcast their Service Set Identifier (SSID)—the name designated for a specific wireless local area network by default. The SSID's factory setting is usually DEFAULT, and it typically doesn't have a password set on the Administrator account. Changing the default SSID helps protect your network. Leaving the default SSID and password on WAP is like using admin and password for the login and password on a server. You can easily change a WAP's SSID to connect to an existing wireless network or to establish a new wireless network.

Use MAC filters

You can also use MAC filters to allow or deny computers access to the network based on their MAC addresses. Enabling MAC address filtering on access points limits unauthorized wireless NICs. Many access points allow you to control access based on the MAC address of the NIC attempting to associate with it. If the MAC address of the NIC isn't in the table of the access point, it won't allow access.

Enable 802.1x

802.1x is the recommended method of authentication and encryption for enhanced security on computers running Windows XP and Windows Server 2003. The use of 802.1x offers an effective solution for authenticating and controlling user traffic to a protected network, as well as dynamically varying encryption keys. 802.1x ties EAP to both the wired and wireless LAN media and supports multiple authentication methods, such as token cards, Kerberos, one-time passwords, certificates, and public key authentication. You configure 802.1x encryption from the IEEE 802.1x tab of the policy setting's Properties dialog box.

Use Wi-Fi Protected Access

Most WAPs have a configuration mode of *Wi-Fi Protected Access (WPA)*. WPA authorizes and identifies users based on a secret key that changes automatically at a regular interval. WPA uses TKIP (Temporal Key Integrity Protocol) to change the temporal key every 10,000 packets. This insures much greater security than the standard WEP.

Finally, don't forget to remove any unused wireless connections (access points). These just provide another way for an intruder to access your network resources without your knowledge.

Do it!

D-3: Configuring a wireless access point (instructor demo)

Here's how	Here's why
1 Open Internet Explorer and enter the IP address of your WAP	You're prompted for administrator credentials on the WAP.
2 Enter the appropriate username and password for your WAP and click **OK**	
3 Activate the Wireless Settings tab	
In the SSID box, edit default to read **warehouse**	
For SSID broadcast, select **Disabled**	
For Security, select **WEP** and record the WEP key	WEP key: _____
Check **Apply**	The device restarts itself.
4 Activate the Tools tab	
In the New password and Confirm password boxes, enter **!pass4321**	
Check **Apply**	
5 Activate the Advanced tab	
Select **MAC filters**	
Choose **Only allow computers with MAC address listed below to access the network**	
In the Name box enter your computer's name	
In the MAC address box, enter your computer's MAC address	
Check **Apply**	
6 Close Internet Explorer	

You need a wireless access point installed on your classroom network to complete this activity. The steps were written for a D-Link WAP. If your WAP is different, alter the steps accordingly.

You also need your computer's MAC address.

Let students know that they'd continue to add MAC addresses for all computers to which they want to allow access to the WAP.

Wireless clients

Explanation

The wireless client must submit its credentials with the authenticating server before wireless network access is established. When the client computer is in range of the WAP, it tries to connect to the WLAN that's active on the WAP. If the WAP is configured to allow only secured or 802.1x-authenticated connections, the WAP issues a challenge to the client. The WAP then sets up a restricted channel that allows the client to communicate only with the RADIUS server. The RADIUS server accept a connection only from a trusted WAP or from one that has been configured as a RADIUS client on the Microsoft Internet Authentication Service (IAS) server and provides the shared secret for that RADIUS client. The RADIUS server validates the client credentials against the directory. If the client is successfully authenticated, the RADIUS server decides whether to authorize the client to use the WLAN. If the client is granted access, the RADIUS server transmits the client master key to the WAP. The client and WAP now share common key information that they can use to encrypt and decrypt the WLAN traffic passing between them. How you configure Windows clients to participate in this process depends on the operating system.

Windows XP wireless clients

Wireless Auto Configuration dynamically selects the wireless network to which a connection attempt is made, based on configured preferences or default settings. Computers running Windows XP support *Wireless Zero Configuration*, which enables computers to connect automatically to available wireless networks. Windows XP client computers can choose from available wireless networks and connect automatically, by default, without user action. Wireless Zero Configuration automatically configures items, such as TCP/IP settings, DNS server addresses, and IAS server addresses. Wireless Zero Configuration includes support for 802.1x authentication and encryption. The default preferences for Wireless Zero Configuration using IEEE 802.1x authentication include:

- Infrastructure before ad hoc mode and computer authentication before user authentication.
- WEP authentication attempts to perform an IEEE 802.11 shared key authentication if the network adapter has been preconfigured with a WEP shared key; otherwise the network adapter reverts to the open system authentication.

Although the IEEE 802.1x security enhancements are available in Windows XP Professional, the network adapters and access points must also be compatible with this standard for deployment.

You can change the default settings to allow guest access, which isn't enabled by default. You shouldn't turn on guest access on a laptop using Wireless Zero Configuration. An unauthorized user could establish an ad hoc connection to the laptop and gain access to confidential information on it.

Windows 2000 wireless clients

Computers running Windows 2000 don't support Wireless Zero Configuration. You can configure a wireless network card for connection, using EAP-TLS or PEAP authentication, just as you can when configuring Windows XP computers. Only Windows XP computers natively support IEEE 802.1x authentication. Microsoft provides an 802.1x Authentication Client download that allows Windows 2000 computers to use the 802.1x standard. This download can be found at
http://www.microsoft.com/windows2000/server/evaluation/news/bulletins/8021xclient.asp.
Microsoft also provides 802.1x Authentication Clients for Windows 98 and Windows NT 4.0 Workstation to customers with Premier and Alliance support contracts.

Windows CE wireless clients

Palm-top computers running Windows CE .NET include Wireless Zero Configuration and similar manual configuration options to those found on Windows XP. They support 802.11a and *Native Wireless Fidelity (Wi-Fi)*. You can configure older Windows CE palm-top computers for wireless networking. The settings and configuration are similar to those for Windows 2000.

With the differences in configuration and the ability to use Wireless Zero Configuration, when you configure client policies, place Windows XP computers into a separate OU. Define policies that apply only to these computers in a GPO linked to this OU and policies that apply to Windows 2000 computers in a GPO linked to the OU in which these computers are located.

Do it!

D-4: Configuring a wireless client (instructor demo)

Your WAP is set to allow your computer access as directed in the previous activity.

Here's how	Here's why
1 Click **Start** and choose **Control Panel, Network and Network Connections, Wireless Network Connection**	You'll configure the client to connect using the settings on the wireless access point.
Click **Properties**	
2 Activate the Wireless Networks tab	
Under Preferred Networks, click **Add...**	
In the SSID box, enter **warehouse**	
Check **Data Encryption (WEP enabled)**	
3 Click **OK** twice	
Click **Close**	

Topic E: Network troubleshooting

This topic covers the following CompTIA A+ 220-603 exam objective.

#	Objective
4.3	**Identify tools, diagnostic procedures and troubleshooting techniques for networks**
	• Identify names, purposes, and characteristics of command line tools, for example:
	• IPCONFIG.EXE
	• PING.EXE
	• TRACERT.EXE
	• NSLOOKUP.EXE
	• Diagnose and troubleshoot basic network issues, for example:
	• Driver/network interface
	• Protocol configuration
	• TCP/IP (e.g. Gateway, Subnet mask, DNS, WINS, static and automatic address assignment)
	• Permissions
	• Electrical interference

Troubleshooting wired connections

Explanation

There can be many sources of problems with wired connections. Some are physically based, such as a bad network cable; and some are software-based, such as an invalid TCP/IP address.

Electrical interference

One common network problem that degrades data signals is electrical interference. *Network noise* is any electrical signal on the network cable that isn't part of the sender's original. Noise is generated both internally and externally.

Internally, twisted-pair cables produce relatively little electrical interference: the twists cancel each other out. Any variation in the thickness of the wire, in the cable insulation, or in the capacitance of wires or insulation causes a mismatch and creates noise between the pairs. When you use good quality cables, you minimize the internally produced noise but don't remove it altogether.

Electrical interference can come from many external sources. You should always install cables in separate conduits away from items such as electric motors (like those found in lifts/elevators), fluorescent lights, and air conditioners. In areas where there's an abundance of electrical noise, you can use shielded cables or other technologies, such as fiber optic cables to avoid interference.

When a data signal travels down a conductor, it creates an electric field, which interferes with any wires close by. This is called *crosstalk*. Crosstalk gets larger at higher frequencies and with parallel wires. The twists in twisted pair cables cancel this effect. However, it's important that the twists are symmetrical and that adjacent pairs have different twists. There are different types of crosstalk, as described in the following table:

Crosstalk	Description
Near End Crosstalk (NEXT)	Crosstalk that originates up to 30 meters from the source of the signal. This is a typical problem on cable connectors or patch panels, where you untwist the wires to make the connection. Always keep the section of untwisted cable to a minimum; even a very short piece of untwisted cable can introduce a large amount of crosstalk
Far End Crosstalk (FEXT)	Crosstalk that occurs at the far end of the cable. FEXT is greater on short cables than on long cables, because signals attenuate by the time they reach the far end of the cable and are weaker.
Equal Level Far End Crosstalk (ELFEXT)	A calculated value of the crosstalk between pairs measured at the far end of the cable. ELFEXT takes into account the amount of signal loss and is calculated for each pair of cables. ELFEXT is slightly different for each pair. If you have a very high ELFEXT, it indicates excessive attenuation or high far end crosstalk
Pair-to-Pair Crosstalk	The value a signal on one pair of cables has on the others. To calculate pair-to-pair crosstalk, you place a signal on one pair and then measure the disturbance on the others. You calculate 12 sets of measurements— each pair at the near and far ends. Measure NEXT for pairs 1 to 2, 1 to 3, and 1 to 4; measure NEXT for pairs 2 to 3, 2 to 4, and 3 to 4. Repeat at the other end of the cable. The worst value you calculate out of the 12 sets is the crosstalk for the cable.

NIC drivers

Hardware devices, such as NIC cards, are manufactured by a variety of vendors. Because different vendors use different processes, components, and standards, specialized software is required for a device to work with an operating system. This software is generically referred to as a device driver.

Device drivers act as intermediaries between hardware devices and an operating system. They contain the instructions necessary in order for the operating system to use the full capabilities of the hardware correctly. Once installed, device drivers load automatically for all enabled hardware as part of the Windows boot process.

In some cases, a driver not specifically designed for your NIC still allows the device to function. This is because many of the basic capabilities of a particular type of device are similar and follow common standards.

However, installing or using the wrong device driver usually results in less than optimal performance and generally doesn't allow you to take advantage of the advanced features of the device. What's worse, the driver might have problems supporting some functions, which can affect the stability of the whole system.

As with any software, NIC vendors often update device drivers after they're initially released. Sometimes this is to fix a flaw. Sometimes additional features or capabilities are added. Because of this, the driver software originally provided with your NIC card (usually on an accompanying disk) is often not the best driver to install, as it may be outdated. Vendors typically post updated drivers to their Web or FTP sites, so that you can get the latest version. When hardware isn't performing optimally or is generating errors, installing an updated driver is often the only solution.

Device Manager

You access Device Manager from the Hardware tab of the System program in Control Panel or from the Computer Management administrative tool.

If a specific device, such as your NIC, is missing or isn't functioning, you have two methods of troubleshooting or fixing the problem:

- Obtain a new driver from the manufacturer's Web site and then install it from within Device Manager.
- Use the Hardware Update Wizard to guide you through the task of selecting and installing an updated device driver.

Troubleshooting wireless connections

The following table lists common problems with your wireless connection that you might encounter:

Symptom	Probable cause	Suggested solution
Unable to connect to infrared wireless device	Out of range, obstructions blocking ports, infrared serial port disabled in BIOS or operating system.	Move closer. Remove obstructions and gently clean the infrared ports windows. Use the BIOS setup utility and Device Manager to confirm that the infrared port is enabled.
Unable to connect to radio wireless device	Out of range, interference from electrical motors or equipment, drivers not installed, wireless router turned off, security settings prevent connections.	Move closer and move away from sources of interference. Use Device Manager to confirm that the wireless device is installed and that there are no conflicts. Confirm that your router is turned on. Confirm that you have sufficient permissions to connect to the wireless device.
Unable to connect to Bluetooth wireless device	Out of range, interference from electrical motors or equipment, drivers not installed, security settings prevent connections.	Move closer and move away from sources of interference. Use Device Manager to confirm that the wireless device is installed and that there are no conflicts. Confirm that you have sufficient permissions to connect to the wireless device.

Do it!

E-1: Verifying the NIC device in Device Manager

Here's how	Here's why
1 Click **Start**	
Right-click **My Computer** and choose **Properties**	
2 Activate the Hardware tab	
3 Click **Device Manager**	
4 Expand **Network Adapters**	
Double-click your LAN adapter	
5 Observe the Device Status	Device status This device is working properly. If you are having problems with this device, click 'Troubleshoot' to start the troubleshooter. Troubleshoot...
	The NIC card should be working properly. You click Troubleshoot to open the Help and Support Center to help you find problems with the device.
6 Activate the Driver tab	
Observe the Driver Provider, Date, Version, and Digital Signer information	Driver Provider: Broadcom Driver Date: 3/12/2004 Driver Version: 4.23.0.0 Digital Signer: Microsoft Windows Hardware Compatibility Publ
7 Click **Driver Details...**	To view more information about the driver, including its filename and location.
Click **OK**	
8 Click **Update Driver...**	To start the Hardware Update Wizard. If you have a new driver on CD or downloaded from a manufacturer's Web site, you can use this wizard to install the driver.
Click **Cancel**	

9 Activate the Resources tab

Observe the Conflicting
Resources list

Conflicting device list:

No conflicts.

If the device settings conflict with any other
device, it would appear in this list. You could
then use the Resource settings box to make
changes to one or the other device to resolve the
conflict.

10 Click **Cancel**

Close Device Manager

Click **Cancel**   To close the Systems Properties box.

Troubleshooting TCP/IP

Explanation

One of the most common complaints you hear from users is that they can't get to something on the network or "the Internet is down." When you hear a complaint about network connectivity, your first step should be to check the user's network connection and TCP/IP settings.

If you find that there's a problem on the client computer, it's your job to fix it, usually by correcting TCP/IP properties. If you suspect a problem with the network as a whole or with a particular server on the network, you need to contact the appropriate individual (typically the network administrator) to escalate the problem.

TCP/IP utilities

TCP/IP includes a group of utility tools that can be used to troubleshoot problems with TCP/IP. The following table lists the utilities and the purpose of each.

Utility	Purpose
ARP (arp.exe)	Manages the IP-to-Ethernet address translation tables that are used to find the MAC address of a host on the network when the IP address is known.
Getmac (getmac.exe)	Displays the NIC's MAC address (new in Windows XP.)
IPConfig (ipconfig.exe)	Displays the IP address of the host and other configuration information. Some parameters are:
	`ipconfig /all`—Displays all information about the connection.
	`ipconfig /release`—Releases the current IP address.
	`ipconfig /renew`—Requests a new IP address.
	`ipconfig /?`—Displays information about ipconfig.
FTP (ftp.exe)	Transfers files over a network.
Nbtstat (nbstat.exe)	Displays current information about TCP/IP and NetBIOS when both are being used on the same network.
Nslookup (nslookup.exe)	Displays information about current TCP/IP connections.
Ping (ping.exe)	Verifies a connection to a network between two hosts.
Route (route.exe)	Allows you to control network routing tables manually.
Telnet (telnet.exe)	Allows you to communicate with another computer on the network remotely, entering the commands, on the local computer, that control the remote computer.
Trace Route (tracert.exe)	Traces and displays the route taken from the host to a remote destination; tracert is one example of a trace-routing utility.

Most of these commands are entered from a command prompt. You can access a command prompt using either the Run dialog box, or a Command Prompt window. A disadvantage of using the Run dialog box (as opposed to the Command Prompt window) is that the results of most commands are difficult to read, because they quickly appear and then the DOS window automatically closes.

If you use a Command Prompt window, the results appear, but the DOS window remains open, so that the user can read the results of entering a command.

To access a Command Prompt window in Windows XP, click Start, and choose All Programs, Accessories, Command Prompt. You can also access the Command Prompt window by typing cmd in the Run dialog box, and then click OK.

From the Command Prompt, you can enter a Windows or DOS command, including any of those in the previous table. You can view the results of the command in the window.

To solve problems that occur when first connecting to the Internet, the most useful utilities are:

- Ipconfig
- Ping

Do it!

E-2: Identifying TCP/IP utilities used for troubleshooting

Questions and answers

1 A user opens a browser window and attempts to contact your intranet server at www.inetplus.class. They receive a message that it can't be found. What's the first TCP/IP utility you should try?

Try to ping the server at www.inetplus.class from a command prompt. If that fails, try to ping the server's IP address. If that's successful, you know the problem lies with DNS.

2 You check a user's computer and find that it's using an APIPA address. What TCP/IP utility should you use?

Ipconfig /release to release the APIPA address; then ipconfig /renew to attempt to get a new address from the DHCP server.

3 You're attempting to connect a Windows XP computer up to your ISP through a DSL connection. The customer service rep wants the MAC address of your NIC card. What command in Windows XP gets you that information?

getmac

4 You're working on a UNIX server hosting your company's intranet site. It has two NIC cards connected to two different subnets. You want to disable one of the NIC cards so that you can troubleshoot a connection problem with just one subnet. What command can you use to do that?

ifconfig

5 You've received complaints from users in one location that load time for the company's intranet Web site is slow. No one in any other location is reporting a problem. What TCP/IP utility can you use to diagnose the problem?

You can use tracert from a computer at multiple locations and compare the hop count. You'll probably find that the hop count is higher in the location reporting slow intranet performance.

Ipconfig

Explanation

When a user complains of network problems, you should first check the TCP/IP settings on the user's computer. When using Windows 2000 and Windows XP, use Ipconfig to display and modify the current configuration of the TCP/IP stack. Several switches can be added to the Ipconfig command line that can display information (Ipconfig /all), release the IP address (Ipconfig /release), and renew the IP address (Ipconfig /renew) for all connections. For a list of all the Ipconfig switches and their meanings, at a Windows 2000 or Windows XP command prompt, type Ipconfig /?.

Check to see if the IP address and subnet mask are correct, and verify the default gateway and DNS server addresses. When you verify this information, you might find that the computer has no IP address configured or has configured itself with an APIPA address. If so, you have a couple of options:

- If IP addressing information is assigned by a DHCP server, suspect a problem with the DHCP server itself or with the network between the user's computer and the DHCP server. First, verify that the network card is working correctly and is attached to the network cable, which is, in turn, plugged into the appropriate network port on the wall or floor. Try to release and then renew the IP address from the DHCP server. If you can verify these things, and you can't get an IP address from the DHCP server, then escalate the call to the appropriate network administrator.

- If IP addressing is assigned manually, assign the correct information and test to see if connectivity is restored.

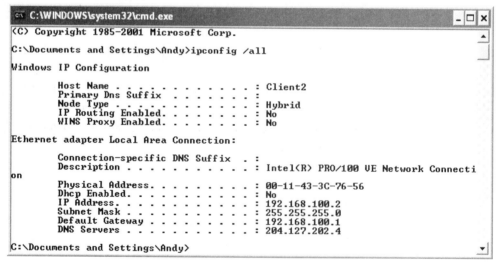

Exhibit 6-20: Ipconfig in Windows XP

SNMP Agent

For more information about SNMP, see RFC 1157 at www.rfc-editor.org.

In addition to the utilities that are automatically installed with TCP/IP, another useful utility for Windows is Microsoft SNMP Agent. *SNMP (Simple Network Management Protocol)* provides system management for networks. A system manager can monitor remote connections to computers running Windows with SNMP Agent.

In Windows 2000 and Windows XP, you can add this utility through Control Panel, using Add or Remove Programs, Add/Remove Windows Components, Management and Monitoring Tools.

Note the Release and Renew buttons at the bottom of the IP Configuration window. If a device isn't assigned an IP address through a DHCP server, these buttons are dimmed. For devices that do have dynamic IP addresses, you can click Release to cause the device to disconnect from the network and then click Renew to renew the connection. If the computer is dynamically assigned IP addresses by a remote host, such as when connecting to an ISP or a proxy server on a LAN, a new IP address is assigned when you click Renew. Sometimes, this action fixes a failed connection. If you release the connection and then attempt to renew it, but the system fails to get a new IP address, use Ping to test for connectivity with the remote host that's to assign you the IP address.

Unix Ifconfig

A command similar to Ipconfig used by UNIX is called Ifconfig. Like its Windows counterparts, this UNIX command displays the IP address of the host and other configuration information. You can also use ifconfig to disable and enable network cards and release and renew the IP addresses assigned to these cards. For example, at a UNIX command prompt:

- Type `ifconfig -a` to show all configuration information.

- Type `ifconfig en0 -168.92.1.1` to release the given IP address from the TCP/IP connection named en0. In this example, en0 indicates the first Ethernet connection of the system.

- To assign a static IP address to this Ethernet connection, type `ifconfig en0 168.92.1.1.5`.

E-3: Using Ipconfig to display TCP/IP settings

Here's how	Here's why
1 Click **Start**, choose **Run**, and enter **cmd**	To open a Command Prompt window. You're going to use Ipconfig to view your IP address settings, and then you're going to use Ipconfig to release and renew a DHCP-leased address.
2 At the command prompt, enter `ipconfig`	To view your current IP address, subnet mask, and default gateway, as shown here.

```
Connection-specific DNS Suffix  . :
IP Address. . . . . . . . . . . : 192.168.100.185
Subnet Mask . . . . . . . . . . : 255.255.255.0
Default Gateway . . . . . . . . : 192.168.100.1
```

This is a quick way to find a computer's basic IP address information.

3 At the command prompt, enter `ipconfig /all`	To view extended IP addressing information, as shown here.

```
Windows IP Configuration

        Host Name . . . . . . . . . . . . : osclient01
        Primary Dns Suffix  . . . . . . . : APlusOS.class
        Node Type . . . . . . . . . . . . : Unknown
        IP Routing Enabled. . . . . . . . : No
        WINS Proxy Enabled. . . . . . . . : No
        DNS Suffix Search List. . . . . . : APlusOS.class

Ethernet adapter Local Area Connection:

        Connection-specific DNS Suffix  . :
        Description . . . . . . . . . . . : Intel(R) PRO/100 VE Network Connecti
on
        Physical Address. . . . . . . . . : 00-11-11-8B-0B-91
        Dhcp Enabled. . . . . . . . . . . : No
        IP Address. . . . . . . . . . . . : 192.168.100.185
        Subnet Mask . . . . . . . . . . . : 255.255.255.0
        Default Gateway . . . . . . . . . : 192.168.100.1
        DNS Servers . . . . . . . . . . . : 192.168.100.254
```

It can be easier to view this information at the command prompt than to click through a few dialog boxes to find the same information in the Windows GUI.

4 Open the Network and Internet Connections window	You're going to use DHCP to obtain a new IP address.
Click **Network Connections**	
5 Right-click **Local Area Connection** and choose **Properties**	
6 Double-click **Internet Protocol (TCP/IP)**	To open the properties of TCP/IP.

7 Select **Obtain an IP address automatically** Select **Obtain DNS server address automatically**	To configure the computer to use DHCP.
8 Click **OK** twice Close the Network Connections window	
9 At the command prompt, enter `ipconfig`	To see what your IP address is now. When you enabled DHCP, the computer immediately broadcast a request for a DHCP server on the network. The DHCP server responded with IP addressing configuration.
10 Enter `ipconfig /release`	To release the IP address. Your IP address should now be 0.0.0.0. You may also see a message in the system tray telling you that the local area connection has limited or no connectivity.
11 Enter `ipconfig /renew`	To request a new IP address from the DHCP server.

Students may have to wait a few moments to receive an IP address from the DHCP server.

Ping and basic TCP/IP connectivity

Explanation

The name comes from submarine sonar, which broadcasts a signal, called a ping, that hits surrounding objects and makes a sound revealing the object's size and position.

While you're in the MS-DOS prompt or Command Prompt window, you can use another tool to verify basic TCP/IP connectivity. *Ping (Packet Internet Groper)* is a simple program that allows one computer to send a test packet to another computer and then receive a reply. You use Ping to discover if another computer is available for communication on a TCP/IP network.

After you've verified that the computer has a valid IP address, you can use the `ping` command to see if you can communicate with another computer on the network. You'll need to know the NetBIOS name, DNS name, or IP address of the other computer— perhaps a router or server that you know is operational. At the MS-DOS or command prompt, enter

```
ping computer
```

where `computer` is the other computer's name or IP address. An example of a successful result is shown in Exhibit 6-21.

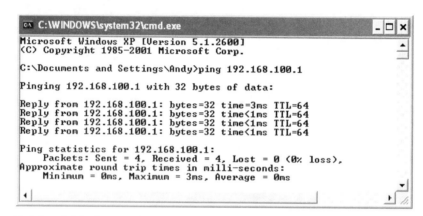

Exhibit 6-21: Successful Ping results

When you issue Ping from the command prompt, followed by an IP address or a domain name, Ping communicates over a TCP/IP network to another node on the network. Packets are exchanged and then reported on the screen to verify connectivity on the network. If Ping works, you know that the two nodes are communicating at the Transport layer of the OSI model. If communication is happening at this layer, you also know that all layers underneath the Transport layer are working.

If you can't use Ping successfully, try these options:

- If you tried to Ping using a domain name, use the IP address of the remote host instead. If that works, the problem is with name resolution.
- Try to Ping another computer. Can you communicate with any other computer on the network?
- If not, use Winipcfg or Ipconfig to verify that the computer has been assigned an IP address.
- Verify all the configuration settings in the Network dialog box.
- Reboot the computer to verify that TCP/IP has been loaded.
- Try removing TCP/IP and reinstalling it. Perhaps the initial installation was corrupted.
- Check the physical connections. Is the network cable plugged in, or is there a telephone connection? Do you get a dial tone?

If all these fail to produce results, you might need to turn to a network technician or computer technician to solve the problem.

To help determine where the network problem is, ping the computer you're troubleshooting, and then ping a computer on the local subnet, the computer configured as the default gateway, a computer on another subnet, and a computer on the Internet. If you can't ping yourself, consider the computer's network adapter as the problem. If you can't ping another computer, the problem is a network error somewhere between the computer you're on and the destination you tried to contact. You can then report network problems to the network administrator.

E-4:   Testing TCP/IP connectivity

Here's how	Here's why
1 Open a Command Prompt	
Type **ping 127.0.0.1** and press [← ENTER]	This is the loopback address and verifies that TCP/IP is working on this computer. Pinging the loopback address tests a computer's own basic network setup.
	You should receive four successful responses.
2 Type **ipconfig /all** and press [← ENTER]	Record your IP address and your default gateway address.
	IP address:
	Default gateway address:
3 Ping your IP address	This verifies that TCP/IP communication can be sent out onto the network cable from your NIC card and back in again.
	You should receive four successful responses.
4 Ping **192.168.100.254**	This is the classroom server, which is on the local subnet. It verifies that you have connectivity to other computers on your local subnet.
	You should receive four successful responses.
5 Ping the IP address of your classroom's gateway	This verifies that you can reach the gateway that connects you to other subnets.
	You should receive four successful responses.
6 Ping **198.80.146.30**	This is the IP address of www.course.com. It's located on the other side of your gateway. This verifies you have connectivity through the gateway to other networks.
	You should receive four successful responses.
7 Ping **www.course.com**	This verifies that DNS is working correctly to translate DNS names to IP addresses.
	You should see the IP address in brackets and then receive four successful responses.

Explain to students that, with a TCP/IP connectivity problem, they can use ping to test connectivity from their computers out, verifying successful communication closest to them first.

Other network settings

Explanation

If a user tells you he or she can't access resources on the network, verify that the user's computer has the correct network client installed: either Client for Microsoft Networks or Client for NetWare Networks. Verify that the client software is configured properly. You should also check File and Printer Sharing on the computer the user is trying to access to ensure that it's installed and enabled.

You can also perform a couple of additional tests on the network:

- You can use the command-line tool Nslookup to verify name resolution (DNS) settings. At an MS-DOS prompt or a command prompt, enter `nslookup` *servername* to verify name resolution settings. Entering just `nslookup` returns the name of the DNS server you're configured to use.

- The Tracert command can be used to check the network path between two computers. At an MS-DOS or command prompt, enter `tracert` *computer*, where *computer* is the name or IP address of a destination.

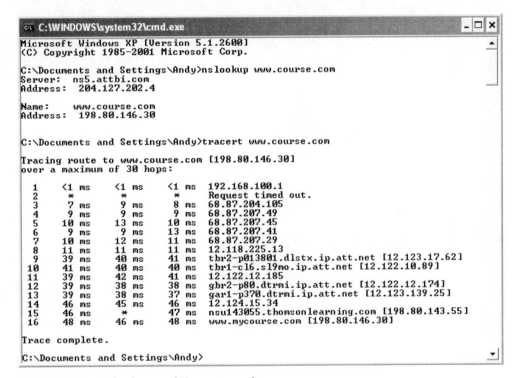

Exhibit 6-22: Nslookup and Tracert results

Any unusual results should be reported to the network administrator. Exhibit 6-22 shows an example of results for Nslookup and Tracert.

Do it!

E-5: Using Nslookup and Tracert to verify settings

Here's how	Here's why
1 At the command prompt, enter `nslookup`	To test your DNS configuration. Depending on your configuration, you might see a DNS server name and IP address returned, or you might see just an IP address and an error message telling you that Nslookup can't find the server name. This is a DNS server configuration issue.
2 Enter `nslookup` followed by a Web address	Try www.yahoo.com. You should see DNS addressing information for that domain.
3 Enter `exit`	To exit Nslookup.
4 Enter `tracert 192.168.100.254`	To trace the path to the DNS server in your network. This is a short path, so the results are returned promptly.
5 Enter `tracert www.yahoo.com`	To trace the route to Yahoo's Web server. This might take a while longer. If you see an error while using Tracert, contact the network administrator.
6 Close the Command Prompt window	

Be prepared to offer another DNS server's IP address, if you didn't use this IP address during setup.

Troubleshooting permissions

Explanation

Sometimes, users have a functioning network connection and are able to communicate with the computer hosting a network resource but not be able to use the resource. When troubleshooting cases such as this, you should check the user's permissions to the resource. This includes Share permissions and NTFS permissions on the resource.

To check Share permissions:

1   Right-click the network resource and choose Properties. (You can also choose Sharing and Security to open the same dialog box.)
2   Activate the Sharing tab.
3   Verify that Sharing is enabled.
4   Click Permissions.
5   Verify that the user, or a group the user is a member of, is listed with the appropriate permissions.

If the user doesn't have share permissions granted, the owner of the network resource or a network administrator has to add them to the list.

In versions of Windows prior to Windows XP, one of the more complex and tedious tasks was determining a user's effective permissions for network resources. Because the permissions that actually apply to a user can be the result of membership in a variety of different groups, this task could often be very complex and involve a great deal of research. In environments that included thousands of users and shared resources, the amount of time and effort required to make this determination could quickly become unmanageable.

To determine easily the effective NTFS permissions that apply to a user or group, Windows XP includes the Effective Permissions tab in the Advanced Security Settings dialog box for a file or folder:

1   In a Windows Explorer windows, right-click the network resource the user is having trouble accessing.
2   Choose Properties.
3   Activate the Security tab.
4   Click Advanced.
5   Activate the Effective Permissions tab.
6   Click Select
7   Enter the name of the user who's trying to access the resource.
8   Click OK.

The permissions granted to this user individually and through group membership are checked. If the user doesn't have the appropriate NTFS permissions, the owner of the network resource or a network administrator has to add them to the list.

Do it!

E-6: Determining effective NTFS permissions

Here's how	Here's why
Students have an NNShare folder that's shared with the default permissions to Domain Users.	
1 Open My Computer	
2 On the C drive, right-click **NNShare**	Where *NN* is your initials. You shared this folder, granting the default share permissions to the Domain Users group.
Choose **Properties**	
3 Activate the Security tab	
Click **Advanced**	
4 Activate the **Effective Permissions** tab	
Click **Select**	
5 In the From this location box, verify that RSTDomain.class is listed	
6 In the "Enter the object name to select" box, type **administrator**	
Click **OK**	
7 Review the Effective permissions	
Close all open windows	

Do it!

E-7:   Joining a workgroup

Here's how	Here's why
1 Right-click **My Computer** and choose **Properties**	You're going to re-join the TECHSUPPORT workgroup.
2 On the Computer Name tab, click **Change**	
3 Select **Workgroup** and enter **TECHSUPPORT**	
4 Click **OK**	
Enter **Administrator** and **Pa$$321**, and then click **OK**	To remove the computer from the domain.
5 Click **OK** twice	
6 Click **OK**	To close the System Properties dialog box.
Click **Yes**	To restart your computer. Your computer is now a member of the TECHSUPPORT workgroup.

Unit summary: Networking

Topic A   In this topic, you learned how to configure a LAN connection. You learned about the various **networking models** and the computer roles in each. You installed a **network interface card** and configured it to communicate using **TCP/IP** and **NWLink**. You joined a **Windows domain** and learned how to view resources on the network.

Topic B   In this topic, you learned how to **share resources**, such as files, folders, and printers, on a network. You controlled access to the resources using **share permissions**. You installed the **Client for NetWare Networks**, so that you could use resources on a NetWare network.

Topic C   In this topic, you learned how to create an **Internet connection**. You identified the various connection technologies available and their appropriate uses. You also discussed the various **WAN bandwidth technologies**.

Topic D   In this topic, you learned how to configure **Windows Firewall** and secure your wireless network.

Topic E   In this topic, you learned how to **troubleshoot** network connection problems. You learned how to update your **NIC driver**. You used **TCP/IP utilities** to test network communication on a TCP/IP network. You also learned how to determine **effective permissions**.

Review questions

1 Which networking model requires that each individual user has an account on all computers he or she wishes to access shared resources on?

   Peer-to-peer networking model.

2 What's the Windows 2000/2003 Server feature that uses a hierarchical organization to provide an administrator with a single place for all system administration, including user and computer configuration and management; follows the client/server model; and allows users to access network resources from any computer on the network?

   The Active Directory.

3 Which is the service that translates computer names, called host names, into IP addresses on a local area network (LAN) and on the Internet?

   A DHCP.

   B DNS.

   C WINS.

   D Active Directory.

4 Which is the built-in identifying address coded into a NIC by the manufacturer?

   A IP address.

   B Subnet mask.

   C MAC address.

   D I/O address.

5 Which communication protocol isn't routable?

    A TCP/IP.

    B IPX/SPX.

    C AppleTalk.

    D NetBEUI.

6 What are the two components of an IP address?

    Part of the IP address defines the network address, also known as the subnet; the other part defines the computer address.

7 What are the two components of a DNS name?

    DNS host names include a NetBIOS-type computer name plus the DNS suffix of the DNS domain that the computer is a member of.

8 What are the three settings that IPX/SPX (NWLink) requires?

    An external network number, an internal network number, and a frame type.

9 If a user can't share files and folders, which client software is probably not installed on their computer?

    File and Printer Sharing for Microsoft Networks.

10 A user can't assign NTFS permissions in addition to the share permissions he or she has assigned to a shared folder. What do you suspect is the problem?

    The drive where the shared folder is located is formatted to FAT or FAT32, not NTFS.

11 What's the Universal Naming Convention (UNC) format for connecting to a share?

    The format for the UNC is \\computername\sharename.

12 What's the protocol used to send e-mail to an e mail server?

    A POP.

    B IMAP.

    c SMTP.

    D HTTPS.

13 Which is a public-key/private-key encryption protocol used to transmit data securely across the Internet over TCP/IP?

    A SSL.

    B HTTP.

    C HTTP-S.

    D Telnet.

14 Which is a fast data transmission technology; affordable for home use; offers a direct connection rather than a dial-up connection; is a broadband technology that uses ordinary copper telephone lines and a range of frequencies on the copper wire that aren't used by voice, making it possible for you to use the same telephone line for voice and data at the same time?

A PPPoE.

B ISDN.

C DSL.

D Bluetooth.

15 What are the components necessary to create a valid network connection through the LAN to the Internet?

At a minimum:

- *A working network card.*

- *An IP address.*

- *A subnet mask.*

- *The IP address of a gateway.*

You might also need to add the IP addresses of one or more DNS servers.

16 When a computer on the network accesses the Internet and goes through a server, router, or other device that substitutes its own IP address for that of the computer requesting the information, what's the name of the device?

A DNS server.

B DHCP server.

C Proxy server.

D Gateway.

17 What's the name of the device that ensures that all communication is received from outside users and computers that are legitimate?

A Firewall.

B Proxy server.

C Gateway.

D NAT.

18 Name the two major Wireless security methods.

Wired Equivalent Privacy (WEP) and Wi-Fi Protected Access (WPA).

19 What are eight steps you can take to secure your WLAN?

    a Enable WEP.

    b Change default access point administrative passwords.

    c Change default SSIDs.

    d Disable broadcast SSID.

    e Separate wireless network from the wired network.

    f Put the wireless network in a DMZ.

    g Disable DHCP in WLAN.

    h Enable MAC address filtering.

20 What steps can you take to minimize electrical interference on your wired LAN?

Install cables in separate conduits away from items such as electric motors (like those found in lifts/elevators), fluorescent lights, and air conditioners. In areas where there's an abundance of electrical noise, use shielded cables or other technologies, such as fiber optic cables, to avoid interference.

21 What might be the cause if you're unable to connect to a radio wireless device?

- *You're out of range.*

- *There's interference from electrical motors or equipment.*

- *Drivers aren't installed.*

- *Wireless router is turned off.*

- *Security settings are preventing connections.*

22 Which command displays the IP address of the host and other configuration information?

    A Getmac.

    B Ipconfig.

    C Nslookup.

    D Ping.

Independent practice activity

1 Your instructor will introduce a network connectivity problem or problems with your computer.

2 Identify the source of the problem.

3 Resolve the problem.

4 Verify that you have connectivity to the Internet.

5 If you don't have Internet connectivity, continue to identify and resolve problems until you can successfully access the Internet.

Unit 7
Security

Unit time: 90 minutes

Complete this unit, and you'll know how to:

A Configure operating system and file system security and understand authentication and encryption.

B Audit and log security events.

C Install and use a fingerprint scanner and card reader and discuss biometric and other security devices.

D Manage the human aspects of computer security.

Topic A: Operating system security

This topic covers the following CompTIA A+ 220-603 exam objectives.

#	Objective
5.1	**Identify the fundamental principles of security** • Identify the names, purposes, and characteristics of access control and permissions • Accounts including user, admin, and guest • Groups
5.2	**Install, configure, optimize, and upgrade security** • Install and configure hardware, software, wireless, and data security, for example: • Authentication technologies • Data access (e.g., permissions, security policies)
5.3	**Identify tools, diagnostic procedures, and troubleshooting techniques for security issues** • Diagnose and troubleshoot software and data security issues, for example: • Data access issues (e.g., permissions, security policies) • Encryption and encryption technology issues

OS security

Explanation

Operating system security begins with determining who's using a computer. Once the user is identified, operating system features can be employed to permit or deny access to resources. This authentication is enabled by users and groups.

User accounts

A user account is an object that represents all of the information that defines a user. The information may include a first and last name, password, group membership information, and other data.

Any person who needs access to the computer needs a user account. By creating user accounts, you can administer and maintain the security of the computer. Through accounts you can:

- Require authentication for users connecting to the computer.
- Control access to resources, such as shared folders or printers.
- Monitor access to resources by auditing the actions performed by a user.

When creating user accounts, it's important that your organization set standards for the various elements of a user object. For example, you might establish a user account naming convention or password complexity requirement.

You might also establish other security conventions. For example, you might require users to have password-protected screen savers, such that, to awaken an idle computer, the users have to enter their passwords.

User account types

Windows supports multiple levels of user accounts, including:

- User—A regular user of the computer. User accounts have limited permissions to prevent inadvertent or intentional misuse or damage to the computer.
- Administrator—An unlimited account, used when managing the computer.
- Guest—An account with very limited permissions. Guest users typically use the computer for just a short time or infrequently.

When performing day-to-day activities, you should log on using a user-level account. Should you need to perform management tasks, you should log off and then log on as an administrator. If you were to log on regularly as an administrator, you create the potential for inadvertent system changes that could affect you and other users of the computer.

Groups

Although user accounts represent the primary method used to identify users on a network, trying to configure permissions or rights for multiple users within their individual accounts can quickly become unmanageable, especially in large environments. For this reason, most operating systems, including Windows XP, include the ability to aggregate user accounts into entities known as groups.

With groups, you assign permissions to groups rather than to individual user accounts. When you want to assign that set of permissions to a user, you simply add his or her account to the appropriate group. For example, you might add a new user to the West Coast Sales group in order to grant him or her access to printers, storage, and other resources used by that team.

Windows supports multiple levels of groups, and typically includes the following:

- Users—The standard group for regular users.
- Administrators—A group to which administrator users belong.
- Power Users—A group used to assign elevated permissions to a select set of individuals.

Active Directory

Active Directory is a management framework for networks of Windows computers. By using Active Directory, administrators can manage all of the computers and peripherals in an enterprise. Active Directory is built on a centralized database of security settings and other information.

Rather than managing individual computers, users, and groups on each of those PCs, the administrator manages Active Directory. All computers that participate in Active Directory immediately inherit those settings.

Active Directory is made up of:

- Domains. Administrative units that group together network resources for management convenience.
- Forests. One or more Active Directory domains that share a schema and global catalog.
- Organizational units. Active Directory containers used to group and organize network resources, such as users, groups, computers, and other organizational units.

Effective Active Directory design requires that you fully understand your organization's requirements for services as well as data access. The way that you plan your domains, forests, and organizational units plays a critical role in defining your network's security boundaries and your ability to push security policies out to your computers effectively.

Do it!

A-1: Securing access to the operating system

Here's how	Here's why
1 For your day-to-day tasks, to what type of account should you log on?	*You should log on as a regular user for routine computer use.*
2 Name at least one purpose for groups	*The biggest purpose for groups is to ease system administration. By changing the permissions assigned to a group, all users obtain those settings the next time they log on.*
3 Log on to your computer using your RSTADMIN## account	
If necessary, click **Cancel**	To skip configuring NetWare client service properties.
4 Click **Start** and choose **Control Panel**	
Click **User Accounts**	![User Accounts icon] **User Accounts**
5 Click **Create a new account**	

These steps assume that the students' computers aren't part of a domain.

6 Type **Jdoe**	To enter a name for the account.
Click **Next**	
7 Select **Limited**	To make this user account a standard user rather than a computer administrator.
8 Click **Create Account**	To create the account.
9 Observe your new account	
10 Click **Jdoe**	
11 Click **Create a password**	
12 Enter **p@ssword**	To enter a password for this account. It won't display as you type. Instead a series of black dots are shown to hide the password from onlookers.
Press ⌷TAB⌷	
Enter **p@ssword**	To confirm your initial entry.
13 Click **Create Password**	To create the password for this account. To use this computer as Jdoe, you now have to enter the password you created.
14 Close User Accounts and Control Panel	

Encryption

Explanation

Encryption is the scrambling of data so that only the permitted people can unscramble and read it. Encryption prevents data alteration or replacement during storage and transmission.

Public key cryptography

Currently, the most powerful form of encryption is public key encryption. In *public key encryption*, two keys are used to encrypt and decrypt data. These keys work in pairs, such that whichever key is used to encrypt data, the other must be used to decrypt it.

For example, with e-mail transmission, public key encryption works like this: Someone wanting to send encrypted data to a user obtains his or her public key, encrypts the information, and sends it to the user. The user, by using his or her private key, can decrypt the message. The public key can't be used to decrypt the message, which means that no one else can decrypt the message other than the holder of the private key.

Encrypting File System

You can use the Encrypting File System (EFS) to protect files. Using EFS enhances the security provided by NTFS permissions on files and folders. Should an intruder gain access to your computer, he or she can't open any encrypted files or folders.

Windows XP Professional supports file encryption. Encryption is transparent, which means that you don't have to decrypt files before using them. You can open and use them within your applications, as you would use any unencrypted file. Windows manages decrypting the file in the background.

Do it!

A-2:   Encrypting files

Here's how	Here's why
1 Copy Marketing Document.txt to My Documents	
2 In My Documents, right-click **Marketing Document.txt** and choose **Properties**	
3 Click **Advanced...**	
4 Check **Encrypt contents to secure data**	
5 Click **OK** twice	You'll be asked whether to encrypt the file and its parent folder or just the file.
6 Select **Encrypt the file only** Click **OK**	Other files in this folder aren't encrypted.
7 Double-click **Marketing Document.txt** Close Notepad	Even though it's encrypted, it opens in Notepad as usual.
8 Close My Documents	

Authentication

Explanation

Authentication is the process by which your identity is validated against a database that contains your account. That validation is subsequently used to grant or deny access to network resources.

Authentication mechanisms

The typical mechanism for authentication is the user name and password. Provided that the password remains secret, this system provides reasonable assurance that the person logging in is who he or she claims to be.

Other authentication mechanisms exist for situations that require greater safeguards:

- Biometric devices—fingerprint scanners are the most common biometric devices, but retinal scans and other systems are available for ultra-secure systems.

- Smart cards—typically used in banking and retail environments, a user passes a card through a reader and enters a password (typically called a PIN, or personal identification number).

- Fobs—the typical fob is a keychain sized device that displays a continually changing semi-random number. The user must log on with a user name and password and then enter the number created by the fob. Software on the secure system knows which numbers are valid and which aren't. Some online banking systems require fobs, as do some business applications.

- Digital certificates—based on public key cryptography and a trusted registry of identities, a digital certificate is a computer file attesting to the identity of an individual or computer. Certificates are often used on the Internet to verify the identity of a secure system, such as a bank's online banking web server.

Authentication process

The authentication process can be handled in several ways to produce many different results, depending on how the environment is structured. A workgroup environment is managed differently from a domain environment, and authentication uses different methods and produces different results in each.

Interactive authentication

Interactive authentication is the process by which a user provides his or her username and password in the Log On to Windows dialog box. There are two types of logons:

- **Domain:** The username and password are compared to information stored on a domain controller in its Active Directory database. Barring other restrictions, a user can log on to any computer in the domain, because each computer can reference the central database.

- **Local:** The username and password are validated by the SAM database located on the computer, rather than by an Active Directory domain controller. The user must have an account on the computer that he or she is logging on to.

Network authentication

Network authentication is the process by which a network resource or service confirms the identity of a user. For example, when you attempt to access the contents of a shared folder on the network, your credentials must be validated. The manner in which network authentication occurs is different if you logged on to a domain versus a local computer account.

In an environment that uses local accounts, only that particular computer authenticates you. When you attempt to access network resources, such as a shared folder on another computer, you have to supply a username and password to use that resource.

With a domain login, once you log on to a computer, you're also logged on to the domain, and you're authorized to use any other resources to which you're granted access. Each resource references the same credentials and automatically recognizes who you are and what you're allowed to do.

Authentication protocols

In a Windows environment, two primary authentication protocols are commonly used:

- Kerberos version 5 (Kerberos v5)
- NT LAN Manager (NTLM)

Kerberos v5

Kerberos v5 is the primary authentication protocol used in Active Directory domain environments. Microsoft operating systems that support Kerberos v5 include:

- Windows 2000
- Windows XP

NTLM

NTLM is a challenge-response protocol that's used with operating systems running Windows NT 4.0 or earlier. Common examples of when NTLM authentication would be used include:

- When a Windows Server 2003 system attempts to authenticate to a Windows NT 4.0 domain controller
- When a Windows NT 4.0 Workstation system attempts to authenticate to a Windows 2000 or Windows Server 2003 domain controller

Do it!

A-3: Understanding authentication technologies

Here's how	Here's why
1 Logging on to a domain from the console of a Windows XP system is referred to as which type of authentication?	**A** Interactive B Network C Domain D Local
2 What's network authentication?	*The process by which a network resource or service confirms the identity of a user.*
3 Authentication is vital to maintaining the _____ of network resources.	*Security*
4 If a Windows NT 4.0 client doesn't have the Active Directory Client Extensions software installed, then which authentication protocol does it use to log on to a Windows Server 2003 domain?	**A** NTLM B Kerberos C RADIUS

Security policies

Explanation

Windows 2000 and Windows XP support a security tool called security policies. With security policies, you can define such settings as minimum password length, password complexity rules, whether to lock out a user account after some number of failed logon attempts, and so forth.

Policy types

Windows supports various types of security policies. The basic types are described in the following table.

Policy type	Policy	Description
Account Policies	Password Policy	Set password requirements, such as complexity, minimum length, expiration period, and so forth.
Account Policies	Account Lockout Policy	Whether to lock out a user account after some number of failed logon attempts, for how long, and so forth.
Local Policies	Audit Policy	What resources to audit.
Local Policies	User Rights Assignments	Granular rights assignments to users and groups.
Local Policies	Security Options	Granular security options, some of which are applied generally and others to specific users or groups.
Public Key Policies	Encrypting File System	Manage how computers participate in a public key infrastructure. Data recovery agent assignments, which specifies who can recover encrypted files in the event a user's keys are lost.
Software Restriction Policies	various	Settings that control what software can run on your system.
IP Security Policies	various	Settings that control IP Security (IPSec) on client, server, and secure server interfaces of your PC.

Computer vs. domain

If your computer participates in a domain, it might inherit security policy settings from the domain. Settings at the domain level override those made at the computer level. There are also additional policy settings, available for domain controller computers, which override the other policies.

Do it!

A-4: Using local security policies to set password restrictions

Here's how	Here's why
1 Click **Start** and choose **Control Panel**	
Click Performance and Maintenance, and then click Administrative Tools	
Double-click Local Security Policy	
2 Expand **Account Policies**	
3 Select **Password Policy**	Enforce password history Maximum password age Minimum password age Minimum password length Password must meet complexi Store password using reversib The available policies display in the right pane.
4 Double-click **Minimum password length**	The current value is zero, indicating that no minimum length is specified.
5 In the characters box, enter **8**	To specify that passwords must be at least eight characters long.
Click **OK**	Minimum password length 8 characters
6 Open **Control Panel**, **User Accounts**	You'll attempt to change a user's password to test your new password policy.
7 Click **Jdoe**	
8 Click **Change the password**	
9 Type **secret** into the new password and confirmation boxes	
Click **Change Password**	A dialog box tells you that the password you entered doesn't meet password policy requirements.
Click **OK**	
10 Click **Cancel** and close User Accounts and Control Panel	
11 In Local Security Settings, restore the minimum password length to zero	To reset the policy to its default value.

Topic B: Auditing and logging

This topic covers the following CompTIA A+ 220-603 exam objective.

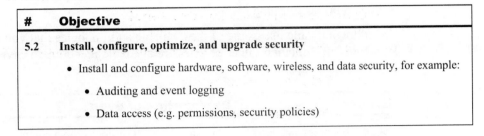

#	Objective
5.2	**Install, configure, optimize, and upgrade security**
	• Install and configure hardware, software, wireless, and data security, for example:
	• Auditing and event logging
	• Data access (e.g. permissions, security policies)

Auditing

Explanation

Monitoring events is a critical facet of any security strategy. Monitoring helps detect potential threats, increases user accountability, and provides evidence of security breaches. Monitoring can also be used for resource planning.

Auditing is used to monitor and track activities. You can specify which events to monitor based on your security or resource planning requirements. When an audited event does occur, a record of it is written to the security log within Event Viewer. The audit entry in the security log provides you with information, such as the user who performed the action, the specific action that was performed (e.g., a logon attempt), and whether it was a success or failure.

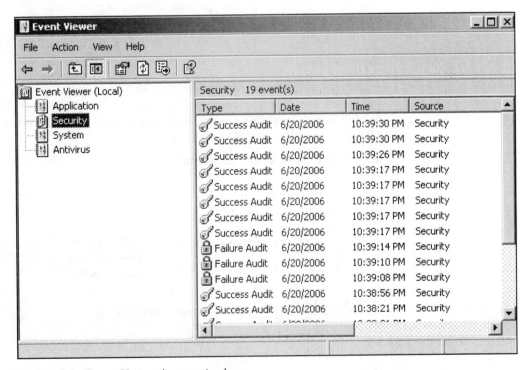

Exhibit 7-1: Event Viewer's security log

Events are stored in the security log of the computer on which the event transpires. Thus, in a domain environment, a logon attempt is logged in the security log of the domain controller computer, not the computer from which the user attempted to log on.

Audit policies

Before you can begin auditing security events or the accessing of network resources, you must first set up an audit policy. An *audit policy* defines the events that are recorded. For example, if you choose to monitor failed logon attempts, an event is written to the security log.

The following table lists some of the available audit policies that you could enable on a Windows XP computer. Other policies are available in a domain environment or with other Windows operating systems.

Event	Explanation of event
Audit account logon events	Activated when a user logs onto a computer
Audit account management	Activated whenever a user or group is created, deleted, or modified, this category tracks successful or unsuccessful password changes
Audit logon events	Activated when a user logs on or off a local computer or Active Directory, audits logon failures to find out if password hacking is taking place
Audit object access	Activated when an object, such as a folder or printer, is accessed; the object must also be configured for auditing successes and failures
Audit system events	Activated when a system event takes place, such as when the computer restarts

Object events

If your files and folders reside on an NTFS volume, you can set up auditing to monitor user access. For example, employee records or financial data may be confidential. To maintain a high level of security for this information, you should audit which users are attempting to access such files or folders.

Auditing guidelines

Excessive auditing can seriously degrade the performance of servers and workstations. Audit only those events that provide you with valuable information. Here are some additional auditing guidelines:

- Audit only events that provide useful information; unnecessary auditing increases overhead and fills up the security log with useless information
- Review the security log regularly, so that you're aware of any security issues
- Audit sensitive and confidential information
- Audit the Everyone group instead of the Users group, because the Everyone group includes unauthenticated users
- Audit the use of user rights assignment, so that administrative users are more accountable for their actions
- Always audit the Administrators group, so that you can track changes made by users who are members of this group

Do it!

B-1:   Enabling an auditing policy

Here's how	Here's why
1 Expand **Local Policies**	

Local Security Policy should be open.

2 Select **Audit Policy**

3 In the right pane, double-click **Audit logon events**

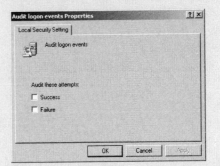

4 Check both **Success** and **Failure** | You'll audit both successful and unsuccessful logon attempts.

Click **OK**

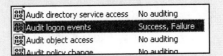

5 Close Local Security Settings and Administrative Tools

Do it!

B-2: Auditing an event

Here's how	Here's why
1 Log off	
2 Attempt to log on using the *wrong* password	You'll create a failure event in the logs.
3 Log on using the correct password	You'll create a success event in the logs.
4 Right-click My Computer and choose Manage	
Expand Event Viewer and select Security	To display entries in the security log.
5 Observe the failure event	Your unsuccessful logon attempt was recorded in the security log.
6 Observe the success event	You can see your successful logon was also recorded.
7 Close Computer Management	You'll now disable logging.
8 Open Local Security Policy	
9 Expand **Local Policies**	
10 Select **Audit Policy**	
11 In the right pane, double-click **Audit logon events**	
12 Clear both **Success** and **Failure**	To turn off logging for both types of events.
Click **OK**	
13 Close Local Security Settings and Administrative Tools	

Tell students the account and password to use

Topic C: Security hardware

This topic covers the following CompTIA A+ 220-603 exam objective.

#	Objective
5.2	**Install, configure, optimize, and upgrade security**
	• Install and configure hardware, software, wireless, and data security, for example:
	• Smart card readers
	• Key fobs
	• Biometric devices
	• Authentication technologies

Hardware-based security

Explanation

In some applications, user names and passwords provide insufficient security or are unmanageable. For example, an ATM card provides a greater level of security than a user name and password—you must both possess the physical credit card and know the secret PIN number.

Security devices

Biometrics

A biometric device authenticates (identifies) a user through the examination of a biological trait, such as a fingerprint, retinal vein pattern, and so forth. Fingerprint scanners are the most common biometric devices. With these scanners, you place a finger over a sensor window. The device scans your fingerprint and matches it to its database of user names and passwords. If a match is found, you're logged into the computer, web page, or application.

Microsoft, APC, and other vendors sell fingerprint scanners. Most are USB devices and come with software for gathering, verifying, and storing fingerprints. In most cases, with one of these fingerprint scanners installed, you can still enter user names and passwords via your keyboard as well as scan your print to access a secure resource.

Exhibit 7-2: A fingerprint scanner

C-1: Installing a fingerprint reader

Here's how	Here's why
1 Follow the manufacturer's instructions to connect and install the fingerprint scanner to your computer	
2 If necessary, install the manufacturer's software	You might need to restart your computer during the installation.
3 Using the software supplied with the scanner, scan your fingerprint and add it to the software's database of prints	You'll probably need to choose which finger to scan and then scan your finger repeatedly.
4 Log off	
5 Log onto Windows using the fingerprint scanner	Each vendor's software differs, but with some, all you need to do to log on is to place your finger on the scanner. You might not even have to select which user account to use. The software matches the fingerprint and user account and then logs you in.
6 Uninstall the software and fingerprint scanner	

You could also demonstrate ways to access password-protected web sites with the fingerprint scanner.

Card readers

Explanation

Smart cards are credit card-sized plastic cards with an embedded microprocessor. Smart cards typically have RAM to store up to 8 KB of data. Additionally, these cards have a small amount of ROM memory for storing programming code, which, among other things, controls the encryption of data on the card.

When inserted into a reader, the card draws power from the reader and boots up its embedded operating system. Then, the card's processor establishes communication with the PC. Typically, card readers interface with the PC over a USB or PC Card (PCMCIA) interface. A card reader and smart card are shown in Exhibit 7-3.

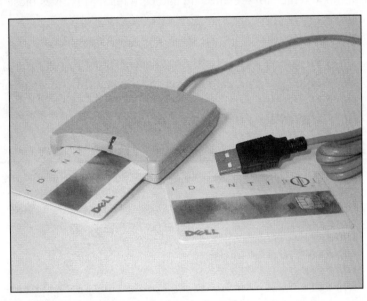

Exhibit 7-3: Smart card reader and cards

In comparison, a credit card or ATM card simply stores a unique identifier number on a magnetic strip. All processing and intelligence must be built into the host PC and applications. Smart cards, on the other hand, can store data and code, such as health insurance records, bank account data, security certificates, and so forth.

Smart cards are more popular in Europe than in the USA. These cards are most commonly used in banking applications in place of the "dumb" ATM card used in the US. According to HowStuffWorks.com, every German citizen has a smart card used for health insurance.

Components

To enable smart card-based security, you need a card reader, a card, and a software host application. Given the current state of the market for these devices, you typically have to purchase each component separately.

SCM Microsystems, RSA Security, and CryptoCard all make smart card readers. Oberthur Card Systems, RSA Security, and Sharp Electronics make smart cards. Software solutions range from Java platform programming environments, such as the Java Card Framework, to pre-packaged security solutions, such as the IdentiPHI Stand Alone Client from IdentiPHI LLC.

IdentiPHI security software

IdentiPHI security software replaces Windows security components to enable smart card, biometric, and other forms of authentication. After installing this software, you get different logon dialog boxes as you log on and off your system.

IdentiPHI Basic also includes a Single Sign-on component, which synchronizes your smart card and PIN with passwords required by other applications. With this component enabled and configured, you don't need to log on to the various applications, provided your smart card is inserted in the reader.

Installing the IndentiPHI software and card reader involves these steps:

1 Installing the card reader and its drivers.
2 Installing the IdentiPHI Basic software.
3 Configuring IdentiPHI Basic to accept smart cards.
4 Enrolling a smart card and setting a secure PIN for that card.

Do it!

C-2: Installing a card reader

Here's how	Here's why
1 Examine the smart card provided by your instructor	You'll notice that it differs from a regular credit card in that it includes a metallic, typically gold, contact area on its face and no black magnetic stripe.
2 Use your browser to visit `http://www.scmmicro.com/security/pcs_product_drivers.html`	
3 Click **End-Users License Agreement ("Agreement")**	To open a pop-up window containing SCM Micro's license agreement.
Click **Accept**	To accept the agreement. You must accept this agreement before you can download the drivers.
4 In the SCR331 row, click where indicated	

Alternatively, have the drivers downloaded and available on a share or CD. Then, pick up with step 8.

The version number might change. Help students locate the correct link.

```
SCR331
SCR531
CCID     V5.18    V4.30.00.01
(USB)
```

To download the SCR331 driver. The version number might change from that shown above.

5 Click **Click here for HTTP Download**	
6 Click **Open**	To download the file and open it.
7 Copy the Win2KXP folder to your desktop	
Close the Zip file window	

8	Plug the smart card reader into your USB port	The Found New Hardware Wizard opens.
9	Select **Install from a list or specific location**	
10	Click **Browse**	
11	Select the **Win2KXP** folder	(On the desktop.)
12	Click **Next**	To install the driver.
13	Click **Finish**	
14	Delete the Win2KXP folder from your desktop	

Do it!

C-3: Installing the IdentiPHI Basic software

Here's how	Here's why
1 Insert the IdentiPHI Basic installation CD into your optical drive	
2 Click **Install IdentiPHI**	An installation wizard begins.
Click **Next**	
3 Accept the license agreement and click **Next**	
4 Click **Next**	To specify to install both the advanced authentication and single sign-on components.
5 Clear Install biometric support and then click **Next**	To install the smart card component but not the biometric device support component. The IdentiPHI software can manage authentication via smart cards, biometric devices (fingerprint scanners), and user name and password.
6 Click **Install**	
7 Clear the view release notes check box and click **Finish**	
8 Restart your computer	
9 Log on	You must now configure the software to use the smart card reader.

Do it!

C-4: Configuring IdentiPHI Basic to accept smart cards

Here's how	Here's why
1 In the system tray, right-click [icon] and choose **System Settings**	
2 Enter your password and click **OK**	By default, you must provide your credentials to be able to reconfigure the authentication options.
3 Click **System**	
4 Next to Smartcard / key, select **Enable**	
Click **OK**	The IdentiPHI software is now configured to use smart cards.
5 Click **User**	To set user level configuration options.
6 Next to Smartcard / smartkey, check **Allow**	
Check **Auto self enroll**	To enable users to enroll their own smart cards.
7 Click **OK** twice	To save your changes and close all dialog boxes.
8 Restart your PC	While the software might not prompt you to restart, you can't continue to use the smart card until you do so.

Card enrollment

Explanation

In order to use a smart card to access your computer and applications, you must enroll the card with the IdentiPHI software. Through this process, you create a logon certificate and download it to your smart card. You also set a password that needs to be provided when you (or someone else attempts to) use your smart card.

Do it!

C-5: Enrolling a smart card with IdentiPHI

Here's how	Here's why
1 Log on	You'll be prompted to enter your smart card pin.
2 Insert your smart card into the reader	
3 Enter **password**	The default password for new cards is "password."
4 Click **New certificate**	To create a new security certificate, which will be saved on your smart card.
5 Select your certificate and click **Next**	
6 Click **Finish**	Your card is now ready for use. However, it's configured with the default password, which you should change.
7 In the system tray, right-click and choose **Change Smartcard PIN**	
8 In the Current PIN box, enter **password** Enter **pa$$123** into the new and confirm boxes Click **OK** twice	To set your PIN (password) to the much more secure pa$$123.
9 Log off	
10 Remove your card from the reader	

Smart card use

Explanation

Smart cards are a form of two-factor authentication. Such authentication methods combine something you have with something you know. A user name and password is a form of two-factor authentication: you have a user name (though anyone else could know it, too) and you (and hopefully only you) know your password.

With smart cards, you have the card. You also need to supply a PIN or password. With the IdentiPHI software, your PIN can be any alphanumeric password with between four and eight characters.

To log on with a smart card and the IdentiPHI software, simply insert your card into the reader and enter your PIN when prompted.

To lock your workstation, simply remove your smart card from the reader. You have to insert your card and re-enter your PIN or enter your user name and password to log back on.

Do it!

C-6: Using a smart card

If the card can't be read, tell students to remove it and reinsert it.

Here's how	Here's why
1 Insert your smart card	
2 When prompted for your PIN, enter **pa$$123**	
Click **OK**	To log on.
3 Remove your smart card	Your workstation is automatically locked to prevent unauthorized use. You could log on with your password or reinsert your card to log on with it.
4 Insert your smart card	
Enter **pa$$123** and click **OK**	To log on.

Do it!

C-7: Uninstalling the smart card reader and software

Students need to uninstall this software to prepare for upcoming activities.

Here's how
1 Using the Control Panel, Add/Remove programs application, uninstall the IdentiPHI Basic software from your system.
2 Restart your PC when prompted.
3 Using the Safely Remove Hardware system tray utility, stop the smart card reader.
4 Unplug the smart card reader from your PC.

Fobs

Explanation

The typical fob is a keychain-sized device that creates a continually changing, seemingly random number, what's called a rolling code. In some cases, the user must log on with a user name and password and then enter the number created by the fob. In other cases, the user simply uses the fob to unlock a secure area. For example, your car's keyless entry system and garage door opener use fobs with rolling number generators.

The generated number isn't random but instead follows a secret progression started with a random seed number. Both the fob and the secure system know the sequence of numbers (or how to generate the next valid number in the sequence). As long as the receiver receives the code it expects, it opens your car, garage door, and so forth.

Visit http://auto.howstuffworks.com/remote-entry2.htm for more information about the way keyless entry systems work.

Topic D: The human aspects of security

This topic covers the following CompTIA A+ 220-603 exam objectives.

#	Objective
5.2	**Install, configure, optimize, and upgrade security**
	• Install and configure hardware, software, wireless, and data security, for example:
	• Software firewalls
	• Wireless client configuration
	• Unused wireless connections
5.3	**Identify tools, diagnostic procedures, and troubleshooting techniques for security issues**
	• Diagnose and troubleshoot software and data security issues, for example:
	• Software firewall issues
	• Wireless client configuration issues
5.4	**Perform preventative maintenance for security**
	• Recognize social engineering and address social engineering situations

People—the weakest point of security

Explanation

The weakest point of any security system is the people who use the system. Ways that you can alleviate some of the security risk are to:

- Restrict physical access to sensitive systems and data
- Manage social engineering attacks

Physical access restrictions

An inexperienced user could inadvertently shut down your main corporate server if the server were simply sitting in a cubicle where anybody could access it. A determined attacker could reboot your server using a floppy disk or CD-ROM in order to attempt to bypass operating system-based security. He or she might simply steal the entire server (or external storage device) in order to gain access to your corporate data. Someone bent on sabotage could simply damage your servers and equipment to hurt your company.

By restricting physical access to a computer, you eliminate a very large potential for security breaches. Some of the restrictions you might consider include to:

- Lock server rooms with key or key card locks. Use separate rooms for low-security computers and high-security systems and carefully manage who has keys to the various locations.
- Lock PC cases (available with some models) to limit access to the system to those who have the key
- Use cameras or motion-sensor alarms to monitor spaces during non-business hours
- Station guards near ultra-sensitive systems.

Do it!

D-1: Implementing physical access restrictions

Here's how	Here's why
1 Describe the physical access restrictions in place at your company or companies where you've worked	*Answers will vary.*
2 Were those access restrictions effective? If not, why not?	*Answers will vary.*
3 What physical access restrictions that you've seen in a spy movie would be practical for a real business environment (if they weren't too expensive)?	*Answers will vary.*

Social engineering attacks

Explanation

A common means to gain access to the network is to use a social engineering attack. In such attacks, hackers attempt to trick users into divulging their user names and passwords or giving up valuable data files. For example, a malcontent might pose as a help desk technician and ask an unsuspecting user for his or her user name and password.

Visit securityfocus. com/infocus/1527 for an interesting article on social engineering.

Phishing, a growing problem on the Internet, is another example of a social engineering attack. With phishing, hackers send emails or create web sites that mimic a legitimate site to gather user names and passwords. For example, an e-mail message might purport to come from a person's bank and request them to log on to a web site to perform account maintenance. In reality, the web site would simply collect the person's user name and password and present fake messages about the account maintenance. Later, the hackers would drain the person's account by logging into the bank's real web site.

Other examples of social engineering include:

- "Dumpster diving," which involves digging through a company's trash to find information that can assist in gaining access to secure resources.

- "Shoulder surfing," which involves observing calling card numbers, PINs, or passwords by watching over the shoulder of a person who's entering those secret credentials.

- Creating camaraderie or friendship for the purpose of convincing people to share their passwords. This happens often in online gaming or pay-access venues in which a banned or non-paying person convinces a legitimate user to share his or her password.

- Trojan horse attachments, which are programs meant to gather information (such as passwords) but are disguised as legitimate programs or data files.

- Sneaking into the building or secure room by pretending to be an employee who has lost his or her badge.

Malicious software

You might have to deal with various types of malicious software. The common types are described in the following table.

Type	Description	Propagation method
Virus	Destructive or damaging software meant to disrupt the operation of a PC, destroy data, or even destroy hardware.	E-mail attachment, digital media (floppy disks, CD-ROMs, etc.), or web page download.
Worm	A self-propagating program meant to disrupt the operation of a PC. Worms can be used to create zombies, which are infected PCs that can be used to attack remote systems in a distributed denial of service attack (DDOS).	Self-propagating via network ports, shared folders, e-mail attachments, and so forth.
Trojan horse	Software that includes undisclosed functions. For example, a game might log your keystrokes to capture passwords, which it sends to the Trojan's author who breaks into your PC or network.	E-mail attachment or web page download.
Spam	Junk e-mail, officially known as unsolicited commercial e-mail (UCE).	E-mail.
Spyware	Software that monitors and gathers information without the user's knowledge. For example, spyware might log your web page visit history sending the data to an advertiser who then targets you with junk e-mail.	E-mail attachment, web page download, or automatic ActiveX component installation when you visit a web page or open an e-mail message.
Adware	Software that displays advertisements, which might or might not be targeted to your interests.	E-mail attachment, web page download, or automatic ActiveX component installation when you visit a web page or open an e-mail message.
Grayware	A general name for software that has annoying, undisclosed, or undesirable behaviors. Trojan horses are a specific type of grayware.	E-mail attachment or web page download.

SPAM is a registered trademark of Hormel Foods Corporation.

Prevention

Awareness and training are the best way to prevent social engineering attacks. Clear expectations about the type of information that's requested and in what form should be spelled out in your corporate security policy and new employee training materials. Your corporate security policy should clearly prohibit divulging passwords and other sensitive information, whether over the telephone, by e-mail, or in person.

Furthermore, your security policy should clearly state how employees should handle file attachments in e-mail. Many companies prohibit opening attachments. Such companies typically use software to filter e-mail and scan or simply delete file attachments.

Most larger companies mandate virus protection software on employee computers, including home computers that connect to the company network. Typically, these companies centrally manage updates to this software. Security policies typically prohibit with tampering or disabling this software, too. Small companies should follow this practice to safeguard their systems.

A corporate security policy provides a means of protection, too. For example, the policy might state that users should lock their PCs when leaving them. As a result, the IT department would then configure password-based screen savers and instruct users on how to lock their PCs. Such policies and practices help prevent both intentional breaches, such as shoulder surfing, as well as opportunistic breaches, when someone finds an unlocked yet logged-in PC.

Do it!

D-2: Managing social engineering attacks

Here's how	Here's why
1 List some items that might be found in a company's trash that would be useful to a hacker	*Company policy manuals, organization charts, company phone books, printouts of sensitive data, receipts, credit card slips, source code printouts, passwords, and so forth.*
2 If you were a hacker planning to call people to convince them to divulge their passwords, whom would you impersonate? (Give a job title or role.)	*A help desk technician, telephone repair person, executive secretary, a traveling executive, a spouse, and so forth.*
3 Have you ever been the victim of a social engineering attack? If so, describe the attack.	*Answers will vary.*
4 How does your company handle file attachments and virus scanning?	*Answers will vary.*
5 Are you required to use a password-protected screen saver or to lock your PC when you leave your desk?	*Answers will vary.*

Network security

Explanation

When considering the human aspects of security, in addition to the areas covered previously, you should also consider:

- Firewalls
- Wireless networking issues
- Password management
- Account management
- Incidence reporting

Firewalls

A popular form of attack is port scanning. Ports are network addresses available on a computer. Attackers set up computers to scan the ports available at random network addresses hoping to find unguarded ports. Once these are found, operating system vulnerabilities can be exploited, permitting the attacker to gain access to the PC or network.

Your company should run firewalls in two locations to block such attacks. At the network level, where your network connects to the Internet or WAN, a firewall blocks outside attackers. At the PC level, software firewalls block internal attacks.

Software firewalls include those included with Windows XP, as well as third-party applications, such as Zone Alarm. A local PC-level software firewall can also prevent the spread of viruses that transmit themselves (a.k.a. worms) to open ports on other PCs.

Wireless networks

War driving, the act of scanning for unsecured wireless networks, is a popular activity with people looking to steal service and cause trouble. You should disable any unused wireless networks. Wireless networks should always be secured with encryption and authentication options.

WPA-PSK (WiFi Protected Access – Preshared Key) encryption is suitable for most home and small business wireless networks. Larger networks or those that require greater security should investigate custom solutions provided by networking vendors, such as Cisco.

Password management

You must manage passwords on your network. You must ensure that users create passwords that are complex and thus difficult to guess. Of course, users must be able to remember their passwords without writing them down, so you can't require passwords for general-level users to be too complex.

Typically, companies require users to change their passwords periodically. Additionally, people are typically restricted from reusing a password. Or, they can't reuse any of the last ten passwords.

You enforce such password restrictions in two ways:

- Local security policy—This Windows-based feature enables you to enforce password complexity, length, and reuse mandates.
- Corporate security policy—Your corporate policy should clearly spell out your password rules, so that employees know the requirements. Such clarity also helps with remediation or discipline, should users violate the policy.

Account management

One of the authors of this course worked for a Fortune 50 company as a mainframe technician. A year after leaving, his super-administrator level account was still active. He could have logged on and shut down this company's mainframes. Instead, he reminded the IT department to delete his account.

User accounts should be closely monitored. As soon as an employee leaves the company or is dismissed, that person's account should be locked. Doing so helps lessen the risk of the employee's logging on and deleting or damaging data and network resources.

After managers or other designated personnel have had time to migrate the former employee's data, the user account should be deleted. Some companies keep user accounts indefinitely, albeit in a disabled state, so that no one can log on to them.

Incident reporting

If your company experiences a security breach, you should report it immediately. Such reporting includes internal and external notifications. As an IT technician, you should report any suspected breach to your supervisor and to whomever else your corporate security policy dictates.

From there, your corporate security officer should notify the appropriate external authorities. This might include law enforcement agencies, the CERT Coordination Center, antivirus vendors, security consultants, the FBI, and so forth.

By reporting incidents, you do the following:

- Provide a basis for legal remedies, such as the arrest and trial of the offender, or financial judgments against the offender.
- Notify other companies who might be at risk, such as in the case of a virus or denial of service attack.
- Assist state and federal agencies to assess the severity and significance of large-scale incidents. For example, the true impact of virus outbreaks is rarely accurately known, because few individuals whose computers are infected report the incident.
- You might be eligible for technical assistance from organizations such as CERT or your antivirus vendor.
- You act as a good Internet citizen, because reporting security incidents is just the right thing to do.

Do it!   **D-3:   Examining network security**

Here's how	Here's why
1 Does your company have a network-level firewall?	*Answers will vary.*
2 Does your company install software firewalls on end-user PCs and servers?	*Answers will vary.*
3 How do you enforce password rules in your organization?	*Answers will vary.*
4 How long after an employee leaves your company is his or her account suspended or deleted?	*Answers will vary.*
5 What's your company's policy on reporting incidents? Have you had to report any incidents?	*Answers will vary.*
6 If you use wireless networking, is your wireless network secured? If so, how?	*Answers will vary.*

Unit summary: Security

Topic A   In this topic, you learned that operating system security depends on authenticating users, that is determining who they are. You saw how you can use users and groups to control access, and you looked at **encryption**, **authentication**, and **local security policies**.

Topic B   In this topic, you learned that **auditing** is a feature that tracks a wide range of security-related events, such as use of user rights, logon events, object access, system events, and more. You also learned that **Event Viewer Security log** is used to view the audited events.

Topic C   In this topic, you learned about the various security devices, such as **fingerprint scanner**, **smart card readers**, and **fobs**. You installed a **biometric** fingerprint scanner and used your fingerprint to log onto your computer. You installed a **smart card reader**, **enrolled a card**, logged in with your smart card, and **locked your PC** by removing the card.

Topic D   In this topic, you learned that **physical access restrictions** involve keeping unauthorized people out of sensitive areas plus physically securing computers and peripherals. You saw how a **corporate security policy** is an effective tool for ensuring security within your organization. You also examined the various **social engineering attacks** that are used to gain access to systems or secure areas.

Review questions

1   List the three basic types of user accounts provided by Windows.

   User, administrator, and guest.

2   You've completed your corporate security policy and had all employees read and sign it. Are you finished with the security policy?

   No, you should regularly review and update it.

3   When performing day-to-day activities, you should log on using a _____-level account.

   User

4   How can you prevent social engineering attacks?

   Awareness and training are the best ways to prevent social engineering attacks. Clear expectations about the type of information that's requested and in what form should be spelled out in your corporate security policy and new employee training materials. Your corporate security policy should clearly prohibit divulging passwords and other sensitive information, whether over the telephone, by e-mail, or in person.

5   List at least two physical access restrictions you should implement in your workplace.

   Lock server rooms, use separate rooms for low- and high-security computer systems, lock PC cases and peripherals, use cameras or motion-sensor alarms, station guards near ultra-sensitive areas.

6   What's the primary authentication protocol used on modern Windows networks?

   Kerberos v5

7   Describe the purpose of a corporate security policy.

A corporate security policy is a contract between the company and its employees about how company technology resources can be used. It heightens security awareness among company personnel. It also demonstrates the company's commitment to security and the protection of vital information assets.

8   List at least two examples of a social engineering attack.

Tricking users into divulging sensitive information, phishing, dumpster diving, shoulder surfing, Trojan horse attachments, and sneaking into secure areas through deception.

9   What's a biometric device?

A device that authenticates (identifies) a user through the examination of a biological trait, such as a fingerprint, retinal vein pattern, and so forth.

10   How does a smart card differ from a credit or ATM card?

Smart cards include a microprocessor, RAM, and ROM to store data and instructions. Credit and ATM cards store a small amount of data on a magnetic stripe, leaving all processing to the host computer or device.

11   What components do you need to implement smart card-based security?

A card reader and its drivers, smart cards, and host software to manage the authentication and authorization process.

12   List the typical steps for installing a smart card reader and enabling secure access.

Install the reader and its drivers. Install the host software. Configure the host software. Enroll the cards and set their PINs.

13   Why should you migrate archival data off your network?

To keep such data available to meet legal requirements but not generally available where it could be stolen or inappropriately accessed.

14   When should you lock your PC?

When you leave your cubicle or office.

15   Where should you have firewalls on your network?

At the network level, where your network connects to the Internet, and at the PC level to block internal attacks.

16   When should you delete a dismissed employee's user account?

Perhaps never, but you should disable it immediately.

17   Give at least two reasons to report a security breach.

Answers might include:

- *To provide a legal basis for remedies.*

- *To obtain technical assistance from consultants, antivirus vendors, CERT, and so forth.*

- *To notify other companies that might be at risk.*

18   Before you can audit operating system or object access, you must create a(n) _____.

Audit policy

Independent practice activity

1 Create a user named PSmith with the password p@ssword.

2 Add PSmith to the Administrators group.

3 Copy Budget Analysis from your My Documents folder to the root folder (C:\).

4 Explicitly deny PSmith write access to the Budget Analysis file.

5 Log on as PSmith.

6 Open the Budget Analysis and attempt to save changes to the file. PSmith is denied write access, so you shouldn't be able to save changes.

7 Log off.

8 Delete the Jdoe and PSmith user accounts.

9 Delete C:\Budget Analysis.

Unit 8

Professionalism and communication

Unit time: 30 minutes

Complete this unit, and you'll know how to:

A Be professional when interacting with users.

B Achieve customer satisfaction.

C Track problems and their resolutions.

Topic A: Professionalism

This topic covers the following CompTIA A+ 220-603 exam objectives.

#	Objective
6.1	**Use good communication skills, including listening and tact / discretion, when communicating with customers and colleagues**
	• Use clear, concise, and direct statements
	• Allow the customer to complete statements – avoid interrupting
	• Clarify customer statements – ask pertinent questions
	• Avoid using jargon, abbreviations, and acronyms
	• Listen to customers
6.2	**Use job-related professional behavior, including notation of privacy, confidentiality, and respect for the customer and the customer's property**

Professional service

Explanation

The hardware support technician role is often involved with tense situations. When a user has just lost a document or needs to print a document for a meeting in five minutes and the printer isn't working, his or her anxiety level can be quite high. As a hardware support technician, you have to remain calm and focus on the task at hand.

Stay focused

Some users may seem just to be lonely and call for support at the drop of a hat. However, because most companies charge the IT department by the minute for the support given to users, avoid entering into idle chitchat with the user, as that can waste time and end up putting you behind schedule and costing the user money from the support budget. If you're just watching files copy during the support call, and the user is interested in talking about last night's game or the new restaurant that just opened, that would be a fine time to engage in some pleasantries.

Many users like to think of themselves as computer savvy and find it difficult to admit that there are some situations that they just can't resolve on their own. Other users refuse to admit that they understand anything about computers and just throw up their hands when the least little problem occurs. It's up to you, as the hardware support technician, to determine at what level the user can understand what the problem is and give you information about the problem. Be sure not to talk down to the user as well as not to talk over the head of the user.

Speak professionally

Avoid using jargon where plain language would suffice. You aren't out to impress the user with all the technobabble you picked up at the latest conference you attended. You need to speak clearly about the issue and implement the appropriate solutions.

Ask clarifying questions, until you're sure that both you and the customer agree that you understand the problem. Often users don't know exactly what the problem is. They only know that, when they try to do X, Y happens. In their description of problems, they might not accurately explain them. They also might not directly ask the question – they might dance around it, leaving you to figure it out from the various clues they give you.

If the user tried to fix the problem on his or her own and covered up the original problem with attempted fixes or made the problem worse, he or she isn't likely to want to admit this to you. If the user tells you that he or she already tried a particular fix when you attempt to perform a step in your troubleshooting, calmly say that, in order to fix the problem, you need to go through all of the mostly likely possibilities that could fix it in an orderly manner. And, if this includes something that was already tried, then it's possible that some step in between that was performed has altered the outcome of trying that fix again.

If you discover that the user has created a problem through a misunderstanding of how things work, be sure to explain to the user how to perform the task so that the problem doesn't recur. You might recommend an online course or classroom course that the user should consider enrolling in to learn more about using the computer.

Respect the customer

It's critical that you respect the customer's privacy, confidentiality, and property. For example, when in a customer's office or cubicle, you shouldn't read the customer's papers, look through the desk drawers, open computer files (unless required for the troubleshooting task at hand), and so forth. You should refrain from making personal phone calls or text messaging. Don't eat or drink in the customer's space. Avoid surfing the web and other non-work activities in the customer's office.

Never interrupt the customer while he or she is speaking. Listen attentively, showing interest and involvement in the conversation. Make sure to look at the customer while he or she is speaking—avoiding eye contact suggests you don't care about the customer or what s/he's saying.

Don't argue with the customer. Even if the customer did something blatantly foolish, never be judgmental or insulting. Don't belittle the customer or minimize the importance of his or her computer problems.

Stay up to date

Keep up to date on the hardware you support, as well as learning about new equipment on the market that could benefit your company and users. Sources to monitor on a regular basis for current information include:

- magazines
- forums
- newsgroups
- Web sites

Do it!

A-1: Maintaining professionalism

Here's how	Here's why

1 You receive a call from a customer named Joe and visit his cubicle to provide assistance. Joe believes himself to be pretty computer-savvy and tells you all the steps he's taken to solve his printing problem. In fact, he becomes irate when you try to send a test print job to the queue before doing any further troubleshooting. What's the best way to respond to Joe?

    A   Tell him that you're the expert and you'll solve the problem.

    B   Tell him that you want to make sure that a problem really exists.

    C   Tell him that you're trying to follow a methodical troubleshooting plan and the first step is to try printing.

    D   Tell him that, before arriving, you degaussed the fuser and primed the piezoelectric elements, so that the print device should be operational.

2 List your three favorite sources for keeping up to date on industry news and information

Sources will vary.

3 List at least three activities that you shouldn't engage in while in a customer's cubicle or office

Answers might include making personal calls on your cell phone, reading their papers, eating or drinking, opening their computer files, browsing the Internet, and so forth.

4 While troubleshooting Jill's computer, you find that she spilled coffee into the keyboard, causing it to fail. How might you inform Jill of the problem?

    A   Sternly tell her that it's against corporate policy to consume food or drink near company computers and equipment.

    B   Tell her the source of the problem and suggest she keep food and drink more than an arm's reach from her computer.

    C   Replace the keyboard without telling her why it failed.

    D   Tell her boss what she did.

5 A user calls distraught that the report she's been working on all day for the meeting in five minutes has disappeared from her computer. Prepare a script on how you would respond to the user and then role-play it with a partner.

Answers will vary.

6 You receive a trouble ticket for a user who has had a string of problems with a new system. When you call the user, he's quite upset that the system still isn't stable. Prepare a script on how you'd respond to the user and then role-play it with a partner.

Answers will vary.

7 A technically savvy user calls the support hotline about a problem with the database she's using. She has only been using the database for a week but is a programmer and former hardware technician who's comfortable around computers. Prepare a script on how you'd respond to the user and then role-play it with a partner.

Answers will vary.

Topic B: Customer satisfaction

Explanation

A problem isn't resolved until both the technician and the user agree that the problem has been resolved. Keeping a customer satisfied during a long troubleshooting process can be a difficult task, especially for a technician who's better at dealing with hardware than with people. Such a technician needs to work on people skills to be successful in the support role.

Service Level Agreements

Many companies develop a Service Level Agreement (SLA) that specifies how clients and support personnel are to interact, what to expect from each other, and timeframes for the resolution of issues. The following are just some of the important concerns that an SLA should cover.

Item	Description
How to contact tech support.	Phone, Web-based application, e-mail, or some other method. It might also specify contact methods that aren't to be used. For example, some companies might not accept E-mail requests for assistance or stopping techs in the hallways to ask for support.
How soon the user can expect a response.	This is usually just an e-mail message or other correspondence to let the user know that the request has been received and queued up for resolution.
How soon the user can expect a tech to attempt to fix the problem.	The tech might need to do something behind the scenes to resolve the problem, might be able to walk the user through the problem over the phone, or might need to meet with the user in person.
	In some companies the response time is in minutes or hours. In others, it's in days.
What happens if the tech can't initially fix the problem.	This often includes how much time the tech is allowed to spend trying to resolve the problem before escalating it.
	It also might specify whether the user gets a loaner system (to use if his or her system is completely down) or other workarounds to the problem.
Escalation of the problem.	Usually there are three tiers of support. This often starts with a help desk via phone, then a deskside hardware technician, and finally to a backroom technician who works at a bench making repairs.
	Each tier of support usually has more experience, as well as access to additional resources, to help resolve the problem.

The course, A Guide to Customer Service Skills for the Help Desk Professional, 2nd edition, is available if you'd like more in-depth coverage of this topic.

Do it!

B-1: Ensuring customer satisfaction

Here's how	Here's why
1 A problem is resolved when ____	*Both the customer and the technician agree that it's resolved.*
2 What's a service level agreement?	*A policy that specifies how clients and support personnel are to interact, what to expect from each other, the timeframes for resolution, and processes to be followed to escalate issues that aren't solved to the customer's satisfaction.*
3 Does your company have an SLA and, if so, what does it contain?	*Answers will vary.*

Topic C: Problem and resolution tracking

Explanation

It's important to maintain information about the problems that you need to resolve and the resolution to those problems. Of course, you must keep track of all open issues so that you and your support technician teammates don't let customers slip through the cracks. Additionally, having a record of past resolutions assists you when you encounter similar problems in the future.

Tracking options

The options for tracking problems and resolutions are nearly endless. You can do something as simple as a pen and paper-based system in a 3-ring binder to an off-the-shelf problem-tracking and resolution database system to a custom-built application. It all depends on the size of the user base you're supporting and the needs of the organization.

It's recommended that, whichever system you use, you maintain a backup copy in a secure location so that, if something happens to the original, you have access to the copy from another location. A system on a server could be unavailable due to server problems, network problems, or computer workstation problems. Any system could be unavailable due to fire or natural disaster problems.

The following is some of the important information you should consider tracking in your system:

- User name
- User location
- Operating system
- Hardware platform
- Date call was received
- Date user was visited
- Time spent on problem
- Date problem was resolved
- Detailed description of the problem
- Detailed description of steps to resolve the problem
- Summary of problem (using keywords or a one-line summary)
- Summary of resolution (using keywords or a one-line summary)

Help desk software

Many vendors offer software to help manage problem tracking and help desk functions. Companies like IBM, Computer Associates, and others offer large-scale commercial problem-tracking applications.

Many smaller companies offer similar packages aimed at smaller company needs or for targeted vertical markets. For example, you can find applications designed specifically to support the tracking needs of Web site hosting companies or software developers.

Visit www.helpdesk.com/software-helpdesk.htm for a long list of help desk software publishers and their Web sites. Further information, particularly on the smaller vendor products, is also available at http://linas.org/linux/pm.html.

Do it!

C-1: Tracking problems and resolutions

Here's how	Here's why
1 What problem tracking solution is in use at your company?	*Answers will vary.*
2 Have you used any software applications to track problems and resolutions? If so, what were the program's strengths and weaknesses?	*Answers will vary.*
3 Looking at the preceding list of information to track, what additional information would you track? What wouldn't you bother to track? Why?	*Answers might include tracking software updates applied, hardware type and version affected, user account information (user name, group membership, etc.), technicians who worked on the issue, and so forth.*

Unit summary: Professionalism and communication

Topic A   In this topic, you learned that being professional, courteous, and respectful is critical to success as a support technician. You learned to stay focused, speak professionally, respect the customer, and stay up to date.

Topic B   In this topic, you learned that a problem isn't resolved until both the technician and the user agree that the problem has been resolved. You also learned about service level agreements that specify how clients and support personnel are to interact.

Topic C   In this topic, you learned that problem and resolution tracking is important to longterm success. Tracking problems and resolutions helps you make sure all problems get resolved and saves you time in the future when you encounter similar issues.

Review questions

1 List at least five pieces of information that you should track about an open trouble ticket.

   Answers might include: the customer's name, the customer's contact information, problem description, problem reporting date, technician assigned, operating system version, and application version.

2 List at least five pieces of information that you should track about a resolved trouble ticket.

   Answers might include: the customer's name, the customer's contact information, problem description, problem reporting date, technician assigned, operating system version, application version, problem resolution description, resolution date, and time spent on the issue.

3 List at least three activities you should avoid while in a customer's office.

   Answers might include making personal calls on your cell phone, reading their papers, eating or drinking, opening their computer files, browsing the Internet, and so forth.

4 You should _____ the customer and his or her property.

   Respect

5 When speaking to a customer, you should speak simply and clearly and not use _____.

   Jargon or technobabble

6 When a customer describes a problem, you should ask _____ to elicit complete details.

   Clarifying questions

7 Never _____ the customer while he or she is speaking.

   Interrupt

8 A problem isn't resolved until _____.

   Both the technician and the user agree that the problem has been resolved

9 A policy that describes how clients and support personnel are to interact is called a(n) _____.

Service level agreement

10 List at least two sources to monitor to stay up to date on technical and market issues.

Web sites, newsgroups, forums, and magazines.

Independent practice activity

1 Search the Internet to locate the Web sites for at least two commercial problem-tracking or help desk management applications.

2 Compare the applications. Which would be better for your company's needs? Which is less expensive? Which vendor seems better able to support their software and customers?

3 Repeat the search, this time looking for an open source tracking application. Would it meet your needs better than either of the commercial applications? What compromises would you need to make, if you were to choose the open source application?

Appendix A

Certification exam objectives map

This appendix provides the following information:

A CompTIA A+ 220-603 exam objectives with references to corresponding coverage in this course manual.

Topic A: Comprehensive exam objectives

Explanation   This section lists all CompTIA A+ 220-603 2006 exam objectives and indicates where each objective is covered in conceptual explanations, activities, or both.

1.0 Personal computer components

Objective	Conceptual information	Supporting activities
1.1 — Install, configure, optimize, and upgrade personal computer components		
Add, remove, and configure display devices, input devices and adapter cards including basic input and multimedia devices	Unit 1, Topic A Unit 1, Topic B	A-1, A-2 B-1, B-2
1.2 — Identify tools, diagnostic procedures, and troubleshooting techniques for personal computer components		
Identify and apply basic diagnostic procedures and troubleshooting techniques, for example:		
• Identify and analyze the problem/potential problem	Unit 1, Topic D Unit 2, Topic B Unit 3, Topic B	D-1 B-2 B-6
• Test related components and evaluate results	Unit 1, Topic D Unit 2, Topic B Unit 3, Topic B	D-1 B-2 B-6
• Identify additional steps to be taken if/when necessary	Unit 1, Topic D Unit 2, Topic B Unit 3, Topic B	D-1 B-2 B-6
• Document activities and outcomes	Unit 1, Topic D Unit 2, Topic B Unit 3, Topic B Unit 8, Topic C	D-1 B-2 B-6 C-1
Recognize and isolate issues with display, peripheral, multimedia, specialty input device and storage	Unit 1, Topic D Unit 2, Topic B Unit 3, Topic B Unit 3, Topic C	D-1 B-2 B-6 C-2
Apply steps in troubleshooting techniques to identify problems (e.g. physical environment, functionality and software/driver settings) with components including display, input devices and adapter cards	Unit 1, Topic D	D-1
1.3 — Perform preventative maintenance on personal computer components		
Identify and apply common preventative maintenance techniques for storage devices, for example:		
• Software tools (e.g., Defrag, CHKDSK)	Unit 2, Topic B	B-1
• Cleaning (e.g., optics, tape heads)	Unit 2, Topic B	B-2

2.0 Operating systems

Unless otherwise noted, operating systems referred to within include Microsoft Windows 2000, XP Professional, XP Home, and Media Center.

Objective	Conceptual information	Supporting activities
2.1 — Identify the fundamental principles of using operating systems		
Use command-line functions and utilities to manage Windows 2000, XP Professional and XP Home, including proper syntax and switches, for example:		
• CMD	Unit 4, Topic A	A-1
• HELP	Unit 4, Topic A	A-1
• DIR	Unit 4, Topic A	A-1
• ATTRIB	Unit 4, Topic A	A-7
• EDIT	Unit 4, Topic A	A-6, A-8
• COPY	Unit 4, Topic A	A-4
• XCOPY	Unit 4, Topic A	A-4
• FORMAT	Unit 2, Topic A	A-3
• IPCONFIG	Unit 6, Topic E	E-3
• PING	Unit 6, Topic E	E-4
• MD / CD / RD	Unit 4, Topic A	A-2, A-3, A-4, A-5
Identify concepts and procedures for creating, viewing, managing disks, directories and files in Windows 2000, XP Professional and XP Home, for example:		
• Disks (e.g. active, primary, extended and logical partitions)	Unit 2, Topic A	A-1 through A-5
• File systems (e.g. FAT 32, NTFS)	Unit 2, Topic A	A-1, A-3, A-4
• Directory structures (e.g. create folders, navigate directory structures)	Unit 4, Topic A	A-2, A-3, A-4, A-5
• Files (e.g. creation, extensions, attributes, permissions)	Unit 4, Topic A Unit 6, Topic B	A-6, A-7, A-8, A-9 B-1, B-2

Objective	Conceptual information	Supporting activities
2.1 (continued)		
Locate and use Windows 2000, XP Professional and XP Home utilities and available switches		
• Disk Management tools (e.g. DEFRAG, NTBACKUP, CHKDSK, Format)	Unit 2, Topic A Unit 2, Topic B Unit 5, Topic A	A-3, A-4, A-5 B-1 A-1
• System Management tools		
– Device and Task Manager	Unit 1, Topic C Unit 1, Topic D Unit 3, Topic B Unit 4, Topic B	C-1, C-2 D-2 B-2 B-3 through B-7
– MSCONFIG.EXE	Unit 5, Topic B	B-3
– REGEDIT.EXE	Unit 4, Topic D	D-1, D-2, D-3
– REGEDT32.EXE	Unit 4, Topic D	
– CMD	Unit 4, Topic A	A-1
– Event Viewer	Unit 4, Topic C Unit 7, Topic B	C-1 through C-5 B-2
– System Restore	Unit 5, Topic A	A-4, A-5
– Remote Desktop	Unit 5, Topic B	B-8, B-9
• File Management Tool (e.g. Windows Explorer, ATTRIB.EXE)	Unit 4, Topic A	A-2 through A-9
2.2 — Install, configure, optimize and upgrade operating systems		
Identify procedures and utilities used to optimize the performance of Windows 2000, XP Professional and XP Home, for example:		
• Virtual memory	Unit 4, Topic E	E-1, E-2
• Hard drives (i.e. disk defragmentation)	Unit 2, Topic B	B-1
• Temporary files	Unit 4, Topic A	A-9
• Services	Unit 4, Topic B	B-8
• Startup	Unit 4, Topic B	B-8, B-9
• Applications	Unit 4, Topic B	B-3, B-9, B-11
2.3 — Identify tools, diagnostic procedures and troubleshooting techniques for operating systems		
Recognize and resolve common operational problems, for example:		
• Windows-specific printing problems (e.g. print spool stalled, incorrect/incompatible driver form print)	Unit 3, Topic B	B-6
• Auto-restart errors	Unit 5, Topic B	
• Bluescreen error	Unit 5, Topic B	

Objective	Conceptual information	Supporting activities
2.3 (continued)		
Recognize and resolve common operational problems, for example:		
• System lock-up	Unit 5, Topic B	
• Device drivers failure (input/output devices)	Unit 5, Topic B	B-1
• Application install, start or load failure	Unit 5, Topic B	B-1
Recognize and resolve common error messages and codes, for example:		
• Boot (e.g. invalid boot disk, inaccessible boot device, missing NTLDR)	Unit 2, Topic B Unit 5, Topic B	B-2 B-1
• Startup (e.g. device/service has failed to start, device/program references in registry not found)	Unit 5, Topic B	B-1
• Event Viewer	Unit 4, Topic C Unit 7, Topic B	C-1 through C-5 B-2
• Registry	Unit 4, Topic D	D-1, D-2, D-3
• Windows	Unit 4, Topic B	B-10, B-11
Use diagnostic utilities and tools to resolve operational problems, for example:		
• Bootable media	Unit 5, Topic B	B-4, B-5, B-6
• Startup modes (e.g. safe mode, safe mode with command prompt or networking, step-by-step/single step mode)	Unit 5, Topic B	B-2
• Documentation resources (e.g. user/installation manuals, internet/web-based, training materials)	Unit 1, Topic D	D-1
• Task and Device Manager	Unit 1, Topic C Unit 1, Topic D Unit 3, Topic B Unit 4, Topic B	C-1, C-2 D-2 B-2 B-3 through B-7
• Event Viewer	Unit 4, Topic C Unit 7, Topic B	C-1, C-2, C-3, C-4 B-2
• MSCONFIG	Unit 5, Topic B	B-3
• Recovery CD / Recovery partition	Unit 5, Topic B	B-5
• Remote Desktop Connection and Assistance	Unit 5, Topic B	B-8, B-9, B-10
• System File Checker (SFC)	Unit 5, Topic B	B-7
2.4 — Perform preventative maintenance for operating systems		
Perform preventative maintenance on Windows 2000, XP Professional and XP Home including software and Windows updates (e.g. service packs)	Unit 5, Topic A	A-1 through A-8

3.0 Printers and scanners

Objective	Conceptual information	Supporting activities
3.1 — Identify the fundamental principles of using printers and scanners		
Describe processes used by printers and scanners including laser, ink dispersion, impact, solid ink and thermal printers	Unit 3, Topic A Unit 3, Topic C	A-1, A-2, A-3, A-4
3.2 — Install, configure, optimize and upgrade printers and scanners		
Install and configure printers and scanners		
• Power and connect the device using network or local port	Unit 3, Topic B Unit 3, Topic C	B-2 C-1
• Install/update the device driver and calibrate the device	Unit 3, Topic B Unit 3, Topic C	B-2, B-5 C-1
• Configure options and default settings	Unit 3, Topic B Unit 3, Topic C	B-3, B-5 C-1, C-3
• Install and configure print drivers (e.g. PCL™, Postscript™ and GDI)	Unit 3, Topic B	B-2
• Validate compatibility with OS and applications	Unit 3, Topic B Unit 3, Topic C	B-2 C-1
• Educate user about basic functionality	Unit 3, Topic B	
Optimize scanner performance for example: resolution, file format and default settings	Unit 3, Topic C	C-3
3.3 — Identify tools, diagnostic procedures and troubleshooting techniques for printers and scanners		
Gather information required to troubleshoot printer/scanner problems	Unit 3, Topic B Unit 3, Topic C	B-6 C-2
Troubleshoot a print failure (e.g. lack of paper, clear queue, restart print spooler, recycle power on printer, inspect for jams, check for visual indicators)	Unit 3, Topic B	B-6

4.0 Networks

Objective	Conceptual information	Supporting activities
4.1 — Identify the fundamental principles of networks		
Identify names, purposes, and characteristics of the basic network protocols and terminologies, for example:		
• ISP	Unit 6, Topic C	C-1
• TCP/IP (e.g. Gateway, Subnet mask, DNS, WINS, Static and automatic address assignment)	Unit 6, Topic A	A-4, A-5
• IPX/SPX (NWLink)	Unit 6, Topic A	A-8
• NETBEUI/NETBIOS	Unit 6, Topic A	
• SMTP	Unit 6, Topic C	C-1
• IMAP	Unit 6, Topic C	C-1
• HTML	Unit 6, Topic C	C-1
• HTTP	Unit 6, Topic C	C-1
• HTTPS	Unit 6, Topic C	C-1
• SSL	Unit 6, Topic C	C-1
• Telnet	Unit 6, Topic C	C-1
• FTP	Unit 6, Topic C	C-1
• DNS	Unit 6, Topic A	A-5
Identify names, purposes, and characteristics of technologies for establishing connectivity, for example:		
• Dial-up networking	Unit 6 Topic C	C-2
• Broadband (e.g. DSL, cable, satellite)	Unit 6, Topic C	C-2
• ISDN networking	Unit 6, Topic C	C-2
• Wireless	Unit 6, Topic C	C-2
• LAN/WAN	Unit 6, Topic C	C-2, C-3
4.2 — Install, configure, optimize and upgrade networks		
Establish network connectivity and share network resources	Unit 6, Topic A Unit 6, Topic B Unit 6, Topic C	A-1 through A-7 B-1 through B-6 C-4

Objective	Conceptual information	Supporting activities
4.3 — Identify tools, diagnostic procedures and troubleshooting techniques for networks		
Identify the names, purposes, and characteristics of command line tools, for example:		
• IPCONFIG.EXE	Unit 6, Topic E	E-3
• PING.EXE	Unit 6, Topic E	E-4
• TRACERT.EXE	Unit 6, Topic E	E-5
• NSLOOKUP.EXE	Unit 6, Topic E	E-5
Diagnose and troubleshoot basic network issues, for example:		
• Driver/network interface	Unit 6, Topic E	E-1
• Protocol configuration		
– TCP/IP (e.g. Gateway, Subnet mask, DNS, WINS, static and automatic address assignment)	Unit 6, Topic E	E-2, E-3
– IPX/SPX (NWLink)	Unit 6, Topic A	A-8
• Permissions	Unit 6, Topic E	E-6
• Firewall configuration	Unit 6, Topic D	D-1
• Electrical interference	Unit 6, Topic E	

5.0 Security

Objective	Conceptual information	Supporting activities
5.1 — Identify the fundamental principles of security		
Identify the names, purposes, and characteristics of access control and permissions	Unit 7, Topic A	
• Accounts including user, admin and guest	Unit 7, Topic A	A-1
• Groups	Unit 7, Topic A	A-1
• Permission levels, types (e.g. file systems and shared) and actions (e.g. read, write, change and execute)	Unit 2, Topic A Unit 6, Topic B	A-1 B-2
5.2 — Install, configure, optimizing and upgrade security		
Install and configure hardware, software, wireless and data security, for example:		
• Smart card readers	Unit 7, Topic C	C-2
• Key fobs	Unit 7, Topic C	
• Biometric devices	Unit 7, Topic C	C-1
• Authentication technologies	Unit 7, Topic A	A-3
• Software firewalls	Unit 6, Topic D	D-1
• Auditing and event logging (enable/disable only)	Unit 7, Topic B	B-1, B-2
• Wireless client configuration	Unit 6, Topic D	D-4
• Unused wireless connections	Unit 6, Topic D	D-3
• Data access (e.g. permissions, security policies)	Unit 6, Topic B Unit 7, Topic A Unit 7, Topic B	B-2 A-4 B-1, B-2
• Encryption and encryption technologies	Unit 7, Topic A	A-2
5.3 — Identify tools, diagnostic procedures and troubleshooting techniques for security issues:		
Diagnose and troubleshoot software and data security issues, for example:		
• Software firewall issues	Unit 6, Topic D	D-1
• Wireless client configuration issues	Unit 6, Topic D	D-4
• Data access issues (e.g. permissions, security policies)	Unit 7, Topic A Unit 7, Topic B	A-4 B-1, B-2
• Encryption and encryption technologies issues	Unit 7, Topic A	A-2
5.4 — Perform preventative maintenance for security		
Recognize social engineering and address social engineering situations	Unit 7, Topic D	D-1, D-2, D-3

6.0 Professionalism and Communication

Objective	Conceptual information	Supporting activities
6.1 — Use good communication skills, including listening and tact / discretion, when communicating with customers and colleagues		
• Use clear, concise and direct statements	Unit 8, Topic A	A-1
• Allow the customer to complete statements – avoid interrupting	Unit 8, Topic A	A-1
• Clarify customer statements – ask pertinent questions	Unit 8, Topic A	A-1
• Avoid using jargon, abbreviations and acronyms	Unit 8, Topic A	A-1
• Listen to customers	Unit 8, Topic A	A-1
6.2 — Use job-related professional behavior including notation of privacy, confidentiality and respect for the customer and customers' property	Unit 8, Topic A	A-1

Appendix B

CompTIA A+ acronyms

This appendix covers the following
information:

A Acronyms appearing on the CompTIA A+
exams covering 2006 objectives.

Topic A: Acronyms list

Explanation

The following is a list of acronyms that appear on the CompTIA A+ exams covering 2006 objectives. Candidates are encouraged to review the complete list and attain a working knowledge of all listed acronyms as a part of a comprehensive exam preparation program. Relevant exams include:

- CompTIA A+ Essentials
- CompTIA A+ 220-602
- CompTIA A+ 220-604
- CompTIA A+ 220-603

CompTIA A+ Acronyms v1.5. Copyright © 2006 by CompTIA. All rights reserved.

Acronym	Spelled out
AC	alternating current
ACPI	advanced configuration and power interface
ACT	activity
ADSL	asymmetrical digital subscriber line
AGP	accelerated graphics port
AMD	advanced micro devices
AMR	audio modem riser
APIPA	automatic private internet protocol addressing
ARP	address resolution protocol
ASR	automated system recovery
AT	advanced technology
ATA	advanced technology attachment
ATAPI	advanced technology attachment packet interface
ATM	asynchronous transfer mode
ATX	advanced technology extended
BIOS	basic input/output system
BNC	Bayonet-Neill-Concelman or British Naval Connector
BRI	basic rate interface
BTX	balanced technology extended
CD	compact disc

Acronym	Spelled out
CD-ROM	compact disc-read-only memory
CD-RW	compact disc-rewritable
CDFS	compact disc file system
CMOS	complementary metal-oxide semiconductor
CNR	communication network riser
COM1	communication port 1
CPU	central processing unit
CRIMM	continuity-rambus inline memory module
CRT	cathode-ray tube
DB-25	serial communications D-shell connector, 25 pins
DC	direct current
DDR	double data-rate
DDR RAM	double data-rate random access memory
DDR SDRAM	double data-rate synchronous dynamic random access memory
DFS	distributed file system
DHCP	dynamic host configuration protocol
DIMM	dual inline memory module
DIN	Deutsche Industrie Norm
DIP	dual inline package
DMA	direct memory access
DNS	domain name service or domain name server
DOS	disk operating system or denial of service
DB-9	9 pin D shell connector
DRAM	dynamic random access memory
DSL	digital subscriber line
DVD	digital video disc or digital versatile disc
DVD-RAM	digital video disc-random access memory
DVD-ROM	digital video disc-read only memory

Acronym	Spelled out
DVD-R	digital video disc-recordable
DVD-RW	digital video disc-rewritable
DVI	digital visual interface
ECC	error correction code
ECP	extended capabilities port
EEPROM	electrically erasable programmable read-only memory
EFS	encrypting file system
EIDE	enhanced integrated drive electronics
EISA	extended industry standard architecture
EMI	electromagnetic interference
EPP	enhanced parallel port
ERD	emergency repair disk
ESD	electrostatic discharge
ESDI	enhanced small device interface
EVGA	extended video graphics adapter/array
EVDO	evolution data optimized or evolution data only
FAT	file allocation table
FAT12	12-bit file allocation table
FAT16	16-bit file allocation table
FAT32	32-bit file allocation table
FDD	floppy disk drive
FERPA	Family Educational Rights and Privacy Act
Fn	Function (referring to the function key on a laptop)
FPM	fast page-mode
FRU	field replaceable unit
FTP	file transfer protocol
GB	gigabyte
GDI	graphics device interface

Acronym	Spelled out
GHz	gigahertz
GUI	graphical user interface
GPRS	general packet radio system
GSM	global system for mobile communications
HCL	hardware compatibility list
HDD	hard disk drive
HDMi	high definition media interface
HPFS	high performance file system
HTML	hypertext markup language
HTTP	hypertext transfer protocol
HTTPS	hypertext transfer protocol over secure sockets layer
I/O	input/output
ICMP	internet control message protocol
ICS	internet connection sharing
IDE	integrated drive electronics
IEEE	Institute of Electrical and Electronics Engineers
IIS	Internet Information Services
IMAP	internet mail access protocol
IP	internet protocol
IPCONFIG	internet protocol configuration
IPSEC	internet protocol security
IPX	internetwork packet exchange
IPX/SPX	internetwork packet exchange/sequenced packet exchange
IR	infrared
IrDA	Infrared Data Association
IRQ	interrupt request
ISA	industry standard architecture
ISDN	integrated services digital network

Acronym	Spelled out
ISO	Industry Standards Organization
ISP	internet service provider
KB	kilobyte
LAN	local area network
LC	Lucent connector
LCD	liquid crystal display
LED	light emitting diode
LPT	line printer terminal
LPT1	line printer terminal 1
LPX	low profile extended
LVD	low voltage differential
MAC	media access control
MAN	metropolitan area network
Mb	megabit
MB	megabyte
MBR	master boot record
MHz	megahertz
MicroDIMM	micro dual inline memory module
MIDI	musical instrument digital interface
MLI	multiple link interface
MMC	Microsoft management console
MMX	multimedia extensions
MP3	Moving Picture Experts Group Layer 3 Audio
MPEG	Moving Picture Experts Group
MSCONFIG	Microsoft configuration
MSDS	material safety data sheet
MUI	multilingual user interface
NAS	network-attached storage

Acronym	Spelled out
NAT	network address translation
NetBIOS	networked basic input/output system
NetBEUI	networked basic input/output system extended user interface
NFS	network file system
NIC	network interface card
NLI	not logged in or natural language interface
NLX	new low-profile extended
NNTP	network news transfer protocol
NTFS	new technology file system
NTLDR	new technology loader
NWLINK	Netware Link
OEM	original equipment manufacturer
OS	operating system
OSR	original equipment manufacturer service release
PAN	personal area network
PATA	parallel advanced technology attachment
PCI	peripheral component interconnect
PCIe	peripheral component interconnect express
PCIX	peripheral component interconnect extended
PCL	printer control language
PCMCIA	Personal Computer Memory Card International Association
PDA	personal digital assistant
PGA	pin grid array
PGA2	pin grid array 2
PIN	personal identification number
PnP	plug and play
POP	post office protocol
POP3	post office protocol 3

Acronym	Spelled out
POST	power-on self test
PPP	point-to-point protocol
PPTP	point-to-point tunneling protocol
PRI	primary rate interface
PROM	programmable read-only memory
PS/2	Personal System/2 connector
PSTN	public switched telephone network
PVC	permanent virtual circuit
QoS	quality of service
RAID	redundant array of independent (or inexpensive) discs
RAM	random access memory
RAS	remote access service
RDRAM	RAMBUS® dynamic random access memory
RF	radio frequency
RGB	red green blue
RIMM	RAMBUS inline memory module
RIP	routing information protocol
RIS	remote installation service
RISC	reduced instruction set computer
RJ	registered jack
RJ-11	registered jack function 11
RJ-45	registered jack function 45
ROM	read only memory
RS-232 or RS-232C	recommended standard 232
RTC	real-time clock
SAN	storage area network
SATA	serial advanced technology attachment
SC	subscription channel

Acronym	Spelled out
SCSI	small computer system interface
SCSI ID	small computer system interface identifier
SD card	secure digital card
SDRAM	synchronous dynamic random access memory
SEC	single edge connector
SFC	system file checker
SGRAM	synchronous graphics random access memory
SIMM	single inline memory module
SLI	scalable link interface or system level integration or scanline interleave mode
SMB	server message block or small to midsize business
SMTP	simple mail transport protocol
SNMP	simple network management protocol
SoDIMM	small outline dual inline memory module
SOHO	small office/home office
SP	service pack
SP1	service pack 1
SP2	service pack 2
SPDIF	Sony-Philips digital interface format
SPGA	staggered pin grid array
SPX	sequenced package exchange
SRAM	static random access memory
SSH	secure shell
SSID	service set identifier
SSL	secure sockets layer
ST	straight tip
STP	shielded twisted pair
SVGA	super video graphics array

Acronym	Spelled out
SXGA	super extended graphics array
TB	terabyte
TCP/IP	transmission control protocol/internet protocol
TFTP	trivial file transfer protocol
UART	universal asynchronous receiver transmitter
UDF	user defined functions or universal disk format or universal data format
UDMA	ultra direct memory access
UDP	user datagram protocol
UPS	uninterruptible power supply
URL	uniform resource locator
USB	universal serial bus
UTP	unshielded twisted pair
UXGA	ultra extended graphics array
VESA	Video Electronics Standards Association
VFAT	virtual file allocation table
VGA	video graphics array
VoIP	voice over internet protocol
VPN	virtual private network
VRAM	video random access memory
WAN	wide area network
WAP	wireless application protocol
WEP	wired equivalent privacy
WIFI	wireless fidelity
WINS	windows internet name service
WLAN	wireless local area network
WPA	wireless protected access
WUXGA	wide ultra extended graphics array

Acronym	Spelled out
XGA	extended graphics array
ZIF	zero-insertion-force
ZIP	zigzag inline package

Course summary

This summary contains information to help you bring the course to a successful conclusion. Using this information, you'll be able to:

A Use the summary text to reinforce what students have learned in class.

B Direct students to the next courses in this series, if any, and to any other resources that might help students continue to learn about hardware.

Topic A: Course summary

At the end of the class, use the following summary text to reinforce what students have learned. It's intended not as a script, but rather as a starting point.

Unit summaries

Unit 1

In this unit, students installed **video adapters**, **sound cards**, and **modems**. Students then installed and removed **PC Cards** and **mini-PCI cards**. Students installed **legacy devices**, and they learned to override **Plug and Play** settings in Windows XP and Windows 2000. Finally, they learned how to troubleshoot **expansion cards**, and they examined common symptoms of failures and the probable causes and suggested solutions.

Unit 2

In this unit, students learned about the components of a **hard drive** and about the **FAT, FAT32**, and **NTFS** file systems Then, they physically installed a hard drive into a PC and learned that there are three steps to preparing a hard drive for use by the operating system: **low-level formatting, partitioning**, and (high-level) **formatting**. Next, students performed basic disk maintenance, and they learned how to troubleshoot hard disk issues.

Unit 3

In this unit, students learned about the various types of printers, including **dot matrix** and **impact** printers, **inkjet** printers, and **laser** printers. Students then examined the **Windows print process**, and they installed a local printer. They also installed printer **add-ons** and **upgrades**, and they learned to troubleshoot printer issues. Finally, students installed and optimized a **scanner**, and they learned to troubleshoot scanner problems.

Unit 4

In this unit, students learned to manage **files** and **directories**. They also learned to monitor and manage a Windows operating system, using **Windows Diagnostics, Task Manager**, and **Computer Management**. Next, they learned to use **Event Viewer** to monitor a computer, and managed Event Viewer **log files**. Students also accessed **Registry** files and searched through the Registry to find a specific piece of information, and they managed virtual memory.

Unit 5

In this unit, students learned how to perform operating system **maintenance** tasks that can help prevent problems from occurring with Windows 2000 Professional and Windows XP computers. These tasks include **backing up** and **restoring** data manually and on a schedule; creating a **system restore point** and restoring to a restore point; installing Windows **service packs** and **hotfixes**; and configuring Windows XP computers for **automatic updates**. Students also learned how to use Windows troubleshooting tools, and they identified the symptoms and causes of common startup errors. Finally, students learned to troubleshoot problems remotely, using **Remote Desktop** and **Remote Assistance**.

Unit 6

In this unit, students configured and installed a **network interface card** and configured it to communicate using **TCP/IP** and **NWLink**. Students also joined a Windows **domain** and learned how to view resources on the network. Next, they shared resources on a network, including a folder and a printer, and they restricted access to shared resources, using **NTFS permissions** and **share permissions**. Students then learned how to create an Internet connection, and they learned about various **WAN technologies**. Finally, they configured the **Windows Firewall**, and they learned to troubleshoot network connection problems using utilities, such as **Ipconfig**, **Tracert**, and **Ping**.

Unit 7

In this unit, students learned that operating system security depends on authenticating users, that is determining who they are, and they looked at **encryption**, **authentication**, and **local security policies**. Students also learned how to **audit** local security events. Next, students learned about security devices, such as **fingerprint scanners**, **smart card readers**, and **fobs**. They installed a **smart card reader**, enrolled a card, logged in with a smart card, and locked their PCs by removing the cards. Finally, students learned about the human component of security, and how security policies and training can be used to keep a computing environment secure.

Unit 8

In this unit, students learned that being **professional**, **courteous**, and **respectful** is critical to success as a support technician. Students also learned that a problem isn't resolved until both the technician and the user agree that the problem has been resolved, and they learned that **service level agreements** specify how clients and support personnel are to interact. Finally, students learned how problem and resolution tracking is important to long-term success.

Topic B: Continued learning after class

Point out to your students that it's impossible to learn to use any software effectively in a single day. To get the most out of this class, students should begin working with hardware and Windows XP to perform real tasks as soon as possible. Course Technology also offers resources for continued learning.

Other courses in this series

This course covers all of the material you'll need to know to pass the CompTIA A+ 220-603 exam. Other courses in the A+ series include:

- *CompTIA A+ Certification: Essentials*
- *CompTIA A+ Certification: 220-602*
- *CompTIA A+ Certification: 220-604*

Other resources

For more information, visit www.course.com.

Glossary

802.1X
Protocol is a mechanism to authenticate wireless users.

Active Directory
Microsoft's directory service, included with Windows servers, that provides a single point of administration and storage for user, group, and computer objects.

AGP
The Advanced Graphics Port, a video port used with Pentium-based computers.

AppleTalk
A suite of OSI-upper-layer protocols from Apple Computer for connecting Macintosh computers and peripherals.

Authenticate
Identifying a user by using a set of credentials, typically a user name and password.

Backbone
The main cable of a network to which other network segments connect.

Bandwidth
The amount of data which can travel over a communication line or wireless connection in a given length of time.

Basic partition
A standard, or classic, partition. Compare to dynamic partition.

Binary
The base-2 numbering system.

BIOS
The Basic Input/Output System is a set of software instructions stored on a chip on the motherboard. The BIOS instructions enable basic computer functions, such as getting input from the keyboard and mouse, serial ports, and so forth.

Bluetooth
A short-range radio communications technology, developed by the Bluetooth Special Interest Group.

Cable modem
A device that connects a LAN to an ISP via the cable television connection.

Case
The enclosure for the motherboard and other internal components of a PC.

CD
A plastic disc on which audio or data files are encoded using the pulse code modulation method.

Client-server network
A network in which computers are either a workstation or a server, but not both.

Clusters
Logical collections of one or more sectors. Data storage is managed at the cluster level, rather than the sector level.

CMOS
Complementary metal oxide semiconductor, a type of computer chip manufacturing technology. A battery-backed up area of memory that stores BIOS configuration data.

Coaxial cable
A round cable composed of a central electrically conducive wire, surrounded by an insulating layer, then a mesh layer, and finally the outer insulation layer.

COM ports
Serial ports, which are named COM1, COM2, and so forth.

Compression
Use of an algorithm to make data take up less space.

Computer account
An account that is stored in the domain database and provides a way for a domain member computer to identify itself securely to the domain.

Continuous form
Paper that is either a continuous roll or perforated at the page breaks rather than cut sheets of a specific size.

Controller
The adapter board that plugs into your PC's expansion slot and is used to interface with a hard drive or storage device.

CPU
Central Processing Unit. The chip(s) that processes instructions, manipulates data, and controls the interactions of the other circuits in your computer. Also called the processor.

Crossover cable
A cable wired with the send wired to the transmit signals and vice-versa so that two computers can communicate as if they were connected to a network.

Crosstalk
Interference when two wires running parallel to each other carries a signal in one wire intended for the other wire.

CYMK
Cyan, Yellow, Magenta, and Black. The colors used in inkjet printers.

Default gateway
Connection device between the LAN and the Internet.

Defragging
Optimizing file access speeds by relocating the clusters that comprise the file to contiguous locations on the disk.

Demodulation
The opposite of modulation by which a digital signal is extracted from an analog carrier wave.

DHCP
A method of automatically assigning IP addresses to nodes on a LAN.

Digital Subscriber Line (DSL)
See DSL.

DIP switches
Small, typically rocker-style, switches that were used with older hardware components to configure various options.

Direct thermal printers
Thermal printers that burn dots into specially coated paper.

Directory
A folder.

Diskette
A floppy disk.

DMA
Direct Memory Access, a system by which a support chip manages memory access by hardware components so that the CPU doesn't have to.

DNS
A part of the TCP/IP protocol suite that translates domain names into their corresponding IP addresses.

Domain
A logically structured organization of objects, such as users, computers, groups, and printers that are part of a network and share a common directory database. Domains are defined by an administrator and administered as a unit with common rules and procedures.

Domain accounts
User accounts stored in the Active Directory domain database. Account can be accessed on any computer that has access to the database.

Domain controller (DC)
A Windows server explicitly configured to store a copy of the Active Directory database and service user authentication requests or queries about domain objects.

Domain name
A unique name assigned to a network and registered with ICANN.

Domain Name Service (DNS)
See DNS.

Dot-matrix printers
A printer which creates characters using a set of pins which strike a ribbon coated with ink.

Driver
A form of software that interacts with hardware to enable that device's functionality.

DSL
A high-speed data and voice transmission line that uses telephone wires, but carries the digital data at frequencies well above those used for voice transmission.

Dual-link
A DVI cable that uses two TDMS 165 MHz transmitters.

DVD
Media for recording digital video and high capacity data storage.

Dye diffusion thermal process
D2T. Most dye sub printers actually do go through a liquid state and this is the term to describe that process.

Dye sublimation printer
Printers that print using solid dye contained on a ribbon or roll using a thermal process.

Dynamic Host Configuration Protocol (DHCP)
See DHCP.

Dynamic partition
An enhanced partition type. With this partition type, you can make changes to your partitions and the volumes they contain without restarting the operating system.

Ethernet
The most common form of LAN architecture. It uses bus or start topology and employs CSMA/CD to manage the flow of data on the network.

Expansion bus

The bus to which add-on adapter cards are connected to enhance the functionality of the PC.

Extended partitions

Partitions that contain one or more logical drives, which is what the operating system accesses for file storage.

FDD

A floppy disk drive.

Firewall

Hardware or software that controls the data entering or leaving a computer system. Used to maintain the security of the system.

Flashing

The process of updating the BIOS in your PC by using a special program provided by your motherboard or PC's manufacturer.

Floppy disk

A removable data storage medium composed of a thin, typically brown, plastic disk contained within a stiff or rigid plastic case.

Folder

An organizational unit on a storage medium that can contain files or other folders. Analogous to a file folder in your file cabinet.

Fusing assembly

The components in a laser printer that heat the toner to melt it into the paper.

Hardware

Any physical component of a computer or peripheral device.

Hex

Shorthand notation for hexadecimal numbers or the hexadecimal numbering system.

Hexadecimal

The base-16 numbering system.

Host

A computer on a network.

HTTP

Hypertext Transfer Protocol. Protocol used to send and receive Web pages over the Internet.

I/O address

A section of memory shared between the CPU and a device through which those components can transfer data.

IBM-type Data Connector (IDC)

Connector used on token ring networks to connect the computer to the network.

Impact printer

A printer that produces images by striking an inked ribbon.

Ink dispersion

See inkjet printers.

Inkjet printer

A printer that produces images by forcing ink through nozzles and onto the paper.

Integrated Services Digital Network (ISDN)

See ISDN.

Interface

A communications standard that defines how data flows to and from the disk drive. In practice, an interface is implemented as a circuit board attached to the drive unit.

Interrupt

A signal sent by a device to the CPU to gain the attention of the CPU.

Ipconfig

A TCP/IP utility which displays the computer's adapter address, IP address, subnet mask, and default gateway, and allows the DHCP to be renewed or released by the user.

IPX

Internet Packet eXchange. OSI Network layer protocol that handles moving information over the network. It is a connectionless protocol.

IPX/SPX protocol suite

The protocol suite used by Novell NetWare networks.

IRQ

Interrupt Request Line, a channel over which interrupt signals are transmitted.

ISA bus

The Industry Standard Architecture bus; the 16-bit expansion bus of the IBM PC/AT computers and clones.

ISDN

A technology that uses a telephone line to transmit digital data at a high speed.

Jumpers

Plastic and metal covers that slide over protruding metal pins to configure older hardware components.

Laser printer

A printer that produces images using toner and a laser on an electrophotographic drum. Static is charged and discharged to transfer the image and the toner to the paper, and it is then heated to fuse the toner to the paper.

Laser scanning assembly
Contains the laser which is used to write the image to the drum in a laser printer.

Local accounts
User accounts stored in the computer's local security database and available only on the computer on which they were created.

Local area network (LAN)
A regionally confined network consisting of computers that communicate and share data and services.

Low-level formatting
The preparation step that divides the disk into tracks and divides each track into sectors. With hard drives, this step is performed at the factory.

LPT ports
Line printer (parallel) ports, which are named LPT1, LPT2, and so forth.

Magnetic tape
Media used in tape drives. Usually in a cartridge, but older formats were reel-to-reel.

Mini PCI card
Same functionality as a desktop PCI card, in a smaller format for portable computing devices.

Modems
Devices that convert a digital signal into an analog one through a process called modulation. Modems enable you to connect your computer to another computer through a phone line.

Modulation
The layering of a digital signal over a standard analog wave to produce a composite analog wave that encodes the digital signal.

Motherboard
The main circuit board in a personal computer.

Multimeter
A meter that can be used to measure multiple electrical properties.

Multi-part forms
A blank pre-printed form with several layers fastened together that are printed with an impact printer. The paper either has carbon paper between the layers or uses NCR (no carbon required) paper.

NAT
A service that allows multiple computers to access the Internet by sharing a single public IP address.

NetBEUI
Network BIOS Extended User Interface. A Microsoft proprietary protocol commonly used for LANs.

NetBIOS
An OSI-session-layer protocol that provides name resolution and session management between computers.

Network Address Translation (NAT)
See NAT.

Network interface card
NIC. A device for connecting a node to a network.

Nickel Cadmium (NiCad)
Battery that was used for portable computing devices. Suffers from memory effect.

NWLink
The Microsoft implementation of IPX/SPX protocol suite.

Page file
A file on the hard disk that is used to temporarily store active data that doesn't fit in the RAM installed on your computer. However, the computer can't work with the data in the page file. It must first read the data back into real RAM, while writing some other data to the page file.

Paper control and transport assembly
The components in a laser printer that move the paper through the printer.

Partition
A portion of a disk that contains a volume.

Partitioning
Dividing a disk into one or more logical drives, which are also called volumes.

PC Card
Expansion cards for portable computers that are approximately the size of a credit card.

PCI
The Peripheral Component Interconnect bus, a 32- or 64-bit expansion bus used in Pentium-based and other modern PCs.

PCMCIA
Personal Computer Memory Card International Association. Group responsible for establishing the standards for expansion cards for portable computing devices.

Peer-to-peer network
A network in which computers can act as either a workstation or a server.

Peripherals
External computer components, such as printers, keyboards, mice, and so forth.

Piezo crystal
Crystal that vibrates when an electrical current is sent to it. On outward vibration, ink is drawn from the cartridge, on inward vibration, the ink is sprayed onto the paper.

Piezoelectric bubble
An inkjet technology that forces ink through the nozzles by vibrating a piezo crystal behind each nozzle.

Ping
A TCP/IP utility that enables a user at one computer to determine if that node can communicate with another computer connected to a network.

Plain Old Telephone Service (POTS)
See POTS.

Plotter
Pen-based output devices that create line images.

Plug and Play (PnP)
A system through which devices in your PC are automatically discovered and configured to use non-conflicting system resources. PnP requires cooperation between hardware and software (operating system) components.

Port
A connector into which you can plug cables from external devices, or in some cases plug in the devices themselves.

POTS
The analog phone service to most homes. A common method of connecting home Internet services.

Primary partitions
Partitions that are directly accessed by the operating system as volumes.

Protocol
A set of rules and standards that a network uses to communicate among its nodes.

Protocol suite
A group of protocols that work together to provide services.

RG-58
Coaxial cable used for Ethernet networks. Also known as thin net.

Riser card
A circuit board that connects to a motherboard to provide additional expansion slots or sockets.

RJ-11 connectors
Square, six-pin connectors used with phone, modem, and LocalTalk connections.

RJ-45
A terminating 8-pin connector on a twisted pair cable used for network connections.

Root directory
The highest level folder on the disk.

Routable protocol
A protocol that allows data to be sent to interconnected networks on the Internet.

Router
A device that connects two or more networks and directs the data traffic passing between them.

Scanners
A device that converts pictures or text to digital data.

Sectors
Divisions of tracks in which data is written.

Security Accounts Manager (SAM) database
The local security and account database on a Windows server.

Serial
A transmission technique in which bits of data are sent one at a time across the medium.

Server
A computer or device on a network that provides network services or manages network resources.

Service set identifier (SSID)
The network name for Wireless LANs.

Software
A set of instructions processed by the central processing chip in the computer.

Solid ink printer
A printer that uses sticks of wax that are melted to create the ink for printing.

Speakers
Devices that convert electrical signals into sound.

SPX
Sequenced Packet eXchange. OSI Transport layer protocol that provides guaranteed delivery of packets.

STP
Shielded twisted pair cable used for LANs.

Sublimation
A scientific process in which a solid is converted to a gas without becoming a liquid in between those two states.

Subnet mask

A string of 32 bits that is used to define which portion of an IP address is the host ID and which part is the network ID.

Switch

A device used in a LAN to direct data traffic among the nodes.

Tape drive

Storage device for archival storage of data.

TCP/IP

A protocol suite composed of Transmission Control Protocol (TCP) and Internet Protocol (IP). The most common protocol used to connect networks.

Telnet

A TCP/IP utility that allows a user in one location to access a computer in a remote location as if the user were physically sitting in front of the remote machine.

Thermal autochrome printers

Thermal printers that use special paper with cyan, magenta, and yellow pigments embedded in the paper.

Thermal bubble

An inkjet technology that forces ink through the nozzles by heating the ink.

Thermal printer

Printers that produce output with heat.

Thermal wax transfer printers

Thermal printers that use ink in a wax base.

Toner

Fine particles composed of carbon, polyester, and iron oxide held in a cartridge and used in laser printers to produce images.

Toner cartridge

A container filled with toner, an EP drum, a blade to remove used toner from the drum, and a corona charging assembly to apply a static charge to the drum after the image has printed.

Tracert

A TCP/IP utility that shows the complete path that data packets are taking from the computer to reach any given destination.

Tracks

Concentric or spiral rings on the disk medium that is divided into sectors, which contain recorded data.

Tractor feed

The sprocketed wheels which dot-matrix printers use to feed continuous form paper through the printer.

Transfer corona assembly

The components in a laser printer that transfer the image from the drum to the paper.

Transmission Control Protocol/Internet Protocol

See TCP/IP.

Type I PC Card

PC Card at 3.3 mm thick most often used for memory.

Type II PC Card

PC Card at 5 mm thick most often used for network adapters, modems, and other communications channels such as SCSI, USB or FireWire.

Type III PC Card

PC Card at 10.5 mm thick most often used for additional storage.

USB

Universal Serial Bus, a standardized peripheral specification developed by a consortium of companies. It defines a bus architecture to which you can connect one or more expansion devices.

Volatile memory

Memory that loses its contents when power is removed.

War driving

Driving around in a car with a laptop using a wireless network card and seeing which networks can be connected to.

WEP (Wired Equivalent Protocol)

A protocol built in the 802.11 standards that governs how data can be encrypted while in transit on the wireless network.

Wide area network

WAN. Networks covering large geographic areas, for example counties, states, or countries, or the world, and beyond.

Wi-Fi (Wireless Fidelity)

IEEE 802.11b wireless standard with an 11 Mbps transmission rate.

WiMax

IEEE 802.16 Air Interface Standard, an emerging wireless standard for metropolitan area networks. It offers a range of up to 31 miles.

WINS (Windows Internet Naming Service)

A service used to resolve NetBIOS names to IP addresses as well as store NetBIOS service information.

Windows print process

The processes involved in getting the print request from the user to the printer.

WinModem

A Windows-based combination of simple hardware (basically, just physical components to interface with the motherboard and phone lines) and modem function emulation software.

Wireless access point

Device to which wireless communications computing devices communicate and connect with network services.

Wireless router

A device to which nodes in a wireless LAN can connect using radio waves.

Workgroup

A logical group of computers characterized by a decentralized security and administration model.

Workstation

A computer connected to a network.

WPA (WiFi Protected Access)

A wireless communication protocol that is replacing WEP. It uses a shared key for security.

Index

X

Z